WILLIAM CAREY, ESPECIALLY HIS MISSIONARY PRINCIPLES

WILLIAM CAREY

WILLIAM CAREY

ESPECIALLY
HIS MISSIONARY PRINCIPLES

BY

Dr A. H. OUSSOREN

MINISTER OF THE REFORMED CHURCH AT MIDDELBURG

LEIDEN — 1945
A. W. SIJTHOFF'S UITGEVERSMAATSCHAPPIJ N.V.

Dedicated
to my Parents and my Wife

PREFACE.

At the end of my academic studies, I first of all want to thank the Lord for the desire and the strength he has given me to finish this work.

It is fascinating to study theology and it is still more fascinating to preach the Gospel of Jesus Christ, but to do something for people who still live in darkness and shadow of death is a task for which we cannot be grateful enough.

Yet this task, especially the writing of a dissertation in a large parish, together with difficult war conditions, so that it was not easy to get books badly wanted, laid some stress and strain upon this work. This will be noted by the missionary expert whose benevolent judgment may allow for these facts.

When I look back on all these difficulties, I am still more grateful to the Lord who enabled me to make some contribution to the missionary science.

I am grateful to all those who were my teachers, the Professors of the Theological High School of the Dutch Reformed Churches in Kampen, and the Professors of the Universitas Libera Reformata at Amsterdam.

Special thanks I will render to you, my Highly esteemed and very learned, Professor Doctor J. H. BAVINCK. Your inspiring lead and the new perspectives that opened to me under your stimulating guidance, the help you gave me in the finishing of my dissertation, will be an always happy remembrance.

When I survey all those who gave me help I will mention only a few names: The Provincial Library of Zealand at Middelburg, the Missionary Library at Oegstgeest, the Missionary Library of the Z(endings) S(tudie) R(aad) at Zeist, doctoranda W. A. VERTREGT, Middelburg, and Miss Helen M. L. Row, St. Asaph, N. Wales, whose help was very much appreciated.

As for the biography of William Carey, I like to say that this dissertation does not pretend to give a complete scientific description of the life of this great man.

War conditions prevented composing such a book, supposing we had had the intention to do so. In the second place it would be difficult to give a better biography than men such as W. PEARCE CAREY, MARSHMAN, DEAVILLE WALKER and GEORGE SMITH have done. Especially W. PEARCE CAREY, a great-grandson of William Carey, made it his life work, devoting 12 years to the actual writing of his famous book, full of details, letters etc. It would be only compilatory work to describe his life once more.

We hope that our description of his principles compared with other principles may forward the missionary scientific studies and that above all many non-christians may be brought to the Cross of Jesus Christ as poor sinners.

INDEX.

CHAPTER I.

BIOGRAPHICAL SURVEY.

CHAPTER III.

HIS MISSIONARY PRINCIPLES COMPARED WITH THOSE OF THE PIETISTS, ESPECIALLY THE MORAVIANS.

CHAPTER IV.

CHAPTER I.

a. The times in which William Carey lived.

I. THE 18TH CENTURY IN GENERAL.

Important eras of human progress and national salvation are generally inaugurated and moulded by a man who has understanding of the times, whose ear is open and attuned to respond sympathetically to the sighs and groans of humanity for redemption from the powers of evil, and who has the constructiveness and comprehensiveness of nature, to become a builder of a nation and the hero of a far reaching reformation. [1])

These words may be applied to WILLIAM CAREY. Just like all great leaders of humanity, he not only understood his own time, but also had a clear conception of the times before him. He saw their corruption, their baseness, their frivolity, their deplorable state of affairs in every way.

Significant in this respect are the words of MONTESQUIEU when travelling through England: "In France people argue: "I don't possess religion enough", but in England all men declare: "I am possessing religion too much". In the English Church the vital forces of the Gospel were petrified in Formalism, Scholasticism, and a Church Culture abundant in Mechanism. [2]) If there was still anything of the Puritan spirit it lingered concealed in the rustic houses of the people of the lower and middle classes, but the court and the upper classes lived in immoralities and orgies. The secret of the Whig government was the entrusting of unlimited authority over the country to the squires who acted as uncontrolled judges and to gentlemen-ministers of the Established Church. [3]) Judges were often drunken squires, ignorant of their duty, hostile to evangelists and Dissenters and encouraged their ill-treatment. The situation of the Church and spiritual life were in such a condition that somebody has written: "Never before was there an era for Christian England so void of belief as in the eighteenth century. The Puritans were buried and Methodists not yet born. The world was just like somebody in the morning after a night full of debauchery". [4])

The amusements of that time may give us a good idea of the low spiritual standard of the people : "They were of the most degrading character. The most popular of these was witnessing the executions at Tyburn, when half the population of London assembled to see men, women, and often children hanged on the scaffold, in many instances for crimes of an insignificant nature. Next in attractiveness to this was Bartholomew Fair. This was sometimes prolonged for ten or twelve days. The neighbourhood of Smithfield was transformed into a city of narrow streets, filled with stalls, booths, raree shows, and exhibitions of almost every kind imaginable. Its patrons were deafened with the cries of showmen, blare of trumpets, beating of gongs, clanging of cymbals and a hundred other ear-splitting instruments ; demoralized by drunkenness, wholesale gambling, indecent shows, plays, interludes, lotteries and nameless debaucheries. There repaired the men of "ton" and fashion from the Westend, there were to be found ladies of the Court, skilfully disguised tradesmen and their wives from the city and there also crowded the drunkards, wantons, thieves, and vagabonds from all parts of London and far beyond". [5])

"Drunk for a penny and deaddrunk for two pence" are ornaments above bars. Fathers are writing letters to their sons about the art of seduction. Government is stimulating gambling and drinking in order to raise immense sums for the treasury. In the two parishes of Westminster were "two hundred and ninety six tables for one fashionable game alone". [6])

The situation at the early part of the eighteenth century may be compared with the days of Isaiah speaking to the upper ten of Jerusalem : "Judge the fatherless, plead for the widow. Everyone loveth gifts, and followeth after rewards : they judge not the fatherless neither doth the cause of the widow come unto them." Isaiah 1 : 17.23.

And every one who is interested in the situation of the prisons of these days, may be advised to read the books of HENRY BROOKE and OLIVER GOLDSMITH, the first prison reformers of the country. In their representation of prison-life there is no exaggeration whatever but their pictures are in every respect trustworthy.

JOHN HOWARD spent his fortune and a great part of his life to change this abhorrent condition of the prisoner.

2

We will pass the conditions of the roads and the trials which travellers had to endure especially on account of the highwaymen, we will pass the dangers of the night when "at once beggars recovered with marvellous swiftness from their lameness, blindness, and diseases, and became sturdy assailants of unprotected passengers", we will pass the utmost deplorable social conditions especially in the mine-districts, we will now try to say something of the condition of the Church.

First of all we have to remember, that two acts were recalled, which had made much restriction on the freedom of those, who dissented with the official Church : the Occasional Conformity Act and the Schism Act. The first imposed a fine of £ 40 upon any person who should attend a conventicle, while holding any public office. The Schism Bill provided, that no person should teach in a public or private school, unless he conformed to the Established Church and had a licence from a bishop. A breach of this Act involved three months' imprisonment. The recalling of these terrible Acts was a great relief to the Dissenters, giving them some religious freedom. [7]

The attitude of the Church against the sad situations in the whole country was one of utter helplessness. From the pulpits we are hearing warnings against debauches, ministers are asking for moderation and soberness, but .... vice can't be conquered by virtue. [8]

Among the reasons suggested by Church-writers are : the jealousy of the Nonjurors [9] towards those who had stepped into their places ; the prolonged Deistical controversy against revelation and in favour of natural religion : the misinterpretations of the clergy by the leaders of the evangelical revival in order to place in bright relief the characters and labours of their own heroes. [10] WESLEY, when asked, what is the present character of the English people, answered : "ungodliness". GLADSTONE writes : "that the preaching of the Gospel a hundred years since had disappeared not by denial but by lapse, from the majority of Anglican pulpits is, I fear, in a large measure, an historical truth". [11] The situation in the circles of the Dissenters may have been a little better, but on the whole, the greater part of the nation was totally ignorant of the doctrines of Christianity. Christ did not live in their hearts. Conversion was not necessary.

Among the clergy there may have been purity of life, but sad

3

instances of immorality and of conduct scandalizing their profession are given. STERNE and SWIFT were clergymen, but the first is described by THACKERAY as "a monster gibbering shrieks and gnashing imprecations against mankind, tearing down all shreds of modesty, past all scenes of manliness and shame, filthy in word, filthy in thought, furious, raging, obscene". And of SWIFT he writes: "a wretched wornout old scamp as vain, as wicked as false as he had ever been". [12]) And CRASHAW giving an account of SWIFT's "Gulliver's Travels" may estimate his book as the most powerful and fascinating in literature and SWIFT himself as a tremendous genius—but on the other hand he asserts: "made mad by his own pride and rage and disappointment". [13])

To show that these cases were not standing apart, we may quote Dr. STROUGHTON: "The public have long remarked with indignation that some of the most distinguished coxcombs, drunkards, debauchees, and gamesters who figure at the watering places and all places of public resort are young men of the sacerdotal order." [14])

The more books are read about this period, the more we are convinced, that there is no exaggeration in the above statements. On the contrary: the way of living of the people is a good mirror of the low standard of the clergy. At the time of WESLEY's death there were 11.164 parishes in England and Wales but only 4412 incumbents, just over one for every three parishes. This shows the enormous prevalence of pluralities and absenteism, though it was already a great step forward in comparison with the situation at the beginning of this century. [15]) BURNET, seeing all this, writes in the early part of this century: "I cannot look on without the deepest concern when I see the imminent ruin, hanging over the Church and by consequence over the whole Reformation. The outward state of things is black enough, God knows; but what heightens my fears rises chiefly from the inward state into which we are unhappily fallen. The much greater part of those who come to be ordained, are ignorant to a degree, not to be apprehended by those, who are not obliged to know it. The easiest part of knowledge is that, to which they are strangers: I mean the plainest part of Scriptures. Many cannot give a tolerable account of the catechism itself how short and plain. This does often tear my heart." [16])

Of course notwithstanding these facts, there was still a host of

4

men who fought at the side of the revealed truth against the principles of rationalism and deism. Names such as Dr. RICHARD BENTLY, WARBURTON, Dr. SAMUEL CLARKE, SHERLOCK, JOSEPH BUTLER and others [17]) are of great reputation in all centuries for their defence of the Scriptures against deism and rationalism. But their books, however valuable, did not change the vices and immoralities and life of shame and sin of the multitudes. The books they issued were full of arguments, but they spoke little or not at all of Jesus Christ and Him crucified and the call of men to live a new life, the call of men to go to the nations and preach the gospel.

In this period JOHN and CHARLES WESLEY and GEORGE WHITEFIELD were the instruments in the hand of God to revive, to call to life, to kindle and to stimulate the Church in starvation. The origin of this call to purity and holiness can be traced to their Holy club at Oxford. Together with the above-mentioned men there arose a great number of gifted men who stirred the Church, who exercised a gracious influence upon the Church as a whole and the clergy in particular.

In this period WILLIAM CAREY was born. After the period of dryness and famine there was a cloud out of the sea like a man's hand. A short time later the heaven was black with clouds and wind, and there was a great rain. 1 Kings 18 : 44.

NOTES

[1]) A New History of Methodism by W. J. TOWNSEND D.D., H.B. and WORKMAN M.A. D. Lit. GEORGE EAYRS, F. R. Hist. S. Hodder and Stroughton, London 1909, p. 79.

[2]) Dr. JOH. HEINR. KURZ, Lehrbuch der Kirchengesch. Mitau 1863, p. 607.

[3]) Wereldgeschiedenis. De geschiedenis der menschheid van de oudste tijden tot heden. Deel IV, pag. 170. De Haan, Utrecht. Artikel Dr. J. S. BARTSTRA, 18e eeuw, p. 205.

[4]) Dr. O. NOREL, John Wesley, Voorhoeve, Den Haag 1936, p. 9.

[5]) TOWNSEND, op. cit. p. 89.

[6]) Ib., p. 91.

[7]) History of the Free Churches of England 1688—1891. SKEATS and MIALL, p. 15 quoted by Dr. H. M. VAN NES, John Wesley, p. 15. Cf. TOWNSEND, p. 104.

[8]) NOREL, op. cit. p. 11.

[9]) Non-jurors arose by the accession of William and Mary to the throne in England. Many of the clergy refused to stain their consciences by offering allegiance to the new dynasty. They thought it their duty, to keep their oaths loyally to the old dynasty. These four hundred men of character, called the salt of the church, were robbed of their offices, livings and homes and sent into the wilderness. This bereavement of the non-jurors was an incalculable loss, for they were by far the better part of the church.

[10]) New History, TOWNSEND, op. cit. p. 116.

[11]) GLADSTONE, Gleanings of Past Years VII, 207, quoted by TOWNSEND, p. 117.

[12]) THACKERAY, English Humorists, ed. 1892, p. 146. TOWNSEND, p. 118.

[13]) WILLIAM H. CRASHAW, Litt. D. LL.D. 'The making of English Literature', London 1906, p. 205.

[14]) Dr. STROUGHTON, Religion in England VI, 206. TOWNSEND, op. cit. p. 118.

[15]) TOWNSEND, op. cit. p. 364.

[16]) Ib., p. 120.

[17]) Ib., pp. 129/130.

2. THE 18TH CENTURY IN SHORT OUTLINES.

When we are giving some short outlines of the eighteenth century especially relating to religious influences in England, which played such an important part in WILLIAM CAREY's life, we will also bring forward some other names wel known to nearly all men. In Leipzig e.g. we meet the great musician JOHANN SEBASTIAN BACH (1685—1759), cantor of St. Thomas Church, famous by his immortal fugue's and his "Passionen". A man who in some way may be called super-temporal and who was certainly standing above the spirit of the eighteenth century. Dr. BARTSTRA, describing the eighteenth century in Vol. V of "Wereldgeschiedenis" supposes that Bach was very much influenced by Pietism. His music was indeed the contrary of the frivolous Rococo and took its origin in the religious heart.

In 1755 people began with the excavations of Pompeji. When the intellectual world was confronted with the results of this work there was an immense influence from it upon the whole structure of Classicism and Rococo. For the former love was awakened once more while the latter lost its charm upon the hearts of men. MARIE ANTOINETTE made her boudoir in Fontainebleau in the style of Pompeji!

Another great influence was exerted by Rationalism and Empiricism, as we stated above. We will only mention the names of CHRISTIAN WOLFF (1679—1754), DAVID HUME (1711—1776) with his famous book "Inquiry concerning human understanding", CHARLES DE SECONDAT, baron de MONTESQUIEU (1689—1755) with his determinism in his books "Causes de la grandeur de la décadence des Romains" and "Esprit des lois", FRANÇOIS AROUET VOLTAIRE who propagated the Newtonian experimentalism, and whoseworks "Histoire de Charles XII" and "Essai sur les mœurs et l'esprit des nations" were a glorification of enlightened reasonableness. Names of DIDEROT (1718—84) and D'ALEMBERT, as authors of their Encyclopaedia with its rationalistic tendencies, had an enormous influence upon the Continent of Europe, and also upon England.

Indeed the mediaeval fears of hell, devil, demons and ghosts had been driven away, but that was not all. Rationalism had also robbed a great number of men and women, especially of the upper classes, of their belief in the Holy Scriptures.

The lower and middle classes however maintained their hold on the old truths of the Church and were not so easily shaken by Rationalism as the upper ten.

In this connection we may not omit the name of JEAN JACQUES ROUSSEAU (1712—1778). The reasoning of philosophers and the lack of new morals after the people had been robbed of religion had awakened discontent. Now this man tried to indicate in his "Discours sur l'égalité" the very roots of the failures of his time. Man in general and particularly the children had to break away from the disturbing influences of "grown-ups". "Virtue, duty and love for one's neighbour" were the words by which he tried to give steerage to the hearts adrift. "Emile ou de l'éducation" and "Julie ou de la nouvelle Héloïse" and afterwards his "Contrat Social" had a mighty influence upon his contemporaries, and may be called the forerunner of the French revolution.

As for politics in England, we will only mention the appearance of WILLIAM PITT whose words "I know that I can save this country and that no one else can" were not very modest, but whose achievements were colossal. In this time Fort William in Bengal was taken by nabab SOERADJA-DAULA, mainly chargeable on the half-hearted and uncapable Directors of the East India Company. We may mention here the war between England and its colonies and its dramatic end. On the other side may be recalled the famous voyages of JAMES COOK (1769—1779) who created new means for the colonial expansion of England in different parts of the world.

A revolution in industry was developed by the famous inventions of ARKWRIGHT in 1769 with his spinning jenny and JAMES WATT in 1788 with his steam-engine. ADAM SMITH became famous by his "Enquiry into the nature and causes of the wealth of nations". Germany was full of admiration for the products of GOTTHOLD EPHRAIM LESSING, JOHANN WOLFFGANG GOETHE and last not least IMMANUEL KANT, and in the same period HAYDN made his immortal "Schöpfung" and "Jahreszeiten".

The enumeration of these coryphaei and phenomena may suffice to show in what a revolutionary century WILLIAM CAREY lived.

When we turn our attention to England we will quote the words of the unknown writer of the "Petite Histoire des Missions Chrétiennes" who has good reason to say: "Il fallut plus d'un siècle encore avant que l'église réformée sortît de l'état d'indifférence à l'égard des missions et d'insensibilité envers les païens où elle paraissait enfermée, congelée. La gloire de l'avoir enfin secouée, réchauffée, rendue à sa véritable vocation revient à William Carey, qui mérite une place à part, la place d'honneur dans l'exposé des missions évangéliques: on l'a appelé fort bien, le pionnier de la mission organisée". [1]   To prove the truth of these words we will first turn to the main literary achievements of the century which reflect its spiritual achievements and religious ideas.   Very clear to everybody was the revolt against the authority of Classicism in Literature.   This does not mean that Classicism was easily overrun. On the contrary.   Classicism was as tenacious as it was old.   This conflict lasted till the end of the eighteenth century.   When asked what this revolt against classicism was, we point to the fact, that this phenomenon is commonly called the new Romanticism. CRASHAW, however, states, that it was not only NEW Romanticism. Its sources were not in the spirit of wonder and enthusiasm, created by the Renaissance as was the case with Romanticism of Shakespeare's days.   On the contrary the inward spirit was often something quite new and original, even when the outward form was an imitation.   When CRASHAW investigates, what causes existed to create the type of Romanticism peculiar to the eighteenth century, just as the Renaissance had created the type of Romanticism, peculiar to the sixteenth century, he denotes five movements —the romantic, the naturalistic, the emotional, the so-called democratic, and the religious.   First the naturalistic movement. This movement of the new Romanticism is a current which is "at bottom a passion for personal freedom, an unconscious striving forward, toward that revolutionary spirit, which was to make itself so strongly felt during the later years of the century".   Indeed people desired to be free, free from the bonds of the Church, free from the tyranny of despots, free from artificialities, free from conventions: in short they wished to breathe free air. [2]   So we understand that WILLIAM CAREY is looking for flowers, insects and is making his British museum in an attic of his parental house, when the great poets of nature WM WORDSWORTH and S. T. COLERIDGE are singing their well-known songs.   But not only in this way

8

"the bonds of classic restriction were broken". After that one sees the *democratic spirit* awakening. People wish personal freedom of feeling, of expression for all men. Puritans have been persecuted, Dissenters despised. All Non-Conformists have felt the obloquy of the highchurchmen. Now they are crying for freedom, personal freedom. They wish recognition of personal worth of all men.

And in this way we see something of the *religious spirit* of the second part of this century : it was according to CRASHAW a vigorous protest against mere conformity, authority, and formalism in religion ; it was on the other side a profound sense of the eternal worth of every individual soul, because for that soul Christ had died and God's infinite love had thereby been made manifest.

So two forces came into contact with each other. The force of Classicism and the force of Individualism. Classicism with its authority in Church and State, with its obedience to rules. Individualism asserting the rights of personality against tradition, convention and established order. [3])

When CRASHAW describes the same spirit in the years of 1780—1800 he says : "Poets (especially ROBERT BURNS) bring us into an intimate and living contact with the natural world to which there is no parallel in the literature of the eighteenth century and perhaps no parallel elsewhere." After dealing with Romanticism and emotionalism as both being stronger and more sincere than in the preceding period, he says with regard to religion : "on the side of religion there was no such marked movement as the Wesleyan revival, but the age was on the whole decidedly more religious. There was action from the scepticism so prevalent during the eighteenth century, while Methodism and other Movements had done much to purify and elevate contemporary life. The religious spirit found expression in literature. BURNS's "Cotter's Saturday Night" and other poems reveal the true religious sentiment that lay beneath the surface of that wild and seemingly irreverent nature. It is typical of the age as well as of the man that BURNS poured out his scornful ridicule only upon the religious profession that was false and hypocritical. Finally, the age was one which recognized as no other age had done the value and importance of the common man. The French Revolution set up its motto of "Liberty, Equality, Fraternity" ; and by those ideas more than any others the age was stirred. The standard of modern democracy had been raised ; and if democracy was not yet to triumph, its spirit was in the air presaging future victory. BURNS believed in the individual man and in his right, to work out his destiny in his own fashion. In his poetry, he voiced the faith that the individual imagination should be free, that the individual heart should be free, to cherish and to voice its deepest passions; that the individual conscience should be free, to worship God according to its own dictates; that the individual man should be free, to find in righteous use of his freedom his own fullest development." [4])

As we stated above the eighteenth century is an age of materialism, a period of dim ideals and of expiring hopes. We have already pointed to the mighty leader who headed a new movement towards the middle of this century. Summarizing we may say, that reason dominated alike the intellect, the will and the passions, that politics were self-interested: a clear example is given in the East India Company which even as late as the end of the 18th and the early part of the 19th century deprived India of the Gospel for the sake of its own financial profits. Of course there were some exceptions, but the man whose influence may be called universal, who revived to the utmost the spiritual life in England and abroad, is JOHN WESLEY. To understand his life-work we must look at the difference between the upper and lower classes.

TEMPERLEY describes this difference in his "Age of Walpole and the Pelhams". Here he gives an account of the time of Caroline, Princess of Wales who in 1727 became Queen of England as George II's wife. She gathered around her profound theologians like BUTLER and BERKELEY, deep-read divines like CLARKE and POTTER, wide-minded philosophers like LEIBNITZ, cultured Deists like CHESTERFIELD. She took great interest in theology but it was *primarily intellectual*. She loved theological *arguments* rather than good works, and valued divines for *depth of learning* or subtlety of metaphysics, rather than for fervour of piety. Deism—never popular with the masses or the country-gentry—had an immense vogue at Court." [5])

We see the same thing in the life of WILLIAM CAREY. In England, but still more in India, he has much trouble with the official personages, with the Court of Directors in London, but the simple land-folk are easily stirred by his Divine Message for his purposes: the same difference as between the Court and lower classes in England.

The above mentioned TEMPERLEY tells us that WALPOLE who confessed himself a sceptic in private, was publicly proclaiming his adherence to the Church; that BOLINGBROKE, who in secret was a freethinker on the other side showed a passion for orthodoxy. As we have already stated above, there was a public adherence to the forms of the Church and a private ridiculing of its spirit by the upper classes. They liked theology, but scorned to live according to the commandments of the Lord. MONTESQUIEU said: everybody laughs when you are talking of religion in fashionable society. Religion was a matter not to be experienced, but to be discussed by philosophers and theologians as professional men. There was lip-service to the Establishment says TEMPERLEY, and benevolent neutrality between rival religions.

In contrast to this spirit at Court and among the upper classes was the spirit in the middle and lower classes. Up to the middle of this century the political influence of the Church had been considerable, and a stumbling block to the Whig-party. But gradually the Church was losing its hold upon life and its political significance. Whereas now the Court and the upper classes were losing their grip on the Word of God, the middle and lower classes remained in general religious: the old Puritan spirit lived on unchanged and from these classes burst forth the revival which changed the whole aspect of life in England. Whereas the greater part of the statesmen (and of the Court of Directors of the East India Company) were unbelievers of any form of Christianity, the greater part of the simple folk adhered to the old doctrines. [6])

But together with this phenomenon, we stated the wish for individualism. TEMPERLEY describes this intention of the upper classes desiring to save their own souls in about the same way as CRASHAW "but at the same time in their selfish individualism *they were directed towards saving the bodies and souls of others* in relieving unemployment, promoting education, or providing the needs of the poor." This remarkable reaction against the spirit, which up till then had occupied their hearts, had of course a profound influence upon the great religious movements of JOHN WESLEY c.s. and no less upon the awakening desire for propagating the Gospel. Not the upper classes but the middle and lower classes were to stimulate these religious movements.

One of the great forerunners was GRIFFITH JONES.

His action was the start of a formidable secession from the

Established Church and to mark his purpose we will only cite a passage from his "Serious Call to a Devout and Holy life": "If, therefore, persons of either sex .... desirous of perfection, should unite themselves into little societies, professing voluntary poverty, virginity, retirement, and devotion, that some might be relieved by their charities, and all be blessed with their prayers, and benefited by their example; such persons, so far from being chargeable with any superstition or blind devotion, might justly be said to *restore that piety which was the boast and glory of the Church, when its greatest saints were alive."* [7])

We won't dwell longer upon this soldier in the army of Christ, this man of reaction against the officialdom of the Established Church, we will turn our thoughts to JOHN WESLEY and GEORGE WHITEFIELD. "Les Méthodistes tirent leur origine d'une association de jeunes gens formée à Oxford, en 1729, par JOHN WESLEY et son frère CHARLES, et bientôt surnommée le « Club des pieux » ou des « méthodistes », parceque les membres s'engageaient à suivre une règle de vie, methodus vitae. Les deux frères entrèrent d'abord en relation avec les Hernhuters, puis allèrent par toute l'Angleterre et l'Amérique propager leurs idées. Ils s'adjoignirent en 1732 un prédicateur de grand talent, nommé GEORGE WHITEFIELD, qui fit faire des progrès sensibles à l'association." [8])

In AUGUST GOTTFRIED SPANGENBERG, "Kurzgefaszte Historische Nachricht von der gegenwärtigen Verfassung der evangelischen Brüderunität augspurgischer Confession" we found a list of the places in England where the Moravians and their missions settled as is shown in the following paragraph. "Unter Groszbrittannischer Hoheit sind sowol in Europa als Nordamerica und auf den westindischen Eilanden verschiedene Brüdergemeinen und Missionen: In Londen seit 1742. In Bedford seit 1748, *in Northampton* zu Okbrook, etc. together about 20 places only in England. [9]) From this we understand, how easily the Methodists connected themselves with the Moravians. Well known is the visit of JOHN and CHARLES WESLEY and GEORGE WHITEFIELD to the Moravian brethren after the unhappy missionary journey to America, where they met some of these Pietists. This visit was paid to Graf VON ZINZENDORF at Hernhut in 1737(8). This meeting was a crucial point in his life, for it leads to his conversion in May of the year 1738. From this time onward, JOHN WESLEY becomes the fiery preacher, who tried by all means in his power to revive the Church of England. Moreover he tried to open the eyes of his fellow-countrymen to the immense needs of the heathen. [10])

SPANGENBERG writes in his extensive biography of Graf VON ZINZENDORF, that Von Zinzendorf "Herrn CHARLES WESLEY einen von den Leuten die man Methodisten nennte, kennen gelernt hat. Von da an machte sich eine Bekanntschaft zwischen den Bruedern und den Methodisten, welche eine Zeitlang in Hoffnung dasz sie ihren Nutzen habe würde, unterhalten wurde." [11])

In the same chapter, he mentions the names of JOHN WESLEY and GEORGE WHITEFIELD. But still more interesting is the following : "Die Lehre von der "sinless perfection" oder der Volkommenheit, dabey man sich nicht mehr als einen sündigen Menschen ansieht, gehörte insonderheit unter die Punckte, darinn der Graf mit JOHN WESLEY nicht eins war. Der Graf behauptete dagegen, dasz ein Mensch, wenn er auch noch so heilig wäre, doch in sich eine sündige Creatur sei, die nicht anders, dann durch die Gnade Jesu Christi, bewahrt werden könne. Seine eigenen Worte davon sind die : ,,Wir glauben, dasz die Sünde in unsren Gliedern bleibt, dasz sie aber über uns nicht herschen könne ; weil es so in der Schrift steht : Denn da heiszt es : So lasset nun die Sünd nicht herschen in eurem sterblichen Leibe u.s.w."." [12])

In the second part of this book he mentions Graf VON ZINZENDORF's voyage to England "der am 20ten April auf die Höhe von Dover kam, so ging er auf ein Boot, und lief mit demselben,bey stürmischem Wetter in der Hafen ein ; nich ohne viele Gefahr, da die Ueberfahrt von fünf Uhr Nachmittags bis Nachts um ein Uhr währte ; doch der Heiland erleichterte ihm alle Beschwerden". [13])

From these quotations we gather that before the middle of the eighteenth century there was indeed some imported spiritual life, although little of it is known in the official world of England. We learn from this that there was a congregation of these Moravians in Northampton at a place in the neighbourhood of the native village of WILLIAM CAREY, a fact which explains his close connection with these brethren in his youth and also when he was in India.

From these statements we also notice the close connection between JOHN WESLEY and VON ZINZENDORF as well as their divergencies.

D. CHANTEPIE DE LA SAUSSAYE says in his fine characterizations of Methodism and Pietism this : "Pietism is fruit of the Lutheran Church, Methodism of the Reformed Church. Pietism had about the same influence on the Lutheran Church as Methodism on the Reformed Church. Generally speaking he thinks that the German Reformation wants reconciliation with God, while the Swiss Reformation wants sanctification. He also states that all the good and permanent factors of Puritanism have passed into Methodism while all the good and permanent factors of Pietism passed into the Moravian congregations." [14])

These generalizations are of course only rough approximations, but they are worth considering by those who make a special study of these times.

Above we stated, why JOHN WESLEY c.s were called "Methodists". This nickname indicates, in what way they were regarded by the whole body of the official Church. They disliked these men, they suspected and despised them. But WESLEY stood his ground firmly against all kinds of attack. He had been formed by three great writers: THOMAS A KEMPIS, JEREMY TAYLOR and LAW. Especially LAW seems to have been of material influence upon him. According to LESLIE STEPHAN it was from LAW and the Moravians that there came the external impulses which affected him. [15]) LESLIE STEPHAN gives in her book "Thoughts on the eighteenth century" an accurate account of the relation between these two men, and informs us that this relation passed through several phases. WESLEY never became a mystic, though he was much attracted by some of the mystical teaching of LAW. He not only wrote an angry letter to him on breaking with him (1738) but eighteen years later (1756) he made a formal attack upon LAW's mystical doctrines. In later years he softened towards his old master.

It is not our purpose to give a full account of the development of Methodism nor of the appearance of the Moravians, but we will only try to give these data which have more or less influenced the activities of the Baptist Missionary Society i.c. William Carey.

Nowhere we have found an account of his contact with Methodists in the books dealing with his life. Neither do we know whether he personally met one of these great men. They were much older. But without any doubt the influence of these men on him was great. It is hardly possible that the fiery preacher John Wesley who tried with all his might to revive the Church, should not have affected the spiritual life in the villages, where William Carey lived. But suppose this was not the case, then we may

be sure, that the eyes of WILLIAM CAREY at any rate were directed
to the WESLEYS on account of their efforts to open their countrymen's eyes to the immense needs of the heathen.

ERNST TROELTSCH even thinks that Methodism was such a force
in England, that it was a means "wodurch die englische Welt
gegen den Geist der französischen Revolution immunisiert wurde.
Der Methodismus war zunächst ähnlich wie die Brüdergemeinde
ein Versuch, durch engere erweckte Kreise das Salz der Landes-
kirche zu werden und ist äuszerlich nur durch Verschlieszung der
landeskirchlichen Kanzeln zur Verselbständigung gedrängt worden." [16])

Diese Erweckung, welche die Methodistischen Missionare unter
Gefahren und Mühen, wie einst die Urapostel, und schlieszlich mit
Hilfe groszer Feldpredigten in die Mittel- und Unterschichten
hineintrugen, muszte aber in ihren Ergebnissen gesichert und
gesammelt werden. Hier griff die Organisation ein, in der Wesley,
ein unermüdlicher und unerschütterlicher Missionar wie PAULUS,
und ein herrschgewaltiger Organisator wie IGNATIUS VON LOYOLA,
Meister war. [17])

Soon we see the symptoms of the sect arising in this Movement.
Wesley was urging that adults should convert themselves and
live perfectly. They should *feel*, that they were in possession of
grace and they should control their lives by an exact scheme of
living.

SELL upholds in his book "Christentum und Weltgeschichte"
that "Aufklärung" and Pietism have the same root : viz. individualism. "In diesen religiösen Neuschöpfungen im Gebiete des
Protestantismus steht der Aufklärung scheinbar in völligem Gegen-
satz. Dennoch sind Pietismus und Aufklärung nicht nur Zeit-
sondern auch Bundesgenossen. Im Augenblick wo die Alleinherr-
schaft des kirchlichen Dogmas über das christliche Abendland zu
zerbrechen begann, hat der Pietismus einen neuen Weg gezeigt,
auf dem das alte Christentum in dogmatischer und kirchlicher,
freier, neuer Weise sich behaupten kann." [18]) We should like to
say the same of Methodism, but Sell thinks the influence of Pietism
much greater and of more importance than Methodism ; according
to him it has no "weltgeschichtliche Bedeutung".

We think that "Vaterlandsliebe" may have played some part
in these assertions. We agree with him, that the root of Pietism
and Aufklärung (and Methodism) was : individualism. Of course

this word does not explain all the compound phenomena of this great century, but we venture to say, that it was one of the principal reactions against the ideas which hitherto had taken possession of men's minds in England and on the Continent.

Now we turn again to William Carey. He wants to be free. Free from the official Church. He may have despised the Hackleton meetings at first, later on he loves them. He mentally takes the side of the "rebels" in America. He likes their desire for freedom. When studying the Scriptures, he is individualistic. For he does not subject himself to the opinion of the Established Church, but becomes a Baptist. He wants to be free from their dullness. The official Church makes no attempt to propagate the Gospel. Neither do the Baptists. Quite alone, he sets to work, independent of other people, whatever they may think, or whatever they may assert. Indeed the struggle for freedom was in the air. In what degree the French revolution affected his efforts, we don't know. But there may have been some influence. In the time of his youth hymnists were singing their songs. Some time before the Mission's Marseillaise was born : "O'er the gloomy hills of darkness". Methodist preachers, Moravian poets, they all are awakening a spirit of reaction against the official church and its corruption. Baptist are gathering into Associations in several areas of the Kingdom making a monthly intercession with their leaders and asking God, whether he will give His blessings upon the barren soil. [19]) When William Carey is attending such a meeting, he gives the answer to these men : "If you want the Kingdom of God speeded, go out and speed *yourselves ;* only obedience rationalizes prayer : only missions redeem your intercessions from insincerity."

Of course, they resist. But William Carey dares to stand alone. And the more his country-men resist, the more Carey is stimulated to rouse them to the consciousness of the missionary call. Just like other Missionaries e.g. the Rev. A. MERKELIJN, missionary sent out by the Reformed Church of Middelburg to Magelang on the isle of Java, Netherlands East Indies, who by the grace of God overcame all difficulties in the face of strong opposition. When describing his method of working, he relates to a dessah, where he and his fellow workers were strongly opposed. But then he simply says : "In this dessah we concluded to *continue* our work." [20])

So did William Carey. He gradually acquired his great influence. First of all the flame in his own heart was kindled and then kept burning by the studying of the facts of salvation. Then by bringing fiery coals on the cold altars of others. After that, he is stirring the coals till they are burning and glowing. He protects the faint flame, lest it is extinguished under the ashes of indifference or through the atmosphere of selfishness or separated by the breath of scorn or damaged by the marshes of open hostility. [21])

Freedom was in the air indeed. But freedom not after the Scriptures. For the latter is contrary to the freedom of the sects and wordly minds. Freedom after the Scriptures means bondage to the highest laws of the Lord himself. Freedom after the spirit of revolution and individualism means bondage to the laws of men, made by men. The first means happiness, the latter in their consequent results: death. For this highest freedom William Carey fights.

Many oppose him. He goes on. He prays and works for free schools, free from the officialdom of the Church and education only given to the rich, free from conventions and unnaturalness. He is attracted by the sea-voyages of Captain COOK, whose books open for him a new and unknown world, he will free the heathen from the bondage of sin and is stimulated by the example of the Moravians, and the vigorous preaching of the Methodists. Indeed, freedom is in the air: new poetry, an inclination to get back to nature, new literature, unhampered by Classicism, new politics unbiassed by Toryism, new inventions so that the poor as well as the rich may be free ; under such conditions William Carey tries to fulfil what he deems his duty : to open the hearts of his countrymen for all those who don't know the freedom of Christ Jesus. So William Carey may be called a child of his time, but the times do not govern him, but by the grace of God he governs the times in which God has placed this servant.

NOTES

[1]) Un laïque, Petite Histoire des missions évangéliques chrétiennes. Seconde édition 1929. Société des missions évangéliques. Paris, p. 82.
The writer of this book gives in a few words a fine characterization of this time in these words : "Bien des faits se sont produits, depuis 1664, qui ont modifié, bouleversé les idées et les sentiments des hommes. L'atmosphère morale n'est plus la même. Notons brièvement les principaux événements par lesquels ce premier résultat indispensable a été produit.
Faits d'ordre *religieux* : le Piétisme en Allemagne, le Méthodisme en Angleterre ont impérieusement jeté les consciences en face des exigences de l'évangile, et parmi ces exigences pouvait-on méconnaître longtemps celle d'évangéliser ?
D'autre part, le *Rationalisme*, mettant l'accent sur l'unité de la race humaine, son

identité, sa faculté de progresser à l'infini, ne devait-il pas, ne fût ce qu'indirectement, attirer l'attention sur les membres les moins avancés de cette grande famille ?

Faits d'ordre *géographique :* par une coïncidence frappante, que beaucoup penseront providentielle, les voyages de COOK à travers les mers australes et les îles innombrables, dont elles sont semées, voyages qui se terminent en 1779 par la mort de l'explorateur parlent en même temps sur imaginations et les font voyager vers ces pays nouveaux, si pleins de séductions naturelles et par suite, vers ces hommes, leurs habitants, restés primitifs et païens, que l'inconnu même et le mystère parent d'une décevante, mais irrésistible poésie.

Faits d'ordre *politique :* la Révolution française, la chute soudaine d'une société séculaire, l'avénement d'un monde nouveau à travers des convulsions tragiques, des crimes et des guerres, il avait là encore ample matière pour les âmes chrétiennes à réflexions, à repentir à saints et héroïques résolutions. C'était l'heure où un Carey pouvait paraître et réussir".

²) WILLIAM H. CRASHAW,The making of English Literature. London 1906, pp. 223—224.

Describing Individualism from 1780—1832 he writes : "On the side of religion there was no such marked movement as the Wesleyan revival but the age was on the whole decidedly more religious.   There was reaction from scepticism so prevalent during the eighteenth century while methodism and other movements had done much to purify and elevate contemporary life.   The religious spirit found expression in literature.   It is typical that BURNS poured out his scornful ridicule only upon the religious profession that was false and hypocritical.   Finally the age was one which recognized as no other age had ever done, the value and the importance of the common man.   The French revolution set up its motto : "Liberty, Equality, Fraternity", and by those ideas, more than by others, the age was stirred.   The standard of modern democracy had been raised : and if democracy was not yet to triumph its spirit was in the air presaging future victory. Burns believed in the individual man and in his right to work out destiny in his own fashion. He voiced the faith that the individual imagination should be free, that the individual heart should be free, to cherish and to voice its deepest passions ; that the individual conscience should be free, to worship God according to its own dictates, that the individual man should be free, to find in his righteous use of his freedom his own fullest development, pp. 233—235.

³) CRASHAW, op. cit., pp. 221—225.

⁴) Id., pp. 253—255.

⁵) Cambridge modern History. Vol. VI, p. 77. Cambridge 1909.

⁶) JOHN RICHARD GREEN, History of the English people, pp. 167—179. London, 1908.

⁷) Cambridge modern History, p. 81.

⁸) LAVISSE et RAMBAUD, Histoire Générale VII. 1715—1788.

⁹) AUGUST GOTTLIEB VON SPANGENBERG, Historische Nachricht, pp. 16—19. Barby 1781.

¹⁰) Prof. Dr. J. H. BAVINCK, Zending in een wereld in nood, pp. 116—117. Zomer & Keuning, Wageningen.

¹¹) SPANGENBERG, Leben von Graf von Zinzendorf, Brüdergemeinen, 1774, p. 1044.

¹²) Id., p. 1047.

¹³) Id. Vol. II, p. 1187.

¹⁴) De godsdienstige bewegingen van dezen tijd naar oorsprong geschetst. CH. CHANTEPIE DE LA SAUSSAYE, pp. 115—127. R'dam 1863.

¹⁵) LESLIE STEPHAN, English thoughts on the 18th Century. Vol. II, pp. 383 f.f.

¹⁶) ERNST TROELTSCH, Die Soziallehren der kirchlichen Kirche u. Gruppen, p. 837. Tübingen 1923.

¹⁷) Id., p. 838.

¹⁸) KARL SELL, Christentum und Weltgeschichte, p. 49. Leipzig 1909.

¹⁹) S. PEARCE CAREY. Op. cit. p. 10.

²⁰) A. MERKELIJN, 26 jaren op het Zendingsveld. Herinneringen van een missionair predikant. Daamen, Den Haag, 1941, p. 263.

²¹) De nieuwe Handelingen der Apostelen. Dr. ARTHUR PIERSON in translation. Nijmegen 1898, p. 31.

b. His life in a nutshell.

1. 1771—1783.

In the year 1600 the great East India Company was founded. From that time onward England had carried on a brisk trade with India. The power of the Company had increased very much as the years went by. The English had come into touch with many districts in India for trading purposes, settlements had been established and a large stream of traders and other people went from England to India. Except one class of people : the missionary men. Not one christian missionary was sent to India from 1600 up to the days of William Carey, a space of time of nearly two hundred years. [1]) It is true, the birth-day of Protestant Mission in India is July 9, 1706, when ZIEGENBALG and PLÜTSCHAU landed in Tranquebar [2]), but to Denmark, not England, belongs the honour of redeeming Protestantism from the century long dishonour of not sending missionaries to India.

Just like the Dutch East India Company, the English East India Company loved trade above all things.

The Society for the Promotion of Christian Knowledge founded by ANTON WILHELM BÖHME in 1678 may have given some aid to the Danish missionaries, even increased the support, when CHRISTIAAN FRIEDRICH SCHWARTZ arrived in Tranquebar in 1750, but nobody from England went to India to render personal service to the missionary cause. Neither "the Society for Propagating the Gospel", founded in 1701, nor "the Society for promoting christian knowledge" founded in 1709, sent anybody to India. As stated before, the real reason was : the barreness of the Church of England, due to Deism and Rationalism and by consequence the terrible state of affairs in the towns and the country amongst all classes of society.

Moreover, the real reason for not sending missionaries to India was not the company's hostility to missionary action—in the beginning of its existence no opposition existed. On the contrary, the Company's agents were at first friendly rather than hostile. [3]) In later days the Company was undoubtedly influenced by the conditions in the Established Church. Not through, but in spite of the Church, William Carey was the first of her own missionary sons, whom England sent to India. Though late, the effect was enormous.

Before we consider the effect and the causes of his great success, we will try to give a brief account of his life. William Carey was born *in Paulerspury on the 17th of August 1761*. Dr. GEORGE SMITH gives in his famous book on William Carey the thoughts of Professor STEPHENS of Copenhagen, who traces back the name of Carey to the Scando-Anglican Car, Caer or Care, which became a place-name as Car-ey. As scores of people were called William, William of Car-ey may have been shortened to William Carey, and this may have become the family name. He says that in Denmark the name Caroe is common. The oldest English instance is the Cariet who coined money in London for AETHELRED II in 1016. He asserts that the name in its different forms of Crew, Carew, Carey, and Cary, still prevails on the Irish coast. Depression of trade is said to have driven the family first to Yorkshire then to the Northamptonshire village of Yelvertoft, and finally to Paulerspury. So if there was Norse blood in William Carey, it came out in his persistent missionary daring, and it is pleasant even to speculate on the possibility of such an origin in one, who was during his whole Indian career indebted to Denmark for its protection, which enabled him to work on his schemes.

Dr. George Smith even tries to show that he was akin to the great statesmen, soldiers, scholars and Bishops from Richard the second to Charles the second, who all had the same name as our missionary. But S. PEARCE CAREY, the great grandson of William Carey gives some other story as we will see afterwards.

His father was EDMUND CAREY, born in Paulerspury, tammy weaver, and parish clerk as well as a schoolmaster, an unusual occupation in those days, when schools were scarcely found.

His mother was ELISABETH WILLS.

His grandfather was PETER CAREY "from near Yelvertoft" as Carey tells us, a place unknown in England. He was the first master of the school in Paulerspury, but also a weaver of tammy cloth. He died Aug. 7, 1743 in Paulerspury, shortly after the loss of his first-born son William. This loss was fatal to him. In the entries of the Paulerspury register we find : William Carey, buried July 1743, Peter Carey, buried August 7, 1743.

His grandmother, wife of Peter Carey, called herself 'Naomi' after these terrible losses. Peter Carey had married her Aug. 1722. Her maiden-name was ANN FLECKNOE, who came from another part of the country. The losses were the more terrible as her other son

20

Peter had sailed for Canada and so she was left alone with Edmund, who was to become the father of William. [4])

When asked, whether anything more is known of the genealogical tree of William Carey, we must give a negative answer. But S. PEARCE CAREY tells us "that Peter Carey in coming to Paulerspury was possibly returning to a home of his fathers". For a James Carey was its curate from 1624 to 1629 and of good handwriting. A James Carey again—perhaps the same—was buried there on April 7, 1661 and an Elizabeth Carey in 1665, and a John in 1667—perhaps the curate's wife and son. If from these Peter Carey has descended, then William Carey came of distant parentage of some culture. [5]) But the missing link between these early-Carey's and William's grandfather Peter Carey has not yet been found. However, a remarkable fact is, that of all these Carey's historians tell us that "their handwriting was of no rustic but of some culture". So was William Carey's.

When Edmund Carey (the father of William) was left alone with his mother, he was a child of seven. As soon as possible, he helped his mother in making a living. At twenty-four, he married the above mentioned Elizabeth Wills and together with his mother, they were a very happy family. His mother did not forget the terrible losses of her firstborn son William and her husband, but the pain was softened, especially when on August 17, 1761 a grandson was born, who was called William in remembrance of the William she had lost.

To 'Naomi' he was the little 'Obed'. He was her light in darkness, and when, after two years, a granddaughter was born, called Ann, old Ann happily died praising the Lord.

An event of some importance in William's early life was the return of his uncle PETER from Canada. Young William had a great love for flowers, plants and insects and by good luck, his uncle was a gardener. But not only did he awaken in the mind of his nephew a love for botany, but he also widened his outlook by telling him of peoples from overseas, which interested young William very much and made him long to see these countries with his own eyes.

When William was six years old his father was chosen as master 1767 of the Paulerspury school and as parish clerk at the people's suggestion! In Paulerspury people had seen his devotion to his widowed mother and his exertion for getting a living for her. So his son

William Carey went from the Pury End hollow to the schoolhouse on the hill. Here he received a good knowledge of the three R's: reading, writing, arithmetic and the catechism and Scripture. His sister Mary, commonly called Poll, tells us that he used to work out sums in arithmetic when he was in bed. Soon he showed an avidity for books especially for books on 'science, history and travels'. He loved the travels of Columbus so much, that his friends gave him the nickname of 'Columbus'. And this name was very suitable for him, for just as Columbus discovered the way to America, he discovered the way to Asia. Columbus met much opposition, so did William Carey. Columbus embarked after a hard struggle, so did this missionary.

As a schoolboy, he once fell out of a tree and this is the way in which his schoolmaster talked about the incident : "Columbus has killed himself." "No—but he's broken his head." "He always said, he'd climb that tree." "He got the nest at the top." "He didn't—he fell before he reached it." [6]) 'Columbus' was not dead but badly bruised and had bumped his head severely. So he was confined to his bed ; later he was allowed to sit in the corner of a room. His mother, busy as ever with four children, thought the prisoner safe in the room ; but one day she found the house empty. After some time, 'Columbus' was back again with the bird's nest on his knee. "Will, you don't mean to say you've been climbing that tree again." "I couldn't help it, Mother," was his answer. His will to conquer difficulties however hard marked his whole life.

So he tried to know all about insects, plants, birds etc. and he conquered. "Tek it to Bill Carey ; he will tell you all about it," his mates said recognizing him as a biologist. [7])

This will to conquer, to overcome difficulties, is one of the main features of his character. He himself said afterwards : "Give me credit for diligence and you will do me justice. Anything more will be untrue. But I can plod and persevere. To this I owe everything."

1773   This ability to plod is well illustrated by his way of studying Latin. At the age of twelve he obtained a copy of "Dyche's Latin Vocabulary" and learnt the whole book by heart. Moreover, he studied the small grammar prefixed to it, probably with the aid of a THOMAS JONES, who was sent by his father to Kidderminster Grammar School to become a physician, but he got a dislike for it and became a weaver instead.

22

His outlook was broadened by his reading of the hand-printed weekly : Northampton Mercury. Three copies were sent regularly to the village, one for the squire, one for the rector, one for the schoolmaster. In this way William also got to know it. DEAVILLE WALKER has shown in his book "Missionary, Pioneer and Statesman", that the very books, which influenced William's young life most, were advertised in its columns : the Voyages of Captain Cook, Guthrie's Geographical Grammar, and DAVID BRAINERD. Through this paper he got acquainted with all kinds of topics, such as the slave trade and so on.

Especially the books of Lieutenant JAMES COOK interested him. James Cook was the son of an agricultural labourer in the neighbourhood, who of course became the hero of the boys of Paulerspury. William's interest for foreign countries and peoples was roused once more.

Carey's own desire was to work in a garden. During two years he gave all his energy to it. But in vain. A corporal disorder— a very sensitive skin which couldn't bear to be exposed to the influence of the sun—made him unfit for any work out of doors. So his father entrusted him to the care of CLARKE NICHOLS of Piddington, a shoemaker. [8])

Piddington 1775

1777

By sending his son to this man, he robbed himself of an apprentice in handweaving. Moreover he had to pay this shoemaker for William's apprenticeship, by which he was greatly inconvenienced. But Edmund Carey learned that his job was threatened by the new-machinery and shoemaking became a leading craft. So William started for Piddington to become a cobbler as he afterwards calls himself. But here we may see the governing of his paths by the Lord. For he not only learned cobbling at Clarke Nichols' house, but here he was won for the Saviour. Not by the behaviour of Clarke Nichols who "had a hot temper and a rough tongue and loved drinking bouts", but by JOHN WARR, his fellow-apprentice, and three years his senior. They had much in common, but there was one great difference : William and his father and grandfather were prominent men in the Church of England, but John and his family were zealous Nonconformists.

Now William Carey, according to his own words, was a Churchman and looked down upon Dissenters. He would fain have destroyed the little meeting house in Hackleton, Piddington's hamlet, where John Warr worshipped. Consequently the two apprentices were discussing religious topics all day long. William Carey says of these discussions : "I had pride sufficient for a thousand times my knowledge. So I always scorned to have the worst in debate, and the last word was assuredly mine. I always made up in positive assertion, what was lacking in my reasoning, and generally came off with triumph. But afterwards, I was often convinced that, though I had the last word, my fellow-apprentice had the better of the argument, and I felt a growing uneasiness and stings of conscience gradually increasing ; but I had no idea that nothing but a complete change of heart could do me any good." [9]) William's reaction to these discussions was nihil. In this time he more than ever took an interest not in religion, but in plants and trees and insects. He himself says : "John Warr became importunate with me, lending me books, which gradually wrought a change in my thinking and my inward uneasiness increased." After having occasionally attended Hackleton prayerhouse through the influence of John Warr, he writes : "I also determined to leave off lying, swearing, and other sins, to which I was addicted ; and sometimes, when alone, I tried to pray." [10]) A deep impression was made on his life by the following incident : "I had been to Northampton, where I made some purchases for myself, which amounted to about a shilling more than I was worth. But I had a counterfeit shilling, which Mr. HALL, the iron-monger, had given me as a Christmasbox. I knew it to be a bad shilling but I was strongly inclined to assert to my master, that it belonged to other money, with which he had intrusted me, to purchase things for him, as this would clear my private account. I recollect the struggle I had all the way home, and I prayed to God to excuse my dishonesty and lying for this once : I would never repeat such an action, but would break off with sin thenceforth. My wickedness prevailed, and I told the falsehood, and was detected by my master. A gracious God did not get me safe through. I soon concluded that my theft was known to the whole village. I concealed myself from all, as much as I could, and was so overwhelmed with shame, that it was a considerable time before I went out." [11]) This event is a crucial point of his life. He now felt the need of a Saviour. He now realised the significance of the word 'sin', prayed for conversion, read Holy Scripture. A special help to enlighten his spirit was Mr. Hall's "Help to Zion's Travellers". He found in this book "all that he had picked up by scraps, arranged and illustrated". [12])

So we may conclude that by the grace of God, John Warr and this Mr. Hall were the instruments, used to bring this sheep to the flock. By means of John Warr he had, like Columbus, discovered a new world : the spiritual world. And from this time on, he was developing his powers for the kingdom of God.

Above we mentioned the way in which he learned Latin. Now he turned to Greek. One day, when finding a book on his master's shelves, he could not read the letters. He accurately copied these symbols and then went to his tutor of Latin : THOMAS JONES. He continued, till he was master of the Greek language.

On February 10, 1779 the King had proclaimed a national day 1779 of fasting and prayer. William Carey attended Hackleton meeting-house. A THOMAS CHATER of Olney (in the neighbourhood of Piddington), a novice in lay-preaching, spoke of Hebr. 13 : 13: 'Let us go forth therefore unto Him without the camp, bearing his reproach'. By these words he was convinced he had to go out of the camp of the Established Church and to unite with those whom he once despised so much, and bear the reproach of Christ. [13])

The reason for attending this service may have been political— the struggle between England and America was growing worse and worse for the country and William Carey was like nearly all the Dissenters mentally allied with the resisters—from this time onward he is associated with the Nonconformists and turns once for all his back on the official Church.

In this year 1779, his master died. In October of the same year William Carey passed into the service of THOMAS OLD of Hackleton. In this time too he made the acquaintance of mystics. His belief was shaken. But after a big struggle he pressed the Book still more to his heart and was relieved of men's speculations. [14])

A man, who also must be mentioned as of importance for his further life is THOMAS SCOTT. As soon as he was in Hackleton, he met this young clergyman and they became friends. Whereas THOMAS JONES was his tutor of Latin and later of Greek, this educated man taught him also Hebrew. When possible, they were together, Carey always trying to listen to the preaching of Scott and reading without pause the books he gave him. William Carey himself declares : "If there be anything of the work of God in my soul, I owe much of it to Mr. Scott's preaching, when I first set out in the ways of the Lord." [15])

A great day in his life is the date mentioned in the margin. Then June 10 1781

William Carey married DOROTHY PLACKET, five years older than himself, a bride not able to sign her name, the village being schoolless. [16])
She was of a well known Puritan family. Then two happy years
1783 followed, and their hearts abounded with joy, when Ann was born, but alas Ann died the next year. His master Thomas Old also died suddenly. Now he passes through a very difficult time. For his wife is a younger sister of his late master's wife. So he has the task of supporting this family of a widow and four children and his own. Trying to get through all the concealed difficulties, he opens an evening school, but "the master is mastered by his pupils", as he himself tells us. By the help of his younger brother Thomas and some others, he succeeded in overcoming the difficulties to some degree. Just at this time a great change comes in his life; for from now on, we may see the shoemaker-minister. This we are going to consider next.

NOTES

[1]) Cf. J. N. OGILVIE D.D., The apostles of India. Hodder and Stroughton, p. 292.
[2]) Prof. Dr. J. H. BAVINCK, Ons Zendingsboek, p. 117.
[3]) OGILVIE, op. cit. p. 293.
[4]) Cf. S. PEARCE CAREY, op. cit. pp. 14—18 and Dr. BEUSEKOM, William Carey, pp. 3—8 and JOHN CLARK MARSHMAN, The life of William Carey etc., p. 1.
[5]) S. PEARCE CAREY, op. cit., p. 16.
[6]) L. H. DALTON, "Young man sit down", p. 3. Ed. House Press. 1938.
[7]) S. PEARCE CAREY gives an interesting account of the recollections of MARY CAREY, Williams younger sister, when she was sixty-eight.
She says : "The room that was wholly appropriated to his use was full of insects stuck in every corner, that he might observe their progress. Drawing and painting he was fond of, and made considerable progress in these arts. Of birds and all manner of insects, he had numbers. When he was from home, the birds were generally committed to my care. Being five years younger, I was indulged by him in all his enjoyments. Though I often used to kill them by kindness, yet, when he saw my grief, he always permitted me the pleasure of serving them again, and often took me over the dirtiest roads to get at a plant or an insect. . . . His natural fondness for a garden was cherished by his uncle Peter and he often had his nephew with him not having a child of his own."
Both his brother Thomas and Mary said : "Whatever he began, he finished. Difficulties never seemed to discourage his mind." Op. cit. p. 23.
[8]) Cf. S. PEARCE CAREY, op. cit., p. 27 and MARSHMAN, op. cit. p. 2.
[9]) Ib., p. 30. Cf. Dr. BEUSEKOM, op. cit., pp. 15, 16 and P. H. MULDER, ,,Gedenk uwe voorgangers", Amsterdam, Bigot & Van Rossum, pp. 59, 60. Prof. Dr. J. H. BAVINCK, "Zending in een wereld in nood", p. 122.
[10]) S. PEARCE CAREY, p. 31.
[11]) Ib., p. 32.
[12]) MARSHMAN, op. cit., p. 4.
[13]) MULDER, op. cit., p. 60. Cf. Dr. BEUSEKOM, op. cit., p. 18.
[14]) S. PEARCE CAREY, op. cit., p. 35.
[15]) Ibid., p. 36.
[16]) Dr. BEUSEKOM, op. cit., pp. 19—20.

26

2. HIS CAREER AS A SHOEMAKER-MINISTER. 1783—1791.

When only eighteen years old William Carey appeared for the first time in the pulpit, in Hackleton in 1779. He himself tells of this preaching : "I had joined the church, formed at the time by a few pious men at Hackleton. A sort of conference was begun and sometimes I was invited to deliver my thoughts on a passage of Scripture, which the people being ignorant, applauded, to my great injury." [1]

When twenty-one, William Carey went to Olney, a place in the neighbourhood, to attend the annual conference of the "Association of fellowship and Christian service". He heard ANDREW FULLER's sermon about "Be not children in understanding" which made a very deep impression upon him. As he had not a penny in his pocket to buy a meal, he was feeling very hungry. When walking through the streets of the village, he met some friends from Barton, who invited him to share their simple food, which he gladly accepted. Mr. Chater, the Independent minister of Olney, took a great interest in W. Carey after hearing his views on religion, and at his instigation, the Barton friends called on William Carey soon after and tried to persuade him to become their minister. But Carey contended he had no aptitude for the ministry. However, after much urging on their part, he yielded to their pressure.

When once he had begun, he continued to serve this Olney Church every fortnight for three years and a half. The church members were poor rush-mat weavers who got the reeds out of the marshes, but Carey loved them and on Sundays he walked six miles from Hackleton to Olney and back again over abominable roads "though they could not pay him enough to cover the cost of the shoes and clothes he wore out in their services." [2]

In Paulerspury, his native village, people heard of his fame, and soon they requested him to preach once a month, to which he readily agreed. His father, who was parish clerk of the official church, listened to the preaching of his son, not openly but from a place of concealment, and went home content. His mother accosted by a friend said : "And will my boy make a preacher ?" The reply was : "Yes, and a great one, if God spares him."

At this time, his conviction on the subject of baptism changed. After hearing a sermon of Rev. JOHN HORSEY, he studied this subject in the New Testament and was led to the conviction that baptism by immersion after confession of faith was scriptural and apostolic. After consulting Dr. JOHN RYLAND of Northampton, he was baptized by him in the Nene river below Northampton castle. [3])

Some years later Dr. Ryland said : "On October 5, 1783, I baptized in the Nene, just beyond Doddridge's meeting house a poor journeyman-shoemaker, little thinking that before nine years had elapsed, he would prove to be the first instrument in forming a Society for sending missionaries from England to the heathen world, and much less, that later on he would become professor of languages in an Oriental college, and translator of the Scriptures into eleven different tongues."

1785   After two years of studying, preaching, cobbling, he went to Moulton at the advice of a friend, who informed him that the Moulton schoolmaster had left the village. Now he set up as a schoolmaster again and had as little success as formerly, but he won his pupils' hearts by his knowledge of plants, insects and foreign countries.

Unhappily the Moulton schoolmaster returned, but Carey went on teaching, however on a much reduced scale. So he had to earn his living again by shoemaking, but fortunately the Moulton Baptists asked him to be their minister, their chapel having been closed for some months already. The village of Barton asked him to be theirs. "He consulted his friends, asked admission to the Olney Baptist membership, and agreed to submit the question of his fitness for the ministry to the judgment of that Church." [4])
William Carey was not accepted, as his preaching did not agree
1786 with the taste of the hearers. The next year he preached again and tried to get a place as an orderly minister. Carey himself says of this sermon that it was "as weak and crude as anything ever called a sermon". Then they commissioned him to preach
1787 "whereever God in his providence might call him". On August 1, 1787 he was ordained while RYLAND, SUTCLIFF and FULLER, who became his lifelong friends, laid their hands on him. So he became a minister, his pay being £ 11 a year, to which £ 5 were added from some fund in London.

His conception of his office is given us in these words : "I held the pastoral office the highest honour upon earth." Here not only he showed himself a good shepherd but also a tenacious student of Latin, Greek, Hebrew, Dutch and Italian. After a few

28

months he was also enabled by the loyalty of GOTCH, his employer, to lay down his shoemaking. When bringing his fortnight's labour, Gotch said: "Let me see, Mr. Carey, how much do you earn a week by your shoemaking?" "About nine or ten shillings, sir." Then Gotch said: "Well now, I've a secret for you. I don't mean you to spoil any more of my leather, but get on as fast as you can with your Latin, Hebrew and Greek and I'll allow you from my private purse weekly ten shillings." [5]) So a great burden suddenly fell from his shoulders as by the hand of God.

In Moulton he renewed his acquaintance with Dr. Ryland and Andrew Fuller, two men, who are of great importance for his further life. This will be clear when we consider his missionary ambitions which especially in this Moulton period are growing. For the teaching of his pupils in the Moulton school he had made a leather globe, and for his own geographical studies he had made a large world-map. With the help of these he got to know the regions where people were still living in total ignorance of God. Moreover in 1785 the story of Cook's latest voyage was issued. The reading of this book still further increased his interest in the peoples of the world. On his map he had marked down the results of his reading: the approximate population, the language, customs and religion of the people. So the vastness of heathenism came home to him, and he awoke to a sense of its terrible need, and of the urgent duty which rested on the Christian Church to supply that need. [6])

His next problem was how to impart a sense of this need to his colleagues and of their duty toward it. Soon an occasion arose. As a minister he had admission to the Ministers' Fraternal of the Northampton Association. The above mentioned Dr. Ryland asked him and another new member to give themes for discussion. After much hesitation William Carey gave this theme: "Whether the command given to the apostles to preach the Gospel to all nations was not binding on all succeeding ministers to the end of the world, seeing that the accompanying promise was of equal extent." Dr. Ryland frowned disapprovingly. He sprang to his feet. He thundered out: "Young man, sit down, sit down. You're an enthusiast. When God pleases to convert the heathen, He'll do it without consulting you or me. Besides, sir, can you preach in Arabic, in Persian, in Hindustani, in Bengali? There must first be another pentecostal gift of tongues." [7])

And in later years Andrew Fuller describing his personal feelings at Carey's words, says: "If the Lord should make windows in heaven might such a thing be."

Carey sat down, was silenced—but the resistance stimulated his zeal. His Bible and his globe gave him new power to persevere, his globe being "a word of God quick and powerful". And: "Moulton was his Troas where he ceaselessly heard Macedonia's entreaty." [8])

In this period he read the biographies of JOHN ELIOT, missionary in Robury in New England among the Indians and of DAVID BRAINERD, missionary sent by the Society in Scotland for propagating christian knowledge. The latter "burned himself out for the Indians and God" dying only 29 years old.

1788   In 1788 W. Carey went to Birmingham to visit Mr. POTTS, a rich man, who had had to flee from America, as he worshipped on Sundays with the negroes. This man showed himself a friend of Carey's idea of world mission allowing him some money for the printing of a pamphlet which might possibly awaken interest in the dark heathen lands. On his return from Birmingham he met Mr. Fuller, Dr. Ryland and Mr. Sutcliff, and asked them to kindle their churchmembers for the missionary action. He told them of his pamphlet, and his wish to publish it, but they advised him to revise it. We will consider this pamphlet more closely in the following chapters. Here we only say it contains a mass of knowledge, acquired by his reading of books and papers on geography, history and statistics of the various parts of the world. He called it: "An Enquiry into the obligations of Christians to use means for the conversion of the Heathens."

May 31 1789   On May 31, 1789 he received a letter from the Baptist Church of Leicester, in which they urgently called on him to come to them. [9]) This denomination was in a very bad situation. William Carey accepted the call and removed to that town. At first all went well. People began to attend regularly and the church had to be enlarged. But after a time there came a change. The union became disunion, the love hatred. The shepherd nearly broke down and the flock was scattered. William Carey looked back to Moulton. But Sept. 1790 with the help of God he continued. "He formed the bold plan of at once dissolving the church and constructing a new association, into which none should be admitted but those who agreed to sign a declaration that they would in future adhere with rigid

30

fidelity to the doctrines and the discipline of the New Testament." [10])

From his coming to Leicester till the beginning of 1791 he only served the church on probation. "In the spring of that year he was once more ordained with Ryland, Sutcliff and Fuller around him." [11])

NOTES

[1]) Marshman, p. 4. Cf. S. Pearce Carey, p. 40 and Beusekom, p. 21.
[2]) M. Schuurman, De groote apostel van Voor-Indië. Leiden, D. Donner, pp. 5—6. Cf. P. A. Douwes, W. Carey, schoenmaker, zendeling, professor, taalgeleerde. Zend. Studieraad, p. 11.
[3]) Allgemein Missions Zeitschrift Pastor C. Wallroth, p. 98, 14e Band 1887.
[4]) S. Pearce Carey, op. cit. p. 49.
[5]) Ibid., p. 52.
[6]) Ogilvie, op. cit. pp. 296—297.
[7]) L. H. Dalton, Young man sit down, p. 11. Cf. S. Pearce Carey, p. 54 and Rheinhold Vornbaum, Missiongeschichte, p. 72.
[8]) S. Pearce Carey, op. cit. p. 55.
[9]) A very interesting letter is given by S. Pearce Carey, sent by the Leicester congregation, showing their simplicity :
"Dearly beloved in the Lord,
"It is with a Degree of Pleasure we Inform you That in the Genneral we are at Peace amongst our Selves ; we also earnestly pray the Same Blessing may rest upon you every Community who desire to worship the Lord in the Beauties of Holyness. With respect to our Present Situation as we Believe most of you are in Some measure Aquainted with it, we need not Say anything By way of Informing you that we are without an Under Shepard to go in and out Before us.
Yet we Aacknolage ourselves greatly indepted to Divine Goodness which has Inclined the hearts of So many of the Lord's Sarvants to Supply us in these things. We have in Less than a year Been Visited with Twenty Three Ministers ; which has given us an opportunity of Disearning a Diversity of Gifts. But all by the Same Divine Spirit ; we Trust it is our Prayer that these Labours may not be In-Vain amongst us. And we take this opportuniۍy, to Return our very cincear thanks to all and every one of the Lord's Sarvants for their Kind Assistance to us in our Low Estate. But we Belive a Stated Minister to be a Peculear Blessing : we have taken we hope some Prudent steps to Bring a Bout that Desirable Ende.
We need not Dear Breethern in form you of the Person we meditate upon to Supply us for three months, But Shall only add that we Request an intrest in your Prayers and also your friendly advise in our futer Preceedings : and if the Lord should smile upon our Attempts we shall Rejoyce—on the other hand if he fusterates our Designs, we wish to submit and waite his time. We conclude the a Bove and Join the Apostle ; with what is ritten in 2 Th. 2.16.17. Signed May 31st 1789 By us Behalf of the Church John Purser, Francis Pick Deacons and nine members. N.B. We have a Pointed Bro. Yates for our Messenger."
[10]) Marshman, op. cit. p. 13.
[11]) S. Pearce Carey, op. cit. p. 62.

3. The great turning-point in the life of William Carey and the world's Missionary cause. 1791—1793.

At the Association's Easter meeting, John Sutcliff of Olney, Andrew Fuller and William Carey urged the hearers to see the missionary call as a duty peculiarly binding upon them. Especially William Carey asked that something should be done. But then the 'wise and prudent' men, even Sutcliff and Fuller, drew back from this application of their expositions and advised William Carey only to print his "Enquiry on Missions".

May
30 and 31
1792
The next Association was held at Nottingham May 1792. On Wednesday May 31 at 10 a.m. Carey was in the pulpit taking as his text Isaiah LIV 2.3. "Enlarge the place of thy tent, and let them stretch forth the curtains of thine habitations. Spare not, lengthen thy cords, and strengthen thy stakes; for thou shalt break forth on the right hand and on the left; and Thy seed shall inherit the Gentiles, and Make the desolate cities to be inhabited. Fear not." This sermon is said to be 'a lance-head with eight years' drive behind its thrust. From this text he took two main ideas [1]: Expect great things from God. [2] Attempt great things for God. With such a dynamic force and such a love did he plead for his cause that Dr. Ryland who was present said: "he should not have wondered if the audience had lifted up their voices and wept". [1] Here he led all his collegues to Galilee's mountain of the forgotten commission and laid its obligation on their consciences and hearts. [2] All his mental power was concentrated in this sermon, all his gatherings of years in workshop and study exploded here, with such a power that reaction was bound to follow. Everyone was seized by his energetic words. Everyone was aghast. Everyone felt these words must have consequences. They all agreed with him, but when the next morning they were about to separate, "the old feelings of doubt and hesitation predominated". Then there came an historic moment in the history of missions and mankind: William Carey in agony at this negative result, seized the arm of his colleague Andrew Fuller and inquired: "Is there nothing again to be done, Sir?" Then.... Fuller hesitated, trembled .... and gave his soul to the call of the Master, whom he heard in William Carey. With all his mental power he supported Carey in his appeal to the people's conscience and before the ministers went home the following resolution was arrived at: "That against the Next meeting of ministers at Kettering a plan should be made for the forming of a society for propagating the Gospel among the heathen." [3]

Oct.
1792
This important meeting was held at Kettering on October 2, 1792. First of all they had to discuss the *plan* which Carey had been working out "during the preceding months of that fateful summer while Paris was seething with a mad frenzy of revolution,

32

and the infuriated French mob was besieging Louis XVI in the Tuileries". [4]) But as half of these men had not been present at Nottingham, "many of them were unready to commit themselves to the *idea* of a Missionary Society". [5]) They felt themselves unfit for such an enterprise, their churchmembers being illiterate people. Besides, a long series of wars ending in the loss of the American Colonies had impoverished the Country. In France there was anarchy. In England restlessness which might easily be kindled by a few sparks from the French inferno. [6]) Their inland position in the centre of England was unfavourable for correspondence and action. Besides, not one of these fourteen men had any experience of the founding of a Missionary Association. Some gave the advice "to ask the great central churches to take the initiative and shoulder the burden". Again these men wavered.

But all their objections were overruled by the vigour of William Carey's arguments. He had been a student of the Moravian Missions and a reader of their "Periodical Accounts" from the start. He produced the latest issue and divulged its contents, to wit, a veteran missionary's prosperous latest voyage to the West Indies : a Christian triumphal march of Brainerd's successor accompanied by Indian Christian warriors and chiefs ; hundreds of adult negro baptisms ; three missionaries bound for the Cape ; three others just arrived at Tranquebar ; and a hundred and thirty-five on the active missionary roll of the Brotherhood. [7]) With these examples he convinced his colleagues that something must be done. He told them that the Moravians were poor people merely artisans. That some of them were British and "cannot we at least *attempt* something in fealty to the same Lord ?" he asked.

Then they took the great resolution and constituted aMissionary Society and a committee of five members : consisting of Andrew Fuller, John Ryland, John Sutcliff, Reynold Hogg, and William Carey. Mr. Fuller was nominated secretary, Mr. Hogg treasurer. Ere they separated the following minute was passed :

At the ministers meeting at Kettering, October 2nd, 1792, after public services of the day were ended, the ministers retired to consult further on the matter, and to lay a foundation at least for a society, when the following resolutions were proposed, and unanimously agreed to :

1. Desirous of making an effort for the propagating of the Gospel among the heathen, agreeable to what is recommended in brother

Carey's late publication on that subject, we, whose names appear to the subsequent subscription, do solemnly agree to act in society together for that purpose.

2. As in the present divided state of Christendom it seems that each denomination, by exerting itself separately, is most likely to accomplish the great ends of mission, it is agreed that this society be called *the particular baptist society for propagating the Gospel among the heathen*.

3. As such an undertaking must needs be attended with expense, we agree immediately to open a subscription for the above purpose and to recommend to others.

Subscription list.

		L	s	d
Rev. JOHN RYLAND		L	2	2 0
,, REYNOLD HOGG		L	2	2 0
,, JOHN SUTCLIFF		1	1	0
,, ANDREW FULLER		1	1	0
,, ABRAHAM GREENWOOD		1	1	0
,, EDWARD SHARMAN		1	1	0
,, SAMUEL PEARCE		1	1	0
Mr. JOSEPF TIMMS		1	1	0
Rev. WILLIAM HIGHTON		0	10	6
,, WILLIAM STAUGHTON		0	10	6
,, JOSHUA BURTON		0	10	6
,, THOMAS BLUNDEL		0	10	6
,, JOHN EAYRE		0	10	6
		L 13	2	6

4. Every person who shall subscribe ten pounds at once or ten shillings and sixpence annually, shall be considered a member of the society.

5. That the Revs. John Ryland, Reynold Hogg, William Carey, John Sutcliff and Andrew Fuller be appointed a Committee, three of whom shall be empowered to act in carrying into effect the purposes of this society.

6. That the Rev. Reynold Hogg be appointed treasurer and the Rev. Andrew Fuller secretary.

7. That the subscriptions be paid in at the Northampton ministers' meeting, October 31st, 1792, at which time the subject shall be considered more particularly by the Committee, and other subscribers who may be present. [8])

When looking at the first and second article we mark a striking difference with the older S.P.G. S(ociety) P(ropagating) G(ospel) (1701). This society defined as its character "for the spiritual benefit of *our* loving subjects', while article 1 of this Baptist minute says : 'amongst the Heathen'. So the first is colonial, the second more catholic, deliberately missionary. [9]) That their outlook was very broad indeed is proved by the decision they took about the first harvest of L.13.2.6. : they would forward this sum partly to the Society in Scotland for propagating Christian Knowledge and partly to the Moravians, unless they themselves soon succeeded in starting their work. Looking at the third article we miss Carey's name. The reason is that he was so poor, that he was not able to promise anything. Instead of subscribing for an annual gift he would rather give them the proceeds of his Enquiry.

Here we are at an historical moment in the life of William Carey, for at a glance, we see the ridiculous contrast between the magnitude of the enterprise and the promised annual income. But the bridge between these two was the unconquerable conviction of William Carey that the Lord called the Christians to fulfil their task among the heathen. His irresistible enthusiasm and his noble character, and above all his God and Father were the causes of launching such an enterprise notwithstanding such low means. The foundation being well laid the building can now be constructed. Before we look at the construction we have to glance at the rising of the missionary understanding of this era, first in England, then in India.

Above we mentioned (page 19) that no English missionary was sent from England to India from 1600 up to the days of William Carey. We also noted the fact that there had been some idea, even some action for sending missionaries. In 1649 e.g. the Long Parliament created the Corporation for the Propagation of the Gospel in New England. Even the parishes contributed the sum of twelve thousand pounds. Afterwards in 1691 "The Society for the Conversion and Religious Instruction and Education of Negro Slaves in British West India Island" was founded. In 1698 the above mentioned Society for the Promotion of Christian Knowledge and in 1702 The Society for Propagating the Gospel in Foreign Parts. But whatever they were and whatever their success, nobody was sent from England to the vast territory of India. Some missionaries had been sent from Denmark however. The books of Bartholomew Ziegenbalg and Henry Plütschow were probably the first books on missions to be printed in England. "These books were read by SUSANNAH WESLEY to her children and were the means of interesting her sons JOHN and CHARLES WESLEY (then little boys) in missions to the heathen." [10]) Afterwards England supplied the money and Germany supplied the men for India, e.g. Schwartz. In 1783, the year of the conversion of William Carey, Dr. THOMAS COKE, a friend and helper of John Wesley's issued a plan for the ,,Society for the Establishment of Missions among the Heathens." In 1784 he entered into correspondence with CHARLES GRANT, a director of the East India Company, with a view to founding a Methodist Mission in Bengal. "But Coke landed in Antigua West Indies." [11]) From this survey we may conclude that the original idea of going to India may not have been William Carey's, as we will see afterwards, but for all that he really is the Father of modern Missions. He was not the first Englishman who went to the heathen, but the first missionary who went to India. He was the founder of the Baptist Missionary Society, moreover he was the greatest missionary that was ever sent out, gifted with such talents as only few possessed. There are not many people on record who were gifted with such talents as he had.

The first meeting of the Committee of the Society was held in Northampton, but neither William Carey, nor Andrew Fuller were present. Gifts were coming in. Special mention must be made of the gift and promise of the church of Birmingham: the first contribution of a church. It amounted to £ 70. It is of great importance that the Society "felt it to be their first duty to rouse the whole Baptist Church even as themselves had been aroused by Carey".

Carey, unable to attend the third meeting, wrote this letter: "Ih ave just received a letter from Thomas, the Bengal "missionary" who informs me that he intended being at the Kettering meeting, but forgot at what time it was to be held. He tells me that he is trying to establish a fund in London for a mission in Bengal; he ardently desires to have a companion, and inquires about the result of our meeting at Kettering. The reason of my writing is the thought that his fund for Bengal may interfere with

36

our larger plan : and whether it would not be worthy of the Society to try to make that and ours unite into one fund for the purpose of sending the Gospel to the heathen."

After the reading of this letter it was arranged that Andrew Fuller should make enquiries about John Thomas in London. The result being satisfactory, Thomas was invited to go under the patronage of the Society. This John Thomas seemed to be a man brought providentially into their way. He was a baptist and by profession a doctor. Failing to make a living in London he had started for Bengal. There he became a friend of Charles Grant who in 1786 wanted a missionary for the Indian peoples. He thought John Thomas the right man in the right place but after some years they had a difference of opinion and both Grant and Thomas went to London.

After he had been accepted by the Society, who had perused his letters, Andrew Fuller said : "There is a gold mine in India but it seems almost as deep as the centre of the earth." When he asked : "Who will venture to explore it ?", William Carey instantly replied : "I will venture to go down' ; "but remember that you Fuller, Sutcliff and Ryland, must hold the ropes." "This," said Fuller, ,,we solemnly engaged to him to do." [12])

John Thomas showed himself no financial expert. On the contrary. To the Society he expressed his belief that "a missionary could for sixteen and eighteen shillings build an excellent house with mud walls and straw covering ; fowls could be purchased at the rate of a penny each and ducks for twopence and a lamb for eight pence. The difficulties attending a gospel mission are not insuperable".

Being convinced that God had opened a door in India to them the brethren concluded to accept Mr. Thomas.

The church of Leicester was reluctant to lose the services of their pastor : "We have been praying for the spread of Christ's Kingdom amongst the heathen and now God requires *us* to make the first sacrifice to accomplish it." But many more difficulties arose. Mrs. Carey thought she could not accompany her husband to India : the obstacles seemed insurmountable to her. Fuller and Sutcliff went over specially to Leicester to reason with the poor woman. Without success. Carey's heart was moved, but his purpose fixed. "If I had all the world, I would freely give it all to have you and the children with me ; but the sense of duty is so strong as to overpower all other considerations. I could not turn back without guilt on my soul .... Tell my dear children I love them dearly and pray for them constantly. Be assured I love you most affectionately." DEAVILLE WALKER is right when saying : "Let us honour the firm devotion of the one and sympathize with the very natural fear (expecting motherhood in the near future too) and grief of the other".

1793   To his father William Carey wrote a letter, dated Jan. 17, 1793, which ends with these words: "I consider myself as devoted to the service of God alone and now I am to realize my professions. I am appointed to go to Bengal in the East Indies, a missionary to the Hindoos. I hope, dear father, you may be enabled to surrender me up to the Lord for the most arduous, honourable, and important work that ever any of the sons of men were called to engage in. I have many sacrifices to make, I must part with a beloved family and a number of affectionate friends .... But I have set my hand to the plough. I remain, your dutiful son W. Carey." The first reaction of his old father was : "Is William mad !"

When the day for embarking was near at hand, William Carey wrote the following letter to his beloved wife, a letter which gives us a good idea of his character : "My dear Dorothy, Ryde, Isle of Wight, May 6, 1798.

I have just received yours, giving me an account of your safe delivery. This is pleasant news indeed to me : surely goodness and mercy follow me all days. My stay here was very painful and unpleasant, but now I see the goodness of God in it. *(He had to wait many days before they could sail on account of the Dunkerk pirates.)* It was that I might hear the most pleasing accounts that I could possibly hear respecting earthly things. You wish to know in what state my mind is. I answer, it is much as when I left you. If I had all the world, I would freely give it all to have you and my dear children with me, but the sense of duty is so strong as to overpower all other considerations : I could not turn back without guilt on my soul. I find a longing to enjoy more of God ; but now I am among the people of the world I think I see more beauties in godliness than ever, and I hope, enjoy God more in retirement than I have done for some time past.

"Yesterday I preached twice at Newport, and once in the country. This place much favours retirement and meditation ;

38

the fine woods and hills and sea all conspire to solemnize the mind, and to lift the soul to admire the Creator of all. To day I dined with Mrs. CLARK at Newport, and Felix *(his son whom he took with him)* found Teddy Clark one of his old play fellows, which pleased him much. He is a good boy, and gives me much pleasure. He has almost finished his letter and I intend to add a little to it. He has been a long time about it, and I question whether you can read it when it comes.

"You want to know what Mrs. Thomas thinks, and how she likes the voyage. She is very delicate, brought up very genteel, and cousin to SQUIRE THURSBY OF ABINGTON. But she is in good spirits, and the sea agrees with her very well. She sends her love to you, and is glad to hear the good news concerning your delivery. She would rather stay in England than go to India; but thinks it right to go with her husband. A young gentleman and his sister, cousins to Mr. Thomas, who have been brought up under the Gospel, go with us.

"I shall be glad to hear of you, and how you do, as often as possible. We do not know when we shall go, but expect it will be in a week at farthest. Tell my dear children I love them dearly, and pray for them constantly. Felix sends his love. I look upon this mercy as an answer to prayer indeed. Trust in God. Love to Kitty, brothers and sisters etc. Be assured I love you most affectionately. Let me know my dear little child's name. I am for ever

> your faithful and affectionate husband,
> William."

From this letter we may conclude that William Carey was not a man of stone. On the contrary. Carey's heart may have been heavy and he may often have felt very sad, yet his purpose was set. Cost what it might he could not draw back, having vowed a vow unto his heavenly Father. It must be noted that Mrs. Carey had agreed to let Felix go with his father, a sacrifice which must not be undervalued. It proves that the love for her William 'was so strong that she could not bear to let him go alone'. On the other hand we must well understand the difficulties of this poor woman. She had never seen London. How could she—with three children, the fourth near at hand—go to countries unknown to her and far away. Even in the present time we think this voyage a formidable undertaking. The more so as the voyage had to be made around the Cape, not by steamer but in a sailing vessel. Everybody regarded such a voyage as a banishment from the beloved country and in this respect we must not blame this poor Dorothy for her resolution neither William for his. Both thought they acted according to God's will.

How different however were God's plans from man's ways! All seemed to be settled. William should go out only accompanied by Felix, returning in a year or two for his wife and the other children and Dorothy should remain in Piddington, her native village. Mr. and Mrs. Thomas and their little boy should go with him. Two difficult problems were to be solved. One was the cost of the passage, an uncertain factor as rates were not fixed in those days. The second, how to get to India, a very difficult one, as the East India Company was hostile to missionary work in those days. Moreover the above mentioned Grant who was a Director of the Company raised no objections to Carey's going to India but nobody could induce him to help Thomas. Then, what was to be done, suppose the Company should send them back to England, when they had arrived at Bengal?

Thomas, however, solved one of these problems: He was a friend of the Captain of the East Indiaman the "Earl of Oxford", the ship on which he had formerly been a surgeon. The captain promised Thomas to take Carey and his son, and Thomas and Mrs. Thomas and their son as well whatever the consequences might be. They were to sail about the middle of April. The money question was brought to a good end too.

All this being settled we must now give our attention to Carey's luggage. For from this luggage we can learn what kind of man he was at this early stage of his enterprise. In the Treasurer's account we find: "Books and globes for the use of the missions £ 13.13s." This informs us that before his voyage Carey was thinking of the possibility of mission *schools*. Further his great desire to take John Thomas with him as a surgeon proved he was thinking of the missionary task of *healing*. "And while touring in Yorkshire he met a devoted young printer William Ward, who was deeply interested in the proposed mission. Looking ahead, Carey said to him: "In a few years we shall want you out in India to *print the Bible*. You must come after us". [13])

From these facts we see that this cobbler-minister-schoolmaster had all the missionary principles in his mind before embarking. Principles unknown to the missionary Societies before him, and during his lifetime, principles born in his own mind. He started from England "determined to use medicine and education, translation work and printing as instruments for the more effective presentation of his message to India."

Carey's farewell service was held in his own chapel in Leicester. March 20 1793 In the evening meeting, Hoog preached and Fuller the Secretary of the Society delivered a parting address to the missionaries: "Peace be unto you; as my father has sent me, so send I you." His thoughts were: the objects they must keep in view, the directions they must follow, the difficulties they would encounter, and the reward they must expect. [14]

When all was ready and the "Earl of Oxford" had arrived the missionaries embarked and sailed from the Thames. But at Ryde, Isle of Wight, the Earl of Oxford had to wait for a convoy on account of the privateers of Dunkerk for the Channel was swarming with them.

Then another difficulty arose. Thomas had incurred a debt of £ 500 and his creditors being informed that he was about to leave England, sent a man with a writ and a bailiff to arrest him. William Carey was greatly shocked at this behaviour of his missionary companion, but what was to be done? Thomas when seeing the strangers had immediately fled to London. After some time he returned and told all to his colleague who was bewildered on hearing that he had run into so large a debt. But as the die was cast they had to start, with Thomas and his debts.

Then however the commander of the vessel received an anonymous letter from London, stating that an information should be lodged against him for taking passengers to India without a license and contrary to the express orders of his masters. [15] William Carey was at a loss, but had to leave the vessel with his Felix and the Thomas family and to store his luggage as well as possible. The ship sailed away and the missionaries stood ashore on the isle of Wight.

Fuller, informed of this terrible news, was staggered for a moment. He writes to Dr. Ryland: "We are all undone; I am grieved; yet perhaps 't is best. Thomas' debts and embarrassments damped my pleasure before. Perhaps 't is the best he should not go. I am afraid leave will never be obtained now for Carey or any other—

and the adventure (the supplies in goods for their support) seems to be lost. He says nothing of the £ 250. for the voyage. 'Tis well if that be not lost".

But then the tide turns. On their visit to Mrs. Carey she again refuses to go with William, but when Thomas once more visits her and reminds her of what would be the consequences of her refusal—"her family dispersed and divided, perhaps for ever and that she would repent it as long as she lived" her heart was broken. Amid tears she declares that on condition that her unmarried sister KATHERINE PLACKETT will accompany her, she will go. Katherine hastened upstairs, knelt down in prayer and when she came down she told that she was ready to go.

With a heart abundant with joy and thanks William rushed off to Northampton in order to provide the necessary money for his wife and children. In a few days all is settled. A Danish ship the "Kron Princessa Maria" is to take them to India, a ship commanded by a Captain Christmas. On June 13, 1793 the whole party embarked and "before nightfall they passed the huge white cliffs of Beachy head". Of course the voyage in such a comparatively small vessel was not a pleasant trip, on the contrary. But on Nov. 7th the ship reached Balasure at the mouth of the Hooghi and on the 11th Carey landed in Calcutta, to begin his missionary task.

June
1793

Before we continue our biography of William Carey, we will make an attempt at describing the missionary situation in India, in order to understand the conditions with which William Carey was confronted.

But to understand the conditions in India we first of all have to glance at the political and spiritual world of Carey's days in *England*, especially their attitude to missionary activities.

A good example of the spirit lingering in the Church towards missionary action is given by the London ministers and churches of the Baptist denomination. They stood aloof from the undertaking of William Carey, a country man, who behaved himself like an enthusiast for an obscure enterprise. When a meeting was held in London in order to consider the possibility of forming an Auxiliary Society to that of William Carey, only one minister was prepared to help them. Mr. Fuller described the feeling of the metropolis in this way : "When we began, in 1792 there was little or no respectability among us, not so much as a squire to sit in a chair, or an orator to address him with speeches. Hence good Dr. STEN-NET (who was very friendly towards William Carey) advised the London ministers to stand aloof, and not to commit themselves". [16]) The undertaking seemed to be much too high for such ordinary men as Fuller, Carey and others. One minister must be excepted from this attitude of aloofness : JOHN NEWTON, who advised Carey "with the fidelity and tenderness of a father". Afterwards we shall see what a great mistake these metropolis-men made by their proud attitude towards these country-men. The germs of a world's missionary enterprise were not in their minds but in the hearts and minds of William Carey and Andrew Fuller, to mention only these.

But still more negative was the attitude of the Church in Scotland. According to MARSHMAN a proposition to establish a foreign mission was brought forward in the General Assembly of the Church of Scotland in 1796. The design was called unnatural and revolutionary. The Rev. Mr. HAMILTON asserted that "to spread about the knowledge of the gospel among the barbarous and heathen nations seemed to him highly preposterous inasmuch as it anticipates, nay, reverses the order of nature. Men must be polished and refined in their manners before they can be properly enlightened in religious truths". Happily Dr. ERSKINE contradicted these assertions reminding him that St. Paul had declared himself a debtor not merely to the polished Greeks, but also to the unlettered barbarians. But another member of the Assembly declared that these missionary organizations were highly dangerous to society. And another member said : "as for these missionary societies, since it is to be apprehended that their funds certainly will be turned against the Constitution it is the bounden duty of the House to give the overtures recommending them our most serious disapprobation, and our immediate and most decisive opposition".

From these quotations we may learn that the attitude of the Church as a whole was one of strong opposition against missionary action. The more we must respect the courage and faith of William Carey to continue his task under such adverse conditions.

We may conclude that he had the power to stand quite alone. Even more than his wife and children he loved the Lord, fulfilling the word of our Saviour : "He that loveth father or mother more

43

than me is not worthy of me ; and he that loveth son or daughter more than me is not worthy of me. And he that doth not take his cross and follow after me, is not worthy of me." William Carey was literally prepared to lose his life for the sake of Jesus Christ.

And not only did William Carey dare to stand quite alone, but he also dared to face the opinion of the majority of the official and highly esteemed Churchmen. And the secret of this attitude is the fact that more than his contemporaries he was seized by the call of the Lord to make disciples of all the nations. And it must be especially born in mind that from the very beginning of the home-action of the Baptist Society, this call was meant not only for some separate members of the Church, who were interested in and exerted themselve for mission work, but for all the Churches. Their action was directed to all the denominations of all the Baptist Churches which is an attitude, quite different from the attitude of many other missionary societies which will be proved later on.

Now we are going to consider the missionary situation in India and in this connection I wish again to make some observations regarding the same situation in England. [17])

NOTES

[1]) MARSHMAN, op. cit., p. 15.
[2]) S. PEARCE CAREY, op. cit. p. 85. Cf. GEORG STOSCH Zeugen Gottes aus allerlei Volk, p. 5.
[3]) JOHN BROWN MYERS, The shoemaker who became the father and founder of modern missions. Patridge and Co., London, 1887.
[4]) F. DEAVILLE WALKER, William Carey, Missionary Pioneer and Statesman London, 1926, p. 95. Student Christian Movement Press.
[5]) S. PEARCE CAREY, op. cit. p. 91.
[6]) DEAVILLE WALKER, p. 97.
[7]) S. PEARCE CAREY, p. 92.
[8]) DEAVILLE WALKER, pp. 98—99.
[9]) Cf. S. PEARCE CAREY, p. 93.
[10]) DEAVILLE WALKER, p. 101.
[11]) Ibid., p. 103.
[12]) Ibid., p. 110. Cf. OGILVIE, p. 300.
[13]) Ibid., p. 119.
[14]) Ibid., p. 120.
[15]) MARSHMAN, cf., p. 56.
[16]) Ibid., p. 17.
[17]) For those who take an interest in the History of Christianity in India the following books will be of value :
History of Christianity in India (5 vols) by the Rev. JAMES HOUGH, 1839.
Christianity in India by Sir JOHN KAYE, 1859.
A History of Missions in India, by JULIUS RICHTER D.D., 1908.
The conversion of India by GEORGE SMITH Ll. D.C.I.E.
The Soul of India by GEORGE HOWELLS Ph. D.
These are some of the books OGILVIE mentions in his Appendix of his above mentioned book. For special Period and Topics he gives a long list.

4. Something of the missionary action in India before William Carey.

It would be fascinating to know all the christian missionaries who have worked in India from the very beginning, but these studies would only be remotely connected with our purpose.

Suffice it to say, that on rather good grounds, some scholars maintain that the apostle St. Thomas was the first who preached the Gospel in the Punjab region. [1] Some also assert that the well known Pantaenus of Alexandria, the teacher of Clement of Alexandria, had worked in India as a missionary, circa A.D. 190. From the year 200 "a veil descends on Indian Christianity and shrouds it completely from the view of the Western world. Only at rare intervals the veil is lifted." [2] When e.g. the great council of Nicea was held, one of the threehundred and eighteen bishops was John, bishop of Persia and Great India. When Nestorius was condemned, his disciples went to India as Nestorian missionaries, penetrated into Punjab and taught fishermen of the sea of Aral: in India the Zamorin himself respected their spiritual and courted their temporal authority. [3] Not only on the West coast of Malabar but also on the East coast of Koromandel, the Nestorians preached the Gospel. Marco Polo tells us that the Nestorian Missions from the eighth century till about 1280 were doing well, but then other travellers tell of a gradual decline. In the beginning of the sixteenth century the "only trace of Christianity on the East coast was the church in ruin".

On the Western coast on the contrary, the church flourished. According to the census in 1911, there were only 728.000 Syrian Christians, being only one fifth of the whole Native Christian Population of India.

In 1319 Jordanus, a Dominican friar, left Avignon for the East with four Franciscan friars. These four men were killed by zealous Mohammedans and Jordanus had to continue the work alone. Back in Europe he gave a detailed account of the Syrian Christians and their diversities. In 1330 he once more made the voyage as Bishop of Columbia and carried with him a papal letter inviting the Syrian Christians to be reconciled to the Catholic Church. But Jordanus, full of missionary zeal, was "a voice crying in the wilderness". The year 1498 is of great importance for the whole of India ; then Vasco da Gama who sailed from Portugal dropped

45

anchor at Calicit, on the East Coast of India. The influence of the Christian Church, during these fifteen hundred years from St. Thomas till 1498, on the whole of the vast population of India was almost negligible. The difference between Europe and India is a striking one. All Europe belonging to the christian church, at least nominally, and India with only a few hundred thousand Christians in some coastal districts while the bulk of the population did not know anything of christianity.

Three factors are mentioned by Dr. OGILVIE, for this tardiness of progress. First the lack of continuity of missionary enterprises.

The efforts were intermittent. There was not a permanent base. Secondly the Syrian Church of Malabar never seems to have possessed the missionary spirit in a measure sufficient to impel its sons to missionary endeavour. Just enough to save itself from extinction, but not enough to awake the interest of others. The main reason however was the strength of Hinduism itself. Hinduism is not only a religion but a culture, a complex of views of life, a citadel of gigantic forces, a philosophy looking down with a smile upon christian missionaries who bring the Gospel of Jesus Christ. No wonder that the few spasmodic efforts of some brave men had no or only a little result.

Sir GEORGE GRIERSON called by Dr. Ogilvie one of the most eminent Oriental scholars of to-day and the leading authority on the Bhakti element in Hinduism, states: "It was in the Southern India that Christianity as a doctrine exercised the greatest influence on Hinduism generally. Although the conceptions of the fatherhood of God and of Bhakti were indigenous to India, they received an immense impetus owing to the beliefs of Christian communities reacting upon the mediaeval Bhagavata reformers of the South. With this leaven their teaching swept over Hindustan, bringing balm and healing to a nation gasping in its death-throes amid the horrors of alien invasion." [4]) This statement of course is of great importance, but we conclude once more that the Christian influence on the whole of India was negligible.

A man of great stature and importance for India is FRANCIS XAVIER (1506—1552). Whereas St. Thomas is called "the apostle of India", this man is honoured by the whole Christian world as "the apostle of the Indies". Born in 1506 at the Castle of Xavier at the base of the Pyrenees in the Kingdom of Navarre, being kin to the royal houses of Navarre in France, he passed his early

days as a gay courtier at the Court of the King of Navarre. [5])
Then he went to the University in Paris at the same time as
Calvin. There he almost became a Protestant which may be
deduced from his letter to his brother: (1535) "I declare in my
conscience as it were under my hand and seal, that my obligations
to Ignatius Loyola are far greater than a whole life devoted to his
service can repay, or even partially satisfy.... But the benefit
he has conferred of highest value is that of fortifying my youthful
imprudence against the deplorable dangers arising from my famil-
iarity with men breathing out heresy, such as are many of my contemporaries in Paris in these times, who would insidiously under-
mine faith and morality beneath the specious mask of liberality
and superior intelligence." In 1534 Loyola formed his bond, later
called "The Company of Jesus", and Xavier was one of the seven
members. The purpose was to convert "unbelievers" such as
Jews, Turks, infidels and heretics. John III, King of Portugal,
was a great friend of this missionary work. Every fleet that made
its annual voyage from Lisbon to India carried many Franciscan
and Dominican friars as well as soldiers for the army of the Portuguese crown. In 1542 Francis Xavier reached Goa, a fine city.
With recommendations of the Pope and the King he went ashore.
But in Goa the Gospel was already known. The city already possessed a spacious cathedral, a bishop and its canons, its Franciscan
convent and its college for training native youths for the service
of the Church. So towards the end of 1542 he went to the extreme
South coast, East of cape Comorin, the inhabitants of which were
humble pearl fishers. Here he worked for some years. His
greatest difficulty was the Tamil language, a difficulty which
oppressed him greatly. According to his own words, he was no
linguist at all. But not only was he ill-prepared for the language,
he also used a method which now-a-days we call old fashioned.
His procedure is told by himself in one of his letters: "I have begun
to go through all the villages of this coast with bell in hand, collecting together a large concourse both of boys and men. Bringing them twice a day into a convenient place I gave them Christian
instruction. The boys in the space of a month have committed
all to memory beautifully. Then I told them to teach what they
had learned to their parents' household and neighbours. On Sundays I called together the men and women, boys and girls into a
sacred edifice.... Then I began with the confession of the Holy

47

Trinity, the Lord's Prayer, the Angelic Salutation, the Apostles' Creed, pronouncing them in their own language with a clear voice. All followed me in the repetition, in which they take an uncommon pleasure.... How great is the multitude of those who are gathered into the fold of Christ you may learn from this that it often happens to me, that my hands fail through the fatigue of baptizing : for I have baptized a whole village in a single day : and often, by repeating so frequently the Creed and other things, my voice and strength have failed me."

The superficiality of this work must strike everybody. After three years' labour he left India. Here we won't dwell upon his method of working. We may conclude once more that there may have been some fruits, but only among the out-casts. Hinduism as a power with its caste-system was unaltered, whatever may have been the great zeal of this noble man.

A very interesting page in the history of Christianity in India is the struggle between the original Syrian Church of Malabar and the Church of Rome, resulting in the accession of 200.000 souls to the Church of Rome. Here we cannot dwell upon this theme, being of no great importance for the description of India as the country where William Carey went ashore.

Well known in the history of Missions is ROBERT DE NOBILIBUS (1606—1741). This great man may be mentioned here as his method of working was quite different from those who preceded him. One of the many criticisms, to which all Missions in the East are subjected, is that Christianity is too Western in its aspects : just adapt Christianity to the Eastern thought, mould it in such a way that the Hindu is not hurt by its Western aspect ; take off its Western dress and retain the essence but give the accidents an Eastern hue. Then Eastern prejudices will be conciliated with Western, the problems of Christianity will be solved and it will spread by leaps and bounds. [6] Robert de Nobilibus tried to solve this problem of adaptation. But in rather a strange way. He was a man of noble birth born in Tuscany in 1577. In 1606 he went to India.

The isle of Madura, the centre of Hinduism for Southern India, was his residence as leader of the missionary work. There 10.000 Brahman students received instruction in the philosophy of Hinduism, studying four or five years. Robert de Nobilibus understood that the handbell of Xavier was of no use among these educated

48

men. There were two things he clearly saw: the power of Caste and the need of a good strategy. His own words, cited by Dr. Ogilvie, are: "To attack from the front would be to close all doors of access: not because these false idols are not worthy of all opprobrium, but for the sake of the salvation of souls. When we chase shadows from a room, we do not make a stir with a broom." [7] Formerly the missionaries in Madura were Portuguese. And the Portuguese were despised as "Parangi". The Portuguese had become the most-hated people of India. Not only by reason of their manners, their display of power, their invasion of the holy Hindu countries, but because they drank wine, they ate cow's flesh, they were friends with pariahs. All this made them despicable men, to whom no fashionable Hindu, especially no Brahman as a leader of the Hindu people would listen. [8]

So he decided to become a Brahman to the Brahmans. He learned their language thoroughly, he studied their books, he became familiar with every detail of the ritual of their religious and social life. As Xavier became a Pariah to the Pariahs so de Nobili became a Brahman to the Brahmans, a much more intricate matter especially when we know something of the complicated way in which all the rites are to be performed. He introduced himself as a "Roman Brahman", declined an invitation of the King "lest his soul should be sullied by his eyes lighting upon a woman". Thousands tried to visit him but only a few were permitted to see the "Roman Brahman" seated cross-legged on a settee as a Sannyasi. In 1609 he declared: "By becoming a Christian one does not renounce his caste, nobility or usages. The idea that Christianity interferes with them has been impressed upon the people by the devil, and is the great obstacle to Christianity. It is this that has stricken the work of Father Fernandez with sterility."

Of further importance is the fact that in 1623 Pope Gregory XV vindicated the Madura missionary and his methods. We will not dwell further on Robert de Nobilibus, but maintain that his method cannot be ours. William Carey, as we shall see, was confronted with almost the same difficulties as Xaverius and de Nobilibus, but he solved these problems in quite another way. This does not mean that we will derogate anything from the great heroism, zeal, power and thoroughness of both these men; on the contrary, but their method cannot be ours. The essence of the Gospel is taught by them in such a way that it must be undervalued by the hearers. In this way adaption is sought at the expense of the Gospel. William Carey's method of missionary work, as we shall see below, is quite different. Moreover the official approval of the method of de Nobilibus by the Roman Catholic Church is the more regretful as this method is still practized in about the same form.

Now we turn to the Protestant Missions in India. It is regretful to acknowledge that a Protestant Mission was hardly known in the first and second century after the Reformation. Luther and Calvin, Melanchton and Beza, Johan Gerhard and many others considered the command of the Lord to make disciples of all the nations as fulfilled by the apostles. Only Bucer and Zwingli felt something of the call of the scriptures. [9] "The Protestants took their Theology from St. Paul, that prince of missionaries, but did not imitate his method of preaching to the heathen the unsearchable riches of Christ." [10] It is noteworthy that Erasmus declared : "It is a hard work I call you to, but it is the noblest and highest of all. Would that God had accounted me worthy to die in such a holy work, rather than to be consumed by a slow death in the tortures I endure. Yet no one is fit to preach the Gospel to the heathen who has not made his mind superior to riches and pleasure, aye, even to life and death itself. The cross is never wanting to those who preach the word of the Lord in truth." This aloofness of the Reformed Churches may be explained by the fact that the countries were in Roman Catholic hands, that their own struggle took much of their spiritual forces, that they expected the Lord in a few years as a Bridegroom to his Church, but it does not excuse their apathy and fundamental attitude towards the command of the Lord.

To Denmark belongs the honour of redeeming Protestantism from the dishonour of apathy and reluctance concerning missionary activity.

The first Protestant Mission in India was established by special desire of King Frederic IV of Denmark. His chaplain Dr. LÜTKENS, was ordered to find some men fit for the great missionary task and so Dr. Lütkens went to Dr. FRANCKE of Halle, centre of the Pietist movement. At his recommendation Ziegenbalg and Plütschau were sent out to the Danish settlement of Tranquebar on November 29th, 1705. [11]

The reception of these first Protestant missionaries was terrible. After their long voyage the ship cast anchor in the harbour of the Danish settlement. Everybody was conveyed ashore, but the two missionaries had to stay on board for several days. The governor J. C. HASSIUS treated them roughly ; a few days later a captain of another ship conveyed them ashore out of sheer pity. When before the gate of the town, the governor himself asked what brought them here. What could they do ? The king knew nothing of their affairs and so they turned their backs on these men. After waiting for some time in the marketplace everybody went home and the doors were closed. So they had to sleep under the stars—in a town of his Majesty the King of Denmark who had sent them—the first Protestant missionaries on Indian soil. Especially the leading officials of Denmark regarded these missionaries with extreme disfavour, fearing that they would injure their commercial interests. But Ziegenbalg and his colleague were nothing daunted. They fought their way through and soon succeeded in studying the Tamil and Portuguese languages. In 1714 a Missionary College was established in Copenhagen and in 1715 Ziegenbalg was introduced to George I of England "who manifested more interest in the success of this effort to promote Christianity among the natives of India than any of his successors had done". Ziegenbalg died in 1719 "a man devoted to his Master and wholeheartedly given to his Master's work of zeal unbounded and of faith unquenchable". His work was indeed maintained and extended by a long succession of able missionaries. [12])

A man of very great importance, a successor of Ziegenbalg is Christiaan Friedrich Schwarz born 1726. He arrived in India 1750 and laboured there till 1798 when he died. He was an adviser even of Indian rulers and of English officials. In the Moravian Churches in India were 35.000 people baptized at the time of his death.

We conclude from the preceding survey that actual missionary work was in progress. But from England nobody had been sent out. Only George I and later the Archbishop of Canterbury as President of the S.P.C.K. showed interest in the work of Ziegenbalg. To the question if in other parts of India there had been any missionary activity at all, the answer is affirmative ; even in Bengal, the part of India where William Carey started his work. So we now turn our attention to this North East part of India.

JOHN ZACHARIAH KIERNANDIER was born at Akstad, in Sweden,

in 1711. Just like Ziegenbalg and many others he was a student of Dr. FRANCKE of Halle. Some years after his arrival, hostilities broke out between the English and the French settlements on the coast, a struggle for supremacy. From these horrors he wished to be freed and tried to reach Bengal. So he arrived at Calcutta in 1758. Here he was enabled to open a school for the education of the poor. He started with forty pupils, English, Armenian, Portuguese, and natives. In June 1759 he began to preach in Portuguese, a tongue much more familiar to him than English and still more than the Bengalee and Hindoostanee languages, which he never learned well. [13]) His wife died shortly after her arrival in India. After some time he married a widow. After her death he became a fugitive as he was in pecuniary difficulties. He fled to Serampore, not far from Calcutta, for protection under the Danish flag. CHARLES GRANT purchased his Church for £ 1000. and appropriated it to the cause of the Mission in connection with the Christian Knowledge Society. [14])

Marshman thinks the real cause of this debacle is his standing security for his spendthrift son. And William Carey when visiting him in 1794 tells us that in 1783 the ardour which he manifested for the conversion of the heathen was very inspiring and that he himself derived the highest encouragement from his exhortations. But his missionary activity seems to have been confined to European settlers in India. His mission was always called the Portuguese mission, as he spoke no other language. Kiernandier had been sent out under the patronage of the Christian Knowledge Society. This Society was now looking for a successor. In 1789 they sent Mr. CLARKE to take charge of the mission. But he soon accepted a Government chaplaincy. Then after an eight years' search the Society sent the Rev. TOBIAS RINGLETAUBE, a German. This man returned after twelve months' lukewarm service.

These two men can scarcely be called missionaries. They did not learn the native tongue. They had no zeal whatever. They were sowing discord among the Christians and as soon as possible they returned to an easier state of life.

Here we must mention that the Rev. DAVID BROWN took up the services in the Mission Church of Kiernandier, a man who at first kept aloof from William Carey but who later on became one of his best friends.

This Rev. Brown found some Christians in Calcutta of whom we should especially mention Charles Grant, the first man connected with the Government of India who ever ventured to advocate the religious improvement of the natives. At this time everything was done in England and India to adjust the administration of India and make it a source of material happiness, but spiritual happiness was practically neglected.

The English East India Company was gradually developing from a mere trade organization into a government power, with its own territories and armies, its administrators and vassal princes.

The morals of nearly all these men were terribly low. Most officials were living in open adultery or had one or more concubines. The separation from home, the heat of India and the general discomforts of life in a tropical country were—according to Deaville Walker—regarded as a sufficient excuse for indolence and loose living.

As we mentioned above trade and not evangelism was the object of the English and Dutch Companies. There was, however, a clause inserted in the Charter of the Company stating that chaplains were to study the vernacular language to enable them to instruct the Gentoos (i.e. Gentiles), but this clause was soon a dead letter.

To change this situation Grant and Brown discussed the plan of bringing the Gospel to the Bengalees. Grant himself would pay for two missionaries. In this way Grant became a friend of the above mentioned physician Thomas.

Grant was the owner of a factory at Gumalti, a village in Bengal and Dr. Thomas was to work among Grant's employees and the villagers. We saw that the friendship of Grant and Thomas was only of short duration. No wonder, for C. B. Lewis, Thomas' biographer denotes him as a great human, a great Christian, a great missionary, a great unfortunate and a great blunderer. And he is right. Afterwards we shall see why. In 1790 Grant withdrew his financial help from Thomas. Then he went to England again. [15])

In 1786 Grant had drawn up a great plan to include Bengal in the missionary work. The Rev. Brown describes this plan as a division of the province into eight missionary circles. In each circle a young clergyman of the Church of England should be established upon a salary of £ 350 a year. He determined to submit the plan to the Governor-General Lord Cornwallis who remarked "he had no faith in such schemes and thought they must prove ineffectual". [16]) His main purpose was to fix the revenue in perpetuity. Then Grant submitted the plan to his attention in person. But without any success.

After some time he tried to get support from England. He sent his scheme to the Archbishop of Canterbury and the Bishop of London. He became the intimate friend of WILBERFORCE, who was then already immersed in the great struggle against slavery. He tried to get him to exert his influence for his own projects. After a short time there seemed to be a good opportunity for him to attain his end. Every twenty years the Charter of the East India Company had to come before Parliament for renewal and that time was approaching. In 1790 Grant himself went to London. He met much encouragement from Wilberforce. The Archbishop however was very cautious in his answers to Grant, but after a long interval the former submitted the plan to the King who "appeared to feel the propriety and even the importance of the scheme, but hesitated to countenance it, chiefly in consequence of the alarming progress of the French Revolution, and the proneness of the period to movements subversive of the established order of things." [17])

In 1793 the renewal of the Company's Charter before the House was due. Wilberforce introduced several resolutions on the subject. The first was that it is the peculiar and bounden duty of the Legislature to promote by all just and prudent means the interest and happiness of the British Dominions in India, and for these ends such measures ought to be adopted as may gradually tend to their advancement in useful knowledge and to their religious and moral improvement. The second resolution referred to the provision of sufficient means of religious instruction for all persons of the Protestant communion in India and the maintenance of a chaplain on every ship of 500 tons burden and upwards. These motions were carried in the House! Marshman tells that Wilberforce made the following note in his journal: "Through God's help, got the East India resolutions in quietly .... The hand of Providence was never more visible than in this Indian affair." Grant was in high spirits. The resolutions were given in the hands of the Attorney and the Solicitor-General. An announcement was made in the papers and William Carey must have seen it at the time when he discovered that the Sheriff's officers were after Thomas. [18])

54

But the victory was only for a moment. The India House was seized with a panic. The Court of Directors held a special meeting and passed a resolution opposing that of Wilberforce. From the beginning of the East India Company till 1757 (the battle of Plassey) the Directors encouraged the missionary undertakings. But after this date when "the merchants became sovereigns and the factory of Calcutta became the capital of a great empire" all things changed. Just like the religous situation in England in the eighteenth century Calcutta presented "a scene of such unblushing licentiousness, avarice, and infidelity as had never been witnessed before under the British flag. England had subdued Bengal, and Bengal had subdued the morals of its conqueror." And especially these Directors, many of whom were old Indians, with a respect for the superstitions of the natives, and a resolute determination not to allow them to be disturbed by missionary fanaticism, were in great consternation when the clause of Wilberforce was carried in the House. One speaker declared, so far from listening to the proposal with patience, that he considered it "the most wild, extravagant, expensive, and unjustifiable project that ever was suggested by the most visionary speculator". Another member declared that "so far from wishing that they might convert ten, fifty, or a hundred thousands natives . . . . he should lament such a circumstance as the most serious and fatal disaster that could happen". They succeeded in creating such an alarm that the clause was withdrawn, with the promise that on a future occasion the House was ready to give it every consideration which its importance required. That future occasion never came and for another twenty years the Company had succeeded in arousing fears and prejudices. Now of course the Company set themselves to prevent missionary work as much as possible in Indian territory.

Wilberforce, "the bold and animated champion of Christianity" as Grant has called him, wrote in his journal after his defeat : "My clauses thrown out. DUNDAS (one of the Directors) most false and double, but poor fellow, much to be pitied. The East India Directors and Proprietors have triumphed ; all my dear clauses struck out last night on the third reading of the bill."

When the bill came before the Lords, the Archbishop of Canterbury and the Bishop of London spoke in behalf of the interests of religion in the East, but the bishop of St. David's questioned the right of any people to send their religion to any other nation. [19])

We may conclude from this survey that it seemed quite impossible to send anybody to India without the support of the Government. And the Goverment when asked for help refused.

Neither did the Church of England take the initiative; it was even with some reluctance that they condescended to answer Grant. The initiative and the support came from an obscure and unknown little society of whom the promotor was William Carey, shoemaker and country parson. Grant is right when afterwards he wrote these words: "Many years ago I had formed the design of a Mission to Bengal and used my humble endeavours to promote the design. Providence reserved that honour for the Baptists."

Now we understand what were the conditions when William Carey, without any support or permission or license went ashore in Bengal. We also understand once more his firm determination to bring the Gospel at all cost and to face the greatest difficulties whatever the consequences might be. He did so in the knowledge of being called by the Lord.

NOTES

[1]) The force of the arguments may not be conclusive, but at any rate they are interesting, e.g.:

a) *Indian Tradition* which gives the story of St. Thomas' Indian career as held by the Syrian Christians of Malabar on the West Coast of India and by the Roman Catholics who are connected with the Portuguese Indian Mission. These Syrian Christians are the oldest existing branch of the Christian Church in India. He had to encounter fierce enmity on the part of the Brahmans and was finally transfixed by the spear of a hostile Brahman. Well known are the references of MARCO POLO who visited India in 1288 and again in 1292 asserting that the body of Saint Thomas the Apostle lies in the province of Malabar. An important argument is that King ALFRED, when London was besieged by the Danes in 883, vowed to send alms to Rome and also to India to St. Thomas, probably a Christian community which venerated the Apostle's name. And Bishop GREGORY of Tours who died 594 A.D. writes in his "In Gloria Martyrum": Thomas the Apostle, is according to the history of his passion, said to have suffered in India. After a long time his blessed body was taken into the city which they called Edessa in Syria and buried there.

b. *Ecclesiastical Tradition*: Eusebius said St. Thomas laboured in Parthia, but Parthia extended to the banks of the river Indus and so included a part of what is now known as India. Jerome wrote in the fourth century: The son of God was present with Thomas in India at all places, with Peter in Rome etc. Hippolytus stated that he suffered martyrdom at 'Calamene', a town in India. Hymns which were made by Ephraem, the famous doctor of the Syriac Church who died in Edessa in the year 393 A.D., begin as follows: Blessed art thou, Thomas the Twin (Didymus) in thy deeds, twin in thy spiritual power: not one thy power not one thy name, etc.

OGILVIE who gives the above mentioned arguments completes them with an apocryphal story coupled with archeological research. But this will do to prove that the arguments in favour of St. Thomas' missionary work in India are of real value, Ogilvie p.p. 5 f.f.

[2]) OGILVIE, op. cit., p. 49.

[3]) NEALE', History of the Holy Eastern Church. Introduction, quoted from OGILVIE, p. 59.

⁴) Ogilvie, p. 86, quoted by Howell in The Soul of India.

⁵) Ibid., p. 89.

⁶) Ibid., p. 166, cf. Prof. Dr. Friedrich Heiler, De Openbaring in de godsdiensten van Britsch-Indië en de Christusverkondiging, p. 17. Dr. Heiler thinks our attitude to Hinduism has been too formal. On the other side he tries to indicate a real connection between the Bhakti religion and Christendom. He disapproves of missionary endeavour as being too much European.

A very useful book to understand this problem of adaptation or accommodation is Dr. Thauren, Die Akkomodation in Katholische Heidenapostolat, cf. Prof. Dr. J. H. Bavinck, op. cit. p. 177. Also Warneck, Evangel. Missionslehre, 3e Abteil. Der Betrieb der Sendung, p. 286.

⁷) Ibid., p. 170.

⁸) Ibid., cf. p. 171.

⁹) Warneck, Abrisz der Geschichte der Protest. Mission, Caput I.

¹⁰) Ogilvie, op. cit. p. 204.

¹¹) Cf. Bavinck, p. 116.

¹²) Ogilvie, op. cit. p. 248.

¹³) Marshman, op. cit. p. 21. See also "Berigten van de Utrechtsche Zendingsvereeniging", 1861, number 8, page 4. This periodical gives also a good survey of the work of Dr. Carcey in Bengal.

¹⁴) Ibid., p. 23.

¹⁵) Ibid., p. 56.

¹⁶) Ibid., p. 32.

¹⁷) Ibid., p. 36.

¹⁸) Cf. Deaville Walker, p. 141 ; Marshman, op. cit. p. 37.

¹⁹) Marshman, p. 49.

5. His second apprenticeship.

The letter William Carey wrote to his father-in-law, when setting out for India, runs as follows :

Dear Father,

We are just going out. The boat is just going out, and we are going on board—Thursday morning at five o'clock—June 14th, 1793. We are all well, and in good spirits. June 13 1793

To Mr. Daniel Placket, Hackleton.

Above we hinted at the difficulties which might be encountered by the family who went to India especially with four little children. The discomforts, however were reduced by the kindness of the captain. He not only reduced the fares, but also helped the family as much as possible. The only reference we make to the voyage is "that Dorothy had many fears and troubles, so that she was like Lot's wife until they passed the Cape". Further that William Carey was preaching and praying and studying. That on board the ship he had already begun to study the Bengali language with the help of Thomas.

So *before* he came to India, he actually felt the importance of a translation of the Bible and of addressing the Bengalees in their own tongue. In Nov. 1793 when the goddess of Reason garlanded with oakleaves was being enthroned on the High Altar of Notre Dame, William Carey, the devoted Baptist Missionary, was sailing within the coast of Bengal. [1])

Nov. 11
1793
The "Cron Princessa Maria" reached the mouth of the Hooghi on Nov. 11, 1793 when William Carey landed in Calcutta. As it was a foreign vessel, the commander was not required to deliver a list of his passengers to the pilot. So Carey and Thomas entered the town without any difficulty, fully aware of the following regulation of Parliament : "If any subject of His Majesty not being lawfully licensed should at any time repair to or be found in the East Indies, such persons were to be declared guilty of a high crime and misdemeanour, and be liable to fine and imprisonment." They rented a house and both families lived together. Ram-boshu, a convert of Thomas, was accepted as a munchi (a teacher of Bengalee) for William Carey. The funds were entrusted to Thomas and here the difficulties arise.

Just as formerly the money vanished more rapidly than it came in. And they had no letters of credit, but only one hundred and fifty pounds. This money had been invested in articles of marchandise. Thomas undertook their re-sale and at first it seemed as if circumstances would favour their settlement in the city. Thomas pursued his medical profession, and Carey tried to secure a living by applying for a post at the Company's Botanical Garden. [1])

In his Enquiry he had given two principles : 1) missionaries must live *among* the people in the simplest manner possible, 2) missionaries must support themselves by agricultural, industrial or some other work.

Being aware that some time would elapse before these principles could be put into practice, the Committee had allowed the above mentioned sum. But before William Carey had been in the country for a month the cost of living in Calcutta proved so high that they had to remove to Bandel, some thirty miles from Calcutta. Here he was introduced to Mr. Kiernander, then eighty-four years old, who encouraged William Carey in his work. In this village they did not succeed in buying a house. So they rented a small cottage and purchased a boat so that they could visit all the river side villages and towns. Here we must point out a mistake : they at once began to itinerate. Daily they went with their boat to other villages, Thomas being in high spirits through Carey's enthusiasm. In this mood he wrote : "Their attention is astonishing. Every place presents a pleasing prospect of success. To see people so interested, inquisitive, and kind, yet so ignorant, is enough to stir up any with the love of Christ in their heart. Last Sunday Mr. Thomas preached to near two hundred in a village. They listened with great seriousness, and several followed to make further enquiries of the heavenly way, and how they should walk therein. The encouragements are very great. I never found more satisfaction than in this undertaking. I hope in a little while to see a Church formed for God." [2]) Then suddenly they all went back to Calcutta. Thomas' creditor was on his track and he thought he had better move to Calcutta and do surgical work there and Carey thought he might get a place at the Botanical Garden made for this city. However all went wrong. The appointment at the Botanical Garden was given to another applicant and his friend Thomas had to appease his creditors by all means possible.

Homeless and without any money they were once more in Calcutta. Carey's wife and her sister complained that they had "to live without the necessaries of life". Dorothy and Katherine and the two elder boys were ill for a month with dysentery—Felix so seriously that his life was in danger. All were longing for their simple cottage in the home-land. So William Carey wrote in his journal : "My wife and sister too, who do not see the importance of the mission as I do, are continually declaiming against me. If my family were but heart in the work, I should find a great burden removed." [3])

1794 Jan.

A rich native offered shelter to William Carey : a small house in Manicktolah, in the southern suburb of Calcutta, "a marshy, malarial, dacoit-ridden district".

Moreover he knew that Mr. Thomas was in danger of arrest. When Carey was offered a piece of land at Deharta, at some distance from Calcutta, he went to Thomas, but this man had incurred a new debt to a money-lender. So he writes Jan. 15, 16, 1794 : "I am much dejected. I am in a strange land, alone, no Christian friends, a large family, and nothing to supply their wants. I blame Mr. Thomas for leading me into such expense at first, and I blame myself for being led .... I am dejected, not for my own sake, but for my family's and his, for whom I tremble." A few days later he finds his colleague living at the rate of two hundred or

59

three hundred rupees per month, he has twelve servants, and is talking to Carey of keeping a coach. "I remonstrated with him in vain," Carey writes in his journal. On Jan. 23 he writes : "All my friends are gone but One, but He is all sufficient. Why is my soul disquieted within me ? Everything is known to God, and He cares for the Mission. I rejoice in having undertaken this work ; and I shall, even if I lose my life therein."

Here again we see the strength of his character. Whatever the difficulties, he continues as a missionary called by the Lord himself. While there is darkness on all sides, he throws himself into his language studies. He begins to translate Genesis into Bengali with the help of his munchi. On Jan. 28 he again went to Calcutta but again it proved a fruitless effort to find a way out of his difficulties. Then he received a letter from Mr. Fuller and the love manifested in that letter "overcame his spirits having not been accustomed to sympathy of late".

Then he called on DAVID BROWN, the Fort William Chaplain. But this man "was an iceberg nor did he offer Carey the least hospitality after his five miles' walk in the sun, for a marked disgust prevailed between him and Mr. Thomas".

Now Thomas with all his faults, showed himself a real help for William Carey on the last day of this bitter month of Jan. 1794. He had managed to borrow one hundred and fifty rupees at twelve Febr. 1794 to June '94 per cent interest to enable Carey to go to Deharta, a place where Ram Boshu's uncle had lived for some years. Though William Carey knew that this jungle was infested with cobras and the fiercest of tigers he resolved to go, and accepted this sum of money. The boat journey lasted three days. The devoted munchi Ram Boshu went with them, right through the jungle with its terrible noises. They travelled, both day and night. On the third morning they reached Deharta where William Carey met with a few Europeans. When he stepped ashore a Mr. CHARLES SHORT came out to meet him, a governmental assistant in the salt department. William Carey told his circumstances and the object which had brought him into the country. Very kindly Short invited him and his whole family to consider his house as his own home for six months or for a longer period, till he would be able to find a suitable place for his family.

Febr. 6 Soon afterwards William Carey chose a piece of land just across the Jubona river, "a very fine and pleasant situation" as he wrote.

We must admire his quiet and fixed determination for "the place was so full of tigers, that before his arrival twenty men had been devoured in the Department of Debharta within a few months". But now again he intended to overcome all difficulties. By the end of February his house, a simple bamboo structure, was almost finished. Daily he crossed and re-crossed the Jubona river with a heart full of joy. He felt he would soon get to know this part of Bengal and be friends with this people. His wife and Felix recovered. Other people who had emigrated for fear of the tigers reinhabited their houses, encouraged by his example. Even a deputation of some Brahmins came to thank him for his arrival. All his future life seemed to lie here. On the river Jubona lay many villages and the people were full of interest for this stranger and his Gospel.

By a providential turn all went quite different from what William March 1 1794 Carey had thought. On the 1st of March he received a letter from Thomas, who had made the acquaintance of Mr. GEORGE UDNEY, a genuine Christian belonging to the Company's civil service. He and Grant had supported the missionary work of Thomas before his arrival in India with William Carey. But like Charles Grant, his sympathies with Thomas had diminished and the friendship was broken. Then Udney's brother and his brother's wife were drowned by the upsetting ot a boat in crossing the river at Calcutta. Thomas who had not ventured to go to Malda where Udney lived, wrote a letter to his old benefactor and to his surprise he received a most cordial reply with the invitation to go to Malda and stay with Udney. Thomas started immediately, dropping his profession in Calcutta. Udney was at that time erecting two indigo factories and proposed that Thomas should manage one of them. Then Thomas told Udney the horrible position in which William Carey found himself in Debharta. Udney agreed that William Carey should manage the other indigo factory. William Carey saw this invitation as a door opened by the Lord himself. His salary fixed, he himself associated with a Christian employer, cooperation with Thomas and money to spare for missionary work. He accepted the offer at once. Now he had to make a long journey of three hundred miles across rivers right through the jungle. From March to May May 23 1794 he is concentrating on his Bengali "a very copious language and abounding in beauty". Then they started on their river voyage, while only Catherine stayed behind. She was married there to

Mr. Short in February. This river journey lasted twenty-three days. On June 15, 1794 they landed at Malda and were welcomed by Udney. Now his financial worries were over. He wrote to England that he did not need support any longer. "At the same time it will be my glory and joy to stand in the same relation to the Society as if I needed support from them and to maintain the same correspondence with them." [4]) Carey had to superintend the workpeople who according to his own plans would be material for missionary work.

The price of the long river journey was paid afterwards: the frail Dorothy, his wife, fell into a fit of melancholia, which later developed into insanity.

June 1794—
June 1796
The factory of which Carey was to take charge was at Mudnabatty, thirty-two miles north of Malda, and Thomas' place at Moypaldiggy was seventeen miles further still.

This factory became for him "his second apprenticeship" for the next six years. First he had his English period, when his great task was to arouse the churches of England to responsibility with regard to the heathen world. The second period begins when he landed in Calcutta and especially in Mudnabatty. God teaches him how to plant and establish the mission in Bengal.

Painful must have been the letter William Carey received from the Society. On hearing that he had accepted the management of an indigo factory they passed the following resolution: "That on the whole we cannot disapprove of the conduct of our brethren in their late engagement, yet, considering the frailty of human nature in the best of men, a letter of serious and affectionate caution be adressed to them."

How little they understood the character of William Carey, nor his missionary aim. He answered them "that after his family had obtained a bare allowance, his whole income goes for the purpose of the Gospel in supporting persons to assist in the translation of the Bible, in writing out copies of it, and in teaching school".

Of his income of 200 rupees a month he devoted by rigid economy one fourth and often one third to missionary objects.

He had ninety people under his control at the factory and of course he considered them as a field of missionary enterprise. He divided his time systematically and devoted it to the management of the factory, the study of the language, the translation of the New Testament and addresses to the heathen. In Sept. 1794 he was prostrate with fever and his life was in danger. He recovered but his son Peter, five years old, died after an illness of a few hours. Mrs. Carey was so deeply affected that she gradually became deprived of her reason, and had to be kept under restraint. It was part of the price William Carey and Dorothy paid for winning Indians for Christ.

In this period many missionary problems arose in his mind. First of all this one : the people listened to the Gospel, but they had not the least inclination to accept it. Sometimes some of them showed more than usual interest, but afterwards they disappointed him. So he wrote to his Society : "The Brahmins fear to lose their gain ; the higher caste their honour ; and the poor tremble at the vengeance of their debtor. Thus we have been unsuccessful." [5]

The second problem was the running of his school. At the end of 1794 he had opened it. But after a few months the parents took their children away. They had to earn money for the people were very poor.

Next there was a social problem. The Indian foremen had hired coolies at two and a half rupees per month, and even from that miserable income deducted two annas for themselves. He had to face these foremen and to help the coolies. In this way he tried to remove their prejudice against Europeans.

Then there was a religious problem : when the natives were to start indigo making, they would make an offering to the goddess Kali that they might have her approbation. Carey of course warned them not to offer a human being. He would like to prohibit it altogether, but he wisely understood that this would mean an obstruction to his purpose. The next day he was informed that they had offered a child to their goddess.

At this time he writes to the Society : "The experience obtained here I look upon as the very thing which will tend to support the Mission. Now I will propose to you what I would recommend to the Society. You will find it similar to what the Moravians do. Seven or eight families can be maintained for nearly the same expense as one, if this method is pursued. I then earnestly entreat the Society to set their faces this way and send out more missionaries. We ought to be seven or eight families together ; and it is absolutely necessary for the wives of missionaries to be as hearty in their work as their husbands. Our families should be nurseries for the Mission : and among us should be a person capable of teaching school, so as to educate our children. I recommend all living together, in a number of little straw houses." [6]) This plan afterwards proved to be of fundamental importance for his missionary work at Serampore.

We may learn from the above mentioned problems he had to face, that indeed this time was one of apprenticeship.

For William Carey problems only meant a stimulus to solve them. So he tried to prevent parents taking their children away from his school by clothing and feeding them at his own expense !

A great deal of his time he devoted to the translation of the Bible for he was convinced of the tremendous importance of this work. So he wrote to England for types to be sent out at his own expense for printing the Bible in the Bengali and Hindusthani languages. Within a year of reaching India he was able to send home a copy of Genesis, Matthew, Mark, and James in the Bengali language with a small vocabulary and grammar of his own composition.

But he was in no hurry to have these printed. He knew very well that his work contained many errors, for a score of Hindu words differ widely from their English equivalent e.g. sin, salvation, holiness. This pioneer understood the fundamental difference in meaning between these words when used by a Hindu or by a Christian.

After he had been in India for two years he found it possible "to preach an hour with tolerable freedom". At this time the people who came to hear him on Sundays, not only the factory-hands but also the people from the villages, a mounted to six hundred. And tactfully, he did not only preach, but also asked many questions e.g. in what kind of temple they worshipped, the name of their god, whether he was dead or alive a.s.o. And when he had gathered some men and women around him he would preach the Gospel to them in their own tongue. He did not take a text, but he began to speak of their gods and their beliefs and then from their own Sahastras, or the nine Incarnations of Vishnu, he passed on to the message of Jesus Christ. [7])

From this we see that he had a definite method of working. He tried to adapt his work as much as possible to the conditions under which he lived, without abandoning the essence of the Gospel. In this period he had not yet a clear insight into the exact course he ought to pursue, but he saw the main facts : translations of the

Bible, erecting schools, social righteousness, living among the heathen and being their friend, not overthrowing their principles but ont the contrary having interest in their religion.

Here we must give our attention to England again. In the year 1795 the London Missionary Society was formed, a large and comprehensive association.. One of the founders said "the torch of this London Missionary Society was lit at the missionary altar which the Baptists had raised." And it was Mr. Carey's communications which kindled the flame and became the immediate occasion of organizing a missionary agency. But this new action once more irritated the Court of Directors of the India Company. The Court had "weighty and substantial reasons which induced them to decline a compliance with the request for permission to proceed to India". [8]) One of the Directors even said : "I would rather see a band of devils in India than a band of missionaries." So the unalterable decision of the Directors was to prevent at all cost "the intrusion of interlopers". The Governor-General, Sir John Shore, fully endorsed the feelings of his masters at home and advised them in 1795 not to allow more than five or six in any one year in India.

Moreover some difficulties arose at William Carey's missionary post. First, Ram Boshu, the teacher and faithful friend of William Carey, had to be dismissed as proven guilty of adultery and embezzlement. (So this man dragged the missionfield into the dust.) Then the master of Carey's native school, vexed at Ram Boshu's dismissal, also left. Under these circumstances he wrote to Fuller : "We are determined to hold on, though our discouragements be a thousand times greater." [9])

1796

William Carey had often asked for more missionaries to be sent out. On Oct. 10, 1796 when he was studying Sanskrit with a new pundit, a stranger suddenly stood before him : his brother missionary called JOHN FOUNTAIN, sent by the Society in England. This young man infected by the principles of the French revolution had sentiments hostile to the existing institutions of government, especially to the India Company. Unable to get a licence he had travelled steerage. His arrival of course gave much joy to William Carey. Soon he became the singing master of the mission's choir of thirty-six boys. But in his letters to the Baptist Society he also sneered at the Company, and it was noticed that many of these

Oct. 10
1796

letters had been opened at the Post Office. So Mr. Fuller became alarmed, and wrote to William Carey : "If these notions continue, it will be a cankerworm at the root of religion as well as a millstone about the Mission." [10]) Even Mr. Fuller threatened that if these letters were to continue he would leave his post as secretary. So we can readily understand the new difficulties which William Carey had to encounter. He had to rebuke Fountain for his daring words against the mighty Company lest they should take notice of his missionary work and forbid it.

Then still other difficulties arose. Mr. Udney had suffered severe financial losses : a business house in Calcutta failed, a well laden ship was captured, the indigo industry had no success. So William Carey wrote to England : "My place cannot be tenable any longer." And here we see the strength of his character again : "There are difficulties on every hand, and more are looming ahead—*therefore we must go forward.*"

In this spirit he asks for more missionaries. He plans a campaign on a larger scale, for he will "attempt great things for God".
Nov. 1796 He clearly understands how the missionary work among the Indian women must be done entirely by the wives of the missionaries or unmarried Christian women. With regard to that he writes to England : "the usages of society in Eastern countries are such as to bar access to the female population, except by their own sex ; and when women are converted to the faith their religious principles and conduct require a constant vigilance and wisdom in their superintendence, different from and far beyond, what man either can or will bestow." [11]) And once more he writes that the way in which all this must be accomplished is by the Moravians' system : some seven or eight families living together, some people cultivating the land, some instructing, some learning, some preaching and the women superintending domestic concerns "but pray, be very careful what stamp missionaries' wives are of".

Even now he urges that the Medical Mission shall complete its equipment. He will not purchase the medicine but they must be furnished gratuitous. "Mr. Thomas has been the instrument of saving numbers of lives," he writes, "whereas his house is constantly surrounded with the afflicted."

As stated, the attitude of the Company became more and more hostile to missionary activity. Now the Bengal Government issued orders that every individual European in the country who

66

was not actually in the service of the Company was to send up annually a statement of his name, place of abode, date of arrival in India and occupation. If permitted to remain in the country each individual had to enter into a covenant and find two securities of two thousand pounds for the due fulfilment of it. [13])

Officially William Carey was called "an assistant to the indigo factory" and Mr. Udney and some other gentlemen had become securities for him. Of course Carey was not afraid to confess himself a missionary but in these circumstances it would mean expulsion from the field.

Meanwhile he calls for more help in the following terms : "What could three ministers do even in England, supposing it now dark and rude as when Caesar discovered it : supposing them also to have the language to learn, before they could converse with any ; and then to have the Scriptures to translate and write out with their own hands ; and this done, to have no other means of making the Scriptures known but by preaching—with printing almost totally unknown, and only here and there one able to write ?   This, brothers, is our case.   May it speed your prompt help.   Staying at home is become sinful for many, and will be more so." [14])

We have shown that Mr. Thomas was a real medical help for the missionary work.   But in business he proved to be an utter failure.   His indigo factory at some distance from Carey's could not make any profit and so after three years he had to leave it. Once more he began his surgical practice in Calcutta.   Here again he was unsuccessful.   After some other efforts he went to Nuddea where he lived in a boat.   There he tried to rent an indigo factory, but the water destroyed all his work.   Then he got a sugar factory. This also went wrong.   Yet amidst all these trials he attempted to evangelize.   He was a great Christian and a great blunderer. He was no business man at all.

In the latter part of the year 1798 he was solaced by a letter informing him, that Mr. W. WARD would come and help him as a printer. [15])   His heart was filled with gladness.   For at this very time he had been able to purchase a second-hand printing press. He bought it for fourhundred rupees, and set it up in his house. One of his English friends gave him the money for it, and lent him a sum in order to purchase type and pay the expenses of the first edition of the Scriptures.   He intended to print the Bible in four volumes and estimated the total cost at £ 2000.   He hoped to sell five hundred sets at Rs 32 each, and then be in a position to give away the remaining five hundred sets. [16])

Sept. 1799
But alas, there soon came a crash. [17]) Mr. Udney was constrained to abandon the ruinous factory of Mudnabatty and Mr. Carey had to look out for another residence and occupation. In order to register his future colleagues as coming out to be his assistants and to lay the foundation of his ideal missionary settlement on Moravian lines, he bought an indigo factory at Khidurpur with the help of Mr. Udney and the Rs 3000. he had saved himself.

When he received intimation of his Society that three if not four families were on their way to him, he began to build houses. Some time later Carey got the news that four new missionaries and Fountain's bride had landed in India. They were William Ward, the Marshmans, the Brunsdons and the Grants and Miss Tidd. Fountain set out by boat to meet them. But suddenly the whole scene changed.

First of all his Khidurpur factory was no success at all. The locality was obscure and unhealthy, and Mr. Udney was succeeded in Malda by a gentleman who was very hostile to the propagation of Christianity. He even inquired if William Carey was not liable to a prosecution for some letter of his, which had been published in England. He even determined to rout out all missionary activity. Moreover the three families and William Ward and Miss Tidd, asked by the pilot at the mouth of the Hoogli to fill in their names and profession, did not report themselves as assistants to Carey but in youthful eagerness they openly entered their names upon the official document as Christian missionaries proceeding to the Danish settlement of Serampore. Of course, it was unwise to wait for a reply and the Captain of the American ship Criterion in which they had sailed, sent them upstream to Serampore. They arrived there on Sunday morning Oct. 13, 1799 just as day was breaking. Marshman immediately went ashore and falling on his knees blessed God for having brought them safely to Indian soil.

Now this was the first instance that the arrival of missionaries had been officially brought before the Government and they naturally thought it a challenge to their authority. On this account the Captain of the Criterion, Mr. WICKES, was ordered to take his four passengers to the police-station. If he refused they would not permit him to unload his vessel. The Danish Governor Colonel BIE, however, resisted the demand of the British authorities and assisted the missionaries as much as possible. Therefore he laid their case before the Governor-General Lord WELLESLY and happily this man appeared to be sensible. He acknowledged that he had no right to punish Captain Wickes merely for bringing four passengers and their families to a foreign settlement. But the next problem was how could they join William Carey. Men of influence in Calcutta tried in vain to obtain permission for the missionaries to travel through British territories. When lodged in a very small and damp house with eight adults and four children, the missionaries invited a number of Christian people to join them for worship on the first Sunday after their arrival. Shortly before the appointed hour the Danish Governor himself and many other gentlemen arrived and speedily filled the room. It was Ward's birthday and he was the preacher. [18]) Such was the attitude of the Danish Governor.

Then a heavy blow fell upon them all. Mr. Grant died suddenly and left a widow and two little children.

Then Carey used all his influence to persuade the British Governor-General to permit the newly arrived families to join him. But all in vain. And the more the British authorities stood their ground, the more friendly became the Danish Governor to them. He assured them that they would be able to do their work without a hindrance. They could open a school. They could set up a press and print the Scriptures and tracts. He offered them the status and privileges of Danish citizens. He even offered to give them passports under his seal, when they desired to travel in British India. They would also be allowed to use the church for the building of which he was just then raising subscriptions. [19])

Monday December 2 was a day of very great importance : Carey has made up his mind to leave all, and follow the call of the Saviour to Serampore. Ward said: "Whilst He opened a door there to us, He has shut all others." On the first morning of 1800 they all left Malda for Serampore, which they reached on Friday the 10th. Carey's apprenticeship was over. His new leadership was to begin. [20])

NOTES

[1]) Mr. CANTON, History of the British and Foreign Bible Society, vol. I, p. 2.
[1a]) JOHN BROWN MYERS, William Carey, p. 42.
[2]) S. PEARCE CAREY, op. cit. p. 147.
[3]) DEAVILLE WALKER, op. cit. p. 151.

[4]) MARSHMAN, op. cit. p. 67.

[5]) DEAVILLE WALKER, op. cit. p. 175.

[6]) MYERS, id., pp. 49, 50.

[7]) Cf. DEAVILLE WALKER, id., p. 178.

[8]) MARSHMAN, p. 73.

[9]) S. PEARCE CAREY, p. 173.

[10]) MARSHMAN, id., p. 77.

[11]) DEAVILLE WALKER, p. 184.

[12]) GEORGE SMITH, The Life of William Carey D.D., p. 104. London 1885.

[13]) DEAVILLE WALKER, op. cit. p. 186.

[14]) S. PEARCE CAREY, p. 180. In his famous book S. PEARCE CAREY gives us some quotations from William Carey's journal, in which he is scourging himself : "Such another dead soul scarcely exists. My crime is spiritual stupidity. I am perhaps the most phlegmatic, cold, supine creature that ever possessed the grace of God. I have no love. O God, make me a true Christian. If God uses me, none need despair. My soul is like the prophet's heath of the desert, which withereth ere its beauty appeareth. I spoke to Mohammedans to-day, but I feel to be as bad as they. I am not one of those who are 'strong and do exploits'. Indeed I dread lest I may dishonour the Mission." And to JOHN NEWTON he wrote in Dec. 1799 : "I know God can use weak instruments, but I often question whether it would be for His honour to work by such as me. It might too much sanction guilty sloth, if I were to meet eminent blessing".

[15]) S. PEARCE CAREY, p. 183. In this period he received the following letter from which may be deduced what farreaching principles he had in mind when still in England : "Dear Mr. Carey. Ewood Hall. Halifax. October 1798. I know not whether you will remember a young man, a printer, walking with you from Rippon's Chapel one Sunday, and conversing with you on your journey to India. But that person is coming to see you and writes this letter. His services were accepted by the Society on the 16th. It was a happy meeting. The missionary spirit was all alive. Pearce set the whole 'meeting' in a flame. Had missionaries been needed, we might have had a cargo immediately. Some time in the spring I hope to embark with the others. It is in my heart to live and die with you, to spend and be spent with you.

I trust I shall have your prayers for a safe journey to you, and be refreshed by your presence. May God make me faithful unto death, giving me patience, fortitude and zeal for the great undertaking. Yours affectionately,

W. Ward".

[16]) DEAVILLE WALKER, op. cit. pp. 190—191.

[17]) S. PEARCE CAREY writing to the Society describes the calamity of the flood in Mudnabati in these words :

"All my attention is required to repair what I can of the ravages of a very calamitous flood, which has just swept away all this year's hopes. About ten days ago I went all over this neighbourhood, and the prospects were charming. The fields were covered with rice, hemp, indigo, cucumbers, and gourds. On Friday night I went over the same parts in a boat, when not a vestige of anything could be seen. All was a level plain of water from two to twenty feet deep. The rivers have made two large lakes, three miles wide and fifty miles long."

[18]) DEAVILLE WALKER, p. 200.

[19]) Ibid., p. 202.

[20]) S. PEARCE CAREY, p. 189, cf. Deaville Walker, pp. 202—203. Here Walker sums up the pros and cons of the proposal to remove to Serampore.

1) I shall be free from Mudnabatty on Dec. 31st, so that then no connection with Mr. Udney can be any hindrance to my joining you.

2) At Serampore we may be unmolested by Government .... here we could only live by connivance.

3) No obstruction will lie in the way of setting up the press at Serampore ; here there may be.

4) In that part of the country there are at least ten inhabitants to one here.

5) Other missionaries may join us there.
On the other hand :

1) I have engaged in a concern which is designed for the use of the Mission, which involved me in a debt of three thousand rupees, about two thousand of which will be paid off in a few days ; and then I am one thousand rupees in debt, and deserting the place.

2) When I have paid that, I have not a rupee to subsist on, except by anticipating a year's allowance.

3) An allowance like mine of a hundred pounds from the Society amounts to only sixty-six rupees per month. At Serampore, houserent alone will come to thirty or forty. If so, how can we subsist on the rest ?

4) Here our Church is formed, and God has given us two Europeans as our hire. A considerable number of natives also have some light though the conversion of any is uncertain.

5) I am now at great expense erecting houses and conveniences, planting a garden, etc., which, with the three thousand rupees, will be entirely lost.

6. The Mission Established.

The fine words of the favourite hymn by A. C. Ainger : "God is working his purpose out as years succeed to years ; God is working his purpose out and the time is drawing near" may be put above this chapter.

In the preceding six years, God gave William Carey the basic knowledge necessary for the establishment of the mission in Serampore. He had learnt to solve all kinds of problems, studied Indian languages, acquired some knowledge of the Indian soul. Moreover he had translated almost the entire Bible into Bengali. God had so far worked his purpose out and now the great time is drawing near that the missionary action will be in full swing. What a contrast : Khidurpur and Serampore.

Serampore in contact with the whole world and situated on the West bank of the Hoogli near Calcutta. Khidurpur only a country place without any culture, Serampore situated on a highway. The town had been purchased by the Danes in 1755. This little settlement had increased in size and importance in the run of years, and just now in 1800 it had reached a climax of prosperity. Here Kiernandier fled from his creditors and here William Carey and his colleagues found refuge and freedom. The principal importance of Serampore was that the site was strategic for the Gospel. Near Calcutta, and in contact with all the sea-faring countries, they reached according to John Fountain more men in a week than in six months in Mudnabatti or Khidurpur.

Now there had been some missionary action in Serampore before. In 1777 two Moravian missionaries went from Tranquebar to Bengal and Serampore : JOHANNES GRASSMAN and KARL FRIEDRICH SCHMIDT. The former as a gardener, the latter as a doctor.

71

In 1781 a carpenter LATROBE joined them. Their only success was a Bengali-German dictionary and they abandoned their missionary task as hopeless.

Now Carey tried to fulfill his Moravian plan. He showed himself a clever hand at knitting six families into one. He knew very well how easily frictions of all kind might disturb their cooperation as had been the case on their voyage from England to Calcutta. While Fuller and Sutcliff held the ropes in England, William Carey was the guiding influence of the missionary families in Serampore. [1]

Here we must note that William Carey tried to carry out his long cherished plan in a somewhat strange way. He tried to buy a piece of ground and intended to live in a range of cheap houses, at an expense not exceeding £ 300. Mr. Fuller had informed William Carey that the balance of the treasurer amounted to £ 3000. Now William Carey advised the Society to remit this money to India to be invested in Government securities which then gave an interest of 12 per cent. "This sum," said William Carey, "would furnish £ 360. a year, without the difficulties and uncertainties of drawing on England." [2] A month later he urged the Society to send £ 4000. "Then the mission could be established without any more labour of begging. Perhaps you may start at the proposal of investing your money in the Company's hands, lest they should become bankrupts or be dissolved. To this I can only say, that in this case the Government of England would, in all probability, become responsible for their debts." This plan of William Carey was not a sound one. And fortunately the project fell to the ground. John Clark Marshman is right when he remarks that an endowed mission of necessity becomes lifeless. And he is also right when asserting 'that a feeling of healthful responsibility to the Christian public periodically enforced, appears to be indispensable to the maintenance of zeal and animation in the missionary system'.

Nowadays it is easy to correct William Carey on this point. Nobody would like a situation in the church 'without any more labour of begging'. But all the more we must admire the insight of this pioneer when after a short time he dismissed the idea of a cheap mission and resolved to carry on the work on a large scale. [3]

In this respect he rejected the Moravian system—a conception which he may have embraced as a result of his own poverty.

Now he purchased a large building at a cost of six thousand

rupees, though they had not half the amount at their disposal. By a loan and by the appropriating of the funds which the missionaries had brought out for their subsistence and by drawing a bill on the Committee the house was paid for. Afterwards when dealing with the principles of William Carey we shall see that he fundamentally differed from the Moravians as regards cooperation with his colleagues. Suffice it to say that he and his fellow-missionaries decided that no breach should divide them whatever their sufferings might be.

They also unanimously agreed that the expenses were to be met from a common fund, that all their earnings were to be pooled, and that each family should receive a small allowance for private needs. Herein they agreed with the Moravian brethren. Carey was made treasurer. He was also in charge of the medicine chest as Dr. Thomas was not with them; Mr. Fountain was made librarian.

Every Saturday night, they had a meeting to regulate family matters, and to adjust any differences that might have arisen during the week. They had instituted a Baptist Church among themselves and on Sundays Carey as their pastor preached.

Their first attention was given to the printing office. Ward set up the types with his own hands and on the 18th of March 1800 March 1800 he was able to present the first sheet of the New Testament to Carey.

They divided their days systematically as follows: about six o'clock they rose, when Carey went to his Botanic Garden behind their house, Marshman to his school at seven, Brunsdon, Felix and Ward to the printing office. Further they write: at eight the bell rings for family worship; we assemble in the hall; sing, read and pray. Then we have breakfast. Afterwards, Carey takes up his translation, or reads the proofs; Marshman goes off to school and the rest to the printing office. At twelve oclock we have lunch; most of us shave and bathe, read and sleep before dinner, which we have at three. After dinner we give our thoughts to a text or question. We have tea about seven and little or no supper. In a letter sent to the Society at home they wrote: "We bless God that as a family we experience His goodness in continuing and we hope increasing, a spirit of unanimity and brotherly love amongst us. We trust we can say we are of one mind, and that our desire is to strive together for the furtherance of the Gospel, and the conversion of the heathen around us." 4)

73

On the first of May 1800 Mr. and Mrs. Marshman opened two boarding schools. They supplied a want which had long been felt by the Europeans in Calcutta and "Marshman's Academy" was quickly crowded with pupils, the financial profit amounting to £ 1000. annually for many years. [5]) On the first of June they also opened a vernacular school for native youth, which also got many pupils.

Then the missionaries hit upon the idea of printing some of the Gospels separately e.g. St. Matthew. This proved a very useful method of evangelizing, an idea quite new to them.

They also issued a paper: "The Gospel Messenger". Carey's old munchi Ram Boshu, who had come back again, was an excellent Bengali scholar and a good writer and became one of the editors. These papers were printed in large numbers and proved a great success.

Meanwhile Carey preached nearly every day. He had numerous conversations with all kinds of people, laboured in the suburbs and in the neighbouring villages, went to market places and addressed Brahmins around temple gateways. Dr. Ogilvie gives us an account of such a conversation: Carey would ask: "What is that mark on your face?" (a white mark of their god gleaming upon their forehead). "It is the Telak," they answered. "Why do you put on such a mark?" continued the missionary. "It is an act of devotion and holiness to wear it. The Shastras commend it," was the usual response. "Tell me about these Shastras. How do you know they are divine?" After telling him of their Shastras, Carey of course produced his "Shastras" and told the Gospel to them.

We may learn from this method of working, that he had grasped the very principles which are the bases of success. Another example may prove how thoroughly he maintained this method. Worshippers are bathing in the river Hoogli. Carey goes to them and asks: "Can any inform us how sin may be pardoned?" By bathing in the holy river," is the answer. Then sitting on the ground he enters into a conversation about sin and remission of sins.

On the 20th of August 1800 Fountain died having laboured with Carey at Mudnabatty for four years. He had been married to Miss Tidd shortly after the arrival of the "Criterion". So the second missionary died on the battlefield of the Lord, far from his family and friends.

74

In the latter half of the first year they printed some six thousand half sheets every week. But after some time they lacked ready money, having but slender means at their disposal. So they concluded to realize the Nottingham watchword of William Carey: "Expect great things from God; attempt great things for God." They ventured to announce in the Calcutta newspapers that they had set up their press in Serampore for the purpose of printing the Bible in Bengali. Now they asked for subscriptions to enable them to carry out the work. Everybody who was in sympathy with their work was asked to subscribe two gold mohurs (four pounds) for a copy. The Governor-General, Lord Wellesley, was inclined to immediate suppression of the press. But after some reflection he consulted Brown. This clergyman assured him that no political questions whatever should be printed and that their attention was only directed to the conversion of the heathen. Moreover he feared that the Bible might do harm to the attitude of the heathen towards the English government as the Bible taught the doctrine of equality to all men. Brown replied that he himself should be responsible for all the mischief the Bible might do in India. From this attitude of the Governor we may conclude the great harm he might have done to the missionary action if they had still been on English territory in Mudnabatty or Khidurpur. We clearly see the Lord had sent them to Serampore. Afterwards, however, Lord Wellesley abstained from intermeddling with their missionary work, he even showed himself ready to foster the work rather than to thwart it.

The Danish Governor was a first subscriber to their Bengali Bible. He also promised Ward his Government printing and urged the Danes to send their children to the Marshmans' schools. The appeal in the Calcutta papers was a great success in such a way that it solved the financial problems. So the first year finished. Lord Wellesley no more hostile, Mr. Brown captivated by Carey's character, the missionary colony well established and last not least the Lord blessing them all.

For seven years Carey had daily preached Christ in Bengali and Dr. Thomas even longer if we include his first term of service in India without there being a single convert. Carey had produced the first edition of the New Testament. He had founded schools, he had the fulfilment of his wish, viz.: a fine Missionhouse and an able staff of workers, he had his own printing house and his own periodical. But to what purpose was all this if the main object was not achieved?

The last disappointment was on the 25th of November 1800, when the first Hindoo offered himself for baptism. After he had returned to his distant home for his child, he appeared no more, probably detained by force.

The task was extremely difficult. In later years Mrs. Marshman showed her daughter Rachel a big tree, "where the Mission has been wont to sing and preach and whence they would sometimes return with bleeding faces from the stones flung at them." [6]) Grassman and Schmidt seemed right: "Preaching at Serampore is ploughing upon a rock." The people mocked them and asked: "If two of you are already dead, has your God indeed commissioned you?" Carey confesses to his colleagues that 'he was almost dried up by discouragement and was tempted to go to his work like a soldier expecting defeat'.

Nov. 25
1800 But on Nov. 25, 1800 KRISHNA PAL, a carpenter, slipped and dislocated his shoulder after his morning prayer in the Hoogli river. He reached his house and sent to the Mission house for Mr. Thomas, who by the way had joined his old friend William Carey some time before. This man was the first Hindu convert. But it was not the first time he heard of the Gospel. First Krishna Pol heard it from one of the Moravians and much later from Mr. Fountain. But now the message of Jesus Christ came home to him with such force through the preaching of John Thomas that one day meeting Mr. Thomas in the street, he said: "Oh Sahib, I am a very great sinner, but I have confessed my sin . . . . and I am free!" When the day of his baptism was fixed, a riot followed. But the Governor placed a soldier before their houses and so he was baptized in the Hoogli at the landing steps near the mission house. So was Felix Carey the eldest son of William Carey.

Before the baptism of Krishna Pal the missionaries had to fight a hard struggle. First of all Krishna's wife and her sister and a friend of his, should also be baptized. They all broke caste by dining together with the missionaries. The meaning of such an act can scarcely be overestimated. Eating with a European, means rupture with the Hindus. And also rupture with the whole social system of India. It meant to be an outcast from this day onward. But for the missionaries it meant that the well closed door to the Gentiles had been opened. That the chain of caste had been broken

76

as Ward puts it. The converts would of course be cursed by the Brahmins. The mob would not spare them either. Once when they were crowded before his house, they shouted: "This man has eaten with the Europeans and has himself become one." The Governor may have forbidden to do them any harm, but yet they snatched Krishna's eldest girl as long ago she had been promised to a Hindu neighbour as a wife.

The neighbours and the kinsfolk pleaded their cause in all possible ways and with success: Krishna's wife and her sister and Gokul withdrew. Only Krishna stood firm. The joy of the missionaries was immense. [7])

But for all that, we learn from these events that the attitude of William Carey and his colleagues towards the Indian castes was negative. Here we only state the fact he took a firm stand against the castes and did not adapt the Gospel to this social and religious order. Whatever the consequences might be: he refused to recognize institutions which are typically paganistic.

And indeed there were consequences: Not only did doctor Thomas, after having waited fifteen years for one convert get such a violant shock that religious mania developed so that he had to be put under restraint, but also was the school for natives in the vernacular tongue left without a pupil the following day. All had been withdrawn lest they should become Christians. Moreover Carey was charged with having desecrated the Ganges. Krishna's Brahmin landlord evicted him: another robbed him of a piece of land partly paid for. So all these men had to suffer. But their joy was heavenly.

On the other side there were also fine consequences: within a fortnight Jaymani, the sister of Krishna's wife, was baptized as the first Bengali woman. In February Krishna's wife and another woman. In March 1801 a bound copy of the New Testament was laid on the Communion Table, a fact of the greatest importance.

Jan. 1801

Febr. March

The highest respect must be paid to Ward and his staff for completing such a huge work in nine months. S. Pearce Carey notes: it was the first people's book ever printed in Bengali and was the fruit of seven and a half years of Carey's toil. [8]) A very interesting letter, especially to Dutchmen, from William Carey to Dr. JOHANNES VAN DER KEMP, the founder of "Het Nederlandsch Zendelinggenootschap" (Dutch Missionary Society) was written in Febr. 1801. Van der Kemp went to Kaffirland as the London

Missionary Society's pioneer. He reached this country in February 1801 and as soon as Carey learned of his presence there he communi-

April cated with him with deep joy. [9]) In the month of April 1801 William Carey was asked to undertake the Bengali professorship at Calcutta. Lord Wellesley was then engaged in a great scheme of establishing a college at Calcutta for the training of the young civilians who came out to India. No post of this three years' training college was more important than the professorship of Bengali. And the only qualified European who could be found was William Carey. Carey hesitated, considering himself unsuitable for such a post. [10]) The letter came from David Brown and after Carey had consulted his colleagues they concluded that it was their task to grasp at once the opportunity of influencing the youths who might ere long be rulers of the country. Carey meeting Brown and Buchanen (another Rev. in Calcutta) told them that he would like to accept on condition that such an appointment must be compatible with his missionary task. Brown and Buchanan who had been appointed as Provost and vice Provost of the College, convinced him that the very interest of the mission should compel him to accept. "I therefore consented with fear and trembling."

Lord Wellesley, hearing that William Carey considered himself above all things a missionary, raised no objection. But one diffi-culty arose : The Statutes of the college laid down that all the professors should promise to maintain the doctrines of the Church of England. Carey as a Nonconformist fell under this restriction. So him was given the status of lecturer with a salary of five hundred rupees a month.

Here again we see Providence guiding his ways. The East India Company had forbidden him to enter Bengal. Had forced him to live in poor conditions for six years. Was the cause that William Carey had to camouflage his work under the pretext of being a business man. Then the same Company forced his col-leagues to stay at Serampore. And now . . . . after all these years of preparation, of modelling he is called to a college to fulfil a duty which was strongly forbidden by the Directors. So against the design and against the desire of the Company he worked out his missionary plan, according to a higher plan : the Plan of the Lord.

May 4 1801 On May of the same year Carey took up his new duties. Soon he also became a teacher of Sanskrit. The task Carey had to face was indeed a very difficult one for never before had any prose-book

78

been written in Bengali. So he had to compose a Grammar and all kinds of books to study this language, which he did with the help of Ram Boshu.

The salary he received was used for the mission and not regarded as his personal income. They were now able to do without the money forwarded from England which they placed at interest.

Carey had been only four mornings in his new appointment when May 8 once more the events distinctly proved how their ways were led by Providence as Marshman puts it. When rising in the morning of May 8 the English flag was flying over the Danish Government buildings. Without "firing a shot or beating a drum" the English troops had crossed the river and captured Serampore : the cause being a war broken out between England and Denmark. The missionaries were summoned to the English Commissioner's House and there they were ordered to pursue their labour as before.

The next year peace was concluded and Serampore restored to the Danes. But by his appointment as a tutor of Fort William College at Calcutta, the missionaries were as safe under the British flag as under the Danish. Here we again see the ways of the Lord : He protected them even against their former enemies. August

In August of 1801 Goluk, a friend of Krishna's, was baptized and in November also his wife followed Christ. Many others followed. Now a difficult question arose : the giving of Christian names to the converts on their Baptism. [11])

William Carey opposed this practice. In the first place because he could not perceive any connection between the rite of Christian baptism and a change of name. In the second place as he could not perceive such a practice in the History of the Church especially not in the apostolic age. All the Roman names of the converts remained.

A fine instance of economic management is given by these men now that Carey's income rose by leaps and bounds. After some months his salary was raised to £ 1500. But all went to the common purse : a fine example of self-denial. "The Marshmans retained only thirty rupees per month for their private expenses, Ward kept twenty rupees, and Carey for himself and his family retained fifty rupees—a little more in order that he might provide himself with suitable apparel for his work at college and for his official appearances at the Government House." [12])

79

Dr. Ogilvie tells us that from the first to the last Carey's contributions amounted to £ 46000 while in the same period the Society procured less than £ 2000.

Another important item is discussed in August 1801, viz. the problem of employing native itinerants in the work of the mission. Ward writes on this problem: "It appears to us all that we ought to make the most of the gifts of our Hindoo friends and we are thinking how to occupy Krishna so as to make himself useful in the vineyard." On their journey they not only preached but also distributed printed books and pamphlets which had never before been seen in the country. [13]

Oct.
On the 13th October Mr. Thomas died at Dingapore. Loving Christ and gifted with zeal for the missionary work but stranded by his great mistakes. Now only three of the missionaries remained: Carey, Marshman and Ward. Many other people were baptized. Fuller was in high spirits and wrote: "Through the medium of their and of your struggles we read the Acts and the Epistles as it were with new eyes and seem to behold the Christianity of the early years as in a mirror. We say: 'Now we live if ye stand fast in the Lord!'" [14]

NOTES.

[1] S. PEARCE CAREY tells us not only of the violent quarrel between the missionaries, but also of the concern they had for the well being of their future family life. I tremble, Ward wrote, almost before we begin to live together. So much depends upon a man's disinterestedness, forbearance, meekness and self-denial. One man of the wrong temper could make our house a hell. Much wisdom will be necessary. It is but here and there that a man makes conscience of strangling his thoughts and of esteeming others better than himself. Only a few are fit to live in such a settlement as ours is to be, where selfish passions must be crushed and the love of Christ swallow up all else, op. cit. pp. 192—193.

[2] MARSHMAN, op. cit. p. 122.

[3] DEAVILLE WALKER, p. 209.

[4] J. B. MYERS, op. cit., p. 65.

[5] MARSHMAN, pp. 130—131, cf. Dr. OGILVIE, op. cit. pp. 308—309.

[6] S. PEARCE CAREY, p. 202.

[7] An interesting letter is given by S. Pearce Carey of the historic Baptism. The letter is Ward's. The words in parentheses are added by S. Pearce Carey. 'Sunday, December 28, 1800.—After our English Service at which I preached on baptism, we went to the river-side, immediately opposite our gate (i.e. in front of the present Mission Church), when the Governor, a number of Europeans and Portuguese, and many Hindus and Mohammedans attended. (Carey says it was nearly one o'clock, the tide compelling this lateness). We sang in Bengali: 'Jesus, and shall it ever be'? (Carey's own rendering.) Carey then spoke in Bengali, particularly declaring that we did not think the water sacred, but water only, and that the one from amongst themselves about to be baptized professed by this act to put off all sins and all "debtahs", and to put on Christ. After prayer he went down the bank into the

water, taking Felix (the son of his heart) in his right hand and baptized him. Then Krishna went down and was baptized, the words in Bengali. All was silence. The (brave old) Governor could not restrain his tears, and almost every one seemed struck with the solemnity of this new ordinance. I never saw in the most orderly congregation in England anything more impressive. 'Ye gods of stone and clay, did ye not tremble, when in the Triune Name one soul shook you from his feet as dust'? When Krishna came from dressing—a quick thing here—a Danish lady took him by the hand, and thanked him from her heart. Brunsdon was ill, but watched all from a palanquin. Thomas alas, was confined in the school, raving mad ! (The bruised reed was broken under the stress of the blessedness. Carey's wife, too, had no power to share her son's and husband's joy.) In the afternoon we kept the Lord's Supper in Bengali for the first time ! 'How amiable are Thy Tabernacles O Lord of hosts !' Krishna said he was full of praise. Felix and I accompanied him to his home. We talked with unusual feeling to the women (and to Krishna's relatives there from Chandernagore and Calcutta). About nine o'clock Krishna came joyfully to the Mission to tell us that they again wished for baptism. Blessed day ! (What a thrilling last Sunday of the year and of the century), p. 209.

8) S. PEARCE CAREY, p. 211, Marshman was in such high spirits that he composed his own hymn for the occasion :

> Hail precious Book divine !
> Illumined by thy rays
> We rise from death and sin
> And tune a Saviour's praise :
> The shades of error, dark as night,
> Vanish before thy radiant light !
>
> Now shall the Hindus learn
> The glories of our King
> Nor to blind gurus turn
> Nor idol praises sing ;
> Diffusing heavenly light around
> This Book, their Shastras shall confound.
>
> Deign, gracious Saviour, deign
> To smile upon Thy Word ;
> Let millions now obtain
> Salvation from the Lord :
> Nor let its growing conquest stay
> Till earth exult to own Thy sway.

9) S. PEARCE CAREY, p. 213. Very dear fellow-helper VANDERKEMP.

The news of your going to the Cape a little before some of us left England to join the Mission caused us to rejoice that God was sending His glorious Gospel to Africa's dark tribes. You and your colleagues are called to a most arduous but important work. You may meet with many discouragements and may have to face many trials : you may labour long with no sign of success : many apparent first fruits may be blasted or for long may seem so. Yet be not weary : you shall reap fruits in due time, if ye faint not. He is faithful who has promised, and will stand by His servants to the end of the world.

Cold reason alone would suggest that a world so beautiful and in many ways so plainly under the government of God, cannot for ever be the theatre of oppression, sedition, slavery and war, and would incite us to hasten the reign of righteousness and peace. Nevertheless, we have little sure hope of their being accomplished, till we read the devine promises, and consider the pledge of their fulfilment in the death of our adorable Redeemer. Then firm rock is felt beneath our feet and we know that the earth shall be filled with the glory of God, as the waters cover the seas.

Seven years have passed since we, who have been here the longest, came first to this country to publish the Gospel. Throughout the faithfulness of God has been our stay and our encouragement :—our only encouragement till last year, save for

His mercy in our family and the conversion of some Europeans, to whom we had access. But now God has begun to add Indians themselves to His Church. We baptized two, some little time ago, and have very lively hopes of three more. Which gives fresh vigour to our spirits—though had we not been blessed with even this success, we should have waited still upon God, assured that all things are under the rule of an infinite wisdom.

Experience has taught us that God's ways are best, and that our little plans are often frustrated in great mercy. As, for instance, in the matter of our settling *here*. Far to the north of this we *were* settled, and to that place every heart was bound, when our colleagues arrived in this country. Not till we could choose no longer, and even then with the utmost reluctance, did we bring ourselves to relinquish what we had begun in Mudnabatty : we only painfully complied with dire necessity. But now we see that the Divine Hand was in it, and are convinced that this is the very place where we ought and are best advantaged to be. Therefore, dear friend, be sure that, even when you are most disturbed, disappointed and discouraged—whilst God leads, you can never go astray. Be strong in Him and in the power of His might. Make mention of His righteousness—even of His only.

We shall greatly esteem a letter from you or from any of your colleagues—telling us where is the seat of your labour, what your success, your difficulties and your prospects. We long to know you intimately, that we may the more sympathize with you affectionately and rejoice with you in a more lively strain, and pray for you more heartily. We wish you to do the same with us. Let us by such mutual communications cement a union between Asia and Africa.

Very affectionately yours in the bonds of the Gospel

W. CAREY, JOSHUA MARSHMAN,
W. WARD, D. BRUNSDON, FELIX CAREY

Serampore Bengal, Feb. 14, 1801.
Cf. BAVINCK, op. cit. p. 128.

[10]) OGILVIE, op. cit., p. 309. MARSHMAN, p. 143, cf. S. PEARCE CAREY, p. 215, who published the letter of Marshman :
Wednesday, April 8, 1801. This morning Carey came to me in great haste almost before I was awake. He had received a note from our very good friend Rev. DAVID BROWN concerning a matter of great moment, to which an immediate answer must be given. 'He wished to propose him as Professor of Bengali in the Governor-General's new College. Would he give his consent ?' Going over to C's room, I found Ward summoned in the same earnest manner. We laid our heads together with the gravity of a conclave of Cardinals. After discussing the subject pretty liberally, we agreed that, as it came unsought, and might in easily-imagined circumstances be of essential service to the Mission we should consent, leaving it to God, to fulfil or frustrate, as was best—there being yet much uncertainty in the business.
[11]) MARSHMAN, p. 151.
[12]) Dr. OGILVIE, p. 312.
[13]) MARSHMAN, p. 153.
[14]) Idem, p. 154.

7. STEADY PROGRESS.

1802

Of very great importance for the whole missionary action was the beginning of 1802. Then the Serampore missionaries had the pleasure of baptizing the first convert of the Kayust or writer caste. To understand the meaning of such an event we must note that there are only four pure classes, divided as follows : The Brahman, the Kshatriyas, and the Vaisya and the Sudra. The three first constitute the three twice-born classes (as receiving a second spiritual birth through investiture with the sacred thread : the poita worn over the naked body) ; the Sudra however is first born, and constitutes the fourth class ; there is no fifth class. From priority of birth, from superiority of origin (in being sprung from the mouth of the Creator), from possession of the Veda (i.e. from the right of repeating, teaching and expounding it) and from a distinction in the reception of the sacrificial thread (as the most important of the twelve Sanskaras or purifficatory rites) the Brahman is lord of all classes.

A Brahman whether learned or unlearned, is a mighty divinity just as fire is a mighty divinity, whether consecrated or unconsecrated. But there is also a more developed social system depicted and a number of mixed castes are described as resulting from the intermarriage of the pure classes. They have a variety of names and are restricted to particular occupations. [1])

Now the Kayust or writer caste is, according to Marshman, second to the sacerdotal tribe though its members are fully equal and generally superior to the Brahmins in wealth, intelligence and enterprise. [2]) The above mentioned convert was PETUMBER SING, a man of nearly sixty years of age. When Krishna and Goluk broke caste, many wondered at it. But then the great majority of Hindus asked disdainfully : Have any of the Brahmins and Kayusts believed in Christ ? What a great thing to have a carpenter and a distiller reject caste ? Then Carey says : "The Lord deprived them of that small consolation by giving us a Kayust and then after some time two more and one Brahmin, too." [3]) A great step forward was the abolition of infanticide, practised by some sections of the Hindus. Every year a great Hindu feast is held at full moon in January. Then thousands of Hindus assemble at Gunga Saugor at the confluence of the Ganges and the sea— and offer children to "the Mother Ganges", mostly a fulfilment of a vow ; Carey was moved with indignation. And so was Udney, his Mudnabatty protector, who had been promoted to the Supreme Council. The latter paid much attention to this cruelty and also directed the attention of Lord Wellesley to these atrocities. The Governor resolved to have this point thoroughly enquired into. He wished the immediate suppression of such a practice, but first he required Carey to investigate whether infanticide rested upon the authority of sacred books. Once more we see how scrupulously he averted all interference with the prejudices of the natives. Carey entered upon this enquiry with enthusiasm. He himself and Thomas had seen cruelties against sick children when they were at Mudnabatty. Buchanan tells us : "If a child refuses the mother's milk, whether from sickness or from any other cause, it is supposed to be under the influence of an evil spirit. In this case, the babe is put into a basket and hung up in a tree for three days. It generally happens that before the expiration of that time the infant is dead . . . . If it be alive at the end of three days, it is taken home and means are used to preserve its life." [4]) His investigation made him quite sure, that this cruel infanticide was not prescribed in any of the sacred books. So he reported the result of his researches and urged just like Udney, that they should be prohibited.

Aug.
1802 At once the General-Governor peremptorily interdicted the drowning of children. Sepoys were stationed near the banks of the river. But already in a few years this action was completely unnecessary, as it had become a thing of the past.

The second great attempt for God was the abolition of female immolation : called sati by the Hindus, which means the burning of the still living widow on the pyre of her decayed husband. [5]) In 1803 only around Calcutta 400 widows were burned in this way and it is estimated that in all the Bengal provinces more than ten thousand widows were killed in the course of one year. It is a pity that results of the investigations of William Carey did not move the Governor-General in such a way that he at once forbade these cruel practices. Carey clearly showed that these customs were not prescribed in the sacred books, but were merely countenanced. However strong his arguments might be, these cruelties went on and he had to wait still many years after this first attempt. Here we must mention another great plan for educating the children of native converts, and of youths who might renounce caste. According to Marshman it was intended to give them instruction in divinity, history, geography, and astronomy, and in the English and Bengalee languages. The main purpose of the missionaries was "to send them out into this part of the heathen world as persons who shall be peculiarly instrumental in turning their fellow-countrymen from darkness to light". [6])

June On the 13th of June 1802 Fräulein RHUMOHR, the daughter of Count Rhumohr of the Duchy of Schleswick, who had been advised to stay in India for her health, was baptized, in the presence of

84

the Governor-General of Serampore, the British Commissioner and many Europeans. Hereafter we shall see that she became the second wife of William Carey.

At the beginning of 1803 the first Brahmin was baptized, viz. 1803 Krishna Prasad. Before his baptism he trampled on his poita to show his rejection of his old religion to the missionaries. Above we mentioned the high value that the Hindus attribute to this holy thread. It places them on an equality with the gods, and through it they are given deep reverence by all the other classes.

This poita is the emblem of the glory of Brahminhood. Now here we must note the attitude of William Carey and his colleagues. They gave this young Brahmin money to buy another poita. They only considered it as a token of social distinction and so the Brahmins were baptized even with the poita around their shoulders! They did not wish to interfere with the national habits and customs. Mr. Ward defends this attitude in this way: "How much better is love and illumination than force. If we had compelled these brethren to leave off their poitas perhaps they might have been attached to them while they lived." After some years they voluntarily renounced the wearing of the poitas. [7])

As for the distinction between the castes, the missionaries resolved to abolish every vestige of it from the Christian community. Other missionaries allowed this distinction to intrude even at the holy communion, when the Brahmins received the elements before the Sudras. But at his first communion Krishna Prasad received the cup directly from the hands and the lips of Krishna Pal!

After this principal attitude was adopted, they could go forward for in April 1803 a Brahmin wedded a carpenter's child! This of April 1803 course was another great step towards total obliteration of the caste distinctions. After the celebration, the bride and bridegroom plighted their faith to each other and signed the agreement, "the first, Mr. Ward remarks, to which a female Hindu had put her name for many centuries".

From many instances given in the biography of S. Pearce Carey we may learn that the missionaries if necessary dared even to excommunicate those who sinned against the law of the Lord and did not show any repentance! But they also rejoiced when the transgressors came back regretful and promised to live as children of their heavenly Father. [8])

A magnificent day for William Carey was Sept. 20, 1804. Above 1804 we mentioned that he was appointed as a teacher of Sanskrit too. Now every year Lord Wellesley wanted to have a speech Day of the College in the Throne Room of the New Government House. Here the students and also the professors had to display their learning in several tongues. At such an assembly the Viceroy and the upper ten of Calcutta were present.

There were even more prominent people than usual, for not only the Governor-General himself, but also his brother the Duke of Wellington, the supreme Council, an envoy from Bagdad, and the city's literati were present. The former shoemaker of Hackleton had as a representative of Oriental scholarship to address this distinguished audience in Sanskrit, which he performed in such a splendid way that Lord Wellesley gave as his comment : "I am much pleased with Mr. Carey's truly original and excellent speech. I esteem such a testimony from such a man a greater honour than the applause of Courts and Parliaments." [9])

From August 1806, he gets equal pay with the Hindustani professor, viz. £ 1500 a year plus the title of Professor. He published six grammars, a Bengali, a Sanskrit, a Marathi, a Punjabi, a Telegu and a Kanarese. His Sanskrit grammar had even 1000 pages. He compiled three dictionaries—a Bengali, a Marathi and a Sanskrit, besides a Bhutia vocabulary. Scholars declare that no language, not even in Europe, could show a work of such industry, erudition and philological completeness as Carey's three-volumed Bengali dictionary with its 80.000 words. Dr. SMITH and Professor H. H. WILSON of Oxford declare that "local terms were here rendered with the correctness which Carey's knowledge of the people's manners and his long domestication amongst them enabled him to attain". In 1805 he made plans of publishing a series of Indian Classics with text, English translation and notes with the help of his Serampore colleagues. They began with the Ramayana. By 1810 they had issued three volumes besides translating some books of the Sankya philosophy. Andrew Fuller called the Ramayana : "that piece of lumber". We once more see how broadminded a man Carey was. He realised that it was necessary to understand the Hindu spirit at its very roots. Therefore he did not begin with the Vedas. Then, he says, the public would be wearied at the very outset. The Ramayana will excite a wish to read it through. William Carey well understood the state of mind of the public. He might grieve over the polytheistic tendencies of the Ramayana, however he admired the beauty of language and the power of expression. He really opened the riches of India to millions of people. William Carey had an eye for the common grace granted to all men, "for the decorum, order, refinement and virtue existing among men, the natural sense of right and the restraints of human laws, universal and powerful". [10])

When Doctor Thomas died, there was nobody to succeed him. But Carey understood the great importance of this branch of missionary work. So he himself had to be a doctor at week ends, just as he had been at Mudnabatti. But of course, he not only gave them medicine for their bodies, but also the best he could find for their souls. In this time Marshman, Carey and chaplains Brown and Buchanan were planning for the establishment of a native hospital in Calcutta : quite a new idea of progressive missionary action.

Meanwhile the missionary staff itself was growing steadily. In 1803 JOHN CHAMBERLAIN arrived from England and at the beginning of 1905 four missionaries more arrived viz. Messrs MOORE, ROWE, BISS and MARDON. Their voyage was not an ordinary one. They had to come via America on account of the hostility of the Company. But the attitude of the Governor and his staff in Calcutta was quite different : they were permitted to land without any difficulty. Felix, the eldest son of William Carey, was also officially recognized as a missionary by the Society at home.

In the course of this year, he clearly sees how many possibilities are given to him through the presence of the many multilingual pundits in Calcutta especially at Fort William College. He agreed with his colleagues that Providence had a hand in it and that they only had to take the opportunity offered to them. So he writes to Fuller in 1804 : "We are engaged in translating the Scriptures into Bengali, Hindustani, Persian, Marathi, and Oriya, and we intend to add more. Perhaps never more there will be so many advantages for rendering the Bible into the Eastern tongues, viz. :

1. The possibility of securing native scholars from all these countries.

2. A large printing establishment and letter-foundry, capable of any expansion.

3. The best library of critical writings to be found in India.

4. An acquired habit of translation and a disposition to do it.

I am more in my element translating the Word of God than in any other employment. [11])

Andrew Fuller was asked to supplement their own resources with £ 1000 a year, and what was the joy of the missionaries when Fuller raised even £ 1300 ! The Bible Society wanted cooperation for the promotion of Bible translation, a fact of very great hope and gladness to Carey and his colleagues.

From this we understand that they were in need of larger premises for the press. Also their own house and the school had to be enlarged. They purchased a fine building for the sum of £ 1420, which they borrowed and repaid from their own earnings. It was their own money, but they vested the property in the Society.

On the 27th of January 1802 the Court of Directors of the Company had issued an order for the immediate abolition of Fort William College. The reason of this terrible blow to Lord Wellesley was really the narrow-mindedness of this Court, while Lord Wellesley, who had a much broader view and a spirit of independence, treated them with contempt. His biographer says : "He was not trained to go in the harness." He strongly insisted on a thorough training of the Company's servants, he wished to promote and complete the education of the civilians in European knowledge and not to confine their studies to Oriental subjects. The college as we have seen was constituted in 1801, but without the permission of the Directors of the Company. So we understand, why such a letter was sent to their "servant" Lord Wellesley. But Lord Wellesley addressed a strongly-reasoned appeal to them in the hope, he said, "that the Court would diligently weigh all the considerations he had placed before them and revise the order for the abolition of the college". In the first week of 1805 Mr. Carey received the cheering news that the Court of Directors had withdrawn their orders. Mr. Pitt, who was at the head of the ministry had overruled their antagonism. In the same year, however, this great man was removed and a period of reaction began. His successor Lord CORNWALLIS died within ten weeks after his landing and then Sir GEORGE BARLOW, a weak man, occupied the Governor-Generalship only to fulfill the wishes of his masters in London: the Court of Directors. [12])

In this time William Carey formed still another plan : the establishment of subordinate missionary stations in Bengal. They brought this plan before their Society in England. His idea was

88

that his native brethren would be able to take their own place in the missionary work, but for some time a European brother would have to oversee them and gently conduct their affairs. As for the cost, they themselves hoped to bear the initial outlay of each station and afterwards all the missionaries would have to pool their earnings in the Common Fund of the Mission. From his letter to the Society we see that he asks for men, who can make paper or glass, print, cloth etc. But he had to arrange some other affairs before this great endeavour for God could take place. Sir GEORGE BARLOW, who had been closely associated with Carey at Fort William College, gave a disappointing reply. He personally favoured the missionary labour, but he had no power to authorize missionary establishments in the country. Then the missionaries tried to forward their work without Government sanction. Of course they had to retire and unfortunately they had drawn unfavourable attention to themselves. Not till 1810 could Carey report that "permission was obtained of Government for the forming of a new station". [13]

In the summer of 1806 they made other great attempts for God. 1806 They opened a 'Calcutta Chapel' in the Lall Bazar, a region of Calcutta full of grog-shops and brothels where sailors of the whole world joined. The preaching in the vernacular awoke no little interest and curiosity. "Multitudes," said Ward, "used to hang upon our lips and would stand in the thickwedged crowd for hours together in the heat." It was the first time the Gospel had been preached to the natives of Calcutta in their own tongue. Unhappily however there was some little disturbance and from this time on Carey had to fight his greatest struggle.

NOTES

[1] Hinduism by Sir MONIER—WILLIAMS, London 1897, cf. Prof. Dr. J. H. BAVINCK, Christus en de mystiek van het Oosten. Kampen, p. 25, 37, 45. Godsdiensten der aarde. Prof. Dr. G. VAN DER LEEUW. Hind. I, 311, 316.

[2] MARSHMAN, p. 154.

[3] Idem, p. 156.

[4] DEAVILLE WALKER, op. cit., p. 244.

[5] DEAVILLE WALKER gives us an eyewitness account, told by WILLIAM CAREY himself : "We were near the village of Noya Serai. Being evening we got out of the boat to walk, when we saw a number of people assembled on the riverside. I asked them what they were met for, and they told me to burn the body of a dead man. I inquired if his wife would be burnt with him ; they answered yes, and pointed to the woman. She was standing near the pile, which was made of large billets of wood, about $2^1/_2$ feet high, 4 feet long and 2 wide, and op the top of which lay the dead body of her husband. Her nearest relation stood by her, and near her was a small basket of sweetmeats .... I asked them if this was the woman's choice, or if she

was brought to it by any improper influence ? They answered that it was perfectly voluntary. I talked till reasoning was of no use, and then began to exclaim with all my might against what they were doing, telling them that it was a shocking murder. They told me it was a great act of holiness, and added in a very surly manner, that if I did not like to see it I might go farther off . . . . I told them that I would not go, that I was determined to stay and see the murder, and that I would certainly bear witness of it at the tribunal of God. I exhorted the woman not to throw away her life ; to fear nothing for no evil would follow her refusal to burn. But she in the most calm manner mounted the pile and danced on it with her hand extended as is in the utmost tranquillity of spirit. Previous to her mounting the pile, the relation whose office it was to set fire to the pile, led her six times round it. As she went round she scattered the sweetmeat above mentioned among the people, who picked it up and ate it as a very holy thing. This being ended and she having mounted the pile and danced as above mentioned (N.B. the dancing only appeared to be to show *us* her contempt of death, and prove us that her dying was voluntary), she lay down by the corpse, and put one arm under its neck and the other over it, when a quantity of dry cocoa leaves and other substances were heaped over them to a considerable height, and then Ghee, or melted preserved butter, poured on the top. Two bamboos then were put over them and held fast down, and the fire put to the pile, which immediately blazed very fiercely. No sooner was the fire kindled than all the people set up a great shout-Hurree-Bol, Hurree-Bol . . . . It was impossible to have heard the woman had she groaned or even cried aloud, on account of the mad noise of the people, and it was impossible for her to stir or to struggle on account of the bamboos which held down on her like the levers of a press. We made much objection to their using these bamboos, and insisted that it was using force to prevent the woman from getting up when the fire burned her. But they declared that it was only done to keep the pile from falling down. We could not bear to see more, but left them, exclaiming loudly against the murder, and full of horror at what we had seen, p. 245—246.

S. Pearce Carey gives in his book very abbreviated sati data, of which we will quote some :

Jan. 30, 1819. Either from the woe of the pain, or in concern for her children, a widow in Benares leapt from the pyre. Her relatives thrust her back, but a chowkidar pitied and saved her.

Febr. 6, 1816. A month before his appointed wedding-day, a man died at Chandernagore. His bride elect immolated herself with him.

Mar. 7, 1819. On the third day after a Brahmin's death, his young wife burned with him,—the delay being occasioned by her youth, since government forbids the burning of those with child, or not 15. Recently a Rajput Raja died, and his thirty-three wives burned with him.

June, 19, 1819. Permission not obtainable for the burning of the widow of Ram Chandra, in her own district, the body was brought to Serampore, and she immolated herself there.

Jund, 1819.—One of a man's two wives at Ballabhpur burned with him. The other, forbidden by her pregnancy, beat herself in with grief, and vowed to burn after her babe's birth. But by then, in her mother's home, she relented—to the vexation of her relatives, who feared a loss of caste.

Aug. 10, 1819.—A widow, who was not held down by bamboo, because she swooned before the pyre was lit, was waked by the fire, and escaped. Sepoys seized her and thrust her back. Again she fled, and again she was thrust into the flame. A third time she escaped, and was saved by Europeans. She has since been outcast., p. 358.

[6]) Marshman, p. 160—161.
[7]) Idem, p. 177.
[8]) S. Pearce Carey, p. 248—249.
[9]) Deaville Walker, p. 241. William Carey said : I have been in the habit of preaching to multitudes daily, of discoursing with the Brahmins upon every subject, and superintending schools for the instruction of Hindu youth. Their language is nearly as familiar to me as my own. This close intercourse with the natives for so long a period has afforded me opportunities of information not inferior to

those which have hitherto been presented to any other person.   I may say indeed, that their manners, customs, habits and sentiments, are so obvious to me as if I were myself a native.   And knowing them as I do, and hearing as I do their daily observations on our Government, character and principles, I am warranted to say (and I deem it my duty to embrace the public opportunity now offered me of saying it) that the institution of this College was wanting to complete the happiness of the natives under our dominion ; for this institution will break down that barrier (our ignorance of their language) which has ever opposed the influence of our laws and principles, and has despoiled our administration of its energy and effect.   Dr. GEORGE SMITH gives the whole speech, p. 223—226.

[10]) HODGE, Systematic Theology, p. 654 etc., cf. S. PEARCE CAREY, p. 228—230.
[11]) S. PEARCE CAREY, op. cit., p. 256.
[12]) MARSHMAN, p. 156—157.
[13]) GEORGE SMITH, op. cit., p. 262, cf. S. PEARCE CAREY, p. 262 and MARSHMAN, p. 196, DEAVILLE WALKER, p. 254, GEORGE SMITH gives the following interesting letter : "Another plan has lately occupied our attention.   It appears that our business is to provide materials for spreading the Gospel, and to apply those materials.   Translations, pamphlets etc. are the materials.   To apply them we have thought to set up a number of subordinate stations, in each of which a brother shall be fixed.   It will be necessary and useful to carry on some wordly business.   Let him be furnished from us with a sum of money to begin and purchase cloth or whatsoever other article the part produces in greatest perfection : the whole to belong to the mission, and no part ever to be private trade or private property. The gains may probably support the station.   Every brother in such a station to have one or two native brethren with him, and to do all he can to preach and spread Bibles, pamphlets etc., and to set up and encourage schools where the reading of the Scriptures shall be introduced.   At least four brethren shall always reside at Serampore, which must be like the heart while the other stations are the members. Each one must constantly send a monthly account of both spirituals and temporals to Serampore, and the brethren at Serampore (who must have a power of control over the stations) must send a monthly account likewise to each station, with advice, etc., as shall be necessary.   A plan of this sort appears to be more formidable than it is in reality.   To find proper persons will be the greatest difficulty, but as it will prevent much of that abrasion which may arise from a great number of living persons living in one house, so it will give several brethren an opportunity of being useful, whose temper may not be formed to live in a common family, and at the same time connect them as much to the body as if they lived together.   We have judged that about 2000 rupees will do to begin at each place, and it is probable that God will enable us to find money (especially if assisted in the translations and printing by our brethren in England) as fast as you will be able to find them."

S. PEARCE CAREY gives us the following important information about these stations : "As for its cost, they themselves hoped to be able to bear the initial outlay of each station, and, for the rest, Carey relied on his fixed policy of partial employment in a profession or trade, for no personal profit—the earnings all pooled for the Mission.   The spirit that was in them breathes in their covenant, dating from these days, and which was to be read thrice a year in each station :

1. To set an infinite value on men's souls.
2. To acqaint ourselves with the snares which hold the minds of the people.
3. To abstain from whatever deepens Indian's prejudice against the gospel.
4. To watch for every chance of doing the people good.
5. To preach Christ crucified as the grand means of conversions.
6. To esteem and treat Indians always as out equals.
7. To guard and build up "the hosts that may be gathered".
8. To cultivate their spiritual gifts, ever pressing upon them their missionary obligation—since Indians only can win India for Christ.
9. To labour unceasingly in Biblical translation.
10. To give ourselves without reserve to the Cause, 'not counting even the clothes we wear our own'.

Let us often look at Brainerd in the woods of America, pouring out his very soul before God for the people.   Prayer, secret, fervent, expectant, lies at the root of all personal godliness. A competent knowledge of the languages current where a missionary lives, a mild and winning temper, and a heart given up to God—there are the attainments, which, more than all other gifts, will fit us to become God's instruments in the great work of human redemption."

8. OPPOSITION FOILED.

1806 Missionaries of sister-societies often visited the brethren in Serampore. They received valuable advice from these experts. E.g. AUGUSTUS DES GRANGES, Dr. JOHN TAYLOR and last, but not least : HENRY MARTYN. "Now let me burn out for God," was his secret prayer, recorded in his journal on landing in Calcutta. From May 16, 1806 to 1812 he laboured in India. That in these few years his influence was so far reaching is due to his intensity and selfdenial. The Chaplain, the Missionary-evangelist, the Scholar, the Champion of the Faith, and the Christian Saint are all according to Dr. Ogilvie, aspects of his life and work that arrest attention by their striking qualities. [1] Henry Martin was very much struck by Carey's proposal of decennial world-mission conferences at the Cape. Carey wrote to Mr. Fuller that such a conference might be very useful as we should understand one another better in two hours than by two years of letters. [2] We see here once more what far reaching plans and what breadth of mind this man had. Only much later have his ideas been realised !

In the same year he asks for more missionaries. He literally says : "We ask the four hundred Home Churches for forty new missionaries to enter these vast lands. And be assured that your best way of securing more money is to send us more men." [3]

Amidst these bold plans e.g. to settle missionary stations throughout Bengal and Orissa and in several parts of Hindustan, severe difficulties arose. Above we mentioned how contrary to the orders of the Government the missionaries had established missionary stations in the country and had to retire. They underestimated public sentiment both at home and abroad in its prejudice against their enterprises. Carey might well feel the necessity of exercising the greatest prudence, for they had really given offence the last few days. Since the departure of Lord Wellesley his enemies had tried to find arguments against the Serampore mission. So it was determined to seize the first possible occasion to put a stop to their labours.

This occasion was given in 1806 in the fortress of Vellore. Two native regiments stationed there had mutinied. The Sepoys massacred several officers and also a great number of soldiers of the European garrison : the colonel and thirteen other officers and men. The opponents of the missionary enterprise connected this mutiny with the presence of the Serampore mission. They therefore asserted that for the sake of peace and even for the preserving of the British possssions it was a duty to keep a close watch upon the Serampore men, to restrict their operations and to command their absolute deportation.

Another incident occurred in these days. CHATER and ROBINSON arrived in Calcutta sent by the Society. But they were not permitted to proceed to Serampore. Carey at once went to enquire but the answer was a special message from the Governor General "that he did not interfere with the prejudices of the natives and he must request Mr. Carey and his associates to abstain likewise from any interference with them". [4])

When the news of Vellore reached England, the antimissionary party in England asserted that the Serampore mission was the cause of the Vellore troubles. Lord Wellesley and Lord William Bentinck (as Governor of the Presidency at that time), Charles Grant and Wilberforce and other men repudiated this crazy idea, but the attack on missions in England was so strong that but for the big struggle of Mr. Fuller and influential men, the Serampore mission would have been forbidden.

After much trouble (Captain Wickes frightened and threatened the magistrates and police-officials with complications with his own U.S.A. Government) the two missionaries who had arrived in Calcutta received a licence to stay at Serampore and the Captain to clear his ship. Carey had also defended his cause to the utmost.

After the storm had abated for a while, the enemies of the mis- 1807 sionaries tried once more in the second part of 1807 to destroy their work. On the last day of July a new Governor General became ruler of India : Lord MINTO. On Sept. 2 William Carey received a letter to attend at the office of the Chief Secretary of the Council. There he was asked whether a Persian tract had been printed by the Serampore Press with many offensive statements against Mohammedanism and its founder. Carey answered that he had not seen such a tract, but he promised to make an enquiry about this question.

Carey discovered that Ward had translated some parts of Sales

93

dissertation on Mohammed into Bengali, but that a Moslem convert, whom he had ordered to translate it into Persian, had inserted offensive comments on his own account. They expressed their sincere regret, sent Ward's original manuscript to the Governor General and withdrew the publication and promised to hand over to the Government the whole edition, save three hundred copies which had been issued.

Lord Minto however, knowing nothing of Carey and his press, and instigated by officials who were hostile to the missionary labour, ordered the immediate transference of the Mission Press to Calcutta. Further he prohibited preaching in Calcutta and the issue of any pamphlets or papers aiming at the conversion of natives [5] Even the Danish Governor General was officially acquainted with these proceedings. When Carey held a conference with his colleagues, they all were deeply dejected. They had a grave fear that Carey might lose his office at Fort William College. Next morning they met for prayer and in that morning session "Carey wept like a child" according to Ward. He understood quite well that the Press, if moved to Calcutta, would not live much longer. Fortunately, however, the Danish Governor Colonel KREFTING stood his ground. He declared that he "would not allow the press to be removed and that if the British authorities resorted to violent measures of compulsion he would strike his flag". [6] Now, William Carey and Marshman agreed to leave the matter in the hands of the Danish Governor General, but Ward did not think this wise and prudent and "as for Col. Krefting we must deprecate the idea of embroiling him with the English government, if we can possibly avoid it." Tender words with the consciences of men on our side go a long way. [7] So Ward advised a personal interview with Lord Minto, with the purpose of presenting a supplicatory memorial to the Governor General. They resolved that Carey and Marshman as the translators of the Ramayana epic should wait upon him, and present him with a copy of this epic as evidence of the Oriental studies they were engaged upon. They also received permission to present him with their memorial and were glad on hearing him promise that he himself would study it before presenting it to the Council. The effect of this visit was that apparently they had made quite another impression upon him than the anti-missionary party had created in his mind, viz. that "they were a group of wild fanatics, determined to forward the conversion of the natives at all cost, even if it set India aflame, and whom it was necessary to set under vigorous laws."

In a Memorial, on which the existence of the Mission humanly speaking was supposed to hang, they remarked among other things that they highly esteemed the principle which guaranteed the natives the full, free and undisturbed exercise of their different religions and opinions and that they were unconscious of having violated it, inasmuch as the solemn engagements of this nature were never supposed to preclude religious discussions. That they had received these views from the provision made in the Charter of 1698 which directed that the ministers of the Honourable Company should learn the Portuguese and native languages to enable them to instruct the Gentoos in the Christian religion. [8]) Together with this memorial the Lord Governor received a letter from Col. Krefting stating that he had prescribed such measures that the issue of anything objectionable was impossible.

After perusing these two documents, Lord Minto changed his mind and came to the conclusion that the missionaries were wise and prudent men. At his suggesion the Supreme Council revoked the press order and accepted the offer of William Carey to submit their edition intended for circulation in the British Dominions to the inspection of the British officers. [9])

There was a special thanksgiving day and Carey went to Lord Minto to thank him for his help. The Council had made a blunder. So they tried to rectify it before their masters in London. But the reply was a well merited rebuke reminding the Government of India that the missionaries were under the protection of Denmark and not living under English authority and further "we rely on your discretion that you will abstain from all unnecessary and ostentatious interference with their proceedings".

So once more they were saved from the actions of the anti-missionary party in Bengal. The struggle had been severe, but the missionaries had been fighting the fight for the Lord and so they had conquered. They had shown themselves brave soldiers but also scientific orientalists. They had won much respect.

During six years not any missionary was sent to India on account of the manifest hatred against the missionaries. Even many missionaries who were sent to the fields were recalled e.g. JOH THOMPSON of the London Missionary Society of Madras. He was instantly ordered to return, whereupon he fell seriously ill and died. When it proved imposible to get passages quickly enough, the missionaries were taken to England almost as prisoners by the Company's fleet. But not only missionaries of other Societies were summoned back, also some of the Serampore mission as Dr. JOHNS and JOHN LAWSON, a trained artist and engraver. Not on account of indiscretion or misdemeanor, but their only misdeed was that they were missionaries. Happily Lawson was permitted to stay for some time to perfect the new metal Chinese types which the Serampore press wanted for the translation of the Bible in Chinese. But Dr. Johns and his wife were cast out. Even Robinson who had been sent to Java by Dr. Carey himself, was ordered back to England.

This policy distressed Dr. Carey very much. So he wrote: "I mourn on my country's account, that preaching the gospel should be regarded in the same light as committing a felony. In every way I have tried to acquit the Government and the London directors of intention to persecute; but I am driven to conclude that, whilst Lord Minto himself is friendly and of liberal enlightenment, the Presidency secretaries are largely infidel and inimical, and that they so shape the information and advice that lay before the authorities as almost to necessitate adverse decisions."

To this distress was added another. When Dr. Johns was in England again he blamed Dr. Marshman that he had not tried to influence the authorities as much as possible "for Lawson was permitted to stay and he had to depart". This demeanour of Dr. Johns "sowed the suspicion of Marshman, whose harvest was tragic", a harvest of ingratitude, of ill-treatment by his own brethren which oppressed Dr. Carey still more than the inimical bearings of the Directors in England.

This does not mean however that the anti-missionary party was silenced. Neither that victory had been complete. The Government might have yielded in the matter of the press, preaching in Calcutta as well as in any station in the country was forbidden. Carey's son William now twenty-one years of age was judged fit for pioneering work. So they made a patient and respectful plea. But in vain. William Grant had left them Rs. 20.000 and another sum of Rs 10.000 towards their translations. So they had power for more big struggles. They tried once more to get the influence of Lord Minto, who personally was still friendly. He even invited Marshman and Carey to his table, but said that he could not find any way to give more freedom to the missionaies. Litera'ly he said : "towards the making of Indians Christians". The remarkable answer of William Carey was : "Do you not misapprehend us, your Lordship ?" We have no faith in 'makings'. You can make hypocrites by pressure ; but not Christians. We only solicit the right to present the Truth to each man's intelligence and conscience, as our Master enjoined." [10]) After this bold plan William Carey began again to make great attempts for the Lord. He writes : "We shall endeavour to evade, that is, we shall run the risk of the missionaries being sent back to Serampore by the magistrate. On this principle we are hoping to send my son William to Chittagong and brother Robinson to Orissa."

Now they were licensed to distribute Bibles at random. But as for Pamphlets etc. they could not print a single sheet without the Government's "Imprimatur". So they felt this as a restriction and by patient but tough perseverance they tried to wear out the opposition party in the Government.

William Carey also tried to mobilize the home front. As a new spirit full of missionary interest was awakening in England, he tried to move Fuller and other members of the Society to present a petition to Parliament. [11]) For the Company's Charter should come before the House in 1813. So they tried in England to make 1813 a united effort. And indeed after bitter fighting and long debating first in the country then in Parliament a clause was embodied by which India was opened to the missionary effort. The long battle was won. Much honour must in this respect be given to the great defender of the cause of Mission : Lord WILBERFORCE. [12]) Before we continue the description of the missionary action of William Carey, we wish to dwell upon his home circle. In January 1807 1807 Carey began his missionary work in Burmah. Amongst others he sent out his son Felix who was a medical missionary of great skill and a scholar in Oriental languages just like his father especially in Sanskrit, and Pali, Bengali and Burman. Very important instructions were given to him, which we will consider afterwards. [13])

On the 8th of March 1807 Carey received the diploma of Doctor of Divinity, from Brown University in the United States. A distinction of his scientific labour and an acknowledgement of his well deserved achievements.

But still greater changes occurred in this year so full of difficulties and struggling against anti-missionary powers. His wife Dorothy Placket died. According to S. Pearce Carey her trouble was not mental illusion but melancholy and misery and violence. We must admire Dr. Carey's tender care that he did not send her to a lunatic asylum though twice she strove to take his life "He was," says Dr. Smith, "her tender nurse." During the fortnight of her last fever Carey watched very gratefully the tender devotion of her Serampore "sisters". She is indeed greatly to be pitied for the price she paid on the field of mission.

1808   In the summer of 1808 Carey remarried : CHARLOTTE RUMOHR, youngest daughter of COUNT RUMOHR of RUNDOFF near Schleswig and of the COUNTESS of ALFEDT. Many of Dr. Carey's friends were distressed at the engagement. They told him that they thought it imprudent. She had a frail health and was somewhat deformed. Yet later on Carey declares to his son : "I could not have found a truer helpmate." To Thomas, Carey's brother, who had an ill paid post at the West India Docks, Dr. Carey sent most of his wife's dowry, to which she heartily agreed. In the same year Carey was very happy to see his second son William start for a mission station in the neighbourhood of Mudnabatti. Of this William, Dr. Carey wrote to his colleague Ward : "William is close and reserved, and a recluse but in his preaching pithy, pointed and savoury. All the Careys are a little obstinate."

Afterwards in 1823 he married a third time, and was happy to find in GRACE HUGHES a most gentle and affectionate wife. After a short time she was baptized and her daughter put her heart into mission work. JABEZ, the youngest son of William Carey was born when they started from England. This young man, who at first had no personal love for the Lord, nor any real interest in missionary work, and "who should be glad to have some employment in the Civil Service", had accepted into his contrite spirit Jesus as his Saviour and Lord in the summer of 1812.

He was sent to Amboyna, one of the Moluccas, gladly devoting himself to this work. In these Moluccas one of Carey's early brilliant students had become the first Resident : BYAM MARTIN. In Batavia Robinson had founded a Baptist church with twenty members. It was the Mission's most Easterly post and the first missionary settlement on Java. 14)

NOTES

1) Dr. OGILVIE, op. cit., p. 347. The biography of HENRY MARTIN is of particular interest to everyone who loves the missionary work. He is an example of whole hearted devotion to the task our Lord gave us.

[2]) A remarkable answer is given to this proposal by Mr. FULLER: I admire Carey's proposal though I cannot say I approve. It shows an enlarged mind, and I have heard say that men dream differently from others! This is one of Carey's pleasing dreams! But, seriously I see no important object to be attained by such a meeting which might not quite as well be reached without. And in the gathering of all denominations there would be no unity(!) without which we had better stay at home, p. 268—269. S. PEARCE CAREY.

[3]) S. PEARCE CAREY, op. cit., p. 270.
[4]) DEAVILLE Walker, op. cit., p. 255.
[5]) MARSHMAN gives us the letter of the Secretary to Government.

"To the Reverend W. Carey.

"Sir,—The substance of your replies to the verbal communications which I had the honour to state to you on the 2nd instant, by direction of Government, having been reported to the Right Honourable the Governor-General in Council, I am directed to request that you will communicate to the Society of Missionaries the observations and suggestions contained in this Address.

"Since the day of your attendance at the Chief Secretary's office various pamphlets and treatises in the Bengalee and Hindustani languages, containing strictures on the religions of the Hindus and Mussulmans, and purporting to have issued from the press at Serampore have been submitted to Government: among them are two pamphlets one in the Bengalee, the other in the Hindustani language, addressed exclusively to the class of Mahomedans; containing the same or similar abuse of the doctrine, books and founder of the Mahomedan religion, as is contained in the Persian pamphlet from which I read to you a translated extract.

"The Governor-General in Council has also been informed that the practise of public preaching on topics of that nature, prevails at a house engaged for that purpose by the missionaries in the town of Calcutta.

"The issue of publications and the public delivery of discourses of the nature above described, are evidently calculated to produce consequences in the highest degree detrimental to the tranquillity of the British dominions in India, and it becomes the indispensable duty of the British Government to arrest the progress of any proceedings of that nature. In the present instance, this obligation is enforced by the necessity of maintaining the public faith, which, under the express injunctions of the Legislature, has been repeatedly pledged to leave the native subjects of the Company in India, in the full, free and undisturbed exercise of their respective religions. To permit the issue and diffusion of printed treatises, and the delivery of public discourses in the languages of the country, replete with the most direct and unqualified abuse of the principles and tenets of the religion of the people is manifestly authorizing an opposition to the full free and undisturbed exercise of it.

"Upon these grounds the Right Honourable the Governor-General in Council deems it necessary to desire that the practise of preaching at the house employed for that purpose in the town of Calcutta, be immediately discontinued.

"The Governor-General in Council also deems it his duty to prohibit the issue of any publications from the press, superintended by the Society of Missionaries, of a nature offensive to the religious prejudices of the natives, or directed to the object of converting them to Christianity; observing that whatsoever may be the propriety of exposing the errors of the Hindu or Mussulman religions to persons of those persuasions who may solicit instruction in the doctrines of the Christian faith, it is contrary to the system of protection which Government is pledged to afford to the undisturbed exercise of the religions of the country, and calculated to produce very dangerous effects, to obtrude upon the general body of the people by means of printed works, exhortations necessarily involving an interference with those religious tenets which they consider to be sacred and inviolable.

"The Governor-General in Council further observes that the press now established at Serampore, being intended for the promulgation of works within the limits of the Company's dominions, it is indispensably necessary that its productions should be subject to the immediate control of the officers of Government. With this view I am directed to desire, that you will signify to the missionaries the expectation of the Governor-General in Council, that the press be transferred to this Presidency, where alone the same control that is established over presses sanctioned by the Government can be duly exercised.

"I am further directed to desire, tha t you will ascertain and report to Government in what manner and in what places the pamphlets and treatises to which this letter refers, or any other of a similar description which may not yet have come under the observation of Government, have been distributed ; and also that the missionaries will employ every effort in their power to withdraw them from circulation."

I have the honor to be &c,

(Signed) N. B. EDMONSTONE,
Secretary to Government.

Fort William, 8th Sept. 1807.

[6]) DEAVILLE WALKER remarks in a note that happily the news had not then reached India that England was even at that hour again at war with Denmark. How fortunate that there were no cables in those days. The tidings reached Calcutta the following January, and Serampore was promptly captured by English troops and held until the restoration and peace after Waterloo in 1815, op. cit., p. 264.

[7]) MARSHMAN, op. cit., p. 321.

[8]) Idem, p. 324.

[9]) Now the same secretary had to write : I am directed to state that the Governor-General in Council is fully convinced of the rectitude of the intentions of the Society of Missionaries, and that the precautions which Government deems it necessary to adopt against the unlimited employment of the press proceed exclusively from the duty imposed on Government of reserving to itself the authority of determining what publications may or may not expose the public tranquillity to hazard. DEAVILLE WALKER, p. 266.

[10]) S. PEARCE CAREY, p. 280—281.

[11]) DEAVILLE WALKERk p. 268 gives the letter WILLIAM CAREY wrote to the Society in England : Be not cast down on our account : the cause in which we are engaged is the cause of God and must prevail. I think, however, that a petition to Parliament might be presented praying respectfully for leave to settle missionaries and for them to be allowed to pursue their labours among the natives, subject in all civil matters to the laws of the country. I doubt not but with a little exertion a million signatures might be procured to such a petition.

[12]) This clause embodied in the Act renewing the East India Company Charter runs literally as follows : "That it is the duty of this country to promote the interests and happiness of the British dominions in India, and that such measures ought to be adopted as may tend to the introduction among them of useful knowledge and of religious and moral improvement : that in the furtherance of the above objects sufficient facilities shall be afforded, by law, to persons desirous of going to and remaining in India, for the purpose of accomplishing these benevolent designs.

Provided always, that the authority of the local Government respecting the intercourse of Europeans with the interior of the country be preserved, and that the principles of the British government on which the natives of India have hitherto relied for the free exercise of their religion, be inviolably maintained." DEAVILLE WALKER, op. cit., p. 268.

A brilliant speech was made by WILBERFORCE, the Christian protagonist of which S. PEARCE CAREY gives the peroration : "These 'Anabaptists' missionaries, as among other low epithets they have been contemptuously called, are entitled to our highest respect and admiration. One of them, Dr. Carey, was originally in one of the lowest social stations ; but, under all its disadvantages, he had the genius as well as the benevolence to devise a plan, which has since been pursued, of forming a society for communicating the blessings of our Christian light to the native peoples of India. His first care was to qualify himself to act a distinguished part in his truly noble entreprise. He resolutely bent himself to the study of the learned languages. After reaching considerable proficiency in these, he applied himself to several of the Oriental tongues, more especially to that which, I understand, is regarded as the parent of them all, the Sanskrit, in which his proficiency is acknowledged to be greater than even that of Sir Wm. JONES, or any other European. Of several of these languages he has already published a grammar ; of one or two of them a Dictionary, and he has in contemplation a still greater literary enterprise. The very plan of these would excite the highest admiration and respect in every unprejudiced literary mind. All this time, sir, he is labouring as a missionary with a warmth of zeal only equalled by that with which he prosecutes his literary labours. Merit like this clould not escape the distinguishing eye of Lord WELLESLEY, who appointed him Professor of Sanskrit and Bengali in the College at Calcutta. Another of the 'Anabaptists' missionaries, Dr. MARSHMAN, has established a seminary (!) for the cultivation of Chinese, a language which he has studied with a success scarcely inferior to that of Dr. CAREY in the Sanskrit. On more than one occasion at the Annual Examinations of the College in Calcutta, the highest eulogiums have been pronounced both on Dr. CAREY and Dr. MARSHMAN by the Governor-General, and the happiest consequences predicted from their literary toils.

It is a merit of a vulgar sort, but to those who are blind to their moral and even their literary excellences, it may afford an estimate of value better suited to their principles and habits of calculation, than these men, and Mr. WARD, another of the missionaries acquiring from £ 1000 tot £ 1500 a year each by the varied exercise of their talents, throw the whole into the Mission's common stock, which they thus support with their pecuniary contributions only less effectively than by their researches and labours of a higher order. Such, sir, are the exertions, such are the merits, such are the successes of these great and good men ; for so I shall not hesitate to term them", p. 329.

[13]) A very important letter containing the instructions given to the Burmah missionaries by Dr. CAREY, is a model for all missionaries. MARSHMAN gives us this letter, p. 288—289, and S. PEARCE CAREY on p. 291, cf. p. 324 and 325, GEORGE SMITH, p. 170—171. Some parts omitted by some of these writers, may be completed by others.

[14]) A fine picture of the character of Dr. Carey is given by S. Pearce Carey when Dr. Carey writes to his son William :

"You are in a post very dear to my remembrance (Mudnabatty) because my first Indian years were spent in its neighbourhood I therefore greatly rejoice in your exertions. The conversion of one soul is worth the labour of a life. Unto us is the favour given that we should preach among the Gentiles the unsearchable riches of Christ. Hold on, therefore ; be steady in your work, and leave the result with God. I have been contemplating a mission to the Afghans of Cabul" p. 294—295.

Again he writes : "There is much guilt in your fears, William. Mary and you will be a thousand times safer committing yourselves to God in the path of duty than neglecting duty to take care of yourselves."

Then once more when according to his colleague missionary Mr. FERNANDEZ made a mistake in following a course in church affairs. William is piqued : but Dr. Carey writes to him :

" *I would rather see you stoop as low as you can to effect a reconciliation than avoid it through any little punctilio of honour or feeling of pride. You will never repent of having humbled yourself to the dust that peace may be restored. Nothing will so completely subdue Mr. Fernandez's dissatisfaction nor make you more respected in the Church of God.*" Cf. also p. 202—203, GEORGE SMITH, op. cit.

Those, who take an interest in the history of Missions in the Dutch East Indies may be advised to read the article of Mr. P. H. VAN DER KEMP, late-director of Tuition, Public Worship and Industry in the Dutch East Indies, in "Mededeelingen vanwege het Nederlandsch Zendelinggenootschap. Tydschrift voor zendingswetenschap", 61e deel, 3e stuk. M. Wyt en Zonen, Rotterdam 1917. It is instructive to compare with it p. 321—327 S. Pearce Carey. As for Java, cf. Prof. Dr. J. H. BAVINCK, Zending in een wereld in nood, p. 138—157.

9. THE LINGUIST, FRICTIONS, EXPANSION, FIRE, SCHISM, DEATH.

In the preceding chapters we mentioned Carey's linguistic proclivities. As a child he had shown his ability for foreign languages and now as a missionary he has become famous by his acquisition of a great number of tongues and his literary achievements. He revised the Bengali New Testament in 1806 and its ninth edition when he was an old man. He also published five editions of the Bengali Old Testament.

Now the Brahmins scorned the Bengali books. They wished to read books in their own sacred language : Sanskrit. So the Sanskrit New Testament was completed in 1808 and the Old Testament between 1811 and 1818.

Some time before he has conceived the bold plan to translate the Bible "in all Eastern languages", viz. in so far as they were known to him. He enumerates them as : the Hindustani, Maharasti, Ooriya, Telinga, Bhotan, Burman, Chinese, Cochin-Chinese, Tongkinese, and Malay.

Now this plan seemed to be realized by two occurrences : first by the action of the Committee in England that raised a fund of one thousand three hundred pounds a year, and secondly by the forming of the British and Foreign Bible Society on March 7, 1804.

Within three months of its foundation this Bible Society asked the Serampore Triad together with George Udney, David Brown and Claudius Buchanan to form an auxiliary Bible Society in Bengal.

When this committee in Bengal had been formed they agreed to pay the Serampore missionaries three hundred rupees a month for this work. Together with the money raised by the Baptist Society it was possible to give a definite shape to their plans.

Heaps of books were issued in all kinds of languages from the famous press. Their achievements were acknowledged by the Brown University in America which conferred the degree of Doctor of Divinity on Marshman in 1811, which title had been conferred on William Carey in 1807.

A large body of pundits and munchis from all parts of India assisted them in translating the Scriptures. Meanwhile Carey was translating the Ramayana from Sanskrit into English. In what way Carey was working may be gathered from his letter to Dr. Ryland informing him that he intends to write grammars and dictionaries and polyglottes etc. [1])

We already stated that Carey was a man of worldwide views. So he had to fight against the narrow mindedness of some members of the Society in England. Even Mr. Fuller e.g. at first did not appreciate his translations from Sanskrit into English at all. But Carey defended his demeanour by saying "that he must be able to read the Shasters for himself" and therefore he also studied the Vedas and the Puranas, he read the Mahabharata, he even carried through the press "the Sanskrit Dictionary of Amara Sinha the oldest Indian lexicographer with an English interpretation and annotations". [2])

Just like Marshman, Carey understood that he had to study the languages to the very root in order to understand the soul of the Indian. In all these labours there arose some friction between the Serampore Triad and Henry Martin. As a highly trained University man Henry Martin was given some translation work. The missionaries, however, felt hurt by being overlooked. Moreover Martin freely criticized their translation work which they did not appreciate, being much older and more experienced.

Whatever the difficulties and frictions may have been, their work was gigantic. Of course many translations were full of mistakes. But they believed "that a faulty translation was better than none".

On March 11, 1812 the mission press was burnt to the ground. March 1812 All was lost save the bulk of the translation-manuscripts as those were kept in a warehouse. Carey was overwhelmed, but here we meet with another instance of Dr. Carey's indomitable spirit when he writes to Fuller : "We are able immediately to begin casting. In a fortnight we shall be able to begin printing again, in one language. Another month will enable us to begin in another and I trust that in six months our loss in Oriental type will be repaired." [3]) This dauntless man standing near the ruins of his and his colleagues' life work e.g. Ramayana and polyglot dictionary of all languages based upon Sanskrit, showed a real missionary spirit : continue whatever the drawbacks might be.

A remarkable fact is that so many people showed sympathy with the Serampore Triad, after this crushing blow. Not only the Calcutta Newspapers spoke of faith in their future labours, but also the Society in England was glad to raise ten thousand pounds.

In 1814 Dr. Carey was able to show a list of twenty-six versions of Scripture and in 1832 Bibles and other books had been issued from the mission-press in forty-two languages and dialects. Now we read in many books that Carey himself made all these translations but his biographers are contradicting this assertion. His munchis and pundits had an important share in this enormous work. But Dr. Carey really was the head master and Dr. Marshman and Ward the assistant masters and so were the pundits and munchis. The Serampore Triad had become a Bible Society by itself.

We add one remarkable revelation of his personal belief in this affair : the text on the Sunday following the disaster was : "Be still and know that I am God. His divisions were : 1. God's right to dispose of us as He pleases. 2. Man's duty, to asquiesce in His will. 4)

Meanwhile the rapid expansion of the mission caused uneasiness in England. Almost everywhere in the East stations were formed e.g. in Java and Mauritius. But just now the Home front was trying to shrink back from the enormous expense this entailed. In connection with this demeanour a letter from Dr. Carey to them is of the utmost importance and of value to every missionary enterprise : "I entreat, I emplore our dear brethren in England not to think of the petty shop-keeping plan of lessening the number of stations so as to bring the support of them within the bounds of their present income, but bend all their attention and exertions to the great object of increasing their finances to meet the pressing demand that Divine Providence makes on them. *If your objects are large the public will contribute to their support ; if you contract them their liberality will immediately contract itself proportionately.*" 5)

Two great plans were still in his mind which he eagerly desired to realize. The first was to establish schools in connection with each mission station and the second was the education of the gifted young men of India as they were convinced that India could only be won for Christ by Indians.

Above we mentioned that Parliament now permitted missionary work according to the new Charter of the Company. Further that the successor of Lord Minto was Lord MOIRA, afterwards the Marquis of Hastings. He was a man who from the very beginning sympathized with the missionary work. He even visited the missionaries and invited them to a private dinner at his residence. In this way the plan of organizing missionary schools in connection with each missionary station could be realized. The Triad seized the opportunity and a great number of schools were established everywhere in the country. In a short time forty five schools were opened.

1818

"They had still greater plans in their minds. Their ideal was a temple of learning, in which the mind should be developed by a liberal course of study in arts and sciences, character formed in an atmosphere of religion, and conducted, inspired by the ethics of Christianity. For those who were willing to undertake it, every facility was offered for specialized study in theology." [6])

The idea of such an education was not new. In 1794 William Carey and Thomas already had a plan to teach the gifted sons of India so that they might be able to communicate their learning to their country fellows. The germ of the later programme and achievement lies in this early period.

In 1802 they again tried to realize the plan "for educating the children of native converts, and youths who might renounce caste". The prospectus of this institution said that "to provide for the education of these native youths in those principles which enlarge the mind (divinity, history, geography, and astronomy) and which lead to the worship of the true God and to a worthy life cannot fail to be essentially advantageous to society and may in a few years be the means of sending out men who shall be peculiarly instrumental in turning their fellow-countrymen from dumb idols to serve the living and true God."

But now in 1818 they not only wanted to have a college which should supply their missionary wants, but which should also consolidate their plans for the spiritual and intellectual improvement of the country.

On the 15th of July they issued the prospectus of "a College for the instruction of Asiatic, Christian and other youth, in Eastern literature and European science". Dr. Marshman had drawn it up and announced that the institution was intended to be a handmaid of evangelisation. He remarked that a more important object could scarcely engage the attention than the propagation of Christianity in India, and that it must be effected by publishing the Gospel in its native excellence, and by comparing it with the system which then held possession of the native mind. Those who were to be employed in propagating it should be familiar with the doctrines which were then held sacred in the country, and this could not be attained without a knowledge of the Sanskrit language, in which they were enshrined. Hence the necessity of a college in which the native Christian teacher might obtain full instruction in the doctrines he was to combat, and the doctrines he was to teach and acquire a complete knowledge both of the Sacred Scriptures, and those philosophical and mythological dogmas which formed the soul of the Buddhist and Hindu systems.   While the native preacher remained ignorant of the principles on which the learned heathen built their arguments, his position as a public teacher was necessarily disadvantageous.   If, he remarked, the apostle Paul had been as ignorant of the philosophy of the Greeks as both European and native teachers, with few exceptions, were of the Hindoo system of philosophy and religion, he could not have urged their own writings against them, or so efficiently fulfilled his mission.   The oriental erudition of a few European missionaries did not supersede the necessity of giving the same advantage to the body of native teachers.   A pundit, foiled by a European disputant, who happened to be versed in the learning of the East, ascribed his discomfiture not to the superior excellence of the Gospel, but to the national superiority of his opponent.   He bowed to the genius of the nation which had established its dominion on the ruin of Hindoo and Mahomedan dynasties.   If ever the Gospel stands in India it must be by native opposed to native in demonstrating its excellence above all other systems.

It is very remarkable that so much stress was laid on the oriental character and that Sanskrit was studied before English literature. On the same principle instruction was to be given in Arabic.   The students were likewise to be thoroughly grounded in European science and knowledge, through the epitomes published in their own language.   But though it would be vain to attempt to enlighten a country through the medium of any language besides its own, it does not follow that English cannot be studied as a learned language, to great advantage, by youths of superior talent. It was therefore intended that, after the student had completed his Sanskrit studies, a select number should be enabled to acquire a complete knowledge of the English language to enable them to dive into the deepest recesses of European science and enrich their own language with its choicest treasures.   Further the school should include the formation of a normalschool, and educate teachers in the science of instruction and qualify them for organising and managing schools.   It was likewise one of the chief objects of the institution to prepare a series of treatises in the vernacular tongues to form the material of education in the schools. But it was pre-eminently to be considered a divinity school, where youths with piety and aptitude for the work of an evangelist, should go through a complete course of instruction in Christian theology. The institution was to be open to native youths from all parts of India, without distinction of caste and creed. Every native who supported himself, or was supported by benefactors, was to be admitted to all the benefits of the college. Christian youths of Asiatic parentage, of every denomination, were to be admitted into it, with the understanding that the instruction should be divested of everything of a sectarian character. A library was to be formed, to include, in addition to works of classical European literature, every manuscript of any value either in Sanskrit or in the vernacular which could be obtained in the country. A philosophical apparatus was also to be provided, and an edifice erected at Serampore suited to the objects of the institution. The government of the college was to be vested in the governor of Serampore for the time being, and the three senior missionaries.

This programme which we derive from Marshman also included an exact calculation of the expense of the establishment: 1960 rs. a month. The missionaries stated that it was highly desirable that an institution, intended to promote the cause of christianity and the interests of literature in India, should receive a character of stability; and they were desirous of raising a sum which, after providing for the expenses of the ground, the building, and the library, should form a fund for the permanent support of the college. They offered to subscribe £ 2500 from their own resources, and asked the public to make such additions to it as to place the institution on a solid basis, and leave only a moderate supplement to be provided by annual subscriptions. [7])

This programme is instructive even for our own time. It is very remarkable that it has some resemblance with the basic principles of the Calvinistic Free University at Amsterdam established in 1880 by the gifted and duly honoured Dr. ABRAHAM KUYPER, a man whose life was devoted to the propagation of the Gospel, as was William Carey's. All missionary societies of every time and every place may see here principles of the highest importance and certainly principles worthy to be carefully studied.

In 1817 Carey wrote to Ryland: "The pecuniary resources and the requisite number of missionaries for the Christian instruction of Hindustan's millions can never be supplied from England, and India will never be turned from her idolatry to serve the true and living God, unless the grace of God rest abundantly on converted Indians to qualify them for mission work, and unless by those who care for India, these be trained for and sent into the work. In my judgment it is on native evangelists that the weight of the great work must ultimately rest." [8])

From this we may deduce that it was the full conviction of these great men that the evangelisation of the country must be accomplished through the vernacular tongues. Sanskrit was necessary on account of the great number of sacred Hindu books in this language but also because it was "the parent of oriental philology and the standard of literary purity and excellence".

The Christian critics at home did not approve of such a broad scheme. They did not see the need of training in Hindu lore etc. But Carey laid it down as a principle that "Those who are employed in propagating the Gospel should be familiar with the doctrines he is to combat and the doctrines he is to teach, and acquire a complete knowledge both of the Sacred Scriptures and of these philosophical and mythological dogmas which form the soul of the Budhist and Hindoo systems." [9]) Moreover the missionaries asserted, as we stated, that in the early ages of Christianity its advocates met the pagan philosophers on their own vantage ground, and combated them with their own weapons; so they hoped to facilitate the propagation of the Gospel in India by a similar system.

Now the prospectus was sent to the Governor (Lord Moira) of Serampore and to the Governor-General of India, Lord Hastings. The former gave his cordial sanction to the establishment of the institution. He agreed to accept the first place in the committee of governors. The latter also expressed his approbation but regretted that the aim seemed to be the conversion of the native students. This step, he said, is so different from the wise and sagacious patience with which the gentlemen at Serampore were securing ultimate success in their object, that he was certain they would excuse his drawing their attention to what they must have overlooked.

Dr. Marshman, however, replied "that the college had two distinct objects. Primarily to educate children of native Christians, and hence the arrangements for Christian instruction had been more expressly set forth. Secondly it was intended to give the benefit

108

of its literary and scientific instruction to other youths, Hindu and Mahomedan, but without placing any strain on their consciences. Perhaps they had not sufficiently guarded against the misapprehension that the particular course of study laid down for pious Christian youths would be compulsory on the students of other creeds. He remarked that the difference between the tuition given in the government and in the missionary colleges consists in this, that in the former Christianity is completely ignored, and the Bible is systematically excluded : in the latter secular knowledge is blended with Christian instruction, and communicated on Christian principles, but without any attempt to interfere with the rights of conscience." [10])

They had not only in India to oppose opinions which were contrary to their scheme but still more in England. The most progressive men in India were alarmed at such thoughts which were contrary to the general opinion of tuition. But still greater was the difference of opinion of the Baptists in England, "so many of whom were shy of college training for even their own ministers, and savouring of incomplete reliance on the Holy Ghost !" The committee in England was in great alarm. They begged the brethren at Serampore with the most affectionate importunity, to pause and in the most calm and serious manner, and in the sight of Him by whom actions are weighed to give the deepest consideration to the subject. The real motive for the writing of these letters was this : the Society in England tried to lord it over their "dear brethren" in India, just like a government over some clerks. We won't dwell here upon this quarrel between the Serampore Triad and the Society, but the contents of the letters from England breathe quite another spirit than of those from India to England.

The Triad felt they could not keep waiting till it should please the Society in England to show their approval of their plans. Feeling that time was due to put their projects into operation, they purchased a piece of land immediately to the south of the mission premises. During the time of the building of a special college house, an old one was used. The project for a suitable building was at once put forward. The missionaries themselves gave two thousand five hundred pounds out of their own earnings. Lord Hastings gave a thousand rupees. They undertook to meet all the expenses, even of board and lodgings etc. They tried to enable the poor as well as the rich to attend the lectures. They made "the college free as the air, not thinking it right that any should be deprived of its benefits for having had the misfortune to be born and brought up within any particular circle : nor that the gates of knowledge should be barred against those who differed in opinion from themselves". There was only this difference : "that whilst the sons of the Indian Christians could dwell together in Serampore, the Hindu and Moslem students, for their own social custom and caste sake arranged to board out." "They were mindful that not only Christians and not only missionaries and preachers were formed but also Hindus, Mohammedans, lawyers, journalists, writers, schoolmasters etc."

The question may be asked whether these *Baptist* missionaries intended to teach *Baptist* principles to their students, and so were bent on getting *Baptist* preachers etc. They themselves state that their purpose is something else : "In a country so destitute and so dependent on us for both political freedom and moral improvement, it is surely our duty to forget the distinctions which divide society in England. It will be time enough a hundred years hence when the country is filled with knowledge and truth had triumphed over error, to think of sects and parties. Every public institution aiming at India's betterment, ought to be constructed on so broad a basis as to invite the aid of all denominations." [11])

Carey was sixty years old when the College building was completed. Then he arranged the library and his museum !

In 1827 Dr. Marshman was granted an interview with FREDERIK VI, and gained from him a charter for the College, with the right to confer degrees in all Faculties, making it the first College in India of its kind and it is still India's only college with power to confer Divinity degrees. [12])

These great men were not only thinking of India's sons but also of India's daughters. Ten schools in the neighbourhood of Serampore were erected at a time when the education of Bengal's girls was not thought of.

But last not least Carey and his friend ventured to issue magazines, one for Indians and one for Europeans and in this way they tried to influence the opinion of the people for the sake of the Lord and to set them against such atrocities as widow-burning and leper-burning etc., cruelties which were still being practised. [13])

In 1815 Andrew Fuller died. The first who brought the news

to Dr. Carey was a ship's officer who had seen it announced in a paper when he lay anchored in Plymouth harbour. Afterwards he received a letter with the communication of the death of the "Mission's Minister of Munitions", as Pearce Carey calls him. Indeed the loss of Fuller was a tremendous blow for Dr. Carey. His doctor said "he was completely worn out by intense application as any one he ever knew in the last stage of consumption." For twenty-three years he had been of one mind and soul with Carey in labour and travail and much patience in journeyings and watchings and fastings in necessities, in hunger and cold. But his greattest achievement of all was his great struggle with Parliament. He had purchased the revised Charter, says Pearce Carey with his very life. Amidst this terrible loss, Carey received intimations from England that the new members of the Society proposed retrenchment in the island mission stations of Java and Ceylon. We mentioned already (on p. 104) in what way Dr. Carey tried to cure this narrow mindedness. Mr. Ward endorsed the axiom of Dr. Carey by saying to them : "I think with Carey that you must not go into the plan of giving up stations because they are costly, unless they are at the same time unnecessary or hopeless. Rather make England, Scotland, Ireland and America ring with the cry of your need."

Then some one at home was stabbing the Serampore Triad in the back by saying that they were making private fortunes. On April 22, 1817 Dr. Carey tries to justify himself and his colleagues by saying : "I confess I am a little indignant at some of the hints in one of your letters about our interested conduct. Beloved Fuller, with one scowl of his brow, would have dissipated a thousand such insinuations ! I have devoted my all to the cause, and so have my colleagues. When Felix loaned from the Mission sums of money, which (through his misfortunes) he could not repay, I became responsible, and with the little private property I possessed through my wife, paid the whole. Nor do I complain.

We are trustees for the public and for God. Had my colleagues wished they could not have remitted the debt ; nor could I have allowed it. I am now in my old age destitute of a rupee. I have become a fool in glorying ; but you compelled me. Were I to die to-day, I should not leave property enough for the purchase of a coffin, and my wife would be entirely unprovided for. We are coarsely clad, and certainly not overfed, and, I believe, he who possesses the most among us has not so much as he contributes to the public stock in four months. I had Rs 6000., but now I have none."

It seemed that especially the Rev. Dyer of Reading, who was successor to Mr. Fuller had tried to officiate the Serampore Triad. For soon we read in the letters of Dr. Carey complaints ot officialism. "That the letters from the brethren at home seemed to be dispatched from the Directors of the East India Company to their servants rather than letters of brethren to brethren." Moreover Secretary Dyer wished to run the mission on the same line as a business concern. Whether this principle is right or wrong we will not discuss here, but we simply state that the Serampore Triad was not accustomed to such a treatment. They felt that they were mistrusted for the "Directors" ordered to send accounts of all the missionary work. More than once Carey is gravely protesting as may be seen in his letters e.g. "We have exerted ourselves to the utmost of our power and in the simplicity of our hearts and have denied ourselves many of the most common conveniences of life to serve the cause of God . . . ." [14])

They really appointed eight British Trustees who had to serve with the Serampore three. Ryland who formerly had written to Dr. Carey : "I tremble for the Ark of God, when it shall fall into the hands of mere counting house men," received a letter from Dr. Carey written under such depression of mind as he had scarcely ever written. "We are yours to live and die with you ; but as your brothers not as your servants. I beseech you therefore, not to attempt to exercise a power over us, to which we shall never submit. Bear with me a little even if I speak foolishly : for my heart is exceedingly wounded at the Society's proposal of the eight British Trustees, and at several concomitant symptoms." [15])

Still more this great man had to endure. His son Felix had toiled in Burmah for some years. Presently the King asked him to establish a mission station with a press in his capital at Ava. Felix went to Serampore. He got his press and vaccine for the prince. But on the 30th of August 1814 when on his way home the ship foundered, his wife and his little boy were drowned. So in one moment he had become wifeless and childless. But not only was Dr. Carey bereaved of his dear grandson, still worse—Felix "shrivelled from a missionary into an ambassador of the King". He had accepted a glorious position but later on he was despised.

After some time he entered Calcutta in the "glory of a golden sword and of a scarlet-silk umbrella with a handle of ivory and gold, and with fifty Burmese attendants". Moreover he began to give way to an excess of wine in such a way that his father was ashamed of his son. This grief was the worst of all for Dr. Carey. But happily after years of praying and struggling the prodigal son came back to his father. We will deal shortly with the schism. Between 1814 and 1817 four young missionaries had joined the seniors. In April 1818 these four left the Seniors to form a missionary auxiliary post of their own. They were all whole-heartedly devoted to the mission. EUSTACE orator and preacher, YATES scholar, LAWSON artist, PENNEY schoolmaster; Pearce "with eyes full of light". [16]) All went well at first. But one of the causes of the friction seems to have been the rule that all brethren were equal and had an equal vote in everything. This was excellent at first. But years had made a gulf of age and experience between the Triad and the young ones. So the friction between them arose on account of this principle. Carey writing to Fuller gives as his opinion that the cause is: the diligence of Marshman opposed to the indolence of some of the younger ones; his acquirements reproach their ignorance, and his accommodating mind not unfrequently excites sentiments of dislike and resentment. [17])

What was the real cause of their coming nobody can tell. Calumny was publicly strewn over Dr. Marshman. Then Penney and Pearce, two of the four juniors "left England under the post-Fuller conditions and apprised the new Committee's point of view and prepared to encourage directer home governance—a sure source of friction". [18]) After some time they withdrew from "Lall Bazar" on their own account, and founded a new church. They established and opened schools in Calcutta, they planted there a press too—in a word they gradually had become a rival missionary action of the juniors contra the seniors, a fact which had every resemblance of competition. In the summer of 1815 the dreaded Schism was complete and the Calcutta Missionary Union was formed and made public. [19]) Carey wrote the following letter to Ryland: "I don't recollect in my whole life anything which has given me so much distress as this Schism.

Many sleepless nights have I spent examining what we have done to give it occasion, but can discover nothing on which I can fix." And later: "The whole might have been prevented by a little frank conversation with us ; and a hundredth part of the self-denial, which I found it necessary to exercise in the first years of the Mission, would have prevented the rupture. But there is no doubt much on both sides to be forgiven."

The effect of this schism was terrible, most of all at home. More than once he had written : "we never considered ourselves as legislators for our brethren but just as their co-workers. If ever the Committee begins to legislate for India, I should expect them to issue a Declaration of Independence, and I should not be sorry if they did." And later : "we have always thought ourselves masters of the funds produced by our own toil. We devote the whole to the cause of God, and wish to do so to our dying day. But the funds we produce though devoted to the same object, have never been merged into the Society's funds so as to put them under other's control. We are your brothers, not your hired servants." So we understand that at the bottom of this difference of opinion lay the question of control. Carey thought that the work done at the bottom of the well as he himself expressed it, whilst others held the rope, did not mean that the descending made him their servant.

Still another factor may have been of influence. Dr. Smith reckons that in all Carey's forty Indian years he did not receive from the Society more than £ 600. for the maintenance of himself and his family, but that in his business years in North Bengal and his Government service in Calcutta he earned not less than £ 46.625, all of which he devoted to the work, apart from grants to necessitous relatives. And Marshman declares in his book that his father earned for and spent on the work between £ 40.000 and £ 50.000 plus a further sum of £ 80.000 by way of public donations. Nobody can reproach the Trio that they did not strain every nerve to settle the differences with the Home base. All in vain however. Ward went home from 1818—1822. Mrs. Marshman from 1820—1821. I. C. Marshman from 1822—1823. Dr. Marshman himself from 1826—1829. After visiting England Ward said that the differences were wide and deep. In 1823 he died, his death being the first breach in the Serampore Triad. When Dr. Marshman met the committee in England, he soon found that they did not intend to yield an inch. And after much self denial Dr. Marshman signed an Agreement of Separation by which he and Dr. Carey were to be left in charge of the College and the grounds attached to it, and all the older mission property was to be vacated and left in the hands of the Committee. The meaning of this was a complete severance from the Missionary Society which Carey himself had founded. [20])

Still other blows followed. In May 1821 his wife died, dearly May 1821 beloved by Dr. Carey. Writing to his son Jabez he says: "Your dear mother truly feared and lived for God. Next to that she lived for me. She never did a thing during the thirteen years we lived together without consulting me, even though she was sure of my consent." At the end of 1822 his son Felix died. He died 1822 with his father's name upon his lips.

In 1823 Ward died of cholera as we mentioned. Carey wrote 1823 to England "He is happy, but oh, what a breach! Who can fill it? We hope in God. We need your prayers."

In the same year Dr. Ryland died, the last of Carey's Covenanters. "It appears as if everything dear to me in England has been now removed. Wherever I look, I see a blank."

Then a staggering blow came upon him after preaching in Cal- Oct. 1823 cutta. Returning at midnight he and a doctor-friend slipped on the Serampore ghat (a landing stage) and Carey was so badly injured that he had to be carried home. Then he fell seriously ill and after his recovery he could not walk for several months.

Then the flood fissured the walls of his house, and destroyed his garden which had become famous both in England and in India; moreover the school buildings of the Marshmans were greatly damaged. And being obliged to support themselves, they were utterly helpless. At last some light broke through the clouds. Some eight students being trained for the missionary service in their own College were about to go to the fields. Other missionaries had arrived, but one of them "would fain have become wholly Indian in food and clothing and dwelling". Of great importance is the attitude Dr. Carey struck against this man: "The master won't thank you for committing suicide; besides, it is yourself and not these externals, that will make the abiding impression." [21])

We mentioned the return of Dr. Marshman. Carey finds him 1829 "looking fifteen years older". Both felt the injustice, the ingratitude bestowed upon them as a great pain. But Marshman "strove to bury it all out of sight and out of reference" and so they were enjoying in the records of his voyages and journeys.

A great day for Dr. Carey was Sunday December 6, 1829. Honour must be given to Lord CAVENDISH BENTINCK immediately, who after assuming government in July 1828 after many consultations formed his own judgment which led to the abolition of the widow-burning. On Sunday Dec. 6, 1829 the edict was handed to Carey as the Government's Bengali Translator. After perusing the edict he at once set himself to translate it with the assistance of his pundit not whishing "to lose an hour with the lives of women at stake". Twenty-five years before he had lodged his first protests and now his heart was full of joy. A Brahmanic petition followed as a protest against interference with the people's religion and accusing the Government of a breach of faith with India, but Lord Bentinck stood his ground. After some time several attempts were made to abolish the verdict. A famous answer was given by the Resident of one of the provinces of India to a son of a rich Indian, who asked the Resident to allow his mother to be burnt together with her dead husband's body as it was a matter of conscience with herself and her family. "Certainly," replied the Resident, "your mother may do as her conscience enjoins her and you as her first born may light the sati fire. Only then you must permit me to follow my conscience and my Government's, and hang you for murder." [22]) The act was irrevocable.

The petition in favour of the sati signed by eight hundred pundits, Brahmins and teachers of holy life in India was presented to the Governor-General and this was followed by an appeal to the King in Council. But neither this nor any other action had result. In a few years the sati had entirely passed away.

The arrival of the young Scotsman ALEXANDEE DUFF in the summer of 1830 was a source of great happiness to Carey. The young missionary finding no ear for his projects with the Calcutta missionaries, went to Dr. Carey, who warmly approved of his plans.

The other disasters followed. We said that the missionaries had to support themselves, but there had been some help from the Baptists of America and the income of the Fort William professorship was of course of the greatest significance. But the Government had to face heavy expenses on account of the war in Burmah. So they had to economize drastically and by consequence the professorships of Fort William were abolished, while Carey received a pension of only three hundred and sixty pounds a year.

Moreover a serious financial crisis arose in Calcutta at the beginning of 1833. Large Calcutta business houses crashed one after the other until "their total losses were estimated at more than sixteen million pounds". The Serampore College having invested nearly all their funds in these crashed firms was at a loss.

Carey who was now seventy-two was shocked. But still he expected great things from God and great things came. Friends in India and friends in England did whatever they could to help these great men, Dr. Carey and Dr. Marshman, not only in words but also in deeds.

In the summer of 1833 he was so weak that he wrote to his sister : "I believe this is the last letter you are likely to receive from me" . . . .

Once more he recovered. His last work was the revision of the Bengali Translation of the New Testament. After finishing this work he remarked : "he had nothing more to do but wait the will of his Lord". The will he made shows once more his great character : "First I utterly disclaim all or any right or title to the premises at Serampore, called the Mission Premises, and every part and parcel thereof : and so hereby declare that I never had or supposed to have any such right or title." [23]

Among those who paid a last visit to him was Alexander Duff. When Mr. Duff left the room and was near the door he was called back. "Mr. Duff," said Carey, "Mr. Duff, you have been speaking about Dr. Carey ; when I am gone, say nothing about Dr. Carey— speak about Dr. Carey's Saviour."

On Sunday June 8, 1834 Marshman knelt by his side for the last time. When Grace Hughes (a widow who had nursed Carey in his old age and whom he had married when she was forty-five years old) asked him whether he knew who was with him, he smiled his "Yes" and pressed his colleague's hand. On the morning of June 9 he passed away.

According to his will "only two lines and nothing more" were inscribed on his wife Charlotte's monument in the Serampore grave yard :

> A wretched, poor and helpless worm
> On thy kind arms I fall."

We may end this survey as Darville Walker does with words of his own : as a leading principle through his life :

> "Attempt great things for God ;
> Expect great things from God.'

[1]) In December 1811 he writes to Dr. RYLAND : "The necessity which lies upon me of acquiring so many languages obliges me to study and write out the grammar of each of them, and to attend closely to all their irregularities and peculiarities. I have therefore published grammars for three of them, the Sanskrit, the Bengali, and the Mahratta. I also intend to publish grammars of the others, and have now in the press a grammar of the Telinga language, and another of that of the Sikhs,and have begun one of the Orissa language. To these I intend in time to add those of the Kurnata the Kashmeera and Nepala and perhaps the Assam languages. I am now printing a dictionary of the Bengali, which will be pretty large, for I have got to 256 pages quarto, and am not nearly through the first letter. That letter however, begins more words than any two others. I am contemplating, and indeed have been long collecting materials for a universal dictionary of the oriental

Year of publication	New Testament	Pentateuch	Histories	Prophets	Hagio-grapha
1801	Bengali				
1802		Bengali			
1803					Bengai
1807				Bengali	
1808	Sanskrit				
1809	Oriya		Bengali		
1811	Hindi, Marathi	Sanskrit		Oriya	Oriya
1812	The year of the fire				
1813		Hindi Marathi			
1814			Oriya		
1815	Panjabi. Balochi (M. Mk. L.) R. Jaipuri (Matt.)	Oriya	Sanskrit		
1816	R. Mewari (Matt.)		Marathi		Hindi
1818	Telugu. M. Konkani. Pashto	Panjabi	Hindi	Sanskrit Hindi	Marathi Sanskrit
1819	Assamese. Lahnda		Panjabi	Marathi	
1820	Gujarati. R. Bikaneri. H. Awadhi (M. & Mk.)				
1821	Kashmiri P. Nepali H. Bagheli. H. Kanouji R. Marwari	Telugu M. Konkani			Panjabi
1822	R. Harauti.				
1823	Kanarese				
1824	Bhatneri. Braj Bhasda	Pashto			
1825	P. Kumaoni (to Col.) Sindhi. (Matt.)				
1826	P. Dogri. B. Maghadi R. Malvi			Panjabi (to Ezek.)	
1827	P. Garhwali. Manipuri. P. Palpa	Kashmiri			
1831	Khasi				
1832			Pashto & Kashmiri (to 2 Kgs)		
1833			Assamese	Assamese	Assamese
	B. means Bihari; H., Hindi, M.	Marathi; P.,	Pahari; R.,	Rajasthani.	

118

languages derived from the Sanskrit, of which that language is to be groundwork, and to give the corresponding Greek and Hebrew words. I wish much to do for the sake of the Bible in the oriental tongues after we are dead.

To Fuller he writes in 1813 : I am never so closely employed as at present. I have just finished for the press my Telinga grammar ; the last sheet of the Panjabi grammar is in the press. I am getting forward with my Kurnata grammar ; indeed it is nearly ready for the press. I am also preparing materials for grammars of the Kashneer, Pushto and Billochi languages, and have begun digesting those for the Orissa. The care of publishing and correcting Felix's Burman grammar is on me, beside learning all these languages, correcting the translations in them, writing the Bengali dictionary, and all my personal and collegiate duties. I can scarcely call an hour my own in a week. I, however, rejoice in my work and delight in it. It is clearing the way, and providing materials for those who succeed us to work upon.

S. PEARCE CAREY gives us the summary of Carey's Biblical translations :

Begali, Oriya, Hindi, Marathi, Sanskrit and Assamese-whole Bibles.

Panjabi New Testament and Old Testament up to Ezek. XXVI.

Pashoto and Kashmiri New Testaments, and old Testaments up to 2 Kings.

Telugu and Konkani New Testaments, and Pentateuchs.

Nineteen other Testaments, and

Five one-or-more Gospels.

That is to say that Carey was given the opportunity, the power and the joy of rendering God's Word, or, at the least, most precious portions thereof, into thirty, five languages to a very empire of peoples, p. 424—425.

On page 426, S. Pearce Carey gives this survey : (see page 118 of this book).

Carey's Biblical Translations.

[2]) DEAVILLE WALKER, op. cit., p. 277.

[3]) His firm belief is revealed in a letter to Mr. FULLER. It runs as follows : "The loss is heavy, but as the travelling a road the second time, however painful it may be, is usually done with greater ease and certainty than we travel it for the first time, so I trust, the work will lose nothing in real value . . . . The ground must be laboured over again, but we are not discouraged, indeed the work is already begun again in every language ; we are cast down, but not in despair." DEAVILLE WALKER, op. cit., p. 284, cf. his letter to Eustace S. PEARCE CAREY, p. 309.

[4]) In the first week of 1813 FULLER writes to Dr. CAREY : "This fire has given your undertaking a celebrity which nothing else, it seems could ; a celebrity which makes me tremble. The public is now giving us their praises. Eight hundred guineas have been offered for Dr. Carey's likeness ! If we inhale this incense, will not God withhold His blessing, and then where are we ? Ought we not to tremble ? Surely, all need more grace to go through good report than through evil. I have less jealousy of you than of ourselves ; but we are all in danger." S. PEARCE CAREY, p. 315.

[5]) DEAVILLE WALKER, p. 288.

[6]) Lord RONALDSHAY, when Governor of Bengal wrote these words : "Their ideal was a temple of learning, in which the mind should be developed by a liberal course of study in arts and sciences, character formed in an atmosphere of religion, and conduct inspired by the ethics of Christianity. For those who were willing to undertake it every facility was offered for specialized study in theology ; quoted by S. PEARCE CAREY, p. 345.

A comparison of Dr. Carey with the founders of the Free University of Amsterdam would be very interesting. Both fighting a spirit which opposed Biblical truths. Both based on principles of the Word of God, but also a college free of the State and free of any denomination. Both scope and outlook agree, the local peculiarities differ.

[7]) MARSHMAN II, op. cit., p. 171.

[8]) S. PEARCE CAREY, p. 346.

[9]) DEAVILLE WALKER, p. 292.

[10]) MARSHMAN II, p. 173.

[11]) S. PEARCE CAREY, p. 352.

[12]) Idem, p. 355, cf. MARSHMAN II, p. 325 etc.

[13]) It was necessary to fight these cruelties by all means. But the papers they

published had first of all to change the minds of the natives. A letter of a friend of Dr. Carey's may prove this. "Last week (Sept. 1812) I saw the burning of a poor leprous man. I got there too late, as he was lifeless before I arrived. I find that it is a very common practice here. The poor man was well enough to go about himself. They had dug a pit about ten cubits deep, in which they made a fire. After all was prepared the poor man rolled himself into it ; but when he felt the fire, he prayed to get out, but his sister and another relation thrust him down again, and he was burned to death. What horrible murder !" That this was not an exceptional case may be proved by the following letter from the Rev. J. G. POTTER : "At Agra I was accustomed to visit the Leper Asylum with Pundit Hari Ram, a Brahmin convert. One day I saw this good man with tears in his eyes, as he spoke to the lepers thus : 'Brothers you owe much to the Lord Jesus. Here you are housed and fed, clothed and cared for by those who are His followers. How different was your condition under Brahmin rule.' At my village of Bisarna, whose priest I was, a leper was once brought to me, and the villagers asked me what they should do with him. I replied : 'Dig his grave and bury him'. Under my instruction the grave was dug, and the leper was forced into it, where he was buried alive." S. PEARCE CAREY, p. 357.

[14]) DEAVILLE WALKER, p. 299.

[15]) S. PEARCE CAREY, p. 338, cf. also p. 339.

[16]) S. PEARCE CAREY, p. 359—360.

[17]) DEAVILLE WALKER gives us some reason of these unhappy differences. He quotes a letter of Dr. Carey to Mr. FULLER running as follows : "You ask me why the young brethren are so much prejudiced against brother MARSHMAN ? I don't know that they have any settled prejudice, yet a suspicion against him is, I confess, soon excited. I believe his natural make is the occasion of it.

Brother MARSHMAN is a man whose whole heart is in the work of the Mission, and who may be considered as the soul and life of it. He is ardent, very sanguine, excessively tenacious of any idea which strikes him as right and important. His labours are excessive, his body scarcely susceptible of fatigue, his religious feelings strong, his jealousy for God great, his regard for the feelings of others very little, when the cause of God is in question. His diligence reproaches the indolence of some ; his acquirements reproach their ignorance, and his unaccomodating mind not infrequently excites sentiments of resentment and dislike. He has also perhaps the foible of dragging himself and his children more into public observation than is desirable. These things, I suppose, lie at the bottom of all the dislike which our younger brethren have felt for him. For my own part I consider him as a man whose value to the Mission can scarcely be sufficiently appreciated and whose death would be a most severe loss. We, viz., Brother MARSHMAN, WARD, and myself live in the utmost harmony.", p. 296 and MYERS, op. cit., p. 144 is right when he says : "The sooner these differences are forgotten the better. But should any reader fell drawn to the investigation of matters relating to the Serampore controversy, we venture to express the opinion that the honour of Carey's noble character would not in the least suffer from such an investigation." Indeed, after reading all the literature relating these quarrels we conclude that MYERS is right. The studying of these differences may have the result that even in the most intricate matters Carey behaved himself as a man of noble character and of lofty spirit.

[18]) MARSHMAN II, op. cit., p. 146—150.

[19]) S. PEARCE CAREY, p. 364, quotes a letter he delighted to write to his son Jabez : "I am sure it will do you pleasure to learn that our long continued dispute with the younger brethren in Calcutta is now settled. We met together for this purpose some three weeks ago, and, after each side had given up some trifling ideas and expressions, we came to a reconciliation which I pray may be lasting. Nothing I ever met with in my life—and I have met with many distressing things—,ever preyed so much upon my spirits as this difference."

[20]) DEAVILLE WALKER, p. 301, cf. S. PEARCE CAREY, p. 360 a.s.o.

[21]) S. PEARCE CAREY, p. 379.

[22]) Idem, p. 383.

[23]) For those who take an interest in his last will in its full length we publish it here as given by MYERS, p. 154—155 : "I William, Carey, Doctor of Divinity, resid-

ing at Serampore, in the province of Bengal being in good health and of sound mind, do make this my last will and testament in manner and form following :

First. I utterly disclaim all or any right or title to the premises at Serampore, called the Mission Premises, and every part and parcel thereof ; and do hereby declare that I never had, or supposed myself to have, any such right or title.

Secondly. I disclaim all right and title to the property belonging to my present wife, Grace Carey, amounting, to 25.000 rupees, more or less, which was settled upon her by a particular deed, executed previously to my marriage with her.

Thirdly. I give and bequeath to the College of Serampore, the whole of my museum, consisting of minerals, shells, corals, insects, and other natural curiosities and a Hortus Siccus. Also the folio edition of 'Hortus Woburnensis', which was presented to me by Lord Hastings, Taylor's Hebrew Concordance, my collection of Bibles in foreign languages, and all my books in the Italian and German languages.

Fourthly. I desire that my wife, Grace Carey, will collect from my library whatever books in the English language she wishes for, and keep them for her own use.

Fifthly. From the failure of funds to carry my further intentions into effect, I direct that my library, with the exception above made, be sold by public action, unless it, or any part of it, can be advantageously disposed of by private sale ; and that from the proceeds 1500 rupees be paid as a legacy to my son, Jabez Carey, a like sum having heretofore been paid to my sons Felix and William.

Sixthly. It was my intention to have bequeathed a similar sum to my son Jonathan Carey ; but God has so prospered him that he is in no immediate want of it. I direct that if anything remains, it be given to my wife, Grace Carey, to whom I also bequeath all my household furniture, wearing apparel, and whatever other effects I may possess, for her purpose and behoof.

Seventhly. I direct that, before every other thing, all my lawful debts may be paid ; that my funeral be as plain as possible ; that I may be buried by the side of my second, wife, Charlotte Emilia Carey ; and that the following inscription, and nothing more, may be cut on the stone which commemorates her, either above or below, as there may be room-viz. :

'William Carey, born August 17th, 1761 ; died . . . .
A wretched, poor and helpless worm,
On Thy kind arms I fall.'

Eighthly. I hereby constitute and appoint my dear friends the Rev. WILLIAM ROBINSON of Calcutta, and the Rev. JOHN MACK of Serampore, executors, to this my last will and testament, and request them to perform all therein desired and ordered by me, to the utmost of their power.

Ninthly. I hereby declare this to be my last will and testament and revoke all other wills and testaments of a date prior to this.

(Signed) WILLIAM CAREY.
(Signed) W. H. JONES, S.M.'intosh.'

CHAPTER II.

HIS MISSIONARY PRINCIPLES AND THOSE OF HIS CONTEMPORARIES.

A. INTRODUCTION.

In the year 1783 William Carey became convinced that baptism by immersion after confession of faith was scriptural and apostolic. We mentioned that he was baptized by Dr. Ryland of Northampton Oct. 5, 1783. As a boy he took no interest in theological books except one : John Bunyan's Pilgrim's Progress. Not on account of the spiritual depth of the book, or its baptist principles, but only on account of the romantic atmosphere in it. We may be fairly certain that his friends Andrew Fuller and Dr. Ryland told him much of their hero. Now the principles of Bunyan and other Baptists were strongly Calvinistic and they laid much stress on the doctrine of predestination. This however does not apply to the former Baptists e.g. the so-called founder of the Baptist sect in England : JOHN SMITH, who took refuge in Holland in 1606 and founded there a new congregation. In his confession of faith (a translation from the Dutch, executed by Professor MÜLLER, from the copy preserved in the archives of the Church at Amsterdam) he is thoroughly Armenian : e.g. article XIV : That God created man with a free will, having the faculty to choose what is good, and to avoid what is evil ; or to choose what is evil and to avoid what is good : and that this liberty of will was a natural power and property, created by God in the soul of man. Article XVIII : That original sin is not a Scriptural term, and that there is no such thing as men intended by the word (Jerem. 18 : 20) ; as God threatened death only to Adam (Gen. 2 : 17),not to his posterity, for their sins, and because God over-rates the soul (Heb. 12 : 9). Article XX. That the infants are conceived and born in innocency, without sin, and that they dying, therefore, are all undoubtedly saved. [1])

This John Smith may have been the founder of the Baptists as some assert. At any rate his influence was wide-spread. He and his followers are called the General Baptists. [2]) Opposite to them were the Particular Baptists. These Particular Baptists had "very much to endure of all kind of obloquy poured out upon them. The atrocities of Munster, heresies of every kind, had been laid to their charge. The civil power had been invoked to crush them, and the Government was blamed for not framing new laws, or enforcing old ones, for their banishment from the kingdom. Of these things the brethren were not ignorant." Therefore in 1644 they issued a Confession of Faith. The title of this document runs thus : "The confession of faith of those Churches which are commonly (however falsely) called Anabaptist. Presented to the view of all that fear God, to examine by the touchstone of the Word of Truth ; as likewise for the taking off those aspersions which are frequently, both in the pulpit and print (although unjustly), cast upon them." The following Scriptures, in full, follow : "Acts IV.20 ; Isa. VIII.20 ; 2 Corin. I.9.10." "London : printed in the year of our Lord 1644." This document is signed by representatives of seven churches in London. Their *adversaries* had represented them as holding *free will ; falling from grace ; denying original sin ; disclaiming of magistracy*, denying to assist them, either in person or purse, in any of their lawful commands ; doing acts unseemly in the dispensing the ordinance of baptism, not to be named among Christians. All which charges we disclaim as *notoriously untrue*, though by reason of these calumnies cast upon us, many that fear God are discouraged and forestalled in harbouring a good thought, either of us or what we profess ; and many that know not God are encouraged, if they can find the place of our meeting, to gather together in clusters to stone us, looking upon us as a people holding such things as that we are not worthy to live." [3])

HENRY C. VEDDER says : The confession of 1644 is outspoken also in the advocacy of religious liberty as the right, and of good citizenship as the duty, of every christian man. The following article is worth quoting in full as the first publication of the doctrine of freedom of conscience in an official document, representing a body of associated churches :

XLVIII. A civil magistracy is an ordinance of God ; set up by Him for the punishment of evildoers, and for the praise of them that do well, and that in all lawful things, commanded by them, subjection ought to be given by us in the Lord, not only for the wrath, but for the conscience sake ; and that we are to makes upplication and prayers for kings, and all that are in authority, that under them we may live a quiet and peaceable life in all godliness and honesty.

"The supreme magistracy of this kingdom we acknowledge to be King and Parliament, and concerning the worship of God, there is but one lawgiver, which is Jesus Christ. So it is the magistrate's duty to tender the liberty of men's consciences. (Eccl. 8 : 8), (which is the tenderest thing unto all conscientious men, and most dear unto them, and without which all other liberties will not be worth the naming, much less the enjoying), and to protect all under them from all wrong, injury, oppression, and molestation . . . . and as we cannot do anything contrary to our understanding and consciences so neither can we forbear the doing of that which our understandings and consciences bind us to do. And if the magistrates should require us to do otherwise, we are to yield our persons in a passive way to their power, as the saints of old have done (James 5 : 4)." [4])

Dr. J. C. CARLILE gives us further information about this document of 1644 in his book "The story of the English baptists". He tells us that in the year 1644 the number of Particular Baptist churches had increased to seven. He also informs us that in the same year these seven churches and one French church of the same faith composed a confession of fifty articles, which gives a brief exposition of Calvinistic theology, and pronounces baptism "an ordinance of the New Testament given by Christ, to be dispensed upon persons possessing faith or who are disciples or taught, who upon profession of faith ought to be baptised", and afterwards to partake of the Lord's supper. He furthermore gives us an account of the way in which the converts must be baptized "by dipping or plunging the body under water, it being a sign. For it must answer to the thing signified, which is that interest the saints have in the death, burial and resurrection of Christ, 'as the word baptizoo signifies to dip or to plunge, yet so as convenient garments be upon both the administrator and subject with all modesty".

Dr. Carlile ends his consideration with these words : "The confession of faith is a distinct landmark in the practice of Baptists, though it should be remembered that it was not set forth to compel or bind the faith of any person ; it was for purposes of information only. It was presented to both Houses of Parliament in the hope that it would silence scandalous misrepresentations as to what was the teaching of Baptists." [5])

The concluding paragraph runs as follows : "Thus we desire to give unto Christ that which is His, and unto all lawful authority that which is their due ; and to owe nothing to any man but love ; to live quietly and peaceably, as it becometh saints, endeavouring in all things to keep a good conscience, and to do unto every man (of what judgment soever) as we would they should do unto us ; that our practise is, so it may prove us to be a conscionable, quiet, and harmless people (no way dangerous or troublesome to human society), and to labour and work with our hands that we may not be chargeable to any, but to give to him that needeth, both friends and enemies, accounting it more excellent to give than to receive. Also we confess that we know but in part, and that we are ignorant of many things which we desire and seek to know ; and if any shall do us that friendly part to show us from the Word of God that we see not, we shall have cause to be thankful to God and them.   But if any man shall impose upon us anything that we see not to be commanded by our Lord Jesus Christ, we should in His strength rather embrace all reproaches and tortures of men, to be stripped of all outward comforts, and, if it were possible, to die a thousand deaths rather than to do anything against the least little of the truth of God, or against the light of our own consciences.   And if any shall call what we have said heresy, then do we with the apostle acknowledge, that after the way they call heresy we worship the God of our fathers, disclaiming all heresies (rightly so called) because they are against Christ, and to be steadfast and immovable, always bounding in obedience to Christ, as knowing our labour shall not be in vain in the Lord."

P. BIESTERVELD, late professor of the Theological High School of the Dutch Reformed Churches at Kampen, informs us in his "Schets van de Symboliek" that the confession of 1644 consisted of 42 articles and agrees with all Calvinistic dogmata except sacraments and church-government. [6])

He also states that the most important confession of the Particular Baptists up till now is the Confession of 1677 entitled : A Confession of faith put forth by the Elders and Brethren of many congregations of Christians baptized upon profession of their faith. Dr. PHILIP SCHAFF gives in "The Creeds of Christendom with history and critical Notes Vol. III" a further explanation of this symbol.   He calls it "The baptist confession of 1688" and in parentheses : "The Philadelphia Confession".   He says : "This is the most generally accepted Confession of the Regular or Calvinistic Baptists in England and in the Southern States of America. It appeared first in London 1677, then again in 1688 and 1689, under the title "A confession of Faith put forth by the Elders and Brethren of many congregations a.s.o. as mentioned above. With an appendix concerning baptism. It was adopted early in the eighteenth century by the Philadelphia Association of Baptist churches, and hence it is also called the *Philadelphia confession of faith*. It is a slight modification of the Confession of the Westminster Assembly (1647) and the Savoy Declaration (1658), with changes to suit the Baptist views on Church polity and on the subjects and mode of baptism. Dr. Schaff gives then only the distinctive features of the Baptist Confession which the Rev. Dr. HOWARD OSGOOD, Professor in the Baptist Theological Seminary at Rochester, N.Y., had selected for his book.

Now Dr. Schaff does not give any other confession of the Particular Baptists. So he himself thinks this Confession by far the most important. We are inclined to think that William Carey maintained this Confession. We are, however, not able to prove this. At any rate : either the Confession of 1644 or the Confession of 1677 (1688) must have been his confession of faith. In our appendix we give this confession of 1677 (1688). [7])

As for the "Philadelphia confession" W. F. WHITLEY M.A. L.L.D.F.R., Hist. S., writes in his book : A history of British Baptists : "One important landmark was the adoption in 1742 by the Philadelphia Association of the confession of 1677, slightly modified by incorporating additions from Elias and Benjamin Keach. This has made that confession far better known among American Baptists than among English."

The same writer gives the following verdict about the confession of 1677 "Baptists were willing now to look more favourably on the masterpiece of Presbyterian erudition, the confession and the shorter catechism of Westminster a generation earlier. So a revision of the Westminster documents with the help of the Savoy Declaration was undertaken, and was published by the London Baptist Association in 1677."

As for the associations of congregations he asserts : "Nearly all these associations found it wise to specify what doctrinal basis they grounded themselves. The confession of 1677 was seldom reprinted , and rarely referred to. A list of ten or twelve doctrines

126

was made, short enough to print in half a dozen lines and this proved sufficient to win the adhesion of one association after another. It was the really vital exposition of what Particular Baptists did esteem important about 1770."

The Rev. J. W. WEENINK, Baptist missionary of Stadskanaal, Holland, thinks the confession of 1677 the most accepted confession in the period from 1768—1814.

From these quotations we may first conclude the great difference between the General Baptists as John Smith c.s., and the Particular Baptists to whom belongs John Bunyan and others. Moreover in the biography of S. Pearce Carey on William Carey, we read that there was a close friendship between the Rev. THOMAS SKINNER a Baptist preacher of Towcester and William Carey. This man had a pastoral heart and he eminently excelled in administering the healing balm. So he soon took Carey to his pastoral heart and lent him a book which indeed proved to be a healing balm to him viz. Senr. Robert Hall's Help to Zion's Travellers. This book was like sweet wine to Carey according to S. Pearce Carey. Just like Robert Hall, William Carey protested against the ultra-Calvinism i.e. the laying of such stress upon the doctrine of predestination that the activities of men are completely ignored. But further this book is really Calvinistic, except the doctrine of baptism. In his missionary principles of Oct. 7, 1805 we found the following statement : "we are firmly persuaded that Paul might plant and Apollos water, in vain, in any part of the world, did not God give the increase. We are sure that only those who are ordained to eternal life will believe, and that God alone can add to the church such as shall be saved."

From these quotations we may further conclude that William Carey just like the defenders of the Baptist confession of 1644, rejects the doctrine of the free will, the falling from grace, the denying of original sin and as we saw in our survey of his life—the disclaiming of magistracy. Generally speaking we found in his life the same spiritual struggle as in the life of John Bunyan : "There was an inward drama in which the three actors are God, Satan, and a solitary human soul. If external influences from events or men affected his spirit, they came as nuncios from God or from the Evil One. Institutions, churches, ordinances, rites, ceremonies, could help him little, or not at all. The journey from the city of Destruction to the Celestial City must be undertaken on a special summons by each man for himself alone ; if a companion join him on the way, it lightens their trials of the road ; but of the companions each one is an individual pilgrim, who has started on a great personal adventure and who, as he enters the dark river must undergo his particular experiences of hope or fear." [8]

These words of EDWARD DOWDEN on John Bunyan may be also used for William Carey. The hero he loves most of all is David Brainerd. When he was still in England he was already perusing the book relating the life of this man. In India he reads and rereads the book. And every one who reads the books on David Brainerd will admire his self sacrifice in his service of Christ, but he also tastes a spiritual atmosphere which is unsound. Personal experiences are sometimes estimated a higher guide than the Word of God and conversion is overestimated. William Carey may not have gone so far, but we don't exaggerate when saying that he is in this respect just like David Brainerd that he is more looking upon the experiences of the individual soul, than upon the work of Salvation of our Lord Jesus Christ. [9] The surety of the Covenant is hardly known to him, neither the importance of the Church and its offices. This may be a reaction against Anglican doctrines. But with a high grade of probability we say that William Carey, who did not give any theological treatise, was a Calvinist, not an Arminianist. That he deviated from the Calvinistic doctrine of baptism, that there was also a Pietistic touch in his general outlook. Later on we will prove that this view of his dogmatic principles is right, when we discuss his "Enquiry".

NOTES

[1] EVAN's Early English Baptist. Vol. I. Bunyan Library. Vol. VII, p. 257. An interesting dissertation describing Baptism in Holland, and also something of English Baptism, is "De opkomst en vestiging van het Baptisme in Nederland" by Dr. G. A. WUMKES. Osinga Sneek 1912.

[2] KOK's Christelijke Encyclopaedie, article "Baptisten" and "Die Religion in Geschichte und Gegenwart", article "Baptiste".

[3] EVAN, op. cit. Vol. II, p. 134—135.

[4] HENRY C. VEDDER, "A short history of the Baptists". Revisch Edition Philadelphia 1887.

[5] Dr. J. C. CARLILE, The story of the English Baptists, published by James Clarke & Co. 1905, London, p. 85—86.

[6] P. BIESTERVELD, Schets van de Symboliek. Kampen 1912, p. 124.

[7] PHILIP SCHAFF D.D. LL. D. The Creeds of Christendom. New York 1905, p. 738—741.

[8] Puritan and Anglican by EDWARD DOWDEN. London 1900, p. 233—234.

[9] Berigten van de Utrechtsche Zendingsvereen. 1861, no. 9 article relating to DAVID BRAINERD, der Apostel der Indianer in Pennsylvanien und New Yersey, von Reinhold Vornbaum, Düsseldorf. 1850.

B. HIS MISSIONARY PRINCIPLES.

In this chapter we take the following order : First we will treat of the principles of Dr. William Carey. Then we will try to describe the principles of the Pietists, especially of the Moravians according to Von Zinzendorf. The main sources for the knowledge of the principles of Dr. William Carey are his "Enquiry" and "The form of Agreement respecting the great principles upon which the Brethren of the Mission at Serampore think it their duty to act in the work of instructing the Heathen". 7 Oct. 1805. Next his biographies.

Par. I. Statement of the motives of Mission.

Dr. JAS. S. DENNIS' words : "Carey's Enquiry marks a distinct point of departure in the history of Christianity. It laid the foundation of Missions in accurate information, careful considera-tion, and wise use of means, as well as in the obligation of Christian duty" are expressing the real worth of the Enquiry. [1] But in order to appreciate this judgment it will be necessary to pay care-ful attention to this most famous writing. We will first look at the division of his Enquiry. [1]

Prof. Dr. WARNECK who made an attempt to give a theory of missions, gives after his preface the following division : "Die Ur-sprung der Christlichen Mission ; Die dogmatische Grundlegung ; Die ethische Grundlegung ; Die missionarische Wurzeln im A.T. ; Die Mission in den Reden Jesu ; Die kirchliche Begründung ; Die geschichtliche Begründung ; Die ethnologische Begründung." [2]

The order of treatment William Carey gives after his introduc-tion is : An Enquiry whether the Commission given by our Lord to his Disciples be not still binding on us. Section II containing a short review of former Undertakings for the Conversion of the Heathen. Section III containing a Survey of the present state of the world and Section IV The practicability of something being done, more than what is done for the conversion of the heathen.

Now it is remarkable that in general the order of the Chapters of this Enquiry of this simple minister-cobbler is the same as the order of the chapters of prof. Dr. G. Warneck's Theory of Missions. Later on we will indicate this once more. But here we at once see the great spirit of this humble man, who was able with such poor means to write such a scientific booklet.

Another remarkable feature of the Enquiry is that the argument of "perishing heathen" is never used. Carey does not paint for our eyes a picture of unhappy souls in the midst of everlasting fire. So his argument is not that we are drawn to propagate the Gospel out of mere charity or mercifulness, on the contrary, the keynote of the book is "obligation". The very beginning is : "An Enquiry into the *obligations* of Christians". All through this pamphlet he uses words and phrases as "obedience". Sometimes : "it becomes us", "it behoves us", "it is incumbent upon us". [3])

Another important feature is that Carey did not dwell upon his Baptist conviction. He simply states that he belongs to the particular Baptist denomination, (P. 84.)

Lastly we are struck by the fact that the beginning and the end of the book contain the same thought : "Thy kingdom come" and "Surely it is worth our while to lay ourselves out with all our might in promoting the cause and Kingdom of Christ".

In his introduction he makes a difference between words and deeds : "As our blessed Lord has required us to pray that his kingdom may come, and his will be done on earth as it is in heaven, it becomes us not only to express our desires of that event by words but to use every lawful method to spread the knowledge of his name." [4]) Living in the eighteenth century, he is fully aware of the fact that the mere use of pious words without pious deeds is hypocritical.

Then he describes the situation in the world of mankind caused by the fall of Adam. Every word is of importance and every sentence can be used in our time. But the pith of the Introduction is this : "One would have supposed that the remembrance of the deluge would have been transmitted from father to son, and have perpetually deterred mankind from transgressing the will of their Maker, but the world changed the glory of the incorruptible God into an image made like to corruptible man, and to birds and four-footed beasts, and creeping things." (P. 4.)

Yet God repeatedly made known his intention to prevail finally over all the power of the Devil, and to destroy all his works, and set up his own Kingdom and interest among men, and extend it as universally as Satan had extended his. It was for this purpose that the Messiah came and died, that God might be just and the justifier of all that should believe in him. When he had laid down his life, and taken it up again, he sent forth his disciples to preach the good tidings to every creature, and to endeavour by all possible methods to bring over a lost world to God. Apostles preached the Gospel near and far, cultured and barbarian peoples alike received it and were blessed. Notwithstanding that a very considerable part of mankind is still involved in all the darkness of heathenism. Some attempts are still being made, but they are inconsiderable in comparison with what might be done if the whole body of Christians entered heartily into the spirit of the divine command. Some think little about it, others are unacquainted with the state of the world and others love their wealth better than the souls of their fellow-creatures.

Section I of the Enquiry deals with the question whether the Commission given by our Lord to his disciples be not still binding on us. The question is asked on account of the attitude of the Reformers, except Bucer and Zwingli. But Calvin, Luther Melanchton and others did not agree with the interpretation of the Words of our Lord in his Mission-call as relating to all Christians. Only the apostles were called as missionaries to the heathen, not the churches founded afterwards. [5])

Contrary to this opinion and the indolence of the 17th and the 18th century is the opinion of William Carey : Our Lord Jesus Christ commissioned his apostles to go, and teach all nations ; or, as another evangelist expresses it, "Go into all the world, and preach the Gospel to every creature." William Carey was a student of the writings and papers of the Moravians who lived also in Northampton. From these studies he knew of course the opinion of Von Zinzendorf and probably of Von Spangenberg. Just like these men, he disagrees with the opinion of the masses "who thought that the commission was sufficiently put in execution by what the apostles and others have done". He says : "It is thus that multitudes sit at ease, and give themselves no concern about the far greater part of their fellow-sinners, who to this day, are left in ignorance and idolatry." (P. 8.)

Next he gives the following observations for the consideration of those who think "that because the apostles were extraordinary officers and have no proper successors, and because many things which were right for them to do would be utterly unwarrantable for us, therefore it may not be immediately binding on us to execute the commission, though it was so upon them": If the command of Christ to teach all nations be restricted to the apostles, or those under the immediate inspiration of the Holy Ghost, then that of baptizing should be so too ; and every denomination of Christians, except the Quakers, do wrong in baptizing with water at all. Secondly if the command of Christ be confined to the apostles, then all ministers who have endeavoured to carry the Gospel to the heathen have acted without a warrant, and run before they were sent. Thirdly, if the command extend only to the apostles, then the promise (Lo, I am with you always, to the end of the world) must be so limited.

He admits of course that there are cases in which even a divine command may cease to be binding. (P. 9). He gives among others the following examples : the ceremonial commandments of the Jewish law. There may be a natural impossibility. It was e.g. not the duty of Paul to preach Christ to the inhabitants of Otaheite, because no such place was then discovered, nor any means of coming at them. But none of these things (he gives some more examples) can be alleged by us in behalf of the neglect of the commission given by Christ.

Some said that the obstacles were such that it was impossible to render obedience. But then he asks : Have not the popish missionaries surmounted all those difficulties which we have generally thought to be insuperable ? Have not the missionaries of the Unitas Fratrum, or Moravian Brethren encountered the scorching heat of Abyssinia, and the frozen climes of Greenland, and Labrador, their difficult languages, and savage manners ? Or have not English traders for the sake of gain surmounted all those things ? He proves this statement by giving many examples and then concludes : "Men can insinuate themselves into the favour of the most barbarous clans, and uncultivated tribes, for the sake of gain ; and how different soever the circumstances of trading and preaching are, yet this will prove the possibility of ministers being introduced there ; and if this is but thought a sufficient reason to make the experiment, my point is gained.

"But some assert he says that there is some secret God's time, for such a world movement, which we can neither hasten nor delay, whose arrival and appearing we must just wait. First the witnesses must be slain and many other prophecies fulfilled. In that case it is also vain to pray for the speeding of Christ's Kingdom ; which who will dare affirm ?" [6])

Still another argument is issued by his opponents. That none shall be converted in the heathen-world till the universal downpouring of the Spirit in the last days. But smilingly he says :

"This objection comes too late. For the success of the Gospel has been very considerable in many places already." (P. 12.)

The last argument of his opponents is that there are multitudes in our nations, and within our immediate spheres of action, who are as ignorant as the South-Sea savages. Carey gives the following answer : "Our countrymen have the means of grace, and may attend on the word preached if they choose it. They have the means of knowing the truth etc. but the heathens have no Bible, no written language, no ministers, no good civil government, nor any of those advantages which we have. Pity not less than Christianity should constrain our instant help." (P. 13.)

Coming to section II *containing a short review of former Undertakings for the conversion of the Heathen* he describes the activity of the apostles from the day of Pentecost onwards as an argument for his purpose : to send missionaries. The first part is an epitome of the Acts of the Apostles. Further he gives an account of the traditional journeyings of the Apostles in Scythia and India, Phrygia and Arabia, Parthia and Ethiopia, Mauritania and Lybia. The labours of Justin Martyr, Irenaus of Gaul, Tertullian of Carthage, Frumentius of Abyssinia, James of Nubia are mentioned and there are references to the evangelistic efforts of Palladius and Columba in Scotland, Patrick and Finian in Ireland.

Then he gives an account of the conversions of "nomads beyond the Danube", of Burgundians and of "Abasgi near the Caucasian Mountains". Then he turns to England. He mentions Augustine and Mellitus, Justus and Paulinus, Ruffinian and Birinus, Felix and Wilfrid. Wild Europe (the northern part) was evangelized by Amandus Gallus, Chelenus, Columbanus, Egidius Gallus, the two Evaldi, in Westphalia, Chilianus in upper Franconia, Boniface or Winifred among the Thuringians, and Willebrord in West Friesland. He mentions the preaching of Ansgarius in Denmark, Gaudibert in Sweden, and Methodius and Cyril in Bohemia. He describes the work of the Portuguese Jesuits in the East Indies,China and Japan, of the Spaniards in South America, the Portuguese in Asia. He mentions the work of Wickliffe, John Huss and Jerom of Prague. In the following century Luther, Calvin, Melanchton, Bucer, Martyr, and many others had to confront all the rest of the world ; they preached and prayed and wrote : and nations agreed one after another to cast off the yoke of popery, and to embrace the doctrine of the Gospel.

When turning to modern missions he mentions especially the work of Mr. John Eliot in New England, Mr. David Brainerd, his beloved missionary whom he often takes as an example, the Danish Missionaries in Tranquebar, the Dutch in Formosa, Malabar, Jaffna, Colombo, Amboyna, Java, Banda, Macassar, Sumatra, and the Cape of Good Hope.

Then he writes: "but none of the moderns have equalled the Moravian Brethren in this good work; they have sent missions to Greenland, Labrador, and several of the West Indian Islands, which have been blessed for good. They have likewise sent missionaries to Abyssinia, in Africa, but what success they have I cannot tell." He ends this second Section with mentioning the efforts of the late Mr. Wesley in the West Indies.

From this survey we see one of the first attempts at a History of Missions. It is highly remarkable that, while none else had studied this aspect of history, this shoemaker-minister gained so much information from books and other sources with his poor means, that he is able to give this picture in order to convince the readers of the possibility, even the necessity of following the example of these great predecessors. So he lays stress upon the principle of our obligation to preach the Gospel to all nations.

In the third Sect. containing a Survey of the present State of the world we meet the map-maker Carey who makes a careful study of the whole world as then known. Twenty-three pages full of statistic tables are shown us as a monument of his indefatigable patience. Close to his bench where he was shoemaking, he had his own-stitched globe of leather. He himself says: in this survey I shall consider the world as divided according to its usual division into four parts, *Europe, Asia, Africa and America* and take notice of the several countries, their population, civilization and religion. (P. 38). S. Pearce Carey remarks: "Sweep of purpose is combined with wealth of detail; the minuteness of the information is almost extravagant." [7])

Every page is divided into five columns showing: 1. Name of the country or island, 2. length in miles, 3. breadth in miles, 4. number of inhabitants, 5. religion.

From page 39—45 he treats of Europe. Every country is treated separately e.g. Great Britain: length 680 miles, breadth 300 miles, number of inhabitants 12.000.000; religion protestants, of many denominations. United Netherlands length 150 miles; breadth

150 miles. Number of inhabitants 2.000.000 ; religion protestants of several denominations. When he discusses Asia he gives all the isles separately : e.g. Java length 580 miles, breadth 100 miles, number of inhabitants 2.700.000, religion Pagans, except the Dutch Christians.

But these tables must serve his purpose. This colossal work is performed in order to move the hearts of his fellow-countrymen. He says : "a few general remarks upon it will conclude this section. 1. The inhabitants of the world according to this calculation amount to about 730 millions. Of these are 420 millions still in pagan darkness ; 130 millions the followers of Mahomet ; 100 millions Catholics ; 44 millions Protestants ; 30 millions of the greek and armenian churches, and perhaps 7 millions of Jews. It must undoubtedly strike every considerate mind, what a vast proportion of the sons of Adam there are, who yet remain in the most deplorable state of heathen darkness, without any means of knowing the true God, except what are afforded them by the works of nature ; they are in general poor, barbarous, naked pagans, as destitute of civilization, as they are of true religion.

His second conclusion is that barbarous as these poor heathens are they appear to be as capable of knowledge as we are. His third conclusion deals with the methods of the Jesuits in China. Their highest aim seemed to be to obtain the good opinion of the heathen ; for the converts were allowed to honour the image of Confusius, their great law-giver, so that the religious state of even heathens has been rendered worse by intercourse with them !

That the greater part of Africa and a great proportion of Asia and Europe are in the hands of the Mahometans, is his fourth conclusion. And his last conclusion is that those who bear the name of Christian show a very high degree of ignorance and immorality. Various baneful and pernicious errors appear to gain ground, in almost every part of Christendom. The last sentence shows the purpose of this section : *all these things are loud calls to christians and especially to ministers to exert themselves to the utmost in their spheres of action and to try to enlarge them as much as possible.*

He was convinced that Christ could save the world if his Church would be faithful. That the darkness and shadows of death would flee if the light of the Church was burning. In this way he summoned his fellow-christians to obey the command of the Master. In the fourth section he treats of the practicability of something more being done for the conversion of the heathen. He recognizes that there are indeed great difficulties in acquainting the pagans with the Gospel, but he confronts all these obstacles. 1 Their distance from us, 2 their barbarous and savage way of living, 3 the danger of being killed by them, and 4 the difficulties of procuring the necessaries of life and 5 the difficulties of the languages. As for the first obstacle : the mariner's compass makes navigation possible as it is shown by the sea-voyages of Cook and others. So navigation, especially that which is commercial, shall be one great means of carrying on the work of God.

As for the barbarism : the apostles were not deterred, did not fear the wildness of Germany and Gaul, and still more barbarous Britons ! He quotes Tertullian : 'Those parts of Britain which were proof against the Roman armies were conquered by the Gospel of Christ.'' (P. 69.) Their watchword was not "civilization first and then Christianity", but "Christianity the royal road to a worthy civilization". Then he cites once more his beloved missionaries Eliot and Brainerd and says : they went forth, and encountered every difficulty of the kind, and found that a cordial reception of the Gospel produced those happy effects which the longest intercourse with Europeans, without it could never accomplish. It does not mean any objection to men of commerce. It only requires that we should have as much love for the souls of our fellow-cratures, and fellow-sinners, as they have for the profits arising from a few otter-skins, and all these difficulties would be easily surmounted. After all, the uncivilized state of the heathen, instead of affording an objection against preaching the Gospel to them, ought to furnish an argument for it. Barbarism baffled no traders. Their very barbarism should move us to swifter help. In a splendid peroration he asks many questions such as the following : "Can we as men, or as Christians hear that a great part of our fellow-creatures are enveloped in ignorance and barbarism ? Can we hear that they are without the Gospel, without government, without laws, and without arts, and sciences ; and not exert ourselves to introduce amongst them the sentiments of men, and of Christians ? Would not the spread of the Gospel be the most effectual means of their civilization ?'' Eliot and Brainerd both subdued and uplifted men ! "If similar attempts were made in other parts of the world, and crowned with a divine blessing, might we not expect to see Divines even amongst those who at present seem to be scarcely human ?

(P. 70.)   The third obstacle is the danger of being killed by them. But should we be reluctant and consult flesh and blood ? Paul and Barnabas hazarded their lives and they were not blamed as being rash, but commended for so doing, while John Mark who through timidity of mind deserted them was branded with censure.   Once more he gives the examples of his heroes Eliot and Brainerd and the Moravians.   But they have been very seldom molested.   Nay, in general the heathen have showed a willingness to hear the word ; and have principally expressed their hatred of Christianity on account of the vices of nominal Christians."

The fourth argument with regard to the difficulties is that of procuring the necessaries of life.   Carey saw the difficulties very well, perhaps better than most of his fellow-countrymen but "a christian is a person who is in a peculiar sense not his own".   He is servant of God.   He engages to go where God pleases and to do or endure what He sees fit to command, or call him to, in the exercise of his function.   He has to venture all, like the primitive Christians, to go everywhere preaching the Gospel.   The next suggestion he makes has been derived from the Moravians as he states afterwards when he is in India and is of great importance for his missionary enterprise in Serampore : "It might be neces sary, however, for two, at least, to go together, and in general I should think it best that they should be married men, and to prevent their time from being employed in procuring necessaries, two or more other persons with their wives and families, might also accompany them, who should be wholly employed in providing for them.   In most countries, it would be necessary for them to cultivate a little plot of ground just for their support, which would be a resource to them, whenever their supplies failed.   Not to mention the advantages they would reap from each other's company, it would take off enormous expense, which has always attended undertakings of this kind ; for though a large colony needs support for a considerable time, yet so small a number would, upon receiving the first crop maintain themselves.   They would have the advantage of choosing their situation, their wants would be few ; the women, and even the children would be necessary for domestic purposes ; and a few articles of stock, as a cow or two, and a bull, and a few other cattle of both sexes, a very few utensils of husbandry, and some corn to sow their land, would be sufficient. Those who attend the missionaries should understand husbandry, fishing, fowling &c, and be provided with the necessary implements for these purposes. Indeed a variety of methods may be thought of, and when once the work is undertaken, many things will suggest themselves to us, of which we at present can form no idea.

As for the fifth obstacle, the languages : the same means would be found necessary here as in trade between different nations. The missionaries must learn the language in one or two years. The idea of learning the languages before the missionaries are sent to the field did not occur to him. Missionaries must be men of great piety, prudence, courage, and forbearance ; of undoubted orthodoxy and must ener with all their hearts into the spirit of their mission etc.

He also gives here a detailed description of the qualities necessary for a missionary : we will treat of this part when we discuss the organs of the mission.

The fifth section enquires into the duty of Christians in general and what means ought to be used in order to promote this work. He deals with the home base and the idea of a Missionary society being a work of the church, of each member of the church. This part, however, will also be treated when we are discussing the organs of the mission.

When we try to summarize what we found in this very useful book, which may be called up-to-date as regards the principles, we state once more that he emphasizes the motives of missionary action. Missionary work is not leisure time-amusement, but duty. Not a favourite pursuit, but ordered by the command of the Lord. The commission of the Lord to his disciples is still binding on us. All the arguments of his contemporaries are refuted. And he appears to have a profound knowledge of their way of reasoning.

The former undertakings are put forward in order to show the possibilities of the present. The description of the past time is an argument ad maiorem for him, as the means of communication are nowadays far better than they were formerly. This first "History of Missions" is a proof of what can be done if christians willingly obey the call of the Lord. This History must be perused by all those who make an investigation into the early protestant description of the activities of missionaries.

The third section deserves still more admiration, when he gives his statistical survey of the present state of the world. Carey shows himself here a sober man. The facts, only the facts he shows to his fellow-christians. And these terrible facts must stimulate his contemporaries to activity. After having reached his conclusions he says : all these things are loud calls to christians and especially to ministers, to exert themselves to the utmost in their several spheres of actions, and to try to enlarge them as much as possible.

But he is not only a sober man, he is also a practical man. He is not an enthusiast without showing us the means of performance. The impediments in the way of carrying the Gospel to the heathen stimulate this man to conquer them.

Neither the distance, the uncivilized and barbarous character of the heathen, nor the dangers or difficulties of obtaining a livelihood or studying the languages are able to subdue his zeal for the propagation of the Gospel. He examines all these impediments and shows to his fellow-christians that they can be removed.

We stated already that the order of treatment of these sections of the Introduction is essentially the same as the order of the chapters of Prof. Dr. G. Warneck.

After his Introduction Dr. Warneck describes the foundation of Mission (Die Begründung der Sendung). Carey does the same. He describes how the commission of the Lord is still binding on us. Then Dr. Warneck describes the dogmatic and ethical foundation. This part is omitted by Carey, just as the chapter dealing with the missionary roots in the Old Testament. But his sermons e.g. Jes. 54 : 2 and 3 of May 31, 1792 are a proof that he also saw the very roots of missionary duty in the Old Testament. Next Dr. Warneck quotes Jesus' own words in giving his command to go to the gentiles, so does William Carey. Then "the theology of missions" of Dr. Warneck, and William Carey describes the labours of St. Paul in extenso. The following chapter of Dr. Warneck gives "the motives of the Church" for missionary action. William Carey gives in his missionary history a description of "the activities of the Church as a motive for renewed action". When Dr. Warneck after this chapter gives the motives of the history, William Carey does the same in p. 14—37 and the last chapter of Dr. Warneck's work "Der Begründung der Sendung" describes the ethnologic motives. William Carey discusses the same subject in the pages 38—66 and 67—77.

Or course each of the two men treats the subjects in his own way. It only proves that the motives for missionary work of both great christians are the same. It proves that the shoemaker-minister when he was still in England, had already professorial thoughts in his mind. Summarizing we state that the motives for missionary action are described in a masterly way, and they may still be used by any scholar studying the principles of missions and by those who have to realize these principles on the fields.

Our conclusions are:

The order of the Chapters in his Enquiry is scientific.

Not charity but obligation is his main argument for the propagation of the Gospel.

As a Baptist, he had an admirable absence of bias in his purpose.

The main thought of his Enquiry is "Thy Kingdom come".

He wants deeds, not mere words.

He is struck by the fact that hardly anything has been done after the action of the apostles.

The Commission of the Lord is still binding upon us.

Traders won the favour of the most barbarous clans for the sake of gain. Then we are able to do the same for the sake of the Lord.

Neither the argument of "God's secret time" nor "of the universal down-pouring of the spirit in the last days" nor "the multitudes in our neighbourhood" makes any impression upon him. We have to obey.

History proves the possibility even necessity of missionary action.

His statistics are given to show the duty of the christians to propagate the Gospel. "Loud calls to christians and especially to ministers to exert themselves to the utmost."

He examines the obstacles and difficulties one by one and shows that they can be conquered.

He advises the Moravian way of living and urges the missionaries to be selfsupporting.

Languages must be mastered on the missionary field as soon as possible.

Par. II. The organs of Missions described by William Garey.

a. The task of the organs at home.

The task of the organs of the home base is described in the last section of his Enquiry. First of all we must pray. The influence of the Holy Spirit may be set at nought, and run down by many, yet it will be found on trial, that all means which we may use without it, will be ineffectual. If a temple is raised for God in the heathen world, it "will not be by might, nor by power but by my Spirit." He gives many examples out of the Scriptures to prove this assertion. With respect to our own immediate connections he says : "We have within these few years been favoured with some tokens for good, granted in answer to prayer, which should encourage us to persist, and increase in that important duty. I trust our monthly prayer-meetings for the success of the Gospel have not been in vain. New opportunities of evangelism have arisen ; there are calls to preach the Gospel in many places where it has not been usually published ; yea a glorious door is opened and is likely to be opened wider and wider by the spread of civil and religious liberty, accompanied also by a diminution of the spirit of popery." Here he makes a hint at France which has begun to break Rome's fetters. The slave trade has been challenged. Sierra Leona on the coast of Africa has become a base for freedom, and promises to open a way for honourable commerce with that country. In this way it may prove the happy means of introducing amongst them the Gospel of our Lord Jesus Christ. Had such prayer been more general in all the denominations, we might probably have seen not only an open door for the Gospel, but many running to and fro, and knowledge increased. Prayer is basic for missionary activities. Many can do nothing but pray, but were the whole body animated by one soul, with what pleasure would Christians attend on all the duties of religion, and with what delight would their ministers attend on all the business of their calling.

The home base must not be contented however with praying, without exerting themselves in the use of means for the obtaining of those things we pray for. Once more he draws a parallel between the trading companies of his time, exerting all powers and trying all means to reach their aim. Let then everyone in his station consider himself as bound to act with all his might, and in every possible way for God. Then comes his great proposal to establish a Missionary Society as the organ for missionary activity.

He also lays much stress upon the attention which must be paid to the views of those who undertake this work. He gives an example of the Dutch East India Company. Some missionaries were sent to the spice Islands, but many of them were attracted by temporal gain. Other men were a scandal to the doctrines which they preached and they were the cause that the Gospel was ejected from Ternate in 1694. (P. 83.)

The next page of his Enquiry is of very great importance for his dogmatic outlook. For here he says : I would therefore propose that such a society and committee should be formed amongst the *particular baptist denomination,* of which denomination he had said some time before that it was *his* denomination. So we clearly see that he does not belong to the General Baptists with their Armenian principles but to the Calvinistic branch of Baptists, who only differ in the doctrines of baptism and who are on the whole Reformed men and women.

But how striking is the next sentence ! "I don't mean by this in any wise to confine it to one denomination. I wish with all my heart, that everyone who loves our Lord Jesus Christ in sincerity, would in some way or other engage in it. But in the present divided state of Christendom, it would be more likely for good to be done by each denomination engaging separately in the work, than if they were to embark in it conjointly. There is room enough for us all, without interfering with each other ; and if no unfriendly interference took place, each denomination would bear good will to the other, and wish, and pray for its success, considering it as upon the whole friendly to the great cause of true religion. But if all were intermingled, it is likely their private discords might throw a damp upon their spirits, and much retard their public usefulness. "How practical this man is. He understands that waiting for unity of the Churches would mean a long delay in missionary activity. Just this and no other is the argument for wishing that a committee should be formed by the particular baptist denomination. S. Pearce Carey is right when he says that we meet here an interesting prophetic glance towards our modern interdenominational missionary co-operation."

He also understands the words of the Lord : "For which of you, desiring to build a tower doth not first sit down and count the cost, whether he have wherewith to complete it ? Lest haply, when he hath laid down a foundation, and is not able to finish, all that behold begin to mock him, saying : 'This man began to build, and was not able to finish." S. Luke 14 : 28—30.

So he proposes that the rich Christians should devote a portion of their wealth to the work. The people in more moderate circumstances were to devote a portion, suppose a tenth, of their annual increase to the Lord ; and the poor should contribute "one penny or more per week according to their circumstances". This would correspond with the practice of the Israelites, of the patriarchs, of our fore-fathers the Puritans. Such giving would supply not only the need of the funds for the home ministry but also for home and world missions.

Then he hints at the slave trade. "Many persons have of late left off taking West India sugar on account of the iniquitous manner in which it is obtained. Those families who have done so, and have not substituted any thing else in its place, have not only cleansed their hands of blood, but have made a saving to their families, some six-pence and some a shilling a week." Carey would indeed never have printed this without doing it himself. The money obtained in this way, should be saved for missionary work.

We will give his last words in full : "We are exhorted to lay up treasure in heaven, where neither moth nor rust doth corrupt, nor thieves break through and steal. It is also declared that whatsoever a man soweth, that shall he also reap." "These scriptures teach us that the enjoyments of the life to come, bear a near relation to that which now is ; relation similar to that of the harvest, and the seed. It is true all the reward is of mere grace, but it is nevertheless encouraging ; what a treasure, what a harvest must await such characters as Paul, as Elliot, and Brainerd, and others, who have given themselves wholly to the work of the Lord. What a heaven will it be to see the many myriads of poor heathens of Britons amongst the rest, who by their labours have been brought to the knowledge of God. Surely a crown of rejoicing like this is worth aspiring to. Surely it is worth while to lay ourselves out with all our might, in promoting the cause, and kingdom of Christ." (P. 86-7.)

Deaville Walker says : "Carey has delivered his message, he has flung down his great challenge, and with the one word 'Finis', he lays down his pen and commits his work to God." [8])

The influence of this pamphlet can scarcely be overestimated. His colleagues were kindled, the denominations were roused to activity, the Baptist Missionary Society was formed (see page 34). This Society may even be called the mother of the London Missionary Society. For George Smith relates that Dr. Ryland, president of the Baptist Miss. Soc., on receiving the ' 'Periodical Accounts relative to a Society formed among the Particular Baptists for Propagating the Gospel among the Heathen", sent for Dr. Bogue and Mr. Stephan, who happened to be in Bristol, to rejoice with them. [9]) The three returned thanks to God and then Dogue and Stephen, calling on Mr. Hey, a leading citizen, took the first step towards the foundation of an organisation of non-Baptists, since known as the London Missionary Society. [10])

Now we have to deal with the question whether the propagation of the Gospel is a task of missionary societies or of the official church. Here we only state the principle of William Carey. In his biography we stated that he roused all his colleagues and church-members to missionary activity. He thought it a duty of all the church-members to give their financial aid to the great cause. But the crucial point : society or church, a question of the highest importance either did not enter his mind, or he gave it an easy solution.

Nowhere did we find even a faint allusion to it. We have placed before us the mere facts of a Particular Baptist Society. When carefully perusing the official title one little word is of great, even of principal importance : "The Society formed *among* the Particular Baptists for propagating the Gospel among the heathen." The Society does not consist of all the church-members, but it is a society among the Particular Baptists, not *of* Particular Baptists. Not the Church of Leicester or any other church of the Particular Baptists is sending missionaries, and managing the home base work, but a society. [11]) We found the same expression in his Enquiry page 84 : "I would therefore propose that such a society and committee should be formed *amongst* the particular Baptist denomination."

We must, however, acknowledge that the conclusion drawn from this title may be denied. For at the famous minister's meeting at Kettering, Oct. 2nd, 1792 the ministers decided to lay a foundation for the Society. In the second resolution unanimously agreed to we read : "this society is called : 'The Particular Baptist society for propagating the gospel.' "Neither the word "among" nor "of" is used. But in the official account from the press of J. W. MORRIS of Clipstone, towards the end of 1794, N° I, the title is as stated above "Society *among* the Particular Baptists." [12]) Now Deaville Walker remarks that after the establishment in Oct. 1792 "another step was taken, for the Society founded at Kettering only included the Particular Baptist Association of

144

Northamptonshire, and the adjacent counties'. Samuel Pearce's people sent £ 70. But they also proposed to form a Birmingham and District Auxiliary, with annual, quarterly, and weekly subscribers, to cooperate with the newly-formed Committee. Thus the first local Auxiliary was organized." [13]) From this we may conclude that indeed it was a Society *among* the Particular Baptists, not *of* the Particular Baptists. This becomes still clearer when we relate that the Society decided to publish a brief narrative of its rise and plan, accompanied with some short address. Of course it was quite impossible that at once all the churches were roused by the issue of the Enquiry or by the establishment of the Society. But the question here is not whether the churches are to be roused, but the question is whether William Carey and his colleagues of the Baptist Society saw the principle that the local instituted church to whom is given the ministration of Word and Sacrament has to send the missionaries and to manage the home base, or whether it is a duty of a Society of Churchmembers i.c. ministers who as an independent power in the Church had to manage all the missionary activities. To the last question we must give an affirmative answer, to the former a negative. The pro's and con's of this principle will be discussed in the third chapter.

We may conclude that the description of the organs of the home base does not come up to our expectation. A form of instructions is not given to the members of the society and committee. Except of course the few rules of Kettering, Oct. 1792. In 1805 we get a more detailed programme, but in this period we have only a few rules in his Enquiry.

And these words are of a general tendency: "Suppose a company of serious Christians, ministers and private persons, were to form themselves into a society, and make a number of rules respecting the regulation of the plan and the persons who are to be employed as missionaries, the means of defraying the expense &c. &c. This society must consist of persons whose hearts are in the work, men of serious religion and professing a spirit of perseverance ; there must be a determination not to admit any person who is not of this description, or to retain him longer than he answers to it. From such a society a committee might be appointed, whose business it should be to procure all the information they could upon the subject, to receive contributions, to enquire into the characters, tempers, abilities, and religious views of the missionaries, and also to provide them with necessaries for their undertakings.

They must also pay great attention to the views of those who undertake this work ; for want of this the missions of the Spice Islands sent by the Dutch East India Company were soon corrupted."

These words are of great value. They demonstrate his principles. But they don't describe the relation between the committee and the missionaries for which we can't reprove William Carey, but which is an omission all the same.

When afterwards, after many happy years of cooperation between the members of the Society (especially with Mr. Fuller) and the missionaries, this bond of cordiality and confidence broke, one of the reasons may have been the influence of a new secretary who had other aspirations than Mr. Fuller, but the real cause is the absence of a description of the relation between the Home base men and the missionaries. Indeed the few resolutions which we gave on page 34 can not be called a program or base of cooperation.

We draw the following conclusions :

The duty of the home base is praying. His monthly prayer meetings have not been in vain. It is basic for missionary activities.

But we must not only pray but we must work too. So the home base must establish a Missionary Society.

Such a Society must pay much attention to the views of the missionaries they send to the field.

The home base activity must not confine itself to its own denomination.

Before sending missionaries the home base must sit down and count the cost.

Rich and poor must give their financial aid to the great cause.

In stead of to the local instituted church to whom is given the ministration of Word and Sacrament, he gives the management of the home base to a Society of Churchmembers as an independent power *in* the Church.

He lacks to give a form of instruction to the members of The Society and Committee, except a few general words.

This lack of an exact description of the relation between the home base and the missionaries will prove to be one of the main causes of the later difficulties.

146

b. The task of the organs abroad.

While we are in want of a description of the task and functions of the organs at home, the organs abroad, however, are given much attention by Carey.

In his Enquiry he puts it in the following way : "The missionaries must be men of great piety, prudence, courage, and forbearance ; of undoubted orthodoxy in their sentiments, and must enter with all their hearts into the spirit of their mission ; they must be willing to leave all the comforts of life behind them, and to encounter all hardships of a torrid or a frigid climate, an uncomfortable manner of living, and every other inconvenience that can attend this undertaking. Clothing, a few knives, powder and shot, fishing tackle, and the articles of husbandry, must be provided for them ; and when arrived at the place of their destination, their first business must be to gain some acquaintance with the language of the natives (for which purpose two would be better than one) and by all lawful means to endeavour to cultivate a friendship with them, and as soon as possible let them know the errand for which they were sent. They must endeavour to convince them that it was their good alone, which induced them to forsake their friends, and all the goods of their native country. They must be very careful not to resent injuries which may be offered to them, not to think highly of themselves, so as to despise the poor heathens and by those means lay a foundation for their resentment, or rejection of the Gospel. They must take every opportunity of doing them good, and labouring, and travelling, night and day, they must instruct, exhort, and rebuke, with all long suffering, and anxious desire for them, and above all, must be instant in prayer for the effusion of the Holy Spirit upon the people of their charge. Let but missionaries of the above description engage in the work, and we shall see that it is not impracticable." Enq. p. 75/76.

Two lines of conduct were put in practice by Carey when he was in India : Just like Paul he was preacher and craftsman. In Malda he tried to till the ground among the natives around the ruined capital of Gour. He engaged Ram Boshu as his pundit and interpreter. But experience soon taught him that Malda is not a land where the white man can be a farmer. Later on he became an indigo planter, a teacher of Bengali, a professor of Sanskrit and Marathi, and the Government translator of Bengali. But he never

147

adhered to the principle of the Jesuit missionaries whose idea of equality with the people was not that of brotherhood in Christ but of dragging down christian doctrine, worship and civilisation to the base level of idolatrous heathenism and deluding the ignorant into accepting the blasphemous compromise. [14])

Another principle is brought forward : viz. a missionary must as soon as possible become indigenous, selfsupporting, selfpropagating, alike by the labours of the mission and of the converts. [15]) On Dec. 26th 1793 he writes the same from Bandel to England : "A missionary must be one of the companions and equals of the people to whom he is sent, and many dangers and temptations will be in his way. One or two pieces of advice I may venture to give.

The first is to be exceedingly cautious lest the voyage prove a great snare. All the discourse is about high life and every circumstance will contribute to unfit the mind for the work and prejudice the soul against the people to whom he goes. And in a country like this, settled by Europeans, the grandeur, the customs, and prejudices of the Europeans, are exceedingly dangerous. They are very kind and hospitable, but even to visit them, if a man keeps no table of his own, would more than ten times exceed the allowance of a mission ; and all their discourse is about the vices of the natives, so that a missionary must see thousands of people treating him with the greatest kindness, but whom he must be entirely different from in his life, his appearance in everything, or it is impossible for him to stand their profuse way of living, being so contrary to his character and so much above his ability. This is a snare to dear Mr. Thomas, which will be felt by us both in some measure. It will be very important to missionaries to be men of calmness and evenness of temper, and rather inclined to suffer hardships than to court the favour of men, and such who will be indefatigable employed in the work set before them, an inconstancy of mind being quite injurious to it." These words are wise and remarkable for a man who makes his first attempts on the field.

We conclude that he saw two great dangers : 1) the danger of living in the same way as the settled Europeans and 2) the danger of living in the same way as the Jesuits. Contrary to these negative warnings he makes his positive statement : a missionary must be a man of calmness and evenness of temper and inclined to suffer hardship. Principles still holding good for our time. As for his Moravian plan of living (see page 137) Ward describes it in a letter of Jan. 18, 1800 in this way : "This week we have adopted a set of rules for the government of the family. All preach and pray in turn ; one superintends the affairs of the family for a month, and then another ; brother Carey is treasurer, and has the regulation of the medicine chest ; brother Fountain is librarian. Saturday evening is devoted to adjusting differences, and pledging ourselves to love one another. One of our regulations is that no one of us do engage in private trade ; but that all be done for the benefit of the mission."

In a letter of August of the same year we read once more the same regulations and moreover a division of labour for every day accurately arranged.

Now S. Pearce Carey states in his biography of William Carey that our missionary derived this plan from "the accepted textbook of Moravian Missions, published in English in 1788". We are glad to have found these instructions and give them as an appendix to this dissertation. When comparing the principles of William Carey with those of the Moravians we will expound their ideas. But here we will say that after all William Carey diverted from the plan of the Moravians as the latter wanted to have a house-fathership, and William Carey founded a cooperation on equality for each, and pre-eminence to none ; these ideas breathed a very democratic, rather a communistic spirit. One of the main causes of the terrible schism lies here.

To his son Jabez who became a missionary in Amboina he wrote a letter full of very useful instructions, and from this letter we clearly see his ideal of a missionary :

1st. Pay the utmost attention at all times to the state of your own mind, both towards God and man ; cultivate an intimate acquaintance with your own heart ; labour to obtain a deep sense of your depravity and to trust always in Christ ; be pure in heart, and meditate much upon the pure and holy character of God ; live a life of prayer and devotedness to God ; cherish every amiable and right disposition towards men ; be mild, gentle and unassuming, yet firm and manly. As soon as you perceive anything wrong in your spirit or behaviour, set about correcting it, and never suppose yourself so perfect as to need no correction.

2nd. You are now a married man, be not satisfied with conducting yourself towards your wife with propriety, but let love to her be the spring of your conduct towards her. Esteem her highly,

149

and act so that she may be induced thereby to esteem you highly. The first impressions of love arising from form and beauty will soon wear off but the esteem arising from excellency of disposition and substance of character will endure and increase. Her honour is now yours, and she cannot be insulted without your being degraded. I hope as soon as you get on board, and are settled in your cabin, you will begin and end each day by uniting together to pray and praise God. Let religion always have a place in your house. If the Lord bless you with children, bring them up in the fear of God, and be always an example to others of the power of godliness. This advice I give also to Eiza *(wife of Jabez)*, and if it is followed you will be happy.

3rd. Behave affably and genteelly to all, but not cringingly towards any, Feel that you are a man, and always act with that dignified sincerity and truth which will command the esteem of all. Seek not the society of wordly men, but when called to be with them act and converse with propriety and dignity. To do this labour gain a good acquaintance with history, geography, men and things. A gentleman is the next best character after a Christian, and the latter includes the former. Money never makes a gentleman, neither does a fine appearance, but an enlarged understanding joined to engaging manners.

4th. On your arrival your first business must be to wait on Mr. Martin (the former English resident, Martin of Amboyna. [16]) You should first send him a note to inform him of your arrival and to inquire when it will suit him to receive you. Ask his advice upon every occasion of importance, and communicate freely to him all the steps you take.

5th. As soon as you are settled begin your work. Get a Malay who can speak a little English, and with him make a tour of the island, and visit every school. Encourage all you see worthy of encouragement and correct with mildness, yet with firmness. Keep a journal of the transactions of the schools, and enter each one under a distinct head therein. Take account of the number of scholars, the names of the schoolmasters, compare their progress at stated periods, and in short consider this as the work which the Lord has given you to do.

6th. Do not, however consider yourself as a mere superintendent of schools, consider yourself as the spiritual instructor of the people and devote yourself to their good. Revise the catechism, tracts, and school-books used among them and labour to introduce among them sound doctrine and genuine piety. Pray with them as soon as you can and labour after a gift to preach to them. I expect you will have much to do with them respecting baptism. They all think infant sprinkling right and will apply to you to baptize their children ; you must say little till you know something of the language, and then prove to them from Scripture, what is the right mode of baptism and who are the proper persons to be baptized. Form them into Gospel churches when you meet with a few who truly fear God ; and as soon as you see any fit to preach to others, call them to the ministry and settle them with the churches. You must baptize and administer the Lord's Supper according to your own discretion, when there is a proper occasion for it. Avoid indolence and love of ease and never attempt to act the part of the great and gay in this world.

7th. Labour incessantly to become a perfect master of the Malay language. In order to this, associate with the natives, walk out with them, ask name of everything you see, and note it down ; visit their houses, especially when any of them are sick. Every night arrange the words you get in alphabetical order. Try to talk as soon as you get a few words, and be as much as possible one of them. A course of kind and attentive conduct will gain their esteem and confidence and give you a opportunity of doing much good.

8th. You will soon learn from Mr. Martin the situation and disposition of the Alfoors or aboriginal inhabitants, and will see what can be done for them. Do not unnecessarily expose your life, but incessantly contrive some way of giving them the Word of life.

9th. I come now to things of inferior importance but which I hope you will not neglect. I wish you to learn correctly the number, size and geography of the islands ; the number and description of inhabitants ; their customs and manners and everything of note relative to them ; and regularly communicate these things to me.

These very important instructions to his son as a missionary are worth to be kept in mind by each member of the home base and the missionaries abroad. They are very clear. To his son William, who went forth to Dinajpoor in 1808 he wrote letters of the same kind full of instructions but more earnestly stimulating him to his missionary task. These letters are given by Dr. G. SMITH in his biography page 180—206. We will only cite a few words of the letter of 3rd August 1811. "The necessities of the mission must be consulted before every other consideration. Native brethren can itinerate, but Europeans must be employed to open new missions and found new stations. For were we to go upon the plan of sending Europeans where natives could possibly be employed, no subscriptions or profits could support them." From this letter we conclude that William Carey laid full stress upon the character and the work of the individual missionary. In our survey of his life we saw his behaviour in difficulties. When troubles came from outside he attracted the younger brethren, Yates and Pearce and healed half the schism which Andrew Fuller's successors in some way had occasioned.

The qualifications of the missionaries must be of a high standard. When William Carey appeals to the Committee in England for help he asks for skilful men and women of understanding, of some erudition, but above all wise and pious men and women with much love for the missionary work.

Many instances of William Carey's noble behaviour might be given in his long career, but we don't think it necessary as many proofs of his wisdom have been given in our survey. That he was a man of character may be shown by a letter of his youngest son Jonathan, two years after his father's death. [17])

Now we hasten to his finest masterpiece, which he unassumingly calls : "Form of Agreement respecting the great principles upon which the brethren of the Mission at Serampore think it is their duty to act in the work of instructing the heathen, agreed upon at a meeting of the brethren at Serampore, on Monday, October 7, 1805." In every word we hear the voice of the shepherd, but the whole Form is placed in the plural, giving his colleagues as much honour as himself.

We have added this Form of Agreement as an appendix to this dissertation. So here we confine ourselves to the articles relating to the qualifications which are thought necessary for the missionaries. As the number of missionaries now residing at Serampore amounted to eight, they were anxious to establish subordinate stations in the country. But previous to this plan, they considered it important to record the leading principles.

This document contains the experience of six years of labour in the missionary field. It is of the greatest value and still up to date.

The first words of this document are : "The Redeemer in planting us in the heathen nation rather than in any other has imposed upon us the cultivation of peculiar qualifications." ROBERT E. SPEER, one of the members of the world Conference of 1910 spoke these fine words : "Christ's leadership prescribes the aim and the principle and the method of the missionary enterprise : the aim, to communicate a life which we have in Christ to all the world ; the principle, a principle of hope which sees in all humanity the possibility of redemption ; the method, a method of love that wins as the Saviour won." [18])

William Carey and Robert E. Speer are both convinced that Christ must be the leader of the missionaries. The missionaries however, must take their example from Paul and Apollos and the disciples.

Carey and his colleagues communicate to all the missionaries that they must bear in mind two great principles : 1. God's decree from eternity and man's responsibility : we are sure that only those who are ordained to eternal life will believe, and that God alone can add to the church such as shall be saved. Nevertheless we cannot but observe with admiration that Paul, the greatest champion for the glorious doctrines of free and sovereign grace, was the most conspicuous for his personal zeal in the work of persuading men to be reconciled to God. In this respect he is a noble example for our imitation.

These words not only prove his Calvinistic outlook, but they also prove that the super-Calvinistic view (as it is commonly called in those days, indicating the one-sided stress upon God's decree from eternity and omitting man's responsibility) is rejected.

In the first article e.g. he thinks it a duty of missionaries to set an infinite value upon immortal souls ; then he describes why we should do so : eternal punishment is threatening them etc. "But while we thus mourn over their miserable condition we should not be discouraged as though their recovery were impossible. He who raised the Scottish and brutalised Britons can raise these slaves of superstition, purify their hearts and make them worshippers of the one God in spirit and truth."

The second article is an instruction for the missionaries "in order to be informed of the snares and delusions in which these heathen are held. The missionaries must try to understand their moods of thinking, their habits, their propensities, their antipathies etc.

This knowledge may be easily obtained by conversing with sensible natives, by reading some parts of their works and by attentively observing their manners and customs."

The third article deals with the problem of adaptation. Dr. H. Kraemer is right when saying: "Hinduism itself, being eminently a social religion of group-solidarity stamps every religion as "foreign" that does not fit in with its whole socio-religious system." William Carey understood this fully. He says: "missionaries have to abstain from those things which would increase their prejudices against the Gospel. Those parts of English manners which are most offensive to them should be kept out of sight as much as possible. Let us be continually fearful lest one unguarded word or unnecessary display of the difference betwixt us in manners, etc., should set the natives at a greater distance from us." He gives the example of Paul, the Moravians and the Quakers.

In the fourth article he orders the missionaries to watch for every chance of doing the people good. We shall always fix in our minds that life is short, that all around us are perishing, and that we incur a dreadful woe if we proclaim not the glad tiding of salvation.

In the fifth article he points out to the missionaries, that it would be very easy to preach nothing but truths and that for many years together, without any well-grounded hope of becoming useful to one soul. The doctrine of Christ's expiatory death and all sufficient merits had been and must ever remain the great means of conversion. Luther, the modern apostles as Whitefield, Wesley, and the most successful missionaries in the world at the present day did and do so.

In the sixth article missionaries are told that they must treat and esteem Indians as their equals. We ought to be easy of access, to condescend to them as much as possible, and on all occasions to treat them as our equals. All passionate behaviour will sink our characters exceedingly in their estimation.

Both the seventh and the eighth article are much longer than the preceding and following articles. In these the missionaries are given instructions to guard and build up "the hosts that may be gathered" and in the eighth to cultivate the spiritual gifts of the converts. We will discuss this eighth article later in this dissertation as belonging to the Purpose of mission (the 5th par. of this chapter). As for the seventh article missionaries are deemed wise when they press upon the heathens as much as possible the great principles of the Gospel, till they be thoroughly settled and grounded in the foundation of their hope towards God.

Then follows an example of the wide outlook of this great man.

"We ought also to endeavour as much as possible to form them the habits of industry , and assist them in procuring such employments as may be pursued with the least danger of temptations to evil. Here we shall have occasions to exercise much tenderness and forbearance, knowing that industrious habits are formed with difficulty by all heathen nations." When we read the 5th Volume of the International Missionary council at Jerusalem in 1928, we meet with similar thoughts. "It is necessary to admit," says Rev. W. PATON, "with absolute candour that Christians in the countries of the West that have enjoyed the Christian tradition for many centuries have not yet succeeded in making effective the application of the Christian ethic to the world of industrial relations. Western Christians are emphatically not in the position of those who, having achieved, desire to make known their achievement and share it with others. They are acutely conscious of failure, and never so much so as when they face the effects in the East and in Africa of their own industrialized civilization." And the statement by the council with the superscription "Christ the Lord of all life" runs as follows : "The international Missionary Council desires to preface its report on industrial conditions by asserting with all the power at its command, its conviction that the Gospel of Christ contains a message not only for the individual soul, but for the world of social organization and economic relations in which individuals live. [20]

In this relation it will be useful to take note of a book of the same writer : "World Community" in which he says that industrialism "means the dissolution of most of the old caste ties and rules." [21] From other sources we know that William Carey established a *savings-bank* on account of the carelessness of the natives and a *Society for promoting agriculture and horticulture.*

We are astonished that W. Carey at such an early period divulged the same thoughts with regard to India.

Regarding their conduct towards the Government "the missionaries observe that it was their duty to honour the civil magistrate and in every state and country to render him the readiest obedience, whether persecuted or protected, and that it was their duty to instruct their native brethren in the same principles."

The faults of the native brethren must be borne, so as to reprove them with tenderness. In walking before native converts, much care and circumspection are absolutely necessary. They know only the Saviour and His doctrines as they shine forth in us. Dr. J. H. BAVINCK points to the same thing in the following words : "When we are investigating the lives of the great missionaries as Nommenson, or Carey or Hudson Taylor, or Scheurer, or any other missionary, we are always touched by the fact that they have conquered not by their words but by their deeds." [22]

Also the following words of M. Carey are still up to date : "We hope—in conversing with the wives of the native converts—always to have the assistance of the females who have embarked with us in the mission. The apostles give the example. Moreover the Asiatic women are shut up from the men, and especially from men of other caste. It behoves us therefore to afford to our European sisters all possible assistance in acquiring the language. A European sister may do much for the cause in this respect by promoting the holiness and stirring up the zeal of the female converts."

In Part V of the Reports of the World's missionary conference of 1910 we read on India : "There is a strong desire among the men for the education of their daughters, sisters, and wives, and the women are generally ready to be taught. The women of India of the various castes are awakening to a sense of need and opportunity. They are seeking education for themselves, and are meeting in conventions for improvement and self-assertion. Here a wide field is opened up for the work of women missionaries and it is not surprising that from all the mission fields the call comes for a great increase in the number of lower and higher grade schools for girls." [23]

From this quotation to which many others could be added we may conclude that from the time of William Carey till our days the need for women-missionaries has been felt. Honour must be given to William Carey that he saw this problem as most urgent, and more clearly than any of his predecessors in India. In the wonderful work of the Moravian Church, women, both married and unmarried have borne their part in the Christian Mission.

In the ninth article he insists upon incessant labour in Biblical translations, but this article will be discussed when we deal with the Means of Missions in this Chapter.

The tenth article is of the utmost importance for any missionary, and home base worker. "That which, as a means, is to fit us for the discharge of these laborious and unutterably important labours is the being instant in prayer, and the cultivation of personal religion. Again we are reminded of the Moravians and especially of Brainerd, who in the woods of America, poured out his very soul to God for the perishing heathen, without whose salvation nothing could make him happy. Prayer, secret, fervent, believing prayer, lies at the root of all personal godliness. A competent knowledge of the languages current where a missionary lives, a mild and winning temper, and a heart given up in a closet religion, these are the attainments which more than all knowledge, or all other gifts, will fit us to become the instruments of God in the great work of human redemption. Let us then ever be united in prayer at stated seasons, whatever distance may separate us, and let each of us lay it upon his heart that we will seek to be fervent in spirit, wrestling with God, till He famish these idols and cause the heathen to experience the blessedness that is in Christ."

Splendid, beautiful words, worth to be read to each missionary when sent to the field, words inspired by a heart which loves the Lord.

Finally he writes: "Let us give ourselves unreservedly to this glorious cause. Let us never think that our time, our gifts, our strength, our families, or even the clothes we wear, are our own."

To keep these ideas alive in our minds, we resolve that this Agreement shall be read publicly at every station, at our three annual meetings, viz., on the first Lord's day in January, in May, and October."

To the question whether William Carey never relaxed in his extreme zeal for the missionary task given to him, the answer may be given in a letter of himself which I add in a note [24]).

He clearly saw the ideal of a missionary. He did not come up to this high standard himself, but he tried his utmost and expected the same of his colleagues.

We may draw some conclusions after this description of William Carey relating to the qualifications of the missionaries.

Missionaries must be pious men and be prepared to great sacrifices.

They must be preachers and craftsmen and must adhere to the idea of equality with the people.

Missionaries must as soon as possible become self-supporting and must not try to live in the same way as the rich Europeans, nor must they try to live with the natives in the same way as the Jesuists.

They must be men of calmness and evenness of temper, and live like the Moravians : equality for each and pre-eminence to none. (But he rejected the idea of a leader.)

They must at all times pay attention to the state of their own mind both towards God and men and must let love be the spring of conduct towards their wives. So they must be affable and genteel to all, but not cringing. They must be firm and manly.

They must begin their work as soon as they are settled and devote themselves as soon as possible to every branch of work on the field.

They must labour incessantly to become perfect masters of the language of the heathen and try to understand the situation and disposition of the aboriginal inhabitants, and see what they can do for them and make a careful description of customs, manners etc. of the people to whom they are sent.

Necessities of the mission must be consulted before every other consideration.

Missionaries must acknowledge Christ as their leader, but must take Paul and the disciples as their examples ; they must bear in mind : "God's decree from eternity and man's responsibility", and for that reason set an infinite value upon immortal souls. They must be well informed about the snares and delusions in which the heathen are held and abstain from those things which would increase the prejudices of the heathen against the Gospel. Those parts of English manners which are most offensive to them must be kept out of sight.

Missionaries must not "tell truths" to the people but Christ and his expiatory death must remain the great means of conversion and first of all they must press upon the converted heathen the great principles of the Gospel as a foundation of their hope towards God.

They must endeavour as much as possible to form the heathen in the habits of industry, and assist them in procuring such employments as may be pursued with the least danger of temptations to evil. (That with "industry" he really means industrialism and not only to be industrious is illuminated by his exertions to establish all kinds of work for the natives.)

They must bear the faults of their native brethren, and reprove them with tenderness and conquer the heathens by their personal examples, not only by their words.

Missionaries must try to get the assistance of the women-missionaries, and they must pray, secret, fervent, believing."

[1]) Dr. JAS S. DENNIS quoted by S. Pearce Carey (without mentioning the title of the book), op. cit., p. 68.

[2]) Dr. G. WARNECK, Evangelische Missionslehre. Ein missiontheoretischer Versuch. Erste Abteilung. Die Begründung der Sendung. Gotha 1897, p. XIII—XVI.

[3]) Cf. DEAVILLE WALKER, op. cit., p. 80, cf. the definition of Prof. Dr. J. H. BAVINCK : "Zending is die werkzaamheid van de kerk, waardoor zij in blijde en nederige gehoorzaamheid aan het bevel van Christus, het evangelie van Gods genade predikt aan alle volken. Missionary work is the activity of the Church in preaching the Gospel of Grace to all peoples in glad and humble obedience according to the command of Jesus Christ., op. cit., p. 5, 6, 7. G. WARNECK, Evangelische Missionslehre : "Unter Christliche mission, verstehen wir die gesamte auf die Pflanzung und Organisation der christlichen Kirche unter Nichtchristen gerichtete Thätigkeit der Christenheit." p. 1.

[4]) WILLIAM CAREY, An Inquiry etc. Reprinted in Facsimile from the edition of MDCCXCII. London. Hodder and Stoughton MDCCCXCI, p. 3.

[5]) WARNECK, op. cit., p. 182. Begründung der Sendung, cf. also Dr. J. H. BAVINCK, Ons Zendingsboek, p. 109—110.

[6]) Cf. S. PEARCE CAREY, p. 72 and DEAVILLE WALKER, p. 84.

[7]) S. PEARCE CAREY, op. cit., p. 73.

[8]) DEAVILLE WALKER, op. cit., p. 91.

[9]) GEORGE SMITH, The life of William Carey, p. 114. Cf. also p. 115 where Dr. George Smith says : "Scotland was the next to take up the challenge by Carey ; then he relates the establishment of the Scottish Missionary Society, and also of the Church Missionary Society, of the Nederlandsch Zendelinggenootschap by Dr. VAN DER KEMP, who had studied at Edinburgh University and the establishment of the British and Foreign Bible Society. All these activities came ultimately from the same source : the Inquiry of William Carey.

[10]) MARSHMAN, op. cit. Vol. I, p. 395.

[11]) A most interesting article is a report of W. H. GISPEN in ,,de Macedonier, Algemeen Zendingstijdschrift Leiden 1890". 8e jaargang. p. 280.

[12]) Dr. G. SMITH, op. cit., p. 113.

[13]) DEAVILLE WALKER, op. cit., p. 106.

[14]) Dr. GEORGE SMITH, op. cit., p. 80.

[15]) Ibid., p. 80.

[16]) Mededeelingen vanwege het Nederlandsch Zendelinggenootschap. By P. H. VAN DER KEMP. Rotterdam 1917.

[17]) In principle my father was resolute and firm, never shrinking from avowing and maintaining his sentiments. He had conscientious scruples against taking an oath ; and condemned severely the manner in which oaths were administered, and urged vehemently the propriety of altogether dispensing with them. I remember three instances in which he took a conspicuous part with regard to oaths, such as was characteristic of the man. On one occasion when a respectable Hindoo servant of the college of Fort William, attached to Dr. Carey's department, was early one morning proceeding to the Ganges to bathe, he perceived a dead body lying near the road : but it being dark and no person being present, he passed on taking no further notice of the circumstance. As he returned from the Ganges after sunrise, he saw a crowd near the body, and then happened to say to one of the watchmen present that in the morning he saw the body on the other side of the road. The watchman took him into custody, as a witness before the coroner ; but, when brought before the coroner, he refused to take an oath, and was, consequently, committed to prison for contempt. The Hindoo being a respectable person, and never having taken an oath, refused to take any nourishment in the prison. In this state he continued a day and a half, my father being then at Serampore ; but upon his coming to Calcutta, the circumstances were mentioned to him. The fact of the man having refused to take an oath was enough to make him interest himself in his behalf. He was delighted with the resolution the man took—rather to go to prison than to take an oath ; and was determined to do all he could to procure his liberation. He first applied to the coroner, but was directed by him to the

sheriff. To that functionary he proceeded, but was informed by him that he could make no order on the subject. He then had a interview with the then chief judge, by whose interference the man was set at liberty.

Another instance relates to him personally. On the occasion of his last marriage, the day was fixed on which the ceremony was to take place—friends were invited—and all necessary arrangements made; but three of four days prior to the day fixed, he was informed that it would be necessary for him to obtain a license, in doing which he must either take an oath, or have banns published. To taking an oath he at once objected, and applied to the then senior judge who informed him that, as he was not a Quaker, his oath was indispensable; but rather than take an oath, he applied to have the banns published, and postponed the arrangements for his marriage for another three weeks.

The duties connected with the College of Fort William afforded him a change of scene, which relieved his mind and gave him an opportunity of taking exercise, and conduced much to his health. During the several years he held the situation of professor to the college, no consideration would allow him to neglect his attendance; and though he had to encounter boisterous weather in crossing the river at unseasonable hours, he was punctual in his attendance, and never applied for leave of absence. GEORGE SMITH, op. cit., p. 419.

[18]) ROBERT E. SPEER D.D. Christ the leader of the missionary work of the church. History records and addresses World missionary conference 1910. Vol. IX, p. 153.

[19]) Prof. Dr. H. KRAEMER, The Christian message in a non christian world. London 1938, p. 366.

[20]) Rev. W. PATON. Industrialism an international Issue Vol. V. Christianity and the growth of Industrialism in Asia, Africa and south Amerika. Jerusalem 1928. Oxford 1928, p. 12—13, 181—182. Cf. also "Evangelische Missions-Zeitschrift". Fünfter Jahrgang. Heft 2, p. 255 with article 2 of the Form of Agreement.

[21]) W. PATON. World Community . London 1938, p. 30, cf. Verslagen der Ned. Afdeeling van het Zend. Genootschap der Engelsche Baptisten te Serampore in Oost-Indië. First Report, p. 10 by Mr. MULLER.

[22]) Dr. J. H. BAVINCK, op. cit., p. 50.

[23]) Carrying the Gospel World missionary conference 1910. Vol. I, p. 151—152. Cf. also Vol. V where Miss A. H. SMALL, principal of the women's missionary college of Edinburgh, issues a short paper dealing with the principles which have guided her in the work of this college. Very interesting is also Chapter XI of Vol. VI in which chapter we found a description of the women's work at the home base, p. 201—206. Cf. also London Missionary Conference. Vol. II, p. 140—160.

[24]) MARSHMAN, op. cit., p. 432. Vol. I. publishes a letter of William Carey in which he gives an honest confession of his struggles and difficulties. The letter is written about 1810. "When I first entered on the translation of the Scriptures into the Bengalee language, I thought that if ever I should live to see it completed, I could say with Simeon, 'Lord, now lettest thou thy servant depart in peace, according to thy word'; but he has preserved me not only to see the version finished, but has given me an opportunity of making many corrections, in succeeding editions, in various parts of it, and also has preserved me to see portions of the Bible printed in Orissa, Sanskrit, Hindoostanee, Mahratta, Carnata, Telinga, and Punjabee, Matthew in Chinese, and a beginning in the Burmese translation." Then in a letter of a later date he says : "I have often thought that the work must be obstructed by me and that the God who aboundeth in all wisdom and prudence in the dispensations of his grace, could not give a blessing from that wisdom and prudence which he always observes. I have often been discouraged on account of that apparent want of every pre-requisite for publishing the Gospel, both natural and moral, of which I am undoubtedly the subject. A natural backwardness for spiritual conversation, a perpetual vagrancy of mind, and uncommon barrenness of idea, a great prevalence of unsanctified affection, to which I may now add a great decay of recollection, have long pressed me down, and convinced me that the ministry of the Gospel is not the work for which I am fitted. I have for years been obliged to drag myself on, to subject myself to rules , to impose the day's work upon myself, to stir myself up to my work, perhaps sometimes several times in an hour and after all, to sit down in confusion at my indolence and inertness in all to which I set my hand. I often

compare myself with my brethren, particularly Brethren Marshman and Ward, with whose daily conduct I am best acquainted. The first of these is all eagerness for the work. Often have I seen him, when we have been walking together, eye a group of persons, as a hawk looks on its prey, and go up to them with a resolution to try the utmost strength of the Gospel reasons upon them. Often have I known him engage with such ardour in a dispute with men of lax conduct or deistical sentiments, and labour the point with them for hours together without fatigue, nay, more eager for the contest, when he left off than when he began, as has filled me with shame. In point of zeal he is Luther, and I am Erasmus. Brother Ward has such a facility of adressing spiritual things to the heart, and his thoughts run so naturally in that channel, that he fixes the minds of all who hear him on what he says, while I, after making repeated efforts, can scarcely get out a few dry sentences, and should I meet with a rebuff at the beginning sit like a silly mute, and scarcely say anything at all. Reflections such as these have occasioned and still do occasion me much distress." These "complexes" are psychologically easy to explain. But we stand aghast when such a man makes such a confession. At any rate : even this great man was a man just like all others : a sinner, with his virtues and vices. Just on this account we love his character all the better and admire his achievements.

c. The education of the missionaries.

When we come to deal with the attitude of William Carey towards the education of the missionaries, we must distinguish between his period in England from that in India.

When in England he laid more stress upon the qualifications of character of the missionaries than upon their educational training. Later on we will see his connection in this respect with the Moravians. Here we only say that it is not quite correct that the Moravians sent uneducated men, and that they accepted almost everybody who wished to go to the missionary field. [1])

But as a whole he adhered to the principle of the Moravians. He had studied their Periodicals and had without doubt met their missionaries in Northampton. When in England he wanted Ward and Marshman, who only had qualifications of character, but they were not educated men.

When in India his thoughts changed materially upon this point. His contact with the Brahmins, his own difficulties with the languages of the Indians, his growing understanding of the task of a missionary, were factors in his changed vision upon educational training of missionaries.

There may have been still another cause. For when Wellesley arrived at Calcutta "he had been shocked by the godless vice and sensual ignorance of the Company's servants. Sunday was universally given up to horse-racing and gambling. Boys of sixteen were removed from the English public schools where they had hardly mastered the rudiments of education to become the magistrates, judges, revenue collectors, and governors of millions of natives recently brought under British sway. At a time when the passions most need regulation and the conscience training, these lads found themselves in the presidency towns or interior of India with large incomes, flattered by native subordinates, encouraged by their superiors to lead lives of dissipation, and without the moral control of even the weakest public opinion. The Eton boy and Oxford man was himself still young, and he knew the world, but he saw that all this meant ruin to both the civil and military services, and to the Company's system." [2])

Marshman even says: "The men who were to undertake the important offices of judges, magistrates, collectors, and ambassadors were considered sufficiently qualified for their duties, if they were versed in the mysteries of the counting house, wrote a legible hand, and understood book-keeping by double entry. Some of the writers, as the young civilians were called, consisted, however of youths who had been educated at the public schools in England ; but they were withdrawn from their studies at the premature age of fourteen or fifteen, before their education was completed. No arrangements were made by the local government to prepare the civilians, after their arrival in Calcutta, for the discharge of the important duties, which were to devolve on them ; and they were nominated to the highest posts of government without any evidence of their qualifications for them." [3])

In our survey of the life of William Carey we mentioned that Lord Wellesley after having written his magnificent state paper of 1800, which he termed "Notes on the necessity of a special college training of civil Servants", established the famous College of Fort William. The curriculum of study included Arabic, Persian, and Sanskrit ; Bengali, Marathi, Hindosthani, Telugu, Tamil and Kanarese, English, the Company's, Mohammedan and Hindoo law, civil jurisprudence, and the law of nations ; ethics ; political economy, history, geography, and mathematics ; the Greek, Latin and English classics, and the modern languages of Europe ; the history and antiquities of India ; natural history, botany, chemistry, and astronomy. [4])

We also mentioned that Mr. Brown urged Carey to take charge of the Bengali and Sanskrit classes as "teacher", which office was entirely in the line of the constitution of the missionary brotherhood. He writes to Dr. Ryland on June 15, 1801 : "I always highly approved of the institution, but never entertained a thought that I should be called to fill a station in it. I had just time to call our brethren together, who were of opinion that, for several reasons, I ought to accept it, provided it did not interfere with the work of the mission. Both Brown and Buchanan were of opinion that the cause of the mission would be furthered by it ; and I was not able to reply to their arguments.''

From these facts we conclude that gradually the necessity of good education for missionaries was realized. Of course he knew the bad training of the officials of government. But yet his friend had to urge him to accept the "professorship", which advice he reluctantly followed, "not being able to reply their arguments".

Afterwards he reaps the fruits of his professorship when many of the students are influenced by him in such a way that they become his faithful helpers. [5]) In a later period he established his famous Serampore college for the education of natives. But we won't discuss this now as it belongs to the paragraph of "The Means of the missions". We only wish to state here, that he gradually grew conscious of the necessity of some education of the missionaries themselves. Dr. George Smith says : "As planned by Carey in 1793, the constitution had founded the enterprise on these three corner-stones : *preaching the Gospel* in the mother tongue of the people, *translating the Bible* into all languages of Southern and Eastern Asia, *teaching the young*, both heathen and Christian, both boys and girls in vernacular schools. But Carey had not been a year in Serampore when he began to see that a fourth must be laid some day in the shape of a college. This, however, does not mean that he wanted to have thoroughly educated *missionaries*. The fourth enterprise is a College for *the natives*. Afterwards many missionaries came from England without a special training for missionary activity. There are indeed excuses for William Carey. Nevertheless we must conclude that he did not lay enough stress upon the training of the missionaries at *home*, whatever may have been his accomplishments in India.

Dr. H. Kraemer states that Dr. ADRIANI pleaded for the appointment of a teacher of languages at the Missionary school at *Oegstgeest, Holland*; this means at the Home base and that he propagated the idea that fundamental knowledge is a conditio sine qua non for a *missionary*. [6])

And Dr. BROUWER writes in his pamphlet "De Opleiding onzer zendelingen": In England and America they are now ($\pm$ 1910) preparing for some special training for missionaries. Up to this time very little has been done in this respect for missionary preparation. There may have been some shortened academic preparation in comparative history of religion and mission, but they lacked knowledge of the country, of the people, of the language. Often they preached the Gospel by means of an interpreter. Therefore Prof. Warneck once said, according to Dr. Brouwer, "It seems that our English brethren understood the commission of our Lord in this way : 'Go and teach all peoples English'."

Dr. Brouwer goes on to say that the complaints of the ignorance of the missionaries were many. And that the warning of Dr. ALEXANDER P. CAMPHOR is of importance : "Africa suffered very much in the past time from ill-prepared missionaries." One of the results of the Edinburgh conference has been that they will try with all means to correct this mistake. Dr. Brouwer gives in a note further evidences of these facts. [7])

We may draw our conclusion and say that William Carey when in England, laid more stress upon the qualifications of character than upon educational training. But when in India he gradually saw the necessity of missionaries as educated men from his own experience of their inadequacy and from the bad example of government officials.

He held no plea for a special college training for missionaries in England, but established a college for native missionaries at Serampore.

d. The financial support of missionaries.

From the very beginning of his missionary activities at home we may state that he adhered to the convictions of the Moravians relating to the support of the missionaries. On page 136/137 we indicated his opinion as shown in his Enquiry relating to the difficulties of procuring the necessaries of life. As one of the tasks of the committee he states that they have to provide them with the necessaries for their undertakings. [8])

We can understand his opinion at once when we quote a letter written by him to his sister on the 11th of March 1795 : "It was always my opinion that missionaries may and must support themselves after having been sent out, and receive a little support at first, and in consequence I pursue a very little wordly employment which requires three months' closest attendance in the year ; but this is in the rains—the most unfavourable season for exertion. My manner of travelling is with two small boats ; one serves me to live in, and the other for cooking my food. I carry all my furniture and food with me from place to place, viz. a chair, a table, a bed, a lamp. I walk from village to village, but repair to my boat for lodging and eating." [9])

Later on when he is in Serampore he adopts a better way of living. But his principle of missionary economy remains the same.

S. Pearce Carey says : "He believed in the Moravian plan of communal settlements—for at least, as he said, a mission's early years—as best securing economy, fraternity and efficiency." And later he says : "The Settlement's salvation lay in their unanimous agreement to disallow all trading and labour for personal gain, to pool all earnings, to distribute for each family according to its necessities, and to consecrate the whole surplus to the Mission's advance. Herein they strictly followed Moravian precedent." [10]) About 1800 the missionaries determined to engage in business for their own support and to throw their profits into a common stock, but without reserving anything for themselves, as Marshman states. Neither the Christian Knowledge Society nor any other missionary Society thought it their duty to send missionaries to support them in such a way that they could live without care. But some of the missionaries were able to accumulate a little independence, which they disposed at their discretion. And neither the London Miss. Society nor the Christian Knowledge Society dreamt of assuming any control of the earnings of the missionaries. Marshman gives the example of SCHWARTZ who bequeathed his money to people of his own choice and his colleague GERICKE left £ 5000 at his death. When there was a deficiency missionaries were advised to make up this deficiency by taking pupils as KIERNANDER had done before. But the Serampore missionaries adopted the novel principle of divesting themselves of all right of property and consecrating it exclusively to the cause in which they had embarked by the formation of a common stock. [11])

Fuller did not agree with this principle of self-denial. He thought they had carried it too far. When he proposed that the missionaries should appropriate their income for one year, the members of the Committee demurred at the proposal, although they had not either by express stipulation or by analogy of missionary arrangements the slightest control in the matter. When the missionaries at Serampore heard of these discussions Marshman wrote to Fuller, who wanted the missionaries to express their own desires without restraint : "I cannot but feel your kindness in the most sensible manner. I am glad however, you did not resolve on what you intended. So far from having any wish of the kind, I myself— and I am sure I can answer for Mrs. Marshman and my dear brethren — esteem it as one of the greatest favours conferred upon me that I am permitted, by the labour of my hands, to contribute in any small degree to the support of His cause, to whom I owe 'my life, my soul, my all'."

Ogilvie states in his biography, that the grants promised from the Society amounted only to £ 360 a year for all the six families. That during the first three years of their residence in India, Carey and his companions received in all only £ 200 from home ; and he gives the reason of this attitude : "the missionaries being supposed not only to preach the Gospel, but also as far as possible to support themselves". Apostolic lines were followed : hence the farming in the Soondarbuns, hence the indigoo factory at Mudnabatti, and hence the practice of more than Spartan economy. Simplicity of living was a sheer necessity, and by adopting the Moravian Brotherhood system, they sought to reduce the expenses to a minimum. [12])

We have mentioned before that Carey received for his service to the Government a salary of £ 600, which soon afterwards was raised to £ 1500. All went into the common purse. From this fund the Marshmans received thirty rupees per month for their private expenses, Ward twenty and Carey for himself and his family fifty. I also stated that from first to last Carey's contributions amounted to over £ 46.000 while from the Society at home the donations in the same period did not come up to £ 2000. To his son Jabez William Carey writes in 1814 : "Remember that the money which you will expend is neither ours nor yours, for it has been consecrated to God. In building especially remember that you are a poor man and have chosen a life of poverty and self-denial, with Christ and his missionary servants. If another person is profuse in expenditure the consequence is small because his property would perhaps fall into hands where it might be devoted to the purposes of iniquity : but missionary funds are in their very circumstances the most sacred and important of anything of this nature on earth."

Later on disharmony arose between the home Committee and the old Missionaries. Indeed they had all their earnings vested in the Society. They only asked to be trusted in their holding and use. They wished to be left free to choose their own colleagues, to appoint their successors, and they wished to be the unchallenged masters in their own domain. The home Committee on the other hand asked full control after the death of Fuller. On this account Carey and his colleagues felt themselves mistrusted.

Now all these difficulties might have been prevented if arrangements and stipulations had been made beforehand. The attitude of the home Committee towards the Missionaries in Serampore was a vague one. Hence the disharmony.

We conclude that while the pecuniary task of the home Committee was limited to the necessaries for the voyage and the first expenditure on the field, the missionaries were on the other hand expected to support themselves as soon as possible.

e. The marriage of missionaries.

We have already quoted the words of Carey to his son Jabez when he wrote to him : "A gentleman is the next best character after a christian, and the latter includes the former." We also mentioned the sufferings of William Carey, caused by the ill temper and dementia of his wife. Some biographers try to excuse her for her reproachful tongue and her misdemeanour towards Carey in difficult days, but whatever the excuses may be, never did reproach or complaint escape from the lips of William Carey. On the contrary, he was a tender guardian even when she tried to kill him. Later on he was married to Lady Rhumohr and still later to Grace Hughes.

He enjoyed a complete oneness of mind with these women, particularly with Lady Rhumohr.

In his early days as a missionary he writes many letters emphasizing the need to send missionaries and women who are a real help to their husbands. Women with a wise heart who have great love for the missionary work, etc.

As regards the question whether a missionary must be married or not, he does not give his opinion as far as we can judge.

We have the impression that he preferred married missionaries to unmarried. Most of the men who came to him were married. As Carey showed himself a very wise man, we venture to guess that his advice would have been : send married missionaries to the field, as the temptations of the unmarried, especially in the India of his days were very great. Definite conclusions, however, are impossible.

f. Auxiliary missionairies

When we deal with the question of auxiliary missionaries, we don't mean the natives who after some instruction help the missionaries, or who act as itinerant booksellers. The question is here whether from the home base some professional workers should be sent to the missionaries to assist them. [13] The answer given to this question by Carey is a strange and rather difficult one. On the one side he gives an affirmative answer, on the other side a negative one. Negative when more than once he asks the home-Committee to send *missionaries*, no coadjutors ; but affirmative when on closer inspection they prove to be no missionaries at all e.g. Ward was a printer and Marshman was a schoolmaster.

The cause of this ambiguous attitude lies in his love for the Moravian conception of missionaries. Here we only state that his idea of a missionary was : a man (or woman) sent by the committee to the field who was willing to live with them according to the Moravian plan. But with one great difference : he wished them to act upon the principle : 'call no man master'. Bishop SPANGENBERG wanted a House father to suppress dissensions etc. But Carey diverged from this scheme by determining that there should be equality for each, pre-eminence to none ; rule by majority, submission to that rule ; allocation of function by collective vote ; superintendence by each in monthly rotation, including as quickly as possible, purchase of supplies, presidency of the common table, keeping accounts, direction of the servants, interviewing callers, and the conduct of the weekly English service. [14]

When these missionaries were called to be one in the team they indeed trembled almost before they began to live together. Ward wrote a letter, which clearly speaks of his scruples. For no less than five and a half years William Carey had been the sole authority on the missionary field and now he had to be one of the team and "to be treated as a freshman", as equal with the others.

From this we understand that the problem of coadjutors and of missionaries subordinate to himself did not exist. He contemplated the helps as missionaries ; it never entered his mind to look upon Marshman and Ward as his assistants. They were his colleagues.

Later on when juniors were sent they were treated in the same way as the senior missionaries. The latter had managed to steer their ship through the most violent tempests. They had shown a combination of the highest prudence, and energy. Now according to his Moravian plan the junior missionaries had to take the helm, whatever were their abilities and prudence. We are not surprised that Dr. Ryland writes in one of his letters to Carey and his colleagues : "Who of us (members of the Committee at home) ever advocated the democratic nonsense of every apprentice we send you being equal the moment he set his foot on Bengal ground ? You may have had such notions ; we never infused them into your mind." [15])

Then Fuller writes to the missionaries "that they think it their duty to counteract that baneful system" and to the juniors "that if such factious antagonism was not discontinued, the committee would feel it their painful duty to recall those who appeared so impracticable."

Then Carey held a meeting of all the missionaries. It was unanimously agreed that "the brethren at Serampore, as well as those at subordinate stations, should hereafter choose their own *coadjutors*". Marshman tells us further that each station should be independent as to its family connections, and that those who formed it should be associated together only by their own consent ; that these distinct families and stations should constitute one general Mission, with a committee and a secretary to transact business at Serampore. The three senior missionaries formed the Committee, and ROWE was appointed for the secretary. The deviation from the Moravian plan was executed after they had experienced its inadequacy.

Moreover the Moravian system in its original form was far better than the "democratic" system of William Carey. This may be still more conclusive as some of the missionaries sent by the committee were "raw men, perhaps religious adventures." One of "their colleagues" told Ward, once wanted to go to the West Indies as a clerk, or something in a plantation ; then to become an officer ; last of all he became a missionary. Ward ends this report : "He is really a good man, but to him the Missionary is a sinecure." [16])

Here we learn once more that the idea of a missionary was not a definite one either with the Committee nor with William Carey.

On account of this failure we can't speak of auxiliary missionaries as Warneck does. The young "missionaries" were made "auxiliary missionaries", when they were in India. But the home committee did not send helpers to the real missionaries.

Later on in 1808 difficulties arose again. Therefore the controlling authority was delegated to the Serampore three. They were able to act with more decision in the government of mission as the representatives of the Society. But the pooling of all the money into one purse involved a great limitation of personal freedom and great sacrifice of personal and social comfort. Then the juniors complained that Dr. Carey and his colleagues had created a system of Moravian self-denial without Moravian equality. The Society, however, regarded the seniors more as fathers than as masters to their younger brethren. But to no effect. The senior missionaries were at last overpowered by opposition of the juniors and driven to adopt a new constitution for the mission. Marshman gives the contents of this document. In a letter received from the Committee the missionaries (seniors) were requested to act as managers of the mission for life, whereas the choice of their successors would be regulated by the Society. The time, they said, has now arrived for their missionary brethren to serve the cause in the separate stations, and, in reality, to form distinct missions. The number of missionaries embraced in this new plan, was seven, and it was proposed to fix the allowance at seventy rupees a month for each missionary and his wife, ten rupees a month being added for the first and seven rupees for each succeeding child. The expense of the seven missionaries would thus—at the exchange of the day—amount to £ 1000 annually. Out of this salary, the missionary was at liberty to reserve a small sum, not exceeding ten rupees a month as a personal allowance(!), and he was to furnish a detailed account of the expenditure of the rest, to be transmitted to the Society. Any surplus which might remain out of this very scant provision was not to be considered in the light of individual property, because this would be repugnant to the leading principle of the mission, and by encouraging a sordid concern for petty savings, eat out every missionary feeling. Every sum obtained by the labour of any of the missionaries was to be inserted in the monthly accounts as mission property. The children of the missionaries were to be educated, free of all expense to the parents, at Serampore, where an asylum and a suitable allowance were, also to be provided for the widows and the orphan. [17])

A few years after the death of Fuller it expired. But as an example of self-sacrifice this document is worth keeping in memory. We described in our survey of the life of Carey that once more struggles arose between the juniors and the seniors. We don't think it necessary to recall them. The real cause of all these struggles is clear. Stipulations regulating the relation between the missionaries are absent. Instructions definitely describing the task of all the junior missionaries towards the seniors are not given by the committee. So we conclude that there really were auxiliary missionaries, but the Moravian plan of working brought them on the level of "missionaries". Later on they were called "auxiliary missionaries", but their attitude towards the missionaries remains ambiguous. Absence of accurate prescriptions are the main cause of the disharmony.

As for the women auxiliaries we refer to the preceding paragraph. Here we only state that neither the Committee nor William Carey made accurate prescriptions for these women. But he highly appreciated the work of the "first woman missionary to India". She is called HANNAH MARSHMAN. Grand-daughter of the Baptist minister of Crockerton in Wiltshire, she proved to be for forty-six years a loving wife, and the equal of the three missionaries of Christ, whom she aided in the common home, in the schools, in the congregation, in the Native Christian families, and even, at that early time, in purely Hindoo circles. Without her the mission must have been one-sided indeed. It is still an occasion of pathetic interest to us to turn to her household books, where we find entered with loving care and thoughtful thrift all the daily details which at once form a valuable contribution to the history of prices, and show how her "prudences" combined with the heroic self-denial of all to make the Serampore mission the light of India. This statement was made in 1800. But in 1827 we read in the Brief Memoir of the Brotherhood much more of this woman-missionary : "The education of females, till within these few years, had never been attempted ; and not a few were disposed to regard the experiment as one which must prove altogether in vain. This, however, was a great mistake. In Serampore and its vicinity there are at present fourteen schools composed entirely of Hindoo females, among which are the Liverpool and Chatham, the Edinburgh and the Glasgow, the Stirling and Dunfermline schools etc. Besides these, one is established at Benares, another at Allahabad, a third in Beerbhoom, three at Chittagong, and seven at Dacca ; twenty-seven in all, with 554 pupils on the lists. One of these in the vicinity of Serampore may be regarded as an unprecedented thing : an *adult female school*, in which the women who have entered have shown themselves quite desirous to receive instruction. The daughters of Mohammedans as well as Hindoos, indeed, receive instruction with evident delight : and into these schools, whether for boys or girls, the sacred Scriptures are freely admitted." [18])

In Calcutta, after the separation had taken place, the wives of the two younger missionaries, Mrs. Pearce and Mrs. Lawson, *who had been trained at Serampore* conducted a school on the plan of Mrs. Marshman's, and encouraged the young ladies, some of whom became the wives of missionaries, to open schools for native girls. [19])

We may learn from these quotations that the idea of missionary is airy. Hannah Marshman had indeed very great qualities and has been of the greatest importance for the work of William Carey. But she is not a missionary in the common sense of the word. Her task was limited to school service.

This letter also shows that the education of the "missionaries" took place in India, not in England. When we discuss the instruments or means of the missionary task we hope to speak of some of the ideas of William Carey on schools. Here we only state that women as auxiliary missionaries are not known by him. Men and women are alike in this respect, they are simply missionaries.

NOTES

[1]) Cf. Prof. Dr. J. H. BAVINCK, Ons Zendingsboek, p. 120.
[2]) Dr. GEORGE SMITH, op. cit., p. 213.
[3]) MARSHMAN. Vol. I, op. cit., p. 142. 143.
[4]) Dr. GEORGE SMITH, p. 215.
[5]) Cf. "Tweede Verslag der Nederlandsche Afdeeling van het Zendeling genootschap der Engelsche Baptisten te Serampore in Oost-Indië". Some missionaries have died, but then we read : "Wy kunnen echter met een dankbaar gevoel hierbij voegen, dat de verliezen, welke het moedergenootschap te Serampore geleden heeft, staan vergoed te worden, of reeds weder vergoed zijn door kinderen van de vorige zendelingen en door inlandsche kweekelingen uit de school te Calcutta afkomstig."
We may thankfully add, that the losses, which the Mother-society suffered at Serampore, are about to be repaired or have already been repaired by the children of the former missionaries, and by the native students of the Calcutta college.
[6]) Dr. H. KRAEMER, "Schets en leven van Dr. N. ADRIANI". Paris. A'dam 1935, p. 46.

[7]) Dr. A. M. BROUWER, "De Opleiding onzer Zendelingen", p. 7 and 8. Hollandia Drukkerij. Cf. also Miss. Conference London 1888, p. 3—26, where we find discussions upon this theme.
[8]) Enquiry by WILLIAM CAREY, p. 71.
[9]) Dr. GEORGE SMITH, op. cit., p. 98.
[10]) S. PEARCE CAREY, op. cit., p. 192 and 194.
[11]) MARSHMAN, op. cit., p. 208—211.
[12]) OGILVIE, op. cit., p. 307, 312, 329.
[13]) Cf. GUSTAV WARNECK, Die Organe der Sendung. Gotha 1897, p. 231.
[14]) S. PEARCE CAREY, op. cit., p. 194.
[15]) M. MARSHMAN, op. cit., p. 302.
[16]) Ibid., p. 303.
[17]) Ibid., p. 403—406.
[18]) Dr. GEORGE SMITH, op. cit., p. 360—376.
[19]) Ibid., p. 127 and 403.

Par. III. The Management of the Mission.

A. THE TERRITORY OF THE MISSIONFIELD.

a. The circumference of the missionary field.

The principles relating to the circumference and the limits of the missionary field are very clear.

When writing his Enquiry we are confronted with the dull state of affairs of the whole world. His conclusions, full of statistics purposely aim at *world* missionary action. The last words of these conclusions may suffice to prove this statement : "All these things are loud calls to Christians and especially to ministers, to exert themselves to the utmost in their several spheres of action, and to try to enlarge them as much as possible." (P. 66.) "When on his voyage to India the Captain hastened on and passed Cape Horn instead of putting in at some harbour here, which was a disappointment for Carey. He had planned to seek out some Dutch minister of the Settlement and, with what Dutch he knew, constrain him to disclose to British Christendom and the Kettering Society South Africa's spiritual dearth."

After arriving in Bengal he writes in this way : "I hope the Society will go on and increase, and that the multitudes of heathen in the world may hear the glorious word of truth. Africa is but a little away from England ; Madagascar but a little way further ; South Africa, and all the numerous and large islands in the Indian and Chinese seas, I hope will not be passed over. A large field opens on every side, and millions of perishing heathens, tormented in this life by idolatry, superstition, and ignorance, and exposed to eternal miseries in the world to come, are pleading ; yea, all their miseries plead as soon as they are known, with every heart that loves God, and with all the churches of the living God. Oh, that many labourers may be thrust out into the vineyard of our Lord Jesus Christ, and that the gentiles may come to the knowledge of the truth as it is in Him !''

The next year 1794 he writes : ''I think the Society would do well to keep their eye towards Africa or Asia, countries which are not like the wilds of America where long labour will scarcely collect sixty people to hear the Word : for here it is almost impossible to get out of the way of hundreds, and preachers are wanted a thousand times more than people to preach to. Within India are the Maratha country and the northern parts to Kashmeer, in which, as far as I can learn, there is not one soul that thinks of God aright." [1]) It would be easy to give many more instances of this attitude. We will only state the following facts : when in Serampore he not only tries to convert the whole of India but tries to translate the Bible in *all the languages of the world* as he puts it. Afterwards he sends his sons as missionaries to the Dutch East Indies and other foreign missionary fields. He tries to fulfill the commission of the Lord : ''Make disciples of all the nations.''

The question of the boundaries of the missionary field was not very urgent. Almost the whole world was open to him except a few christian countries, and some territory in the south of India and a few other fields.

We conclude that the question of the circumference of the missionfield is answered in the same way as that of the missionary synod of Middelburg on Walcheren in 1896 : ''To all creatures.''

b. The differences on the missionary territory.

1. LINGUISTIC.

In our survey we more than once considered the linguistic abilities of William Carey and his senior colleagues. The question that concerns us here is this : what must be the attitude of the missionary towards the language of the people he tries to convert. For William Carey the answer is clear. ''The Missionary Magazine'', a periodical publication intended as a repository of discussion and intelligence respecting the progress of the Gospel throughout the world, contains an article of Dr. Carey as the outcome of his first two years' experience, to show ''The Peculiar Advantage of *Bengal*

174

as a Field for Missions from Great Britain". After describing the immense population, the highly civilised state of society, the eagerness of the natives in the acquisition of knowledge and the attachment of both the Mohammedans and Hindoos to their ancient systems as lessening every day, he says the following : "The language of Bengal is spoken over a vast extent of country. The preacher on the coast of Africa, in America, in Greenland, who has learned the language of the heathen, finds himself confined to a few hundreds of thousands of miserable Pagans ; and when he goes beyond the narrow limits of his tribe, or horde, is a barbarian to the neighbouring nations ; but the missionary who has learned the language of Bengal will have more millions to address than the others can find hundreds or thousands. The advantage of this can hardly be overestimated. Without any additional trouble of learning languages, to how wide an extent may he carry the glad tidings of salvation. And a translation of the Sacred Scriptures into this tongue will give millions and opportunity of perusing a book which can make them wise unto salvation, through faith which is in Christ Jesus . . . . But Bengal has a further recommendation. If the Gospel were once planted, and had taken deep root in that province, there would be a pleasing prospect of its being propagated through every part of Hindostan. That immense region contains a hundred and twenty millions of inhabitants. Should Bengal ever be converted to the faith of Christ, the way is plain and easy to every other province of the empire.

He also describes Bengal as in the centre of the southern part of Asia : China at no great distance in the East. Thibet and Tartary on the north. Beyond the ocean, Persia to the West, calls for the consolations of the Gospel, to cheer them amidst the darkness of Mohammedan delusion : while the swarthy sons of Pegu and Siam invite the messengers of peace to come and proclaim the glad tidings of life and immortality." [2])

In his Form of Agreement of 1805 he asserts : "It becomes us also to labour with all our might in forwarding translations of the Sacred Scriptures in the languages of Hindoostan. The help which God has afforded us already in this work is a loud call to us to go forward.

The Mission of Burmah commenced in the year 1807. The instructions given on their departure are as follows : "the language of the country in its different *dialects* and the best means of acquiring it—whether the natives have frequent intercourse with the neighbouring islands, and whether the language of those places could be learnt at Rangoon—must be investigated." [3])

From these quotations it is very clear that he does not only wish that missionaries study the different languages but they also must acquire the dialects of the people. Dr. ADRIANI when he was at Posso on Celebes also urged missionaries to study the dialects. Whatever may be the difficulties and whatever may be the amount of the dialects annihilation of these different tongues would be impoverishment. We conclude : William Carey wishes to address the natives in their own tongue and requires of missionaries that they thoroughly understand the native language.

2. CLIMATIC SITUATION OF THE MISSION FIELD.

The differences between the climate of the home land and the mission field are often of such an extent, that the question must be raised whether the Society at home can bear the responsibility to send men and women to the field.

We mentioned in our survey (page 63) that William Carey was prostrate with fever, and that his life was in danger. That his son Peter, five years old died after an illness of a few hours. That his wife was so deeply affected, also caused by the climatic trials in India, that she gradually became deprived of reason.

Later on when missionaries are sent to him at Serampore, some die on account of the strain put upon them through the hot climate, dysentery, fever and other Indian illnesses.

They did not yet live in the time of accurate medical and psychological research before being sent to India. So we fully understand that many of the Moravians in the West Indies and many of the missionary colleagues of Carey died in Bengal.

Indeed we may raise the question whether the sending of missionaries to India can be justified when we know beforehand that they will suffer or even die.

It is a pity that William Carey did not raise this problem.

3. NATIONAL AND CASTE DIFFERENCES ON THE MISSION FIELD.

In his famous Form of Agreement William Carey had stated that they considered it necessary to abstain from whatever would tend to increase the repugnance of the natives to wards the Gospel,

176

to keep out of sight those English peculiarities which were offensive to their feelings and at the same time avoid any attack on their prejudices by exhibiting any degree of acrimony against the sins of their gods, and on no account to do violence to their images or interrupt their worship—the real conquests of the Gospel being those of love. Article 2 and 3.   Now he struck not only a negative attitude but also a positive by establishing schools.   Especially in this way he hoped to bridge the national differences.   For after a few years he established at Serampore and neighbourhood a hundred vernacular schools.   These vernacular schools were most popular.   After some time they proved to be the feeders of the Church.   The missionaries wrote to England about these schools: "The whole plan must have been nipped in the bud, since, if the natives had not cheerfully sent their children, everything else would have been useless.   But the earnestness with which they have sought these schools exceeds everything we had previously expected.   We are still constantly importuned for more schools, although we have long gone beyond the extent of our funds."   So we understand that Carey very well understood the national feeling of the Indians.   We may even say just like Dr. George Smith: "by using books and tracts and by providing the literary form of the vernacular languages Carey laid down the foundation of the new national civilization." [4]

The foundation of his christian education was laid deep in the very nature of the people.   Foreign influences were omitted as much as possible, though the teachers were foreigners.   We must admire this great architect, who in this way solved the difficult problem of adaptation.   He acted up to his principles by bringing the Gospel and by avoiding any attack upon their prejudices and by building up a national feeling according to Scriptures.

Of course these schools and their results roused the hatred of the Brahmins.   They very well understood that he laid down the axe at the root of the heathen tree.   And when Golook the daughter of Krishna was denied to the Hindoo to whom she had been betrothed from infancy, the Brahmins seeing the whole structure of their society undermined, understood, that he menaced their caste system.   The consequences were that the mob seized some christians and took them before the magistrate.

But whatever the consequences might be, William Carey persisted with his principles and formed a new Christian national system, deprived of the caste differences and other pagan structures. Here we will state already that the missionaries knew very well that their Danish predecessors in South India had allowed converts to retain their caste, and caste distinctions were thus perpetuated within the Church of Christ. After considering the question very carefully, Carey understood that such an attitude does not agree with the principles of the Scriptures. These arbitrary social distinctions, such as the Hindu system imposes, are contrary to the rule of the Gospel: "one in Christ". Ogilvie writes when he discusses the influence of Ziegenbalg: "He laid down the lines on which his successors through the length and breadth of India have worked. It is true there have been many developments as the long years have passed. But except on one point there has been no abandonment of the main methods of missionary work adopted first by Bartholomew Ziegenbalg. The exception concerns his attitude to Caste, and his practical treatment of that problem in the infant church at Tranquebar. In this matter he was severely handicapped by two circumstances. The Roman missionaries had carried the recognition of caste to an extreme, thus prejudicing the native mind as to the pliability of the Christian religion in this connection and making it difficult for the first Protestant missionaries to adapt a radically different position. And, further these same missionaries were at the start entirely ignorant as to the true meaning and importance of caste, and lacked that experience of its evils which had led later Protestant missions, with the single exception of the Leipsic mission, to give it no quarter whatever in the Christian Church. Afterwards troubles arose in the Danish Church in Tranquebar. Separate places were assigned to the Sudras and to the Pariahs. They sat apart and at the celebration of the Holy Communion the Sudras, women as well as men, approached the Table before the Pariahs." [5]) Now we only state the fact.

This problem is of course still of the utmost importance. Different attitudes are taken towards it. Here we refer only to Dr. FRIEDRICH HEILER, who defends the caste system in the Christian Church.

At the London Conference in 1888 the Caste system was a subject of discussion, so it was at the Edinburgh Conference in 1910, in Jerusalem 1928 and in Tambaram 1939. [6])

In our Survey of Carey's life we referred to a Brahmin wedded

178

to a carpenter's child.   Many other examples might be given.   We conclude that the principles laid down in his Form of Agreement of Oct. 1805 were acted up to.   He laid down a sound foundation for a new national life of the Christian Indians by abolishing the arbitrary caste system with its cruel distinctions.   In this respect he showed himself a master-builder.

4. POLITICAL DIFFERENCES ON THE MISSIONARY FIELD.

In his seventh article of the Form of Agreement of 1805 Dr. Carey writes : "As we consider it our duty to honour the civil magistrate and in every state and country to render him the readiest obedience whether we be persecuted or protected, it becomes us to instruct our native brethren the same principles.   A sense of gratitude too presses this obligation upon us in a peculiar manner in return for the liberal protection we have experienced.   It is equally our wisdom and our duty also to show to the civil power that it has nothing to fear from the Progress of Missions, since a real follower of Christ must resist the example of his great Master and all the precepts the Bible contains on this subject, before he can become disloyal.   Converted heathens, being brought over to the religion of their Christian Governors, if duly instructed, are much more likely to love them, and be united to them, than subjects of a different religion."

Dr. Carey adhered to these principles in a remarkable way.   We saw the struggles between the Serampore triad and the East India Company.   We also saw how after the death of Lord Cornwallis Sir GEORGE BARLOW took up the reins of Government.   He was a weak man and very responsive to whatever influences were brought to bear upon him ; the struggles which arose after the arrival of Messrs Chater and Robinson and the Vellore mutiny and the influence of this mutiny in the Houses of Parliament in England are examples of the behaviour of William Carey towards Government even in days when the Governors seem to be unjustified in their measures, cf. p. 92 f.f.

Later on when the opposition which arose from Hindoo animosity was foiled, the attitude of William Carey and his colleagues was openly justified in India as well as in England.

One item is of major importance.   He disobeyed the Directors of the East India Company in going to India, when no missionary could get a license.   When other missionaries came to him, he advised them to come as labourers to his indigo factory. Afterwards we see the same attitude towards other men and women.

So when the question is raised in what measure William Carey obeyed the governors, we can't say: he was not in subjection to the laws of the higher power (Rom. 13 : 1). On the contrary. But when the laws of the Governors were contrary to the laws of God, he tried with all possible means to disobey them. As e.g. when it is not permitted to send missionaries to the stations, and the missionary activity had to be limited to the Danish settlement.

Two questions are raised here. First whether a Government is justified in prohibiting the sending of Missionaries to any missionary field, and secondly does not a Government exceed the limits of its power towards the missionaries and their activities, when it meddles with the affairs of the missionaries? William Carey gave an answer to both.

To the first he gave a negative answer. To the second he answered that the extent of their power reached only so far that whatever their measures, it should not prevent the missionary activities, in so far as these activities did not purposely interfere with reasonable laws.

Further we fully agree with JOHN CLARK MARSHMAN when he states in his preface to his famous work on the Serampore Triad: "It is contrary to all sound policy and to the interests of Christian truth, that Christianity should be propagated in India by the direct instrumentality, or the direct aid, of Government. From every attempt to evangelise the country, it is the bounden duty of Government most conscientiously and most scrupulously to abstain." The spread of the Gospel is the exclusive province of the missionary and he must not appear as the delegate of the state. Dr. Carey in discussing this subject made a remark which should be kept in mind. "Whatever government may do, let it not touch my work ; it can only succeed in making men hypocrites ; I wish to make them Christians." At the same time it would be unworthy of a great, powerful and enlightened government to shrink, as the Government of India has hitherto done, from avowing its Christian character. It is to be lamented that the public authorities in India have been too much disposed to keep their religion in the back-ground, as if they were ashamed or afraid to acknowledge it in the presence of the heathen. It is a fallacy to suppose that we shall lose the confidence of the natives by the manly avowal of our creed. The Hindoos and the Mohammedans are men of such intense religious feeling that they cannot be expected to entertain any respect for those who do not manifest the same strength of attachment to their own religion. They cannot believe in the existence of religious indifference in a government, and our profession of perfect neutrality has only tended to bring our motives under suspicion, and to complicate our relations with them. The soundest policy is to adopt a just and fearless course ; to tell our native subjects that the government of the Crown is a Christian Government, and regulated by christian principles, that, although it believes Christianity to be the only true religion, and desires to see it prevail throughout India, yet, in obedience to its principles, it will employ neither force nor fraud to convert its subjects, but will continue to allow them the fullest liberty of conscience, and to permit every man to profess and practise his own religion without any interference." [7])

The powerful words of Marshman are worth keeping in mind by any christian Government. And they are also of infinite value for every missionary activity at home and abroad.

We conclude that William Carey did not agree with a government when prohibiting the sending of missionaries to India. That he behaved loyally towards Government even when he was treated roughly and unjustly. That he would not permit government to touch his missionary work as the spreading of the Gospel according to his view is the exclusive province of the missionaries in heathen countries.

5. CULTURAL DIFFICULTIES ON THE MISSION FIELD.

In his Enquiry William Carey states "that the missionaries to the Germans and Gauls and Britons did not wait for the ancient inhabitants of these countries to be civilized, before they could be christianized, but simply went with the doctrine of the cross. The uncivilized state of the heathen, instead of affording an objection *against* preaching the Gospel to them, ought to furnish an argument *for* it. Would not the spread of the Gospel be the most effectual means of their civilization ? Would not that make them useful members of society ? Cf. Elliot and Brainerd." (P. 69/70.)

The cardinal question is indeed touched by this great man in this part of his Enquiry. For the question is this : Must the heathen first be civilised and then receive the Gospel or must they receive the Gospel and be civilised in this way. Marshman throws light on this vital question in giving a full account of all the debates held in connection with the renewal of the Charter in 1813. Colonel, afterwards Sir THOMAS MUNRO, the renowned governor of Madras, said : "If a good system of agriculture, unrivalled manufacturing skill, a capacity to produce whatever might contribute to convenience or luxury, schools established in every village, the general practise of hospitality and charity among each other, and above all, a treatment of the female sex full of confidence, respect, and delicacy, were among the signs which denoted a civilised people, then the Hindoos were not inferior to the natives of Europe ; and if civilization were to become an article of trade between the two countries, he was convinced that England would greatly benefit by the import cargo. Its practical tendency, says Marshman, was to perpetuate the moral and religious degradation of India and to impede the progress of Christian civilization." [8])

In the "Baptist Miss. Magazine" 1887, translated into German for "Die Allgemeine Missionszeitschrift" we found the following assertions given by Pundita Ramabai, an Indian widow, the first woman who left India in order to receive a further education. She relates the situation of India's high caste women and girls : "Ein indisches Mädchen darf frei umherlaufen, wird weder erzogen noch unterrichtet und im Alter von neun bis zehn Jahren verlobt. Sie kommt nun in das Haus ihres Bräutigams, welcher je nach Umständen zehn oder fünftig Jahre alt ist, wird hier ganz der Schwiegermutter untergeordnet und ihr Leben meist ein sehr hartes. Nachdem sie bis jetzt in strengste Zucht genommen, sie darf nicht lachen und musz allen Familiengliedern ihres künftigen Mannes gehorchen. Mit 16 Jahren, zuweilen noch früher, wird sie verheiratet und ist von dem einen Wunsche beseelt, Mutter von Söhnen zu werden, weil in Indien eines Mannes Stellung im Himmel davon abhängt, ob er Söhne hat oder nicht und er hat das Recht, sein Weib zu verstoszen, wenn ihr solche versagt bleiben. Eine Frau mit Söhnen wird hoch angesehen, hat sie keine Kinder oder nur Mädchen, so wird sie verachtet.

Eine Witwe aus den höheren Kasten kann nicht wieder heiraten auch nicht, wenn ihr Mann als Bräutigam gestorben ist. Es gibt in Indien einundzwanzig Millionen Witwen (1887), welche ein bejammernswertes Leben führen und deren Behandlung jeder Beschreibung spottet. Eine Frau musz immer ihrem Vater, ihrem Gatten oder jemand unterthan sein und Gehorsam ist ihre erste Pflicht.

Bei Frauen hält man Bildung für überflüssig. Mein Vater, der sehr gut war und mich nicht miszhandelt sehen wollte, hielt mich ausnahmweise zum Lernen an ; aber gewöhnlich wird es nicht gewünscht.

Eine Frau soll ihren Mann als Stellvertreter Gottes ansehen und nur in ihm die Götter verehren. Gehorcht sie ihrem Gatten nicht, so kommt sie nicht in den Himmel ; denn nur durch ihn darf sie hoffen hinein zu kommen. Viele Männer sind aber so bösartig, dasz ihre Frauen sie unmöglich verehren können und während andere Frauen hoffen einst in den Himmel zu kommen, so bleiben indischen, in unglücklichen Ehen lebenden Frauen, nur der eine Trost — sie kommen in die Hölle, wo sie wenigstens von ihren Männern erlöst sind. Es gibt jedoch auch einzelne Ausnahmen, wo es den Frauen gelungen ist, Einflusz auf ihre Männer zu gewinnen.

Die indische Frau hat weder Erb- noch Eigentumsrecht. Hat sie keinen Sohn geboren, so wird sie gezwungen, einen anzunehmen, der als Erbe ihres Gatten eintritt und von dem sie nun in allen Stücken abgenommen, sobald sie verwitwet sind." [9])

We must omit a great deal of this article but we will quote only this : Of the 122 million women in India only 200.000 are able to write and read.   Those who read this article will be struck with the cruel and terrible situation of the women and girls in India.   Now we have the impression that William Carey did not make any difference between culture and civilization.   Nowadays culture is defined as the trained and refined state of the understanding and manners and tastes which are prevalent at a certain time or place, while civilization is the advanced stage of social development.

William Carey used the word civilization in the meaning of culture.   And in this way it is easy to understand that he wishes first conversion then culture.

When the conclusion should be drawn that we only have to push aside all heathen-culture and give a fresh christian culture instead, it would only mean that the real situation of the missionfield or the missionary difficulties is not understood.

We must never forget that the so-called christian culture sometimes is a very bad propaganda for the conversion of the nonchristian.   Many heathens, even primitives, and still more highcultured heathens are often an example of inner discipline for the christians. Each tendency to despise the heathen culture, to look down upon it, is not only foolish, but it is also a proof of bad understanding of the adaptation principles.

Generally speaking the words of Sir Munro are not right. But yet he felt that the fine Hindoo culture has a stamp of its own. And that it is quite impossible to change it in a simple way for the christian culture. Friedrich Heiler felt the same. And so did William Carey. He appreciated the culture of the Bengalees. "When he reached India, Bengali, as a cultured tongue, was almost extinct, by reason of the contemptuous roughness of the Moslems. There was not a book to be read in its prose. But Carey revived it by translating the whole Bible into its speech, and demonstrating its unbound capacity to become the refined vehicle of a great literature, and to express the deepest truths with simplicity and grace." This quotation of S. Pearce Carey shows that William Carey really understood that we may not despise the heathen culture as such. He was right when he stated in his Enquiry that the spread of the Gospel is the most effectual means of the civilization of the heathen. But on the other hand be felt that this problem is not solved by simply stating that we first have to christianize and then civilize. As culture also can he defined as the sediment, resulting from the struggle in the spiritual and material provinces of life, which was gradually adopted by men, he understood very well that this problem can only be solved after a very long time. Civilization as William Carey saw it, is not only a question of refined manner but first of all conversion of the heart. In this way he tried to build up a totally new culture.

c. Knowledge of the religious situation on the missionfield is necessary.

We more than once cited from letters of William Carey and from his Form of Agreement and also from his Enquiry the words containing this principle : a missionary must be well equipped with knowledge of the whole missionary field. He must try to describe the character of the land, of the people, the vastness of the country, he must try to pry into the soul of the people by learning their language thoroughly a.s.o. All the principles antithetic to the different pseudo-religious systems must be studied. A fine picture of the religious situation in India in 1793 is given by Dr. George Smith and Dr. H. Kraemer. [10] It once more confirms the assertion that their culture and civilization is quite incompatible with the christian view of it, however adaptive and accommodating the Christians may be.

After making his diagnosis he prescribes medicine. "Our ultimate plan is to settle missionary stations throughout Bengal and Orissa, and in several parts of Hindoostan Proper. These stations to be at the distance of 100 or 150 miles from each other, and to be managed by a European missionary. Surrounding each of these as a centre, we wish to settle seven or eight native preachers or catechists, at proper distances from each other, who will be under the management and control of the European minister. The places at which we desire to settle missionaries are at or near to Cawnpore, Benares, Dinagepore, Goalpara, Chittagong, Jessore, Cutwa, Dacca, and Juggernath. At present we are only able to occupy three of the above stations, viz.: Dinagepore, Cutwa, and Jessore. To each of these stations we wish to send a person immediately. For the support of these stations, it is desirable to connect with them some small line of vicinity of a military station; a small manufactory of indigo anotta, or a little trade in cloth would be desirable in other stations. If, however, this would be thought improper, we will endeavour to support them from another fund.

We wish for no privileges or exemptions, but merely for leave to settle, preach the Gospel, and distribute Bibles, or other religious tracts, among the natives, without molestation or prohibition from the magistrate of the district; and for a general license to itinerate for this purpose in any part of the British dominions in India. The latter of these privileges is peculiarly desirable, if it should be thought improper to grant the first. It is our desire to be subject to the laws of the country in every respect; and we shall esteem it a duty to teach the people their obligations to obey magistrates, and pay all respects to the government under which they live." [11])

In our survey we mentioned the terrible infanticide and the burning alive and burying alive of the widows and the lepers. The abolition of the suttees and the reaction upon it in India and in England and the firm stand of Lord William Bentinck against these terrible cruelties are described in detail by Marshman. Enough to state once more that the civilization of the Hindoos desperately needed improvement, and that only the Spirit of Christ in the hearts of the people is able to make these unhappy men and women rejoice in their Lord and Saviour.

d. Choice of missionary field.

Calcutta-Debhatta-Kalutala-Mudnabatti-Serampore are the different "choices" of William Carey. Of course first of all we have to see in his life the Leadership of his heavenly father who made him an apprentice. First in England, then in the wilderness of India. But from this we may learn two things : First of all that the Committee did not make the choice and secondly that William Carey did not see the example of St. Paul and other apostles. St. Paul laboured according to a fixed plan. [12]) Just like a great strategist. First he went to the synagogue ; when the Jews did not agree with his preaching in their sacred places of worship, he went to the heathen. From this we learn that he sought the centres of religious life. So he also did in respect to the towns he visited. He chose the centres, the capitals, not the country. And from the centre he went to the country.

It is true William Carey laboured in Calcutta for a few days at the start of his missionary career. But his aim was not Calcutta but just like Eliot and Brainerd, his exemplars, he would have cheerfully chosen Tahiti or Africa, or some piece of land in the wilderness and then evangelize the heathen living there, itinerating day after day just like his Moravian heroes.

But Gods ways were different from his ways. God took the helm of the ship of his life and steered him to Serampore. In this way the method of Paul as a golden rule is justified in the life of William Carey when he changed Mudnabatti for the Danish settlement. Not through but in spite of William Carey his principle was sound. Later on he indeed made centres of his principal missionary stations. Then he understood the way in which he had to work. But even when he had to choose between Mudnabatti and Serampore he made a balance of pros and cons and in this way he came to this town.

When the question is raised what attitude must be taken towards neighbouring missionary fields of other societies, we must answer that this problem of mutual relation was not yet acute in in his days. Dr. Warneck made a magnificent report concerning this problem on the London Conference of 1888. He gave a threefold reply : I. We must become mutually acquainted with each other. II. We must mutually bind ourselves to avoid all overstepping of borders. III. We must constantly hold out helping hands

to each other.   Principles which he elaborated and which are to
be found in the reports of the Conference. [13])

Our conclusion is that the principle of Scripture was visible
in the life of William Carey, but only by the guidance of the Lord
who made him choose the best method.

B. THE MISSIONARY TASK.

a. The religious character of the missionary task.

Both William Carey's Enquiry and Form of Agreement refer
to the task which the Lord gave his disciples in the words of Matth.
28 : 19/20 "Go ye therefore and make disciples of all the nations
baptizing them into the name of the Father and of the Son and
of the Holy Ghost : teaching them to observe all things whatsoever
I commanded you : and lo, I am with you always, even unto the end
of the world."

In the Introduction to his Enquiry he says that our blessed Lord
has required us to pray that his kingdom may come and his will
be done on earth as it is in heaven, and that it becomes us not only
to express our desires of that event by words, but to use every lawful method to spread the knowledge of his name.

In the first section of this famous pamphlet we are taught that
this commission was as extensive as possible, and laid them under
the obligation to disperse themselves into every country of the
habitable globe, and preach to all the inhabitants, without exception or limitation.

The first sentence of his Form of Agreement of Oct. 1805 is :
"The Redeemer, in planting us in the heathen nation, rather than in
any other, has imposed upon us the cultivation of peculiar qualifications."   And the first article of this Form runs : "It is absolutely
necessary that we set an infinite value upon immortal souls."

The main purpose of our missionary is the making of disciples
of all nations, especially of the Indians to whom he is sent.

SOUTHEY, the famous writer, gives in a fine style his view of
the way in which Carey saw his missionary task : "Carey and his
son have been in Bengal fourteen years, the other brethren only
nine ; they had all a difficult language to acquire before they could
speak to a native, and to preach and argue in it required a thorough
and familiar knowledge.   Under these circumstances the wonder
is, not that they have done so little, but that they have done so

much ; for it will be found that, even without this difficulty to retard them, no religious opinions have spread more rapidly in the same time, unless there was some remarkable folly or extravagance to recommend them, or some powerful wordly inducement. Their progress will be continually accelerating ; the difficulty is the making of a good start. This done the husband may be the means of the conversion of his wife, the son of his parents, the friend of his friend, and every fresh proselyte becomes a missionary in his own neighbourhood. Thus their sphere of influence and of action widens and the eventual issue of a struggle between truth and falsehood is not to be doubted by those who believe in the ultimate victory of the former. Nothing can be more unfair than the manner in which the scoffers and alarmists have represented the missionaries. We, who have thus vindicated them, are neither blind to what is erroneous in their doctrine or ludicrous in their phraseology : but the anti-missionaries cull from their journals and letters all that is ridiculous, sectarian and trifling ; call them fools, madmen, tinkers, Calvinists, and schismatics ; and keep out of sight their love of man, and their zeal for God, their devotion, their indefatigable industry, and their unequalled learning. These low-born and low-bred mechanics have translated the whole Bible into Bengali, and have by this time printed it . . . ." In this strain he goes on. It may be enough to prove that the religious character of the missionary task was well understood by William Carey. He not only understood the commission of the Lord given to him and all christians, but also his task of civilization. In the year 1803 a Christian Brahman was united to a daughter of Krishna Pal, in the presence of more than a hundred Hindoos. Carey sat at the table ; and after a short introduction he explained the character of a christian marriage and pointed out the impropriety of the Hindoo customs in this respect. The next evening they all sat at a table again and some of the neighbours looked on with kind amazement. It was a new and very singular sight in this land in which the distinctions clean and unclean are of so much importance.

Another example of a new civilisation is given by the story of the funeral of Gokool. The usual method of Europeans was to hire a set of men (Portuguese) whose job was to bury the dead. But now the christians did it themselves. A converted brahman, a converted Mussulman, and two other Christians took up the coffin.

Of course all Serampore stood on tiptoe with amazement. But

188

in this way a new principle of Christian civilization was set up as the outcome of his well-understood task of making disciples of all nations. He elaborated this principle much further when he established schools, erected all kinds of useful institutions, paid attention to the rural problems.

So we see that William Carey understood his primary missionary task very well and in consequence of this also the work of civilization such as the establishment of schools, translation of the Scriptures, establishment of missionary stations and other cultural institutions.

b. The missionary task as christianization.

The question to be dealt with here is the significance of the commission of the Lord towards the disciples.

As far as we know, William Carey did not give any scientific exegesis of the words of St Matth. 28 : 19 and 20.

The question raised here is not whether he understood his task and tried to christianize the world—of course he did much better than his contemporaries, but the question here is whether he understood the words of Matth. 28 : 18—20 and other places in their original meaning. We regret to say that he did not prove this. We hope to treat of these places when we shall discuss the principles of William Carey.

c. The missionary task as christianization of the nation.

The same answer must be given here as to the preceding question. For here a scientific question is raised what is the significance of the word "nations".

Another question in this connection is this : whether the missionary task is restricted to the individual or aims at the conversion of the whole nation. The answer is given by Carey in his practice. He understands the commission of the Lord as a command to seek the persons, but in relation to the nation and family in which they are placed by God. Just as the General Synod of Middelburg 1896 expressed it in its report : "It does not suffice to bring the Gospel to some stray Javanese, but we must turn to the centre of the community. Automatic mission only works upon these individual, now living persons ; a mission which directs itself also to the people as nation, is turning over the conscience of the nation and is changing the convictions and giving fruits for the future." [14]

It is a remarkable fact that the advice given by Prof. Dr. J. H. Bavinck in his "Zendingsboek" is just like the practise of William Carey. Prof. Bavinck says : "In order to lay hold on the people as a whole and not on some separate individuals, the best practise will be to convoke a village-meeting. When e.g. in some village somebody is drawn by the Gospel, it may be of the utmost value that all the adults of the village are called together and such a man testifies of his faith in God before his fellow-villagers. It is possible to make it clear in this way that God summons the whole community to a new life." [15])

Of course not in a sense of e.g. Bonifacius or Xaverius who were satisfied with superficial mass-conversions, but missionaries should try to get into contact with the principals of a village or family or tribe and then work from this centre to the circumference. A fine example of such a method is given by the German Neuendettelsauer Mission on New Guinea (Dutch) of which Prof. Bavinck tells in his above mentioned book. [16])

William Carey worked in the same way. He always tried to get influence in the higher ranks especially with the Brahmins and from such a centre he tried to influence the individuals. Of course this does not mean that he neglected the lower castes. On the contrary. But he very well understood this modern way of working as we showed in our survey.

His way of baptizing was another than that of the Reformed Churches. We already showed that he only baptized adults after confession of faith. So he could not baptize a whole family, or a tribe. Later on we will show that he did not see the importance of the Covenant. But all the more we appreciate his attitude towards the whole people, including the children whom he brings together in the schools, trying to bring them into contact with the blessings of the Gospel.

We appreciate this attitude, for as we will see later on he educated the natives in order to use them for the spreading of the Gospel to all the ranks of the Hindoo people, seeing that they were much better adapted for the missionary task than Europeans, at least when guided by the missionaries.

He always tried, from his very beginning till the end of his life, to convert India as a whole. In this respect we may call him the founder of modern missions.

d. The missionary task relating to some important problems.

1. SLAVE TRADE.

From his early days in Paulurspury c.a., William Carey was impressed by the cruelties of the slave trade. His sister writes in a letter A.D. 1786 : "He was always, from his first being thoughtful, remarkably impressed about heathen lands and the slave trade. I never remember his engaging in prayer, in his family or in public, without praying for those poor creatures." [17]

In these days his contemporary THOMAS CLARKSON of Wisbeach made his first efforts to free the slaves. Great Britain was responsible for the existence of 9.000.000 of slaves in India, many of them bought by Hindoo merchants as well as Arabs from Eastern Africa, to fill the hareems and zazanas of Hindoos. Only towards the end of Carey's career he got acquainted with these facts. But his prayers continued daily from 1779, were answered by the deliverance of all the English West India slaves. The hearing of his prayers was manifested in the East in 1843, when the legal status of slavery in India was abolished. [18]

Deaville Walker supposes that his interest in the abolition of the slave trade was already roused when William Carey was eleven years old, when his father was discussing the burning topic of the day and especially Lord Chief Justice Mansfield's famous declaration that on English soil no man can be a slave.

We know that Carey in his early days sympathized with the French revolution and Rousseau's ideas on liberty. Rousseau of course never gave a thought to Christian missions, but Carey was stimulated by this great man to pray for the emancipation of these poor creatures. "The modern slave trade had reached disgraceful proportions ; for Britain had developed what Portugal and Spain had begun. London papers openly advertised children for sale. Two million negroes were shipped to our colonies in a century. Just under two hundred vessels left our ports in 1790 for the West. Half their living cargoes perished on the way through brutality, starvation and disease. The ships were 'floating hells'. Our sins were scarlet. Our crimes cried out to God. Yet public feeling was quiescent. Even religious opinion was little stirred. The Quakers or Friends were the first remonstrants. Then followed the Baptists. Carey, from his very conversion, was violently opposed to this abomination. Under the influence of the poet COWPER he watched the collaboration of CLARKSON and WILBERRORCE, of ZACHARY MACAULY and SHARP; how the Commons faced the question; Fox's stand for abolition; WILBERFORCE's superb effort in the House in 1789 and the subsequent mitigation of the transport atrocities; then, alas! in 1791 came the trade's smashing triumph, in spite of Wesley's dying entreaty, through Parliament's reaction under the turbulence of France." [19]) Carey's answer to this attitude was the abandonment of the use of sugar, that he might cleanse his hands of blood, as we mentioned above.

When he draws his conclusions in his famous Enquiry he says: "Arabian Mohammedanism had bled Africa to death through the slave trade, of which Christian nations shared the guilt".

When Professor at Fort William his wrath was roused on learning that the Jamaican House of Assembly had prohibited both the education of the negroes and their religious assemblies. He wrote to JOHN WILLIAMS of New York, urging him to call his people to prayer to defeat this injustice. He writes "Certainly God's hand will fall heavily on those Isles, whose trade is maintained by robbery and cruelty. When He maketh intercession for blood, He will not forget the sighing of the poor and needy. Yet may these oppressors be rather converted than destroyed." Later on, when writing to Prof. ROGERS Carey says: "I was much shocked at seeing in some American newspapers advts. headed: To be sold a negro Man! I hope no Christian keeps a slave. If this should be the practice (for custom often blinds the eye of even good men) in the Southern parts of the United States, it will not be difficult to answer the enquiry in a certain Association letter you sent me, why the churches are in so languishing a state; but I hope that everyone who names the name of Christ departs from the iniquity of holding their fellow-creatures in slavery, and that it is the practice of those only who are enemies of God." [20])

And to finish this survey of his principal attitude towards slavery we will mention the words of J. C. Marshman who says that a letter reporting that the Cabinet meant to have free trade with India and to emancipate the West Indian slaves was a source of great joy, especially to Carey. In no public question had he taken a deeper interest. With tears in his eyes he thanked God, and proposed that we should give special thankgivings to God for one month in all our meetings.

It is not difficult to know his opinion on this point. During his whole life he had fought for emancipation of our fellow-men, the slaves, by means of prayer and by influencing his students and public opinion. We could not find an accurate detailed definition of slave trade, a scientific treatise of it by his hand.

2. THE MISSIONARY TASK RELATING TO MARRIAGE AND POLYGAMY.

Above we have mentioned already the bad situation of the women in India. We cited a report of a Hindoo woman. Here we will state some more, especially relating to the polygamic situation. "The Hindoo girl spends the first ten years of her life in sheer idleness, immured in the house of her father. Before she has attained this age, however, she is sought after by the ghutuks, men employed by parents to seek wives for their sons. She is betrothed without her consent, a legal agreement, which binds her for life, being made by the parents on both sides while she is still a child. At a time most convenient to the parents, this boy and girl are brought together for the first time, and the marriage ceremony is performed, after which she returns to the house of her father.

If before the marriage is consummated, the boy dies and this girl becomes a widow, she is doomed to remain in this state as long as she lives as law prohibits the marriage of widows. The greater number of these unfortunate beings become a prey to the seducer, and a disgrace to their families. Concubinage, to a most awful extent, is the fruit of these marriages without choice. In some cases as many as fifty females, the daughters of so many Hindoos, are given in marriage to one brahmin, in order to make these families more respectable, so that the parents may be able to say: We are allied by marriage to the koleens." [21]

In our survey we noticed the persecution of the eldest daughter of Krishna Pal, called Golook. She was carried to the house of the Hindoo to whom in infancy she had been betrothed. As a Christian she loathed such a connection which was both idolatrous and polygamous.

In 1803 the missionaries discussed the problem of polygamy. Especially this question : what was to be done with converts whose wives would not join them. They came to this solution : They urged the husband to use every means to induce his heathen wife to join him. If such a wife made a long delay or refused to join him, they counted it a sufficient reason for divorce, and allowed him to marry again. As for a polygamous Christian, they solved

13   193

the problem in this way that they kept him out of office in the church, binding on his conscience that which our Lord taught us in Matthew 19 and Paul in I Corinthians 7. Marshman tells us that towards the close of 1806, the missionaries laid down a principle, which they pursued when the wife of a convert refused to join him, after he had embraced Christianity. Bhagvat, a young brahmin, had been baptized some months before ; his wife rejected all his entreaties to live with him ; and it became desirable, that he should marry again. But the missionaries were unwilling to encourage this course, till every effort to overcome the wife's reluctance had been exhausted. Bhagvat was, therefore, directed to draw up a document stating that he had embraced Christianity, but still continued to consider himself the lawful husband of the woman he had married when a Hindoo, and was still willing to discharge all the duties of a husband towards her affectionately, but that he should consider the connection dissolved if she persisted in refusing to live with him. The document was formally registered in the Serampore Court, and he proceeded with it to his own village. He was not however, permitted to pollute the family mansion by his presence, nor would his wife hold any communication with him. He was obliged, therefore, to stand at the outer door, where he read the paper aloud in the presence of several witnessess, and then sent it to his wife, who was listening from within. He called on her distinctly to state whether she would accompany him to Serampore. After a short pause, she tore the paper in pieces, and declared that from the day of his baptism she had renounced him for ever, and assumed the condition and dress of a widow. He asked for a deed of separation, which was refused, and he returned to Serampore, where Mr. Carey and his colleagues, after maturely weighing the circumstances of the case, determined in accordance with the decision of St Paul : "But if the unbelieving depart, let him depart. A brother or a sister is not under bondage in such a case" that the convert was no longer debarred from contracting a second marriage.

The solution of this difficulty is in concordance with the principle stated in 1803.

He may have practised some more rules but in this effect this will do to prove how on principle he rejected the institution of polygamy. On the other hand he did not adopt rigorous measures against Christian polygamists. They had to try to win their wives

If the latter were reluctant and adhered to their idols, they were free.   Once more we see that he did not give any scientific treatise on this question but solved the problems as they came to him on the missionary field.

3. THE MISSIONARY TASK RELATING TO CASTE.

Incidentally we remarked in par. III page 177 that William Carey formed a new Christian national system, without caste differences, and other pagan structures.   We also mentioned that their Danish predecessors in South India had allowed converts to retain their caste and caste distinctions were thus perpetuated within the Church of Christ.   For the first time caste was broken when Krishna Pal and his friend Gokool ate together with the missionaries and their wives sitting at the same communion table.

William Carey and his colleagues saw much better than the Southern India chaplains and missionaries that the retention of caste was not something of minor importance.   They risked the defiance of the people regarding this inveterate Indian principle and practice, for they saw very clearly that the bulwark of Hinduism diametrically opposed the spirit of the Gospel.   So they refused it the least sanction from the first.   They were aware, says S. Pearce Carey that by this drastic course their progress would be slower, but at least it would be sure.   And wisdom justified their works.   Brahmins and sudras were treated as equals and brothers. [22])

4. THE MISSIONARY TASK RELATING TO POLITICS.

As a Baptist Carey hated militarism.   As a missionary he avoided every political dispute.   Once he became seriously ill.   Afterwards he wrote : "In my delirium I was busily employed, as I perfectly remember, in carrying a communication from God to all the princes and governments in the world, requiring them instantly to abolish every political establishment of religion, and to sell the parish and other churches to the first body of Christians who would purchase them.   Also, to declare war infamous, and military officers the destroyers of the race.   I was attended by angels in all my excursions, and was universally successful.   A few princes in Germany were refractory (!), but my attendants struck them dead !   I also pronounced the doom of 'Rome' to the Pope."   This prophetic dream he dreamed. But the core of it is worth mentioning: his attitude towards militarism.

5. HIS MISSIONARY TASK AND HORTICULTURE AND AGRICULTURE.

William Carey was broadminded. He clearly saw that the Indian people could cultivate their own soil much better than they did. "His missionwork and his horticulture were twin expressions of one aim—to enrich men with God's best. He mourned that both in things material and in things spiritual, in the world of sense as well as in the realm of religion, the multitudes of India knew and possessed only what was fifth-rate and inadequate, whilst a whole wealth of bounty and beauty and blessing might be theirs. He gave his life to supply their double lack." [23])

In "Het eerste verslag der Nederlandsche afdeeling van het zendelinggenootschap der Engelsche Baptisten in Serampore" (The first report of the Dutch section of the missionary Society of English Baptists at Serampore) we read: "Lately Carey established a Society with the purpose of encouraging Agri- and Horticulture, of which Society the Governor would be the patron." [24])

At Jerusalem 1928 a report was given on: "The Christian Mission in relation with the rural problems". Or course the problems of the days of William Carey were different from those in our time. But he understood the heart of the question. He tried to enrich the people materially as well as spiritually.

He also established a savingsbank and a benevolent school and a leper hospital. In every way he tried to elevate the people not only by preaching the Gospel but also by applying the principles of the Gospel in daily life.

NOTES

[1]) Dr. GEORGE SMITH, op. cit., p. 64, 85—86.
[2]) Ibid., p. 335—336.
[3]) MARSHMAN, op. cit., p. 288. Vol. I.
[4]) Dr. GEORGE SMITH, op. cit., p. 154—155.
[5]) OGILVIE, The apostles of India, p. 246—247 on BARTHOLOMEW ZIEGENBALG.
[6]) a. Report of the Centenary Conference of the Protestant Missions of the World London 1888. Third edition, p. 65 and 212. Vol. II; Vol. I, p. 52 and 59.
    b. Reports of Commission IV. The missionary Message in relation to Non Christian religions 1910, p. 157, 164—166, 168, 195. Vol. IV.
    c. The Christian Mission in relation to Rural Problems. Jerusalem 1928, 252f. Vol. V.
    d. The Church and the State. Vol. VI. Tambaram 1938, p. 135.
[7]) MARSHMAN, op. cit. Preface p. XI and XII.
[8]) MARSHMAN. Vol. II, p. 20. Chapter X is very interesting for those who study the politics of that time.

[9]) Baptist Missionary Magazine 1887, p. 92 by PUNDITA RAMABAI, quoted by die Allgemeine Missionszeitschrift 1887, p. 87. Beiblatt.

[10]) Dr. GEORGE SMITH, op. cit., p. 71—74.

On landing in Bengal they found themselves surrounded by a population of heathens (not including the Mohamedans) amounting to at least one hundred million souls. They heard the idolators speak of 330.000.000 gods. There were innumerable temples and services without end. They saw the population prostrate before dead matter, before the monkey, the serpent, before idols which were the very personification of sin. They supposed the world under the sway of beings ignorant, capricious, and wicked. Through their ignorance of heart and the deep turpitude of sin, these people imagined that the waters of the Ganges had virtue enough in them to purify the mind from its earthly stains. Hence they saw the whole population residing in its neighbourhood morning and evening crowding to the river ; they saw the holy water carried for religious uses to the most distant parts, and the dying hurried in their last moments to receive their last purification in the sacred stream. Under the delusion that sin is to be removed by the merit of works, they observed others, undertaking long and dangerous pilgrimages in which thousands perished ; while others were inflicting the most dreadful tortures on their bodies and others were sitting all day and all the year, repeating the names of their guardian deities . . . .

The Hindoos believe that the good or evil actions of this birth were not produced by their own volition, but arose from, and were unavoidable results of the actions of the past birth ; that their present actions would inevitably give rise to the whole complexion of their characters and conduct in the following birth ; and that thus they were doomed to interminable transmigrations, to float as some light substance upon the bosom of an irresistible torrent . . . .

No Bibles were found, no sabbaths, no congregations for religious instruction in any form ; no house for God ; no God but a log of wood, or a monkey ; no Saviour but the Ganges etc.

This is a brief account of note 10 while the description of the widows and infants is about the same as we gave on p. 182—183.

Dr. H. KRAEMER writes in the well known book "The christian message in the non christian world", p. 139 :

"In the light of the dialectical situation of all religious life and of all religious life in Biblical realism, points of contact in the real, deep sense of the word can only be found by antithesis. This means by discovering in the revealing light of Christ the fundamental misdirection that dominates all religious life and at the same time the groping for God which throbs in this misdirection and which finds an unsuspected divine solution in Christ. It is clear that this antithetical way of establishing points of contact is not meant as a negative way of condemnation, but as a deeply positive way of dealing realistically with the dialectical reality of the religion of mankind."

[11]) MARSHMAN, op. cit. Vol. II, p. 399—417.

[12]) Dr. J. H. BAVINCK, Zending in een wereld in nood, p. 29 f.

[13]) London 1888. Missionary Conference Dr. G. WARNECK, Mutual Relations, p. 432 f.

[14]) Historisch Document Zendingsrapport van de Gereformeerde kerken van Middelburg 1896 Bootsma Utrecht, p. 32.

[15]) Prof. Dr. J. H. BAVINCK, Ons Zendingsboek, p. 58.

[16]) Ibid., p. 185.

[17]) Memoirs of the Life and Writings of the Rev. ANDREW FULLER by J. A. MORRIS, 1816, p. 96 quoted by Dr. GEORGE SMITH, op. cit., p. 31.

[18]) Cf. Dr. GEORGE SMITH, p. 292—293.

[19]) S. PEARCE CAREY, op. cit., p. 6—7.

[20]) S. PEARCE CAREY, p. 223.

[21]) Dr. GEORGE SMITH, op. cit., p. 75.

[22]) S. PEARCE CAREY, op. cit., p. 211.

[23]) Ibid., p. 395.

[24]) Het eerste verslag der Nederl. afdeeling van het zendelinggenootschap der Engelsche Baptisten in Serampore, p. 10—11. 1822.

It may be of considerable interest for genealogical researches especially to Dutchmen to peruse the "Naamlijst" (Index of Names) of all the persons who gave their donations to the Dutch section of the Serampore Society at that time e.g. At Amsterdam : Mevr. P. C. TEN CATE, J. CORVER, C. CROMMELIN, J. HUIDEKOPEE. At Rotterdam : de heer MACKAY, de heer E. P. MONCHIJ, de heer VAN ZUIJLEN VAN NIJEVELT. At Middelburg : de heer R. MENALDA en S. REKKER etc.

Par. IV. Missionary instruments.

a. Only the Word.

On page 156 of this dissertation we purposely omitted the treatment of the 9th article of the Form of Agreement and on page 174 dealing with the linguistic differences on the missionary field we only referred to it. Now we will give the contents of it.

William Carey insisted on "labouring with all our might to produce translations of the Sacred Scriptures in the languages of Hindoostan". He says : "It is a bounden duty." "We consider the publication as an object which we ought never to give up till accomplished."

Then : It becomes us to use all assiduity in explaining and distributing the Divine Word on all occasions, and by every means in our power to excite the attention and the reverence of the natives towards it, as the fountain of eternal truth, and the Message of Salvation to men. It is our duty also to distribute, as extensively as possible, the different religious tracts which are published. Considering how much the general diffusion of the knowledge of Christ depends upon a liberal and constant distribution of the Word, and of these tracts, all over the country, we should keep this continually in mind and watch all opportunities of putting even single tracts into the hands of those persons with whom we occasionally meet. We should endeavour to ascertain where large assemblies of the natives are to be found, that we may attend upon them, and gladden whole villages at once with the tidings of salvation.

Here we see his method of working. Before he went to India he had already in his mind the translation of the Scriptures and on his voyage to India he planned for the future : "I am very desirous that my sons may pursue the same work, and intend to bring up one in the study of Sanskrit and another of Persian. May God give them fitting grace for the work !"

In our survey we mentioned his enormous assiduity and capability for studying languages and translating the Scriptures. The following appreciations of his work show that this principle was estimated at the highest value by all christians. In the "Reports of the

Dutch section of the Missionary Society of English Baptists at Serampore", we found as the first and second principle : "The preaching of the Gospel", and "The translation of the Scriptures". In the fourth report dated Oct. 1825 we are informed of the fact that Carey personally supervises all the translations of the Holy Scripture. In the fourteenth report we read in an article to the memory of W. Carey : "He was fitted with extraordinary capacities in studying foreign languages and he enjoyed himself in translating the Holy Scriptures in the dialects of the different natives. A labour in which he succeeded more than any other predecessor."[1]

The Rev. Browne writes in his book "The History of the British and Foreign Bible Society": "From the work 'Contributions towards a History of Biblical Translations in India', a work full of valuable information, it appears that twenty one editions of the Bengali New Testament, besides several of the Old, and innumerable portions of the Scriptures have been circulated over India."

The Committee cannot receive the intelligence of the death of their venerable friend, Dr. Carey, without expressing their long cherished admiration of his talents, his labours, and his ardent piety. At a period antecedent to the formation of the British and Foreign Bible Society, Dr. Carey, and his earlier colleagues were found occupying the field of Biblical translations ; not as the amusement of literary leisure but as *subservient* to the work to which they had consecrated themselves—that of teaching Christianity to heathen and other unenlightened nations.

Following in the track marked out by the excellent Danish missionaries, they set sail for British India intending there to commence their enterprise of zeal and mercy : and there, notwithstanding impediments, which at first threatened to disappoint all their hopes but which were afterwards succeeded by the highest patronage of Government—there for forty years did Carey employ himself, amid the numerous dialects of the East ; first in surmounting their difficulties and compelling them to speak of the true God and of Jesus Christ, whom He hath sent ; and then presenting them in a printed form to the people.

For this arduous undertaking he was qualified in an extraordinary degree, by a singular facility in acquiring languages—a facility which he had first shown and cultivated, amidst many disadvantages, in the retirement of humble life. The subsequent extent of his talents as well as of his diligence and zeal may be judged by the fact, that in conjunction with his colleagues, he has been instrumental in giving to the tribes of Asia the Sacred Scriptures, either partly or in full, in between thirty or forty different languages!

For many years it was the privilege of this Society to assist him in his labours; he was among its earliest correspondents. If for the last few years the intercourse has been less regular, and direct assistance suspended in consequence of difficulties arising out of conscientious scruples on the part of himself and his brethren, still the Committee have not the less appreciated his zeal, his devotedness, his humility; and they feel, while they bow with submission to the will of God, that they have lost a most valuable coadjutor, and the Church of Christ at large a distinguished ornament and friend. [2])

This judgment of the famous British and Foreign Bible Society is of greater value than a great many quotations out of his works etc. The reason why the British and Foreign Bible Society suspended direct assistance to the translations of Dr. Carey is given by W. CANTON in his book "History of the British and Foreign Bible Society" Vol. II p. 114. After stating that Bengali was the language of 30.000.000 people, he says that Dr. Carey restricted the Greek word for baptism to immersion. When the British and Foreign Bible Society asked just like HENRY MARTIN, to change this translation as not being correct, he declined to do so. So the Bible Society regretted that it could give no further assistance to the translations of the New Testament. [3])

Dr. George Smith gives a quotation from the eighty first Report of the British and Foreign Bible Society 1885 in which he expressed his appreciation of this pioneer's work in the following words: "Two new versions of the Bible are in progress, the Tulu, and the Konkani, a dialect of the Marathi. In both these languages some efforts were made long ago—in the case of the Konkani by Dr. Carey; but time and better tools have imposed the duty of advancing upon the achievements of the past, not so much displacing and superseding as building upon them." Later on this Report continues: "In the Great Exhibition held at Calcutta in 1883, Carey's Translations, lent by the College Library at Serampore, were exhibited side by side with the revised versions, to which they gave birth in most instances." [4]) He fulfilled his plan as he had intended to do. "Only the Word" was the principle he maintained from his early beginning as a missionary to the very end of his life. He was fully aware of the deficiency of his work, but he tried to give the best he could and sent out missionaries with these translations in order to distribute the Bibles or some parts of the Bible in the different countries of India.

We mentioned already the Establishment of the Auxiliary Bible Society in Calcutta. Marshman gives a detailed translation memoir and quoted an appreciation by Fuller of the work of Dr. Carey in this respect. [5]) Deaville Walker, S. Pearce Carey, Myers and other biographers gave an extensive description of his translation work. In our survey we also tried to give a summary of this great achievement. It may suffice to say once more that he fulfilled his programme and that he considered the word as an excellent missionary instrument.

b. The demonstrated Word.

The answer to the question in what way William Carey and his colleagues wanted to demonstrate the Word in their personal life, in order to be illustrations of the Gospel, is to be found in the tenth article of the F.o.Agreement of 1805. The things that are indispensable for that purpose are being instant in prayer, and the cultivation of personal religion. Let us ever have in remembrance the examples of those who have been most eminent in the work of God. Once more he gives the example of David Brainerd and goes on : "Prayer, secret, fervent, believing prayer, lies at the root of all personal godliness. A competent knowledge of the languages current where a missionary lives, a mild and winning temper, and a heart given up in closet religion, these are the attainments which, more than all knowledge, or all other gifts, will fit us to become the instruments of God in the great work of Human Redemption. Let us then ever be united in prayer at stated seasons, whatever distance may separate us, and let each one of us lay it upon his heart that we will seek to be fervent in spirit, wrestling with God, till He famish these idols and cause the heathen to experience the blessedness that is in Christ."

These splendid words need no comment. They are bright, clear, serene.

But the preaching of the Word of God requires the permanent illustration of merciful deeds of the Word, especially in the heathen world with its misery. Missionaries must be illustrations of the Word.

On this account William Carey wrote to England already in 1795 that his Medical Mission wanted further equipment. "I submit it to the consideration of the Society, whether we should not be furnished with medicines gratis. No medicines will be sold by us, yet the cost of them enters very deeply into our allowance. The whole supply sent in the "Earl Howe", amounting to £ 35, besides charges amounting to thirty per cent, falls on me ; but the whole will either be administered to sick poor, or given to any neighbour who is in want or used in our families. Neighbouring gentlemen have often supplied us. Indeed, considering the distance we are from medical assistance, the great expensiviness of it far beyond our ability, and the number of wretched, afflicted objects whom we continually see, and who continually apply for help, we ought never to sell a pennyworth. Brother Thomas has been the instrument of saving numbers of lives. His house is constantly surrounded with the afflicted ; and the cures wrought by him would have gained any physician or surgeon in Europe the most extensive reputation. We ought to be furnished yearly with at least half a hundred weight of jesuit's bark."

From this quotation we see that William Carey very well understood the importance of medical help to the afflicted. He even planned the establishment of a native hospital in Calcutta. Later on his son Felix applied himself with success to the study of medicine, and walked the hospitals of Calcutta for several years. He had not long been at Rangoon before he found ample scope for his medical skill, and was thus enabled to obtain favourable access to the heathen. He was the first to introduce the blessing of vaccination into the country, and was delighted to obtain permission, at the outset of his career, to operate on the child of the governor. [6])

These two facts may prove that William Carey indeed saw the great importance of medical help for the sick in India. But we cannot prove that he made a principle of it. He did not see the medical profession and the hospitals as instruments for the preaching of the Gospel. At best he saw the medical service subordinated not coordinated to the central service i.e. the preaching of the Gospel. He called Dr. Thomas a missionary. Not on account of his medical work, but on account of his preaching and talking with the natives. We at least found nowhere any information of his desire to establish such a medical service coordinated with the main service : the preaching of the Gospel.

Later on we shall see that his attitude towards the schools was quite different. But here we already state that he did not make the mistake of considering schools, translations etc. as subordinate to the preaching of the Gospel. On the contrary. He saw them on the same level. He did not, like the Dutch Reformed Mission, distinguish between main service and auxiliary service. To the former belongs the preaching of the Gospel. To the latter the schools and medical attendance in hospitals etc. This differentiation may lead to the thought that the labour in the schools and hospitals should be subordinated to the propagation of the Gospel.

To prevent such an idea prof. Bavinck has suggested in his work "Ons Zendingsboek" to change this divison into centre services and co-ordinated services.

He suggests this idea in order to prevent the opinion that medical help given to the native is administrated only in order to bring him into contact with the Gospel. That the auxiliary service is only considered as a help to the service of the preaching of the Word. Then the Hospital, the school would only lead up to the Church or be an introduction to the main Service.

This is undoubtedly wrong. The centre service (preaching, catechizing and the ministration of the Sacraments) lies on the same level as the hospital service schoolmission, Sunday school, biblelectures etc. But the preaching of the Gospel by the missionaries is the centre and the other services are coordinated with it, not subordinated. [7])

We may draw this conclusion : William Carey tried to illustrate and to demonstrate the Word by all possible means. But he made no principal difference between the services. He simply called all these men and women missionaries and he did not see the medical attendance in hospitals etc. as an important instrument, coordinated with the Gospel-preaching. The preaching by way of healing the sick, nursing the wounded probably did not enter into his mind.

c. The missionary language.

When William Carey and his colleagues erected the Serampore college the cardinal question was whether it should be chiefly Western or Eastern ; and whether its vehicle of communication should be English or Indian. An important item is that young India itself would have chosen a Western university and the English language was wanted for Hindu youths applying for Government clerkships. But William Carey was not "greedy for quick returns of profit". He looked towards the Christian development of India. He did not try to make India after their own British image or likeness, but to quicken its own Indian individuality through Christ for the enrichment of humanity and the advance of the Kingdom of God. [8])

They purposely tried to make the principle that India should be not only self-supporting, but also propagating the Gospel by its own missionaries in its own tongue. Ward said : "We carefully avoid whatever might anglicize our students and converts."

The training of the students should be outstandingly Indian. Only the "especially steadfast and able" should be taught English as a reward. S Pearce Carey says : "India's sacred writings and classics would be disclosed to their students in the original Sanskrit. And he then asserts that this idea was quite revolutionary, for Sanskrit was not only denied to the multitudes of India by the conditions of their lives, but had been forbidden to any of the common people as too sacred for their knowledge and their use. Only Brahmins might possess this treasure."

So they broke not only the wall of the exclusiveness of the Brahmins but also "the mental disfranchisement and bondage". The low-bred Indian would receive the high-bred education of the Brahmins by means of the low-bred Englishmen. The Western sciences would be given in Bengali textbooks ; and the Biblical Scriptures, translated into several Indian tongues. The education should be Indian. [9])

No finer example of broadmindedness can be given in such an early period of missionary activity.

Here we state already that in this respect his stand-point differed essentially from that of the Moravians.

But we may conclude that William Carey principally solved the problem of adaptation.

d. The missionary conversation.

In three ways conversation with natives had been practised : 1 By essaying to prove the truth, by bringing forth the thesis 2 by a controversial way of preaching or 3 by a sympathetic way of preaching. William Carey chose the first way of conversation. But not in such a way that his thesis repelled the people.

By asking many questions e.g. of a Brahmin as we stated in our survey, he drew the attention of the people and at the same time he brought the Gospel. Not as RAYMUNDUS LULLUS (antithetic) not as XAVERIUS (sympathetic) but as PAUL. His conversation was biblical. In order to illustrate his way of applying this principle we will give one example, from Pearce Carey's book. He gives the following conversation : "Friend, can you read ? ' "No, sahib." "Have you any in your family that can ?" "No." "Any in your village ?" "Yes, one." "Then give him this, and bid him to read it to you and your neighbours. It tells you the way of salvation, how your sins can be forgiven, and how you can be blest in life and death." They mostly received them with astonishment and trembling.

Satire was Carey's frequent weapon as is illustrated by the following : "You think you'll be saved by the incessant naming of your god or debtah ? A parrot's holiness and yours is one." Seeing some idol, he would ask : "What is that ?" "Our God," they would answer. He would retort : "Did that make men, or did men make that ?"

These examples may prove that he had a sharp criticism, but the way in which he accomplished this task is of the greatest importance. Jesaiah also used satire. But neither Jesaiah nor Carey were scornful. They used satire, and conversation as an instrument to bring the heathen to the acknowledgment of the frivolity of their idols and to the belief in Christ and him crucified. Once more we see that William Carey acted biblically.

e. The missionary preaching.

The very beginning of his Enquiry is this : Our Lord Jesus Christ, a little before his departure, commissioned his apostles to go, and teach all nations ; or, as another evangelist expresses it, go into all the world, and preach the gospel to every creature.

In article 5 of his Form of Agreement we saw that he stated that the duty of missionaries is to preach "Christ Crucified" as the great means of conversion.

On page 154 of this dissertation we gave a summary of this article. He sees as the vital part of his preaching Christ crucified. The expiatory death and all sufficient merits have been and must remain the great means of conversion. So far as our experience goes we must freely acknowledge, that every Hindoo among us, who has been won for Christ, has been won by the astonishing and all constraining love exhibited in our Redeemer's propitiatory death. O then, may we resolve to know nothing among the Hindoos and Mussulmans but Christ and Him crucified. Ward writes to the Society in 1800: "Carey and I went to a village this morning. Our congregation was noisy; but, whilst he was relating the sufferings and death of Christ, there was all attention. He (i.e. Carey) is more and more persuaded that this is the one net for the catching of converts. Redeeming love is more and more his theme." [10])

To his son Felix he writes: "Preach the never-failing Word of the Cross." [11]) To his son William he writes: "Unto us is this favour given that we should preach among the Gentiles the unsearchable riches of Christ. Hold on therefore: be steady in your work etc." [12])

Many other instances might be given. Still one example may be of interest: The preaching of the doctrine of the Cross in addresses purposely directed to the people, or on special occasions, always remains one of the best ways to reach our purpose. Many European and Native missionaries are labouring without pause throughout the country visiting the cottages and palaces, religious feasts and assemblies, in order to form the highest interests for christ and his Gospel. This quotation from "Het Verslag der Nederlandsche Afdeeling der Engelsche Baptisten te Serampore", shows that the preaching is not limited to the Europeans but also the natives themselves preach the Gospel. But we will discuss this topic in a following paragraph.

It is well known that Carey laboured in India for seven years without making a single convert. But the soil was exceptionally hard and Bengal was a stronghold of Hinduism. The vastness of the population made a few individual conversions of little avail as a lever for moving the whole. But nevertheless he continued preaching the Gospel and when God's time came, Krishna Pal made the great step in 1800 and by the year 1810 there had been 300 baptisms, and every successive year saw an increase. [13])

In his early period in Calcutta and Mudnabatti he made itinerant missionary journeys, but soon he understood that a fixed station as a centre would be better.

Here we may conclude that he laid much stress upon conversion by showing the expiatory work of Christ. Also that his way of preaching was biblical, which is shown in his way of addressing the people and in trying to find a connecting link between their own religion and the Gospel he brought, as was the manner of St Paul.

f. The missionary school.

Carey realized that schools were essential for the missionary work. So he planned the raising of schools from the very first. These plans culminated in the establishment of Serampore college in 1818. But at the same time we must mention as a result of Carey's activity the primary school circles under native christian inspectors, a system carried out ever since the Mutiny of 1857 by the Christian Vernacular Education Society and adopted by the state departments of public instruction. [14])

Already in 1795 he writes to the Society in England : "Mr. Thomas and I have formed a plan for erecting two colleges ; one here, (Mudnabatti) and the other at his residence, where we intend to educate twelve lads, viz. six Musselmans and six Hindoos at each place. A pundit is to have charge of them, and they are to be taught Sanskrit, Bengali, and Persian ; the Bible is to be introduced, and perhaps a little philosophy and geography. The time of their education is to be seven years, and we find them meat, clothing, lodging, etc. We are now inquiring for children proper for the purpose."

Very important is his ninth article of the Form of Agreement of 1805 : "The establishment of native free schools is also an object highly important to the future conquests of the Gospel. Of this very pleasing and interesting part of our missionary labours, we should endeavour not to be unmindful. As opportunities are afforded, it becomes us to establish, visit and encourage these institutions, and to recommend the establishment of them to other Europeans. The progress of divine light is gradual both as it respects individuals and nations."

In July 1803 the first Sunday school was opened, which was superintended by Felix and William Carey and John Fernandez. It confined itself to teaching catechisms in Bengali and English.

Boarding-schools were opened already in 1800 especially for the children of the Armenians, the Portuguese, and the Eurasians, as well as for the natives of India. The boys' school was soon followed by a girls' school, through which a stream of Christian light radiated forth over resident Christian society, and which schools turned out many a missionary.

There were also many children of Europeans by native women, several of which were well educated, and nearly all of Protestant confession. These children, whether children of English, French, Dutch or Danish fathers, are called Portuguese. But these children are never admitted to table in the company of Europeans and are treated by the English as inferior species of beings. They may be regarded as a connecting link between Europeans and natives. For these children Carey established the "Benevolent Institution for the Instruction of Indigent Children", "one of the monuments of active and indefatigable benevolence towards Serampore. [15]) In "Het tiende verslag der Nederlandsche Afdeeling van het Zendelinggenootschap der Engelsche Baptisten", we read : "The Benevolent institution has been a great blessing for the poor and destitute children. The number of the pupils amounted to one hundred an eighty-five, the number of the girls from sixty to eighty. Further we are informed in this report of two lads who were saved by industrious reading of the Scriptures, together with their neighbouring families." [16])

In our survey we mentioned the native schools at the many stations in the country. We also gave an account of his famous Serampore college. Carey's last report at the close of 1832 may be of particular interest. Dr. George Smith asserts that this report was a defence of what has since been called *educational missions*, or Christian Colleges, which were not always duly appreciated outside India and Scotland. But Carey on the contrary preferred a special divinity college for Asiatic Christians, a *divinity faculty* as p a r t of an Arts and Science College, in which the converts study side by side with their inquiring countrymen, where the inquirers are influenced by them as well as by the Christian and secular teaching in a Christian spirit, and the Bible consecrates the whole. The Free Church of Scotland has, in India as well as in Africa, proved the wisdom, the comprehensiveness, and the spiritual advantage of Carey's policy. When the Society (in England) opposed him, scholars like Mack from Edinburgh and LEECHMAN from Glasgow rejoiced to work out his Paul-like conception. When not only he, but also Dr. Marshman had passed away, Mack bravely held aloft the banner they bequeathed, till his death in 1846. In a note Dr. George Smith gives his further information : "In 1834, the year Carey died, there were in the College ten European and Eurasian students learning Hebrew, Greek, Latin, Bengali, mathematics, chemistry, mental philosophy, and history (ancient and ecclesiastical). There were forty-eight resident native Christians and thirty-four Hindoos, chiefly sons of Brahmins, learning Sanskrit, Bengali, and English. The Bengal language is sedulously cultivated. The Christian natives of India will most effectually combat error and diffuse sounder information with a knowledge of Sanskrit. The communication, therefore, of a thoroughly classic Indian education to Christian youth is deemed an important but not always an indispensable object."

Besides all these institutions we will mention one more : a free school, under a Bengali master for the children of India's very poor. They had already founded boarding-schools for the sons and daughters of well-to-do Europeans and East Indians to make money towards the cost of printing Scriptures, but these schools for the very poor were a pure joy to Carey and his colleagues.

From all we mentioned in this summary we clearly see the principle of William Carey : He tried to get hold of the Indian youth of all classes in order to get a hold on the future life of India.

He clearly understood that the Serampore college should not be a seminary, but a kind of Indian University for India. His principle of adaptation could never be better demonstrated than here. His preaching by means of the schools was one of the mightiest instruments in the fulfilment of the commission of the Lord.

He did not see the schools and college as subordinate to his preaching of the Gospel : the central service. On the contrary : he called the schoolmasters, the lecturers, the professors who tried to convert heathen by means of their influence missionaries. Thomas' medical skill could be a help to his work, but schools were not only a help but they were an indispensable part of the missionary work.

He saw the school service as coordinated with the central service : the preaching of the Gospel.

g. The written Word.

Above we mentioned his colossal work of translation. Here we only refer to his writing and distributing tracts and pamphlets, editing papers etc.

When he has been only a few days in India, he tries to buy a second-hand press, in order to print the Bible, tracts etc. In making his itinerating journeys he and his fellow-missionaries preached in various villages on the route and excited great interest by the novelty of their addresses to the heathen and more especially by the distribution of printed books and pamphlets, which had never before been seen in the country. The demand for books exceeded their highest expectation. The natives crowded around the boat, asking for them with great importunity; and if the supply had been five times as large, it would speedily have been exhausted. From this report of Ward dating 1801 we conclude that at the early start of his work, William Carey clearly understood the great importance of the colportage of books.

On page 93 of our survey of his life we mentioned a pamphlet which had been issued from the Serampore Press containing strictures on Mohammedanism and its founder. For the words of abuse in this pamphlet, however, neither Dr. Carey nor his printers were responsible. Mr. EDOMONSTONE was assured that measures would be immediately adopted to suppress the pamphlet which had appeared obnoxious to the Government.

This quarrel shows us the great influence attributed by Government to these pamphlets. Government would never have been excited if these pamphlets had been considered negligible.

The importance of the use of the Bengali language is illustrated by Dr. George Smith in his eleventh Chapter. But here we have not to deal with the literary but with the missionary influence of William Carey. It is difficult to distinguish between the two influences. E.g. when he translates the famous Ramayana and constructs his grammars, he is influencing the country in a missionary way as well as in a literary way. His dictionary of 80.000 words began to appear in 1815. And knowing that in the long run the literature of a nation must be of indigenous growth, he at once made the natives join in the work.

RAM BOSHU was a well known pundit, who wrote the "Gospel Messenger" and described the Life of Raja Pratapaditya, the last king of Sagar Island, for William Carey. Later on newspapers appeared: the Samachar Darpan on the 31st of May 1818 "the first newspaper ever printed in any Oriental language". Lord Hastings declared on his return from fighting the Pindarees: "that the effect of such a paper must be extensively and importantly useful." Also the natives welcomed the newspaper with enthusiasm. The paper influenced the development of the Bengali language as well as the moral and political education of the people. Later on other papers and periodicals were issued. This may do to show once more how broadminded William Carey was.

He took in hand both the printing and distributing part of the Colportage-service. Also in this respect he may be called a founder of modern missions.

h. Baptism.

In our survey we more than once stated that William Carey did not adhere to the principles of the Reformed church regarding Baptism. "Baptism is an ordinance of the New Testament ordained by Jesus Christ to be unto the party baptized a symbol of his fellowship with Him in his death and resurrection ; of his being engrafted into him ; of remission of sins ; and of his giving himself up unto God, through Jesus Christ to live and walk in newness of life.

Those who actually profess repentance towards God, faith in and obedience to our Lord Jesus, are the only proper subjects of this ordinance.

The outward element to be used in this ordinance is water, wherein the party is to be baptized in the name of the Father and the Son and the Holy Spirit.

Immersion, or dipping of the person in water, is necessary to the due administration of this ordinance." (Baptist confession of 1688.)

The significance of the promises of the Lord to all his people living under the Covenant was not clear to William Carey.

But he was fully convinced that his stand-point was correct. We mentioned his dispute with Henry Martyn and also with the British and Foreign Bible Society. But this dogmatic principle did not interfere in such a way with his missionary task that it was detrimental to his work. On the contrary. He was always prepared to collaborate with other denominations. And he advised his son Jabez to be prudent with the propagating of baptist principles.

People were baptized by him if they showed love to and had some knowledge of the Biblical truths as we saw in the case of Krishna Pal.

He never baptized children. Only adults who were immersed after having confessed their faith.

A question may be raised in this connection : the question of the renaming of the converts. When the converts were received in the church by baptism, should the convert adopt another name at this ceremony? William Carey opposed this practise. It was not the custom in the apostolic age and he himself could not see any connection between the rite of Christian baptism and a change of the name, as not usual in the apostolic age. See p. 79 of this book.

Par. V. Missionary purpose.

a. The problem.

One of the greatest problems is the question what must be done with the natives after being baptized.

In what way are they to be made useful. Are they to join in the missionary labours. The seventh article of the Form of Agreement of 1805 is a detailed answer to this difficult question. We may refer to our Appendix where we find this article in full.

Of course William Carey did not raise these questions at the outset, but he studied them later on when he was an experienced missionary.

b. The cooperation of the natives.

A definite plan of cooperation of the native brethren occupied their attention in Dec. 1803. Then they plan to set up a number of subordinate stations, in each of which a brother was to be settled. They furnish him with translations of the Bible, pamphlets etc., while to every brother in such a station one or two native brethren are added, in order to do all they can to preach and spread Bibles, pamphlets, etc., and to set up and encourage schools where the reading of the Scriptures shall be introduced. The whole belongs to the mission, and no part will ever be reserved for private trade or private property. The gains may probably support the station. Four brethren must constantly send a *monthly account* of spiritual and temporal matters to Serampore, and the brethren at Serampore (who must have a power of *control* over the stations) must likewise send a monthly account to each station, with advice, etc., as shall be necessary. The four brethren at Serampore must be like the heart while the other stations are the members. This plan may be extended over a circular surface of a thousand miles' radius, and a constant communication kept up between the whole.

We already stated in our survey that this plan could not be executed because *Government* refused to give its consent, but Carey anticipates its approval in spite of *the Company's* determined hostility in England. [17])

In this connection it may be of interest to quote the words of Ward to Dr. Ryland: "Be assured that whatever Europeans may say about the impossibility of converting the Hindoos (as the Moravian missionaries), there wants nothing more, as respects human means, but a few men of gifts and real powerful godliness. Hindoos and Mahomedans will as surely fall under the doctrine of the Cross as Greenlanders and Hottentots. The reason why this work has never been done yet is, because the means have never been suited to the end. It will be in vain to expect that the Gospel will ever spread widely in this country, till God so blesses the means as that *native men* shall be raised up, who will carry the despised doctrine, brought into the country by the Mlechas, into the very teeth of the brahmins, and prove from the Scriptures that this is indeed the Christ that should come into the world. We hope we shall see the dawn of this". [18])

Later on no report was issued from Serampore without enforcing the necessity of native agency, and the subject was taken up in 1818 with increased vigour. They represented the European missionary as possessing qualifications which were wanting in native converts, and which fitted him to become ,,the soul of a missionary circle". But the employment of *native itinerants* was indispensable even on the ground of economy. The sum required for the support of a European with a family would be sufficient to meet the wants of twenty *native labourers*, who, under his guidance, might itinerate through a large district and fill it with Scripture knowledge. And one missionary thus supported by a body of native labourers, would unquestionably be able to accomplish more than two or three Europeans without that aid. [19])

Dr. Beusekom remarks in his "William Carey, de grondlegger der hedendaagsche zending" that William Carey lays much stress upon the principle of *"naturalising* Christianity in India", and as a remarkable fact, Stanley Jones uses the same term in his "The Christ of the Indian Road": "He (Christ) is becoming naturalised there" [20])

We may come to a conclusion and say that Carey determined to employ the natives of the land. Of course many of these men did not possess the energy of the European character; but they had a thorough knowledge of the character and the habits of the people, and above all they were familiar with the *vernacular tongue.* Moreover, when these men went into the country they could not be deported for want of a license.

We may end the survey of this principle by giving his own words: "We have availed ourselves of the help of native brethren ever since we had one who dared speak in the name of Christ, and their exertions have chiefly been the immediate means by which our church has been increased. But we have lately made a plan for rendering their labours more extensively useful; namely, that of sending them out, two and two, without any European brother. This also appeared to be a most desirable means to interest the whole of the native church among us in this work: indeed, we have found much in them to commend in this respect. In order, then, more effectually to answer this purpose, we had a special meeting of all the brethren on Friday evening, Aug. 8th, 1806, and laid before them the following ideas:

1. Now that they had been called by the Saviour, out of darkness into marvellous light, He meant them to labour to their utmost to advance his cause among their countrymen.

2. That it was therefore their indispensable duty, both collectively and individually, to strive by every means to bring their countrymen to the knowledge of the Saviour: that if we, who were strangers, thought it our duty to come from a country so distant, for this purpose, much more it was incumbent on them to labour for the same end. This was therefore the grand business of our lives.

3. That if a brother in discharge of this duty went out forty or fifty miles, he could not labour for his family: it therefore became the church to support such, seeing they were hindered from supporting themselves, by giving themselves wholly to that work, in which it was equally the duty of all to take share.

4. We therefore proposed to unite the support of itinerant brethren with the care of the poor, and to throw them both upon

214

the church fund, as being both, at least in a heathen land, equally the duty of the church.

These ideas are of the highest value even for our days.

c. The financial self-support of the heathen-churches.

We more than once stated that one of the main principles of William Carey was that the missionary work should be self-supporting, just as *the Moravians* had it. In his Enquiry he had made proposals for contributions. But these had to be used for the voyage and the first expenses. So Carey was at a loss where to find the necessary money as Dr. Thomas spent all in a few days, and they had no other funds. When the Society in England complained of his starting an *indigo factory* he answered : "I may declare that after a bare allowance for my family my whole income, and some months much more, goes for the purpose of the Gospel, in supporting pundits, and school-teachers and the like. The love of money has not prompted me to this indigo-business. I am indeed poor, and always shall be, till the Bible is published in Bengali, and Hindustani, and the people need no further instruction."

We already stated that the common expenses were to be met from the common fund, but each family was to receive a small allowance for private needs. And all the money earned should be paid into the *common cash-box*.

When he erected the stations they themselves hoped to be able to bear the cost of the initial outlay of each station, and for the rest Carey relied on his fixed policy of partial employment in a profession or trade for no personal profit—the earnings all pooled for the Mission. "Therefore he begged *the home base* to send them such as, together with clear spiritual fitness, 'could make paper or glass, print cloth or dye chintz, teach drawing or music, be apothecaries or surgeons etc.'." [21])

Now there seems to have been some change in his opinion, for on the preceding page we noted that he planned to support the native-christians, who were itinerating. But these two statements are not contradictory. When he adheres to the principle of self-supporting he expresses the idea that India shall support India. The home base is only wanted when he is in need of funds, which he pays back again.

215

d. The organization of the congregations.

When William Carey was ordained in Leicester (May 24th, 1791) to the pastorate upon which he had entered some eighteen months ago, he showed himself a clever organiser. In September 1790 he proposed the church's dissolution, and its reformation on the basis of a solemn covenant, which was "to bind them to a strict and faithful New Testament discipline, let it affect whom it might". This was approved by the majority and put into practise. The refractory, holding back, were after two months declared no longer in membership. This shows us that he adhered to the idea of church discipline. Later on his son William excluded two members of the Church in the absence of Mr. Fernandez, the pastor. Then his father vituperates him. Not on account of the exclusion, but it would have been better for William "to have advised them or even to have required them to have kept from the Lord's table till Mr. Fernandez's return, and to have left it over to him to preside over the discipline of the church." 22)

This shows us that he had some Calvinistic idea of church government, and we also know that he practised this principle when natives did not live according to the law of God.

His organizing of the church was, as we saw on page 194, without reference to caste distinctions. Krishna Pal was the first convert to be baptized. Jeymooni, Krishna's wife's sister, was the first Bengali woman to be baptized, and Rasoo, his wife, soon followed. The year 1800 did not close without any fruit of his labour, for Petumber Singh, a man of the writer caste, was moved by one of the tracts of the Serampore press and asked further intruction and was baptized afterwards. The first Mohammedan was Peroo. In Calcutta the first Brahmin who had bowed his neck to the Gospel was Krishna Prasad. In 1804 two more Brahmins were baptized.

Then a church was built by Krishna Pal—the first native meeting-house in Bengal. Carey preached the first sermon in it to twenty natives.

Then the marriage difficulty had to be settled : a Brahmin was married to a sudra in the christian way : Englishmen ate with the married couple and their friends, at the same table, and at a native house. Hindoos say that such a sight has not been in Bengal for millions of years. 23) William Carey abolished caste

216

and settled a new community and laid the foundation for a well established church.

We saw other instances of this when the members of different castes communicated at the Lord's supper and when he buried Gokool, not in a pagan way, but with christian ceremony.

When the question is asked in what way he organised the internal church government, we once more answer in the Moravian way, which gave much trouble when the juniors arrived.

We may conclude this summary by asserting that he tried to establish a christian community, a christian church contrary to the Hindoo systems and life.

This fact is very important, particularly when we look at the practises of other missionaries. In this respect we may call him a founder of new principles in India.

e. The ecclesiastical relations.

The problem here discussed is this : what is the relation of the established churches to each other.

The eighth article of the Form of Agreement gives a detailed answer to this question, to which we may refer here.

This article specially shows that he had a broader outlook than any other missionary of his time, and before him.

In this respect it is also of importance to read the seventh article, especially the last sentences. A real missionary becomes a father to his people. Indeed, just as a father educates his children to independence, so William Carey tried to bring up the native, not as transformed Europeans, but as converted Indians with an Indian life.

NOTES

[1]) Verslagen der Nederlandsche Afdeeling van het Zendelinggenootschap der Engelsche Baptisten te Serampore in Oost-Indië.
We found in these reports not only a summary of the principles of Dr. WILLIAM CAREY as a foundation for his main action, but also the names of the Dutchmen who actually supported the missionary activities at Serampore. Especially the reports one to fourteen are of great interest to anybody who tries to write a biography of Dr. William Carey and also to those who intend to write a History of Dutch Missions. These reports (1—14) are dated from Sept. 1 1822 till April 23 1836.
In the first report we found four principles : 1. The preaching of the Gospel (het verkondigen van den leere des Evangeliums). 2. The translation of the Scriptures (de overzetting namelijk der Heilige Schrift). The Dutch word "namelijk" does not mean namely but especially. For on the same page the writer of this report S. MULLER, mentions the translation of many other books and the edition of Grammars and tracts and also the issue of a magazine : "Brahmaansch Magazijn of De Zendeling en de Bramijn" (Brahman Magazine or the Missionary and the Brahmin).

3. The establishment of schools for the education of the Indian youths (de scholen voor het onderwijs der Indische jeugd). 4. As a fact of the greatest importance is mentioned the establishment of the Serampore College (de kweekschool ter opleiding van Predikers en zendelingen). This verdict is not quite right, as it is only one of the purposes of this famous college.

Of great importance is the information Mr. MULLER gives on p. 10 of the first report when he tells us that WILLIAM CAREY established a savings-bank on account of the carelessness of the natives (om den geest van zorgeloosheid tegen te werken, hebben de zendelingen op hunne woonplaats een spaarbank opgerigt).

Moreover he tells us that Dr. Carey founded a Society for promoting agriculture and horticulture as we mentioned already. (de Heer Carey heeft onlangs een genootschap opgerigt ter aanmoediging van den Land- en Tuinbouw.) Here we see once more the founder of an up-to-date Mission. The second report written by R. KOOPMANS, president and S. MULLER, secretary, dated October 1823 is divided in three parts : the first dealing with the missionary activities in East India on the Continent, and the second part dealing with the East India Islands and the third part dealing with West India. Mr. DIERING of Sumatra and Mr. BRÜCKNER of Java are mentioned and Mr. EVANS of Padang and Mr. BURTON of Battas. The fourth report dated Oct. 4, 1825 tells us that Dr. CAREY himself supervises all the translation of the Holy Scripture ("Hij houdt in persoon het opzigt over elke dezer vertalingen") In the seventh report of Nov. 25, 1828 we read something of the benevolent institution established in 1809 for children of the poor and sailors etc. This institution greatly improved social conditions and roused religious activity especially for the outcasts and the very poor.

The report of Febr. 17, 1831 tells us that the suttee or sati custom has been abolished especially by the activities of Lord WILLIAM BENTINCK. In this report we also read the establishment of boarding-schools. The tenth report tells us that some schools particularly erected for girls are due to be enlarged. In the eleventh report we read that the Benevolent Institution teaches 150 to 160 boys. That three Sunday schools have been established, and further a detailed report of all the stations where the missionaries are labouring. While the thirteenth report is dealing only very shortly with Dr. WILLIAM CAREY, the fourteenth on the contrary gives us the account of his death. At the general Assembly a unanimous declaration was made, praising highly the enormous task he fulfilled and the extraordinary skill for oriental languages and his talent for organisation. These reports are of very great and particular worth for those who take an interest in the whole story of the Serampore mission. And as we stated above : almost all these reports are dealing with the missionary work on Java, Sumatra and Dutch West India. So they are of the highest importance for the History of Missions.

[2] The Rev. GEORGE BROWN, "The History of the British and Foreign Bible Society". Vol. II, p. 140—141.

[3] W. WANTON, "History of the British and Foreign Bible Society".Vol. II, p. 114.

[4] Dr. GEORGE SMITH, op. cit., p. 451.

[5] MARSHMAN, op. cit., p. 230—238.

DEAVILLE WALKER gives in Chapter XXIII of his work a survey of Carey's translation work. Moreover the pages 176, 204, 229, 238, 270—271, 314 should be consulted.

All his biographers give a detailed account of his translations which are among his greatest achievements.

[6] MARSHMAN, op. cit., p. 412.

[7] Dr. J. H. BAVINCK, Ons Zendingsboek, p. 54 and 55.

[8] S. PEARCE CAREY, op. cit., p. 349 f.

[9] Ibid., p. 350.

[10] Ibid., p. 201.

[11] Ibid., p. 291.

[12] Ibid., p. 295.

[13] OGILVIE, op. cit., p. 313—314.

[14] Dr. GEORGE SMITH, op. cit., p. 102 f.

[15] Ibid., p. 152.

[16] Nederlandsch Verslag tiende Juli 1831, p. 6.

[17] Dr. GEORGE SMITH, op. cit., p. 162 f.
[18] MARSHMAN, p. 182 I.
[19] MARSHMAN, II, p.
[20] E. STANLEY JONES, The Christ of the Indian Road, p. 40. London 1930.
Dr. Ir. H. G. VAN BEUSEKOM, De Grondlegger van de hedendaagsche zending, p. 103.
[21] S. PEARCE CAREY, p. 261—262.
[22] GEORGE SMITH, op. cit., p. 202.
[23] Ibid., p. 146.

C. PRINCIPLES OF MISSION OF THE PIETISTS, ESPECIALLY OF THE MORAVIANS.

a. Some historical facts of the Pietistic and Moravian missionary movement.

Dr. Gustav Warneck asserts that the real cause of the powerful missionary movement in the Lutheran church, is unknown. He thinks it highly improbable that the King of Denmark should be the real cause of this movement, although many attribute to him the honour and praise for the enterprise. Now he may have been a religious man, just as his family, but Dr. Warneck contests, that he is the real cause of the Pietistic missionary movement. He may have been an instrument to effect the first lutheran missionary movement, but then more, says Dr. Warneck, on account of his position as a king, than on account of his religious conviction. Dr. Warneck thinks it probable, that the chaplain-in-ordinary of the king, Dr. Lütkens, who went to Copenhagen in 1704, after having laboured in Berlin for seventeen years as a provost, had much more influence on his missionary plan, than is usually accepted. Dr. Lütkens is asserted to have been a friend of PHILIPP JACOB SPENER, the father of Pietism, the writer of the famous Pia Desideria, and these ideas should have particularly influenced Dr. Lütkens. [1]

These thoughts of Dr. Warneck are remarkably confirmed by the writer of "The lives of the missionaries in southern India", who says: "In the early youth of Frederick, his religious instruction had been confided to one of the royal chaplains, Dr. Lütkens, a man of earnest piety, whose soul longed for the conversion of the heathen to Christ. He imparted to his royal pupil a missionary zeal resembling his own, and taught him to look upon his exalted position as a means of endeavouring to advance the kingdom of God upon earth. As soon as Frederick was peaceably settled on the throne, and had brought to an end a disastrous war with Sweden, which troubled the opening years of his reign, he began to form plans for the conversion of the heathen, who dwelt on his own territory of Tranquebar." [2])

It is pleasing to know the way in which the Lord ultimately aroused the missionary interest in the heart of the king. One evening in March, 1705, King Frederick IV. of Denmark was busy in his palace perusing some official papers which had arrived from his over-sea dominions, and a paper which specially interested him was one from Tranquebar. This was an appeal for a pension from the widow of a Danish soldier, who had lost both husband and son in some skirmish with the natives. Out of her sorrow and penury the widow appealed to the King and the royal heart was touched. From considerations of the woman's sad lot, his thoughts turned to the condition and needs of the heathen who had wrought this sorrowful deed. What was he doing for them ? Surely this was a divine leading ! What effort was he making to convey to those Hindus the riches of the Gospel, in return for the material wealth which he and his people were drawing from India ? And he had to answer—nothing. His conscience awoke, and there and then he resolved to atone for past neglect. Dr. Lütkens, his chaplain, was hastily summoned, and heard with glad surprise the King's resolve. When asked where he could find a suitable missionary the good old man replied : "Here am I. Send me." [3])

The king, however, understood that it was impossible to send Dr. Lütkens, being too old and so he was ordered to look out for suitable men for the great enterprise. *This* marked the beginning of a new epoch in the History of missions.

Dr. Lütkens went to Berlin, and there he purposely went in a pietistic direction in looking for a missionary. As mentioned, Dr. Lütkens was a friend of Spener, who had tried to reform the Lutheran church from cold orthodoxism and scholastic dogmatism towards the living theology of the heart, which he expressed in his work "Pia desideria", in the following six points :
1. Dass man darauf bedacht sein möge, das Wort Gottes reichlicher unter uns zu bringen. 2. Die Aufrichtung und fleissige Uebung des allgemeinen Priesterthums. 3. Dass man den Leuten wohl einbilde und sie dahin gewöhne zu glauben, es sei mit dem Wissen im Christentum durchaus nicht genug, sondern das Christentum bestehe vielmehr in praxi. 4. Dass man genauer auf sich Acht

geben sollte, wie man wegen der Religionsstreitigkeiten und Diejenigen sich zu verhalten habe, welche allerdings Ungläubige und Falschgläubige wären 5. Dass die Akademien, wie es billig sein sollte, auch recht als Pflanzstätten der Kirche in alle Ständen und Werkstätten des heiligen Geistes, nicht aber des Weltgeistes, ja des Ehrgeiz-, Sauf-, Balg- und Zankteufels an dem Leben der Studiosorum erkannt wrden möchten. 6. Dass die Predigten so von Allen eingerichtet werden mochten dass der Zweck derselben nämlich der Glaube und dessen Früchte bei den Zuhören bestmöglichst befördet würden. [4]) At home Spener had his well known religious meetings, called "collegia pietatis", where they prayed and tried to explain and apply the Bible. These meetings were imitated by many other leaders of the Pietist movement e.g. AUGUST HERMANN FRANCKE, PAUL ANTON and KASPAR SCHADE, who gave them some different character viz. the explanation of the Bible in the German language. They called these meetings "collegia philobiblica". Francke stirred the dead bones of German orthodoxy marvellously by his numerous institutions as his orphanage, his paedagogium, his seminarium, his Orientale, his Seminarium Nationum and under his influence numbers of young men were trained for christian work and fired with christian zeal. [5]) At Berlin was a friend of Dr. Lütkens, Professor LANGE who was also a friend of Francke. So to professor Lange an appeal was made and he recommended the two pietistic candidates Bartolomaus Ziegenbalg and his friend Heinrich Plütschau. [6])

Francke himself was a universal spirit. He already had missionary ideas by influence of Leibnitz, who intended to christianize China, before the King of Denmark had any idea of Tranquebar. In the archives of mission in the orphanage of Francke a book is found of which the title runs as follows: "Pharus missionis evangelicae, seu consilium de propaganda fide per conversionem ethnicorum maxime Sinensium, prodromus fusioris operis ad potentissimum regem Prussiae Fredericum, in quo veritatis demonstratio, causae moventes, conversionis praeparatoria tentamen legationis evangelicae subsidia necessaria, ut et modus conversionis et conversorum conservatio primis fundamentis delineantur et censurae societatis Brandenburgicae scientiarum ut et eruditorum omnium et piorum seriae deliberationi subiiciuntur."

This book is thought to be written by Francke, as Prof. Warneck asserts. The title of this book proves how Francke was thinking of missions before King Frederick IV had any project at all. Moreover his seminarium universale "an establishment to improve all classes in Germany and outside this country, even in Europe and all parts of the world" proves his broad ideas and his purpose to revive Christianity. Last but not least we must mention here his collegium orientale, to revive the Oriental and Greek Churches. From this college many pupils went to Russia and Constantinople. From the establishment of these institutions we clearly see that there was missionary zeal in this great man, pietist though he was.

Prof. Warneck asserts that this universal spirit was the real cause of the missionary action of Halle. He gradually became the leader in missionary affairs in Europe. He formed in Germany many congregations which were praying for the missionaries he had sent and he was the man who gave all necessary advice to any missionary who wished information. The Danish mission had its real centre in August Hermann Francke and without this man the Tranquebar mission would soon have died.

It is a great pity that the official church in Germany opposed the idea of *church* mission. Most of the opponents even warned against any financial help. When the Wittenberg University had its anniversary the missionaries were called "false prophets", and the Hamburg preacher NEUMEISTER concluded his sermon on Ascensionday with these words : Years ago people said : "God into the world", but now we say : "Stay where God has called you."

But whatever this resistance of the official church might be, the Pietistic movement became the bearer of new missionary life. And whatever may have been the narrowmindedness of A. H. Francke, he was an instrument in Gods hands to move almost all the protestant churches in Europe to new life and missionary action. True, he said : "dass was nicht der Erbauung dient als schädlich gemieden wurde." And HEUSSI pretends : "Damit schrumpfte er das theologische Studium zur erbaulichen Beschäftigung mit der Bibel zusammen, Wissenschaft und Philosophie gerieten in Miszkredit. Die Folge war eine völlige gewissenschaftliche Unfruchtbarkeit. Kinder wurden alle Fröhlichkeit verboten und alles Spielens" [7]), but it is highly remarkable that just such a man had such an influence in the whole world.

For not only Plütschau und Ziegenbalg were sent to India,

but also SCHULTZE, GERICKE, FABRICIUS, SCHWARTZ [8]), all due to the activity of Francke. At Copenhagen they were happy to send some missionaries to Lapland and Greenland. To Lapland : ISAAC OLSEN, THOMAS VON WESTEN, and PER FJELLSTRÖM. To Greenland : HANS EGEDE of Norway.

Closely connected with this action of Halle is the action of Nikolaus Ludwig, Graf und Herr Von Zinzendorf und Pottendorf (1700—1760). As a boy of 10 years he was already in contact with August Hermann Francke at Halle, who educated him in his Paedagogium from 1710—1716. When he was 15 years old he established some kind of missionary society. At Wittenberg from 1716—1719 he became a doctor of law and made a trip to Holland and France where he met many reformed people. Famous are his words : "When der Christ auch sonst von niemand geachtet wird, so will ich mich doch an ihn hängen und mit ihm leben und sterben." Another famous expression is : "Ich habe nur eine Passion und die ist Er, nur Er." A very deep impression was made upon him when he was at Düsseldorf and he saw a picture with these words : "Ego pro te haec passus sum, tu vero quid fecisti pro me ?" [9]) He decided definitely to be at the disposal of his heavenly Father. In 1722 some Moravians fled to his castle and he inspired these men with the same missionary love as he had. [10]) In 1731 he made a journey to Copenhagen to attend the coronation of King Christiaan IV. Some of the Moravian brothers went with him and they met a negro of St Thomas, called Anton. This Mr. Anton made a trip to Hernhut and gave the advice to the Moravians to give his countrymen the education they wanted. At the same time the Moravians heard at Copenhagen of the need of Greenland and the result of these meetings was that at once some of the Moravians were prepared to preach the Gospel in St Thomas and Greenland. But they still had to wait a year and in August 1732, LEONHARDT DOBER and DAVID NITZSCHMAN were sent to St Thomas with one pound of journey-money and in January 1733, MATTH. and CHRISTIAAN STACH were sent to Greenland. In 1733 missionaries were sent to St Croix, 1735 to Suriname, 1737 to the coast of Guinea and to Capeland, 1740 to North America, 1754 to Jamaica, 1756 to Antigua. RUTH ROUSE is right when she says : Zinzendorf was the founder of Unitas Fratrum, the Moravian Church, the most missionary Church in the world. Amongst Moravians, a missionary vocation for their young people has always been considered the normal thing, and in less than two centuries the tiny church, never numbering more than 70.000 sent out 2000 missionaries. The speciality of the Moravian Church has always been missions to neglected, oppressed or dying races. [11])

The action of the Moravian Church is unique in the history of Christianity and Prof. G. Warneck says that the explanation of this phenomenon is only this that the Moravians form a congregation which is founded in the Evangelic faith and which has as its root, love of Christ, a congregation in which the mentality are combined of Mary and Martha. [12])

When they had Holy supper on August 13, 1727 Zinzendorf sung:

> Hernhut soll nicht länger stehen
> Als die Werke deiner Hand
> Ungehindert drinnen gehen,
> Und die Liebe sei das Band,
> Bis wir fertig und gewärtig
> Als ein gutes Salz der Erden
> Nützlich ausgestreut zu werden.

This song has been fulfilled. Hernhut sent according to Prof. G. Warneck, more missionaries in twenty years than the whole remainder of Protestantism in two hundred years. Many of them died, they were sent without money, without education, they went only to the poor and destitute, but their example aroused much esteem in the whole world.

God has used this man Zinzendorf and this little congregation as an instrument in his hand to do wonderful things. Their principles may not be ours and their methods may differ from ours but their achievements were colossal.

We must here see God's hand and without seeing his leading hand, we cannot understand that he used these means to revive the whole church of Europe in order to understand its missionary task.

b. Some difference between the Pietistic and Moravian theological principles.

It is not my intention to describe fully the development of the religious ideas of Zinzendorf, as they fall outside the scope of this dissertation. But we can only understand his missionary principles when we understand some of his theological principles.

For that reason we will give some of his main doctrines here. Zinzendorf was in his early years very much under the Pietistic influence of August Hermann Francke at Halle. But later on, when he was in Wittenberg and when he made his trip to different countries after finishing his studies, he gradually received ideas different from the Pietistic. In 1729 he asserts that the Pietistic way of experiences which leads to trusting upon self-righteousness and own penances in stead of a trust on the merits of Christ, should not be followed. You are a child of God, he says, when you love the Saviour and you trust in Him. But you have to go one step further, he says. You must confess your own sins and have the conviction that you are and remain a sinner, that means a man, who always wants grace and who can never become a being who can stand alone before God. To get this conviction you don't want a penance-struggle. [13]) VON UTTEN-DORFER thinks that from 1729—1734 he gradually became convinced that the Pietistic way was not the right way. In the minutes of the Moravian church of Hernhut, we can read these anti-pietistic words : Living only according to law means a false and melancholic zealoting. One should not keep souls from Christ a long time, but you should show them Christ immediately. An improvement by law is not useful. Conversion is easy, for you only want trust in Christ. Formerly we believed that regeneration was the last station on the way of salvation and that it exists in the perfection of the image of God, but now we believe that even children can have it. [14]) From 1739 he criticized the righteousness founded on human work of the Pietists. "Die Hallenser haben den Artikel von der Rechtfertigung ganz verkehrt und sagen, dass man fromm werden und Christo nachfolgen soll, so werde man Gnade bekommen und selig werden." [15])

More and more he opposes the idea of the necessity of personal penance-struggle "von dem notwendigen eigenen Busskampf". He criticizes Pietism that it lays all the stress on practise and not on belief. For when there is belief the works will follow spontaneously and of their own accord. He does not like a special method to be saved. Pietism wishes improvement of life to prevent abuse of the merits of Christ, but Zinzendorf wishes to make a fable of personal holiness and to preach everywhere the righteousness through Christ's blood only. For that reason, he says, is the Pietist always dejected and only sometimes he has comfort, but the Moravian is saved by the Grace of God and is humbled sometimes when he sees his own sins. He says: the Pietistie way is the right way for melancholic people. What is necessary for penance-struggle our Saviour has done. Our Saviour has wept and has been very anxious and it is despicable for man to be so. [16])

We can say that after 1740 his ideas are fixed and then his main doctrines are the following:

1. His startingpoint is the infinite and absolute sovereign God to whom the finite creature has no admission and who cannot be reached by thinking only.

2. So religion must have another place in the life of the soul than intellect. Religion lies in feeling. Feeling is not according to Zinzendorf some state of mind, but direct, intuitive experience, coming forward from the inmost man, which experience is given, not made. Heart, he says, is the centre of the life of soul, lying in unconsciousness. The religious feeling is in its primitive form fear, but in its developed form it is feeling of something superior, or feeling of dependence towards the Creator. From that feeling grows on one hand obedience towards his will, on the other hand religion, which is worship and adoration.

3. God revealed himself in such a way that human beings can understand it. The highest revelation is the revelation of the Logos, whose work is already seen at creation but still more when he came into man.

4. The essence of sin is that man tried to be independent of God. It is pride.

5. Christ became man, not only to reveal God to man, but also to draw fallen man towards God again. He lays stress upon the true mankind of the Saviour. He has become true man and he has all human infirmities, but he is also the Creator himself, who humbled himself to death on the cross. The whole contents of the divine revelation is according to Zinzendorf this word: The creator is the Saviour. He lays much stress on the result of the death of Christ for fallen mankind. When they think of his death, they experience the judgment of damnation on one hand and on the other hand the endless love of their Creator who died for them, and this changes their animosity in to surrendering

226

love. It is not necessary for them to do penance, for penance *has* been done, they only have to accept grace. A sinner accepts salvation when he grasps the historical fact that the Creator is the Saviour and always sees before him the death of Christ on the cross. It is not possible to prove all this in a philosophic way, for both : fall of man and salvation of man by the love-act of Christ are supra-rational, paradoxical facts.

6. The essence of sin is no more independence, but unbelief, lack of trust in God who came down to us. The separate sins are only fruits of this inward corruption.

7. But we must not only believe in Christ but also love him. God has created man to love him, but the fall of man has broken this love. Fear remained and also the longing of the heart to be able to love God. Man is saved, when he looks upon the suffering Christ, who fills the sinner with love, reverence and obedience. So religion is salvation, salvation through the love of God. When a man acknowledges his misery and in his misery the Saviour, he is saved and does the commandments with happiness.

8. All stress must fall upon the seeing of Christ as crucified and in such a way that the innermost part of a man : the heart is united most intimately with the Saviour. He wishes that there is intercourse with the Saviour. And we want special hours of listening to him. Prayer and intercourse with the Saviour is quite the same for him and it has as its purpose not only to ask something of the Saviour, but in the first place to know his will and to form oneself according to his will.

9. Religion is a personal and experienced bond with God. Personally we must have connection with the Saviour To rely in religious affairs upon a big congregation leads to superficiality. Mass suggestion is not the real means to promote religion. On the other hand the Saviour did not create us to be hermits, but to be social beings and so we must have love to the brothers. This brotherlove develops itself from the love towards the Saviour. When these brothers are one then the Saviour pours his Spirit upon the whole and creates a community spirit, who pervades everybody and creates a harmonious life out of one fountain. This Spirit is a divine gift and cannot be received by human education.

10. We are all poor sinners. Not only worldly people but also Christians. For worldly people have deserved death. But Christians are also poor sinners because they not only pleaded innocence by

227

grace but they also are called poor sinners because there would be a possibility to sin in all eternity, if a christian should forget that he is totally dependent on God. So this idea is related to his main idea of religion : creation is dependent on the creator and God created man to be a means of godly grace and love. [17])

So we see that the whole system of the Pietists Buszkampf-Durchbruch-Versieglung has been broken. He puts aside all the experiences in order to be sure of salvation. He sees the way of salvation, justification and sanctification almost only in the suffering and death of Jesus Christ : in such a way that he does not see the vicarious character of Christ.

But there were also many points of contact with the Pietists His system is a reaction of the feeling against cold intellectualism, of the subject against objectivism, of life against scholastic doctrine. He also wishes knowledge of the heart and not of the head. He lays stress upon the action of a Christian, though in another way than the Pietists. He also formed an ecclesiola in ecclesia, he also became separatist and assembled people from other churches according to his philadelphic oecumenical aspirations. [18])

So the differences may be great, but yet his doctrine is closely related to Pietism and has more points of correspondence with the Pietists than of difference.

NOTES

[1]) Historische schets der Protestantsche zendingen van den tijd der Kerkhervorming tot op heden. Dr. GUSTAV WARNECK, Utrecht, 1882, p. 24.
[2]) Society for promoting christian knowledge. Life of missionaries. London without date, p. 6.
[3]) OGILVIE, op. cit., p. 208—209.
[4]) PHILIPP JACOB SPENER, Pia Desideria. Herausgegeben von KURT ALAND. Berlin 1940, p. 87, 88.
[5]) RINN und JÜNGST, Kirchengeschichtliches Lesebuch. Tübingen 1906, p. 256
[6]) WARNECK, op. cit., p. 24—25.
[7]) HEUSSI, Compendium der Kirchengeschichte 1937, p. 366.
[8]) WARNECK, op. cit., p. 27.
[9]) TH. MÜLLER, Een blik in de geschiedenis der Evangelische broedergemeente Zeist 1925, p. 71.
[10]) TH. MÜLLER, op. cit., p. 48—52.
[11]) RUTH ROUSE, God has a purpose. London 1935, p. 13.
[12]) GUSTAV WARNECK, op. cit., p. 31.
[13]) VON UTTENDORFER, Religiöse Grundgedanken. Hernhut 1935, p. 40.
[14]) Ibid., op. cit., p. 42.
[15]) Ibid., op. cit., p. 43.
[16]) Ibid., op. cit., p. 44.
[17]) Ibid., op. cit., p. 190—198.
[18]) Dr. W. LÜTJEHARMS, Het philadelphisch oecumenisch streven der Hernhutters in de Nederlanden in de 18e eeuw. Zeist 1935, p. 21.

Par. I. Statement of the motives of Pietist Missions especially of the Moravians.

The Danish-Halle missionary action was ultimately the work of the King of Denmark. He ordered the search for missionaries, he took Ziegenbalg and Plütschau in his service. They had his letters, his credentials in their hands, when they landed in Tranquebar, and his motive was to fulfill his duties towards his non-christian people by means of the preaching of the Gospel. They were servants of the King of Denmark who paid their expenses. They were "royal" missionaries.

In Hernhut the motive was different. At least in the very beginning. It was: "Seelen für das Lamm zu werben"; to gain souls for the Lamb. But after some time, the question was raised whether this elementary phrase was sufficient, especially after the first experiences. In order to understand the statement of the motives of Mission we must know something of his conception of the church.

It is well known that there was much struggle among the churches of his time. He would be ashamed, he said, to go to the heathen-world with such a church and preach the Gospel to the pagans. "In Europa trennt man sich aus Not und Liebe, aber den Plunder mit nach Amerika zu schleppen, das ist nicht vernünftig, geschweige denn christlich." He gradually gets the conviction that there is no palpable, visible church on earth, but only secondary schools, and academies with different classes, and with pupils who look down upon each other. Yet all these different sects have their task and whosoever is the servant of the Saviour is saved by Him through all denominations, if only he totally adheres to him: "wenn er's nur ganz mit ihm meint". This phrase "es ganz mit ihm meinen" is the crucial point of all religions. Apart from all these different religions, is the manifestation of the congregation of Christ (der Gemeinde Christi) always getting a new stature in the change of time. It is the task of unitas fratrum to establish this congregation. This unitas fratrum is only an instrument to make visible the vera ecclesia, the true church. His moravian church is called: "Streitwagen", "Bataille-pferd", "Lazarett", "Herberge" (war-car, war-horse, military hospital, inn). But these very words are an indication that he sees the unitas fratrum as a means to the great purpose: the Kingdom of God. [1])

And *here* we get an answer to the question ; What are his motives of mission ? The kingdom of God is the "continuous action", in which action are the Father, Son and Holy Ghost, together with the angels and elected people. The missionaries who are sent to the heathen don't go in order to establish a new Moravian Church, but they go as messengers, as witnesses, as fighters against the darkness, some amongst Roman Catholics, others among other Christian denominations and still others among the heathen of all tongues. Their weapon is everywhere the same : the witness of that, which took possession of their heart. They are fighting, but not their own fight. God fights the fight, He is in "continuous action".

When you, missionaries preach the Gospel, says Von Zinzendorf, then you must not use all kinds of philosophic arguments, but you only have to be witnesses of the Lamb, of the Creator who was crucified for them. For understand "that before you said one word to them, the Holy Ghost prepared them already ten years ago. You only are instruments and give thoughts and words to them to express what they possessed before you came to them. Our task is only to show the light of our message, to set fire to the heart, in which the Holy Ghost did his work long ago. ²)

There is not any place for propagandism, for all preaching must be witnessing of Christ. According to the apostolic example we have, without the dogmatic ballast, "Christum zu treiben", to insist on Christ.

Now Von Zinzendorf makes a clear distinction between 1 Sam. 25 : 29 and Matthew 13 : 47. When he has a meeting in America among the Indians he says : the mission to the heathen must not be a net, but a bundle of life. Does he mean to make a contrast between individual conversion and mass-conversion ? Not at all. He is thinking of the situation in Europe, where he sees the contrast : congregation and sect : Moravian congregation, Unitas fratrum and the sects with all their differences. Now he asks "shall we use the same methods among the heathen ?" Shall we try to christianize the heathen ? That would be a work of the devil. Europe is a warning example of "Generalheidenbekehrungen" of general conversions of the heathen. So we don't want a net, but a bundle. The task of the Unitas fratrum is to be a bundle, to be a roof, to be a mustardseed, a bundle of life. We only have to gather into that bundle souls, who are prepared by the Holy Ghost, and we may not be a net. [3]) When we are like mustard-seed, we can look into the future and expect the Kingdom of God in power and glory. For the "time of the heathen" lies still in the future. When we look back, then we see a ὕστερον πρότερον nations have been conversed, but very few disciples have been made. It first disciples had been made among all the nations, according to the command of the Lord, then the mustard-seed would have been a tree now. We see that a zealot-spirit has made people confess with their lips, before they have taken the Gospel in the heart. Asia and Africa lost these nominal Christians and Europe will lose them too, when impiety will fight these so-called christians. But when the name of Christ is written in the heart, it never can be rooted up. For that reason we must look at the old maxims : make disciples among the nations. You cannot preach to all nations at a time, but who has ears to hear, he hears us, and in this way the elect go out of all nations into the house of God. And in this way the Saviour will receive much more than by the conversion of whole nations. For that reason we say : "It is not our intention to convert the heathen." We are convinced that it is not yet the time of the heathen. We only want to lead a few souls to the Saviour. When people think that it is our intention to convert the heathen, they are wrong. Time has not yet come for general conversions, it is only ἐκλογη and ἀπαρχη just the same in the religions as among the heathen. The time of the heathen has not yet come. It would not be good when masses would be converted, as long as there are the religions and Pietists, who try by all means to convert people.—We are looking for firstlings out of the nations, and even when we have only two till four then we entrust them to the Saviour to do with them whatever he likes.

Von Zinzendorf does not intend to build of these firstlings a congregation of elite-christians, but he only want to see in them an indication towards the time of the heathen which shall come.

How must we see our missionary task ? This I see, he says, as a preparation for the Saviour . For it is not our task, it is not our instruction, that we have to converse nations, countries, islands ; but as we ourselves are a ἐκλογη so we have only a ἀπαρχην out of the heathen, especially out of the unspoiled heathen, that means, heathen who are not in touch with the socalled christians.

Von Zinzendorf feels that the example in the New Testament is different from what he has in his opinion. So he asks : Are not we obliged to make quite a lot of such hermits as the eunuch under Candace, so that they may work at the construction of the Kingdom of God ? The answer is : "Only St. Paul has gathered congregations, but all other disciples have not done this, according to the wish of the Saviour. But both were right. For St. Paul has not done this in many places e.g. in Galatia. The forming of a congregation is not the point, should not be the purpose.

When asked, what he means with the assertion that the time of the heathen has not yet come, then the answer is that this idea is due to his opinion about the kingdom of God. He thinks that the conversion of the Jews precedes the conversion of the heathen. But still more he lays stress upon this opinion : now we live in the time of religions, and if the heathens were converted as a whole just now, then they would come into the way of the religions and lose their purpose.

Once more he says : Our plan does not go further than the firstlings. That does not mean that no more people will be converted. But we will be phlegmatic when the number is reduced from a hundred to twenty and from twenty to ten. We won't make haste with establishing Churches, but we will look at the example of our Lord who had five hundred brothers, but usually he had not more than twelve, and when he wanted something better still : they were four. That was the total amount. And so we know that the terminus a quo, the time from which we rely on national-, or world-conversions to the slain Lamb, is *then* when the devil can no longer seduce the heathen. 4)

Par. II. The Organs of Missions.

In "some historical facts" we mentioned in which way the negro ANTON awakened the missionary action of the Moravians. Not after a long and logical reasoning, not after a rational solution of the missionary problem, but from irrational backgrounds the missionary consciousness was awakened. 5)

It was the same "Zeugentrieb" witness-drive, which drove them with obstinate power to the heathenworld. They felt related to the attitude of the apostles and St. Paul who had to preach, even when they were forbidden to do so. For that reason von

Zinzendorf made a sharp distinction between "der Religion" and "das Apostolat".

The idea of "the religion" is: "I come from the Father. They had the true religion, before other religions arose. We will stick to it."

The idea of "the Apostolate" is: "More people must be saved; Heathen come! Christians come! Men come to the Saviour! When they don't listen in the religions, then we go to the heathen. The Apostolate will arouse hatred in all religions; but we cannot help it. We cannot chain the Gospel."

Von Zinzendorf also says – "We would be extremely glad if that witnessdrive would be seen again: that a man would behave himself like a hound, who as soon as he sees that his master takes his rifle, does not know in which way he shall bound to show his joy. When in this way we only could see brothers who are longing for the saving of souls!"

But when such a witness drive is shown, von Zinzendorf does not like to send him to the mission field at once. First of all it must be examined. It may be years and years, before they are convinced of the genuineness. But when this is assured, all other obstacles must be removed. They ventured to send them away, only possessing the witness-drive. A very remarkable judgment is given by von Zinzendorf, in which he says that this witness is higher than conversion. "Thinking of our missionary action during twenty years, I must state that our first missionaries were not content because they were converted, but they had a burning urge and great courage to do something for the Saviour.

A missionary who fears the sea, or who repents when he is in the harbour should stay in his country."

Gradually however this witness drift was dwindling. For that reason von Zinzendorf is complaining of the lack of love especially about 1750. In the early years, he says, they were sent without knowing the language, without knowing in which country they should come, what their living would be. Now-a-days the enthusiastic form has gone away as the ecclesia plantanda has become an ecclesia plantata.

He does not like to send the missionaries to the field similarly to the Danish-Halle missionaries: paid by somebody, and as a pastor. He does not wish that missionaries are sent as colonists, or that they shall have such economic conditions that they forget their task. "Da sind viele Brüder nach Thomas gegangen, Apostel unter den Heiden zu sein, und haben die Aprikosen, Zypressen usw. im Kopf gehabt." [6] (Many brothers went to St. Thomas in order to be apostles among the heathen, but they had in their mind apricots and cypresses.)

He says our Saviour told us that we should not have any desire except him.

His method is quite different from the method of William Carey. He does not like that the missionary work should be done in this way "that missionaries should come home with large books, with new maps, had discovered some new mark in the compass, they should come home with souls." [7]

a. Qualifications of the missionaries.

The witness-drive is the decisive qualification of the divine call for each missionary according to Von Zinzendorf. But apart from this basic qualification, he asks whether a missionary should have other qualifications. It is a remarkable fact that in the first years there was not any discussion about qualifications A theologian was not put aside, because he was a theologian, nor was he put in the foreground. Von Zinzendorf takes artisans, people who never have left Hernhut, who must try to earn a living in the heathenworld. Later on in 1756 Von Zinzendorf looks back at the early years of their very beginning with some uneasiness. But he comforts himself with these words: The Saviour has seized them and after seizing them, has given them ability.

The Saviour gave these people an analogy of his way of thinking and made them speak a word in due time which was very good, for they showed understanding of the situation. Among the masses of people who went to the field there were artisans, and scientists, young and unmarried, old and married people, even widows. That there were so many artisans is due to the economic conditions of Hernhut, but also to the economic condition of the missionary work. This is the way expenses had to be met; they had to earn their living with their hands during the voyage and on the mission-field.

The little town of Hernhut was of course not able to afford all the workers, necessary for the different missionary fields. Müller states: "Die Mission Hernhuts ist von Anfang an ohne den breiten

234

Hintergrund des deutschen Pietismus nicht denkbar. Es strömten fortgesetzt die Leute herzu die sich mit ans Werk stellten.'' So we see that Pietism made Hernhut's missionary work possible. Even more : the missionaries were from the different parts of Germany. For the same reason Müller tells us that of the 763 missionaries who were sent to the fields from 1732—1832, we don't know the origin of 215 but of 548 he gives the countries from where they came. The greatest amount is given by Saxony, viz. 48, then Würtemberg 30. England gave 31 missionaries and America the same number. Ireland 13 and Holland 2. All the other parts of Germany gave less and this proves that the missionary movement of Von Zinzendorf was only possible through Pietism.

As for the education of missionaries from the very beginning they speak of essential knowledge for the missionfield. But later on we don't hear anything about education. Then they were content with elementary education. The synods of 1818 and 1825 which dealt with missionary affairs, declined the establishment of a missionary college. The synod of 1818 took the following descision : "We think it not in concordance with our purpose to have missionary schools or to prepare brothers by means of some systematic education. The conversion to the Saviour by the Holy Spirit connected with ardent love to souls, proved to be the best preparatory method. It is our task to preach the word of the cross with the greatest possible simplicity to the heathens : it is not necessary to use some educational system nor to deal with polemics. [8] When the heathens had a high culture then they understood that some more education would be advisable. Von Zinzendorf lays not only stress upon the spiritual qualifications necessary for a missionary, he also desired that he shall be a man of character. He must be a man between waiting and hurrying. At the first start they must be fiery, they must be just like a lightning flash and strike into lands and places, and before people understand what happens they must have converted them.

Many of the Moravian missionaries were married. Preferably they sent their children to a boarding school in Hernhut, later to Niesky. [9]

As for the health of the brothers and sisters, Von Zinzendorf thinks it profitable that some doctor goes with them, who can give some help to white and black men. The missionaries were also allowed to go on leave for some time in order to regain health. Especially in those times when the communications were so bad it was necessary for them.

A missionary by profession was unknown. They were not missionaries for their whole life. In the early beginning we see that missionaries go back to their work at home after some missionary period. Von Zinzendorf complains that gradually some class-feeling grew in the missionaries. They despised being servants on the ships taking them to the nations.

But on the other hand he is happy that another feeling was stronger : to be a messenger of the Lord. That feeling was often so strong that he had to warn them against a martyrdom which was longed for. Each witness must be prepared to give his life, says Von Zinzendorf, but he may not lose it by being neglectful. [10])

b. The missionary church.

A very important principle of the Moravian Church is that not some corporation or Society sent missionaries, but the *church* itself. Müller asserts that even the Danish-Halle mission would not have been possible, if there would not have been some circle of friends. The fact that the christian congregation sends the missionaries became a reality in the "Evangelische Kirche" in Hernhut "for the first time". Later on we see in Germany and other countries private missionary Societies, which exist apart from the Church, except the Hermannsburger Mission.

Müller further asserts that the very stormy beginning of the missionary action of Hernhut was only possible by the courageous work of a living congregation, which never had any lack of messengers. It is not accidental, that at any place where missionaries made themselves loose of the congregation their labour made no roots. There must be a congregation to send new man-power, when the stormtroops have fallen. Not only missionary action needs the christian congregation if it will not perish, but also the christian congregation needs the missionary action to inflame the faith of the congregation anew. [11])

A remarkable thing is the casting of lots which had a hidden but very definite part in the managing of the mission. Since 1727 all important decisions were made by drawing lots. The election of missionaries, the place and name of a missionary station, the admission to baptism and supper, even the trifling in-signifances, as e.g. the question whether they should read Old Testament or New Testament, were decided by casting lots. [12])

Now Müller raises the question in which way they decided to cast lots, and how this practise originated. He tells us that the real cause was Von Zinzendorf. In his personal life, he always made decisions by casting lots. E.g. whether he should go to Denmark. He had no money nor any intention to make that journey. But after the decision of the congregation and the lot, he went. Also the lot decided n which way he should travel. The lot decided his way of dealing with affairs in Copenhagen. Four days before he went home again he had to decide whether he should act: "doucement, rigoureusement, indifféremment, ou prudement". The lot decided the last. He thought that his way of dealing was biblical. He founded his opinion on Numbers 27 : 21 and 1 Sam. 28 : 6 where we read of the use of Urim and Tummim, and also in the New Testament Acts of Apostles 1 : 26. He said that human arbitrariness should be put aside and the will of the Saviour should be sovereign. They saw in the lot a very important means to prevent all subjectivism. But this practise does not exclude the using of their minds. On the contrary they have to think about a matter before they draw the lots. But when they draw the lots, then they must know very definitely what they are asking. He puts it in these words: "Wir machen mit dem Heiland erst das quod aus, dann gleich das quomodo." First they put the question about the "quod", then the "quomodo". Sometimes a missionary was reproved when they used the lots in an improper manner. The point of this custom was not to choose paths after their own desire, but to ask: "Lord what wilt Thou that I shall do." [13])

c. The financial support of missionaries.

The great principle of the Moravians is selfsupport. In the early days when DOBER and NITSCHMANN went to the mission field they were sent away with hardly any money. Quite the same attitude was struck when ARWED GRADINS went to Constantinopel in 1739. Only the most necessary expenses were brought together for the journey. But later on when the missionaries established missionary stations and when they had the care of wife and children, this problem became more and more acute.

So VON ZINZENDORF made this rule : the missionaries are sent to the different fields at the charge of the sending congregation. But as soon as they have arrived on the field, they must bear their own expenses and they also have to repay the costs of the journey. So the home front had to bear the costs of the outfit and all the rest had to be paid by the missionaries. [14])

An interesting comparison is given by Th. Müller, who informs us that of the 40 millions of guilders necessary for the expenses of all the missions, a little more than 1 million is used by the Moravians, and of all the protestant missionaries viz. 15.000 were only 300 Moravian missionaries. [15]) About 1750 it became a custom to collect during the meeting for the missionaries, each half year and the collection was announced eight days before.

Another source of financial support were the friends of Von Zinzendorf who were spread all over Germany, and who also gave board and lodging to the brothers when they left Germany for the mission-field. But all the stress was laid on voluntary contributions, and they did not like to make these contributions obligatory.

But contrary to the custom of Von Zinzendorf in Germany is his practise in foreign countries : in Amsterdam, in Copenhagen, in London were quite a lot of people who not only contributed but who really gave the financial support to the mission of Hernhut. [16]) In 1741 A Society for the propagation of the Gospel was established in Amsterdam, but many of the "dominees" (Dutch pastors), and rich merchantmen did not agree. [17]) In the same year a Society for furtherance of the Gospel was established in London. Later on a Heidendiakonie, a Reliefservice for the Heathen was founded (1754) which was a great help to the financial difficulties of Hernhut. Another means was the building of ships for use of missionaries and economic purposes. But they met with bad success.

The great principle of Von Zinzendorf and later on Spangenberg remained the same, whatever they did in foreign countries : to give some aid, as the selfsupport of the missionaries fell short of their wants. All possible means however were tried to make them self supporting and for that reason cobblers, tailors, carpenters, butchers, farmers and doctors etc., were sent to the fields. They also tried to support the mission by means of trade. But Von Zinzendorf saw clearly that it would be very difficult to keep trade and mission apart and he feared that trade would damage mission. "We should make ourselves to servants of men and that is contrary to our principles," he said. [18]) Later Von Zinzendorf warned very strongly against the mixing of mission and trade., "Wir dachten, der Dienst des Evangelii liesze sich in den Ländern, wo der Teufel noch wohnt, mit der Wirtschaft kombinieren. Aber dessen sind wird nun ganz anders überzeugt worden, dasz ich hoffe, wir werden nicht mehr so denken." Our opinion was that the service of the Gospel could be combined in those lands where the devil still lives. But our conviction has changed materially, so that I hope that we won't think so in the future. On the other side we see that Von Spangenberg and JONAS PAULUS WEISZ have another opinion. They agree with trade work when the trade only supports the mission and if kept apart from the mission. [19])

Par. III. Management of Mission.

A. TERRITORY OF THE MISSION FIELD.

It is not our purpose to give a description of the immense work of the Moravians in the different parts of the world. It does not fall within the scope of this dissertation as we only deal with these historical facts, which are of some value for understanding the principles of William Carey.

Now we see at once a great difference between the Danish-Halle mission which sent the missionaries to Danish territory and the Moravian Mission. Germany had no colonies at all. And for that reason Von Zinzendorf tried to find some missionary field in the colonies of Holland and Denmark : Suriname, South-Africa and Greenland. When the call was heard for colonists, the brothers were sent to North-America. Sometimes missionaries were sent to a land without any preparation e.g. the endeavour on the gold coast of Africa.

It was their custom to send some men to a land before the arrival of the missionaries in order investigate the country. Quite the same method was practised when the missionaries wished to go as colonists, in order to know whether the door was open or not. But often missionaries were sent to some fields contrary to the advice of those who had investigated the territories. Later on he disliked this method.

A very important question which was always raised was this :

whether there *were* already missionaries of other Societies. There were two reasons for this attitude : in the first place they did not like to enter into competition with other missionary societies and the second reason is that Von Zinzendorf feared the pernicious influence of the white nominal christians. He always longed to find some field where no white people had worked and spoiled the heathen. [20])

Just like missionary VERHOEVEN who established in West-Java a village of christians only, as an island in the middle of the Mohammedan world, so Von Zinzendorf made his plan of a christian town in which the only inhabitants were conversed Indians in the wilderness of Skehantowa. The language should be German and there should be no contact with the rest of the world, in order to prevent communication with other christians, whom he feared so much. [21])

Von Zinzendorf also planned to make some island in the middle of the ocean for a fine missionary field, in order to prevent all the fatal influences from outside.

Müller says : "Aber man ist dafür bewahrt geblieben, dem Heiland aus der Schule zu laufen und, den Sehnsüchten des eigenen Herzens folgend, ein Wolkenkuckucksheim zu bauen." But the Lord saved them from walking out of the school to follow the longings of their own heart and to build some "cuckoohome in the clouds". [22])

B. THE MISSIONARY TASK.

I. SLAVE TRADE.

One of the most unpleasant experiences of the Moravians when they landed in the foreign countries was the behaviour of the white man towards the coloured man. Europeans behaved often in a shameful and cruel way towards the heathen. They tried to rob them of the local products for little or no money and tried to enrich themselves at the cost of the natives. Of course there were exceptions but the general rule was very bad.

So the white man was hated by a vast majority of the heathens. So when the Moravians came with their Gospel, and with their assertion that the heathen-religion was wrong and that the "European" religion was right they had not a kind reception. On the contrary. Many heathens showed their enmity.

But not only the heathens hated the Moravians, still more the slave traders. They considered the slaves as no human beings, as creations of the devil, as people without a soul, as cattle. Only when considered in such a way, the brutal treatment could be justified.

When the missionaries told these slaves that they must become children of God, when they preached them the riches of the Gospel of Jesus Christ, when they told them that they could be free from all bonds of the devil, the slave-traders were furious. They put all possible obstacles against the missionaries. It must be admitted that there were some christian slave-owners who struck another attitude, but by far the greater part tried to thwart the missionaries as much as possible.

Now we must state here that the attitude of the Moravians was not quite correct, at least their standpoint was not the same as ours is now. They showed themselves children of their own time in their opinion of the slave-trade. They even laid stress upon the idea of the Bible which speaks of slaves. But they did not see that the slaves in the time of the Bible had a quite different treatment from the treatment in their days. [23]) Von Spangenberg calls slave-trade an inhuman thing and the Moravians put the question whether there were special slave-morals : e.g. whether a slave should be allowed to steal when he has not enough to feed and dress himself. A definite line had to be followed for the slave-marriages, as husband and wife were often separated from each other. The law did not acknowledge their marriages but the Moravians did. The Moravians tried to move the Government to acknowledge their marriages but without any success. [24])

It is pretty strange that the Moravians did not like at all to give freedom to the slaves, when Wilberforce and other men were it fighting for il. As some of the causes, Karl Müller mentions their fear for a new enmity against them, as the rebellions which often arose were said to be due to the activity of the Moravians. Moreover the Moravians put forward this principle for slave-trade that the idleness, which teaches much wrong, is prevented in this way and in their distress they learn to call to God in the right way. And they disliked very much the way in which the English tried to solve the problem, who hoped to see in the Moravians champions for the emancipation of the slaves.

2. POLITICS.

F. STAEHLIN gives us many examples in his book about the hostility of the colonial governments. Now the governors welcomed the Moravians most heartily, if only they would behave themselves as colonists. But as soon as they showed themselves missionaries their attitude changed all of a sudden. Except a few e.g. the governor LÖSZNER of Surinam. Von Zinzendorf preferred not to worry about the attitude of the governors. He simply stated that they had a right to preach the Gospel everywhere and for that reason he did not ask permission. "Unsre Art ist es nicht die Bekehrung der Heiden auf Erlaubnis der Obrigkeit zu traktieren. Man geht unter sie, und wenn sie sich bekehren, so fragt man nicht, ob es der Obrigkeit recht ist."

So the problem was solved in a very easy way. He claimed the freedom of religion. That this claim was not met everywhere with the same kindness can be understood. But once more we must esteem his courage. [25] As for the *military service*, the Moravian brothers mostly refused to go into the forces. Especially in North America, where often war broke out. When the brothers refused Von Zinzendorf stated the following in August 1737 : "Je sais que nos Frères ne consentiront jamais ni de gré ni de force à aller tuer les gens dans des païs où ils ne recherchent que le salut des âmes et je m'imagine que l'honneur de la Nation demande de les en dispenser ou de favoriser leur sortie."

They even cast lot about the question whether they were obliged to cut trees in order to help them to make a fortress. The lot defended it and the same sound we hear in 1759 when the minutes of the Synod tell us : "Die Hilfe, die die Welt in solchen Fällen von uns erwarten kann, besteht nur darin, dasz sie von uns ehrlich behandelt wird. Wir machen auch, dasz ihre Leute nicht davonlaufen und wenn einmal Krieg in solchen Ländern wird, so helfen wir ihnen Frieden machen." The help which the world can expect of us in such cases, amounts only to this that it will be treated by us in an honest way. We also prevent their soldiers deserting and when there is war in such countries, we help them to make peace." Which they actually did. [26]

As for the *attitude of the Moravians to other churches* vice versa the Moravians had a hard struggle especially in the beginning of their missionary action. A letter of a Dutch clergyman [27]

242

showed that the Moravians were disliked and even hated in the Dutch colonies. Moreover the attitude of the Moravians was often narrowminded, Pietists as they were at bottom, contrary to the official clergy of the Lutheran Church who looked down upon them, especially as the behaviour of these clergymen was not always correct, to say the least of it. Later on when the esteem of the Moravians was increasing gradually and the governments protected them, their position im proved.

Karl Müller is right when he says that after the first century the battle was won, the terrible hatred had been subdued, the Moravian Mission had stood her ground against state and church and had won an esteemed position in public life. In this way it could do great tasks with power. [28]

As for *polygamy* Von Zinzendorf allowed the Indians to keep their wives. He meant that polygamy was a "schöpfungsmäszige Gegebenheit". A fact which was given in creation, or a datum of creation. He saw also arguments in the Old Testament in which the polygamy was allowed by the Lord God himself, and according to his opinion polygamy was abolished by the Romans, "zum Unsegen", bringing no blessing. Neither did he see any prohibition in the New Testament. He did not allow divorce, and so he did not allow the. converted heathen to send away his second or third wife. The ideal however is, he said to tell the baptized that one man is married to one wife. But it must not be told them in the form of a strong command. The passions must be sanctified and they must learn holy ideas relating married life from Scripture. [29]

NOTES

[1] KARL MÜLLER, 200 Jahre Brüdermission. Das erste Missionsjahrhundert Hernhut 1941, p. 263—265. Herrnhut 1931.
Cf. LÜTJEHARMS, Het philadelphisch oecumenisch streven der Hernhutters in de Nederlanden in de 18e eeuw. Zeist, 1935, p. 20—21.
[2] KARL MÜLLER, p. 267.
[3] Idem   p. 268—269. Cf. Hefte zur Missionstunde no. 12 Die wichtigsten Missionsinstructionen. Zinzendorf's Herrnhut 1913.
[4] KARL MÜLLER, p. 269—274.
[5] Idem   p. 275.
[6] Idem   p. 278.
[7] Idem   p. 279.
[8] Idem   p. 282
[9] Idem   p. 287.
[10] Idem   p. 288.
[11] Idem   p. 292. Cf. Dr. LÜTJEHARMS, Het phil. oec. streven, p. 98.
[12] Idem   p. 294.
[13] TH. MÜLLER, Een blik in de Geschiedenis der Evangelische Broedergemeente.

243

Zeist 1925, p. 121, cf. F. STAEHLIN, Die Mission der Brüdergemeinde I 52. II 2) 13
3) 100, 174, 282. III 1) 3, 5, 29, 48, 181, 236, 238 f, 251, 266, 275, 284 f. 2) 151.
3) 125, 203, 220, 232.

[14]) F. STAEHLIN, see table of contents, p. 341. Missionsgewerbe. K. MÜLLER,
p. 313—314.
[15]) TH. MÜLLER, op. cit., p. 144.
[16]) LÜTJEHARMS, op. cit. gives the articles for the Hernhut congregation at Amster
dam of the year 1736, p. 220—221.
[17]) STAEHLIN, op. cit. See index p. 336 under "Finanzielle Nöte". K. MÜLLER,
p. 315—320.
[18]) STAEHLIN, cf. index "Selbsterhaltung der Mission", p. 341. K. MÜLLER, p.
323—331.
[19]) K. MÜLLER, p. 331.
[20]) Dr. LÜTJEHARMS, p. 105—106.
[21]) Dr. J. H. GAVINCK, op. cit., p. 154 , cf. MÜLLER, p. 290.
[22]) Cf. MÜLLER, p. 290.
[23]) Cf. STAEHLIN, p. 339. Index "Mission unter den Negersklaven". K. MÜLLER,
p. 332—335.
[24]) K. MÜLLER, p. 334.
[25]) STAEHLIN. Index p. 336. Feindseligkeiten. K. MÜLLER, p. 336.
[26]) STAEHLIN. Index p. 338. Landesdienste, p. 343. Waffentragen. K. MÜLLER,
p. 338.
[27]) LÜTJEHARMS, p. 106 and 226.
[28]) K. MÜLLER, p. 341.
[29]) Idem   p. 310—311. Stachlin op cit. p. 113; 123 II² 34 III²; 227 III³.

Par. IV. Missionary Instruments.

a. The preaching of the Word.

When the Hernhut missionaries came to the missionary field
they put this question : how can we give the heathen that which
has taken our hearts completely. Now they had many drawbacks : they hardly knew anything of the language, they had
no sound theological education and could not express themselves
in terms to make themselves understood.

For that reason they took as the base for their teaching the example
of the Halle missionaries. These missionaries had learned the
following : "When you intend to help the heathen, you must
first of all try to preach away from their hearts their polytheism
and destroy the great catalogue of their idols, before you can take
them to the Eternal God. When they believe in God, then it is
necessary to teach them the attributes of God. Further the
misery in which all people are originally, and then the necessity
to rise from that misery and at last it is necessary to show them
the means of grace in Jesus Christ. This is a pure logic and dogmatic
way to open the heart of the heathen."

It is a pity that the Moravians had no other and better method
in the very beginning. But they noticed very soon that this

was a wrong way. They saw that it was not the Gospel but Law they preached. And that the purpose of this preaching was a new moral life without a new-born life, which God alone could give.

For that reason the synod of 1744 made this statement : "One should not take to the heathen a christian idea or morals, but the Gospel." [1])

Von Zinzendorf says : "Bei den Wilden muss man ja nicht zuerst von Gott, sondern gleich vom Heiland reden und seine Herzensfreundschaft und Neigung zu ihm aufzurichten suchen. Und aus dem Heiland heraus geht man hernach in die Idee von der Gottheit." [2])

He further says that we must take the example of St. Paul and not preach in abstract terms but the heathen must know that his Creator in his Saviour.

Every now and then a missionary was instructed in the meaning of this new missionary method. He was told that he had to preach the expiatory death of Christ on the cross. Formerly the hearts of the heathens were closed, and many missionaries almost lost all courage, but now they understood that the Saviour had retarded their work for some years as they had to learn that they should preach his sufferings especially on the cross. From that time onwards, all the work was successful among Hottentots and Greenlanders, in Canada and Brasil.

On the other hand the Moravians also saw that the one-sided stress upon the cross of the Saviour might awake unsound sensibility. Müller acknowledges that this danger really existed, and some heathens showed this sensibility.

He also mentions that many missionaries had a feeling for the actual situation and understood in which way they had *to adapt* themselves to the customs of the heathens. E.g. the Greenlanders have no lambs, no sacrifices, and other customs known to Europeans. But they tried to teach them and tried to understand the individual character of the different peoples.

Von Zinzendorf says in 1745, when some missionaries are sent to the field : "To correct the people in their principles is not our plan but to bring them the image of Christ, always in different and new forms, ... just as if he had been crucified before our eyes, just as if we had seen his last death-look . . . . that is our task. [3])

b. Baptism and Holy Supper.

The division into four classes was usual among the Moravians : Disciples, candidates for baptism, baptized people and communicants. It is interesting that von Zinzendorf warned against too many scruples relating Holy Supper. He asks whether it is not due to an old reformed idea to see the Holy Supper as too great a mystery.

As for Baptism : it was not allowed to baptize a native, if the governor had no information of it, and moreover the Danish Lutheran rite was practised. But apart from these difficulties, the question was raised whether they should baptize reluctantly or with some haste. Von Zinzendorf warned against haste but he also said that a scrupulous examination should not be practised. The form of baptism was different according to the customs of the country. [4]

Exorcism was disliked by Pietism. The Moravians sometimes did not approve of it either, but they often used it on the missionary field e.g. the missionary Caries in Jamaica who practised this form : "In the name of my dearest Lord Jezus Christ, who has destroyed all the Power of Darkness, I command you, ye unclean spirits and all power of Darkness to depart from these servants of Jesus Christ and to give way unto the Holy Ghost." [5]

Children were baptised when the parents were baptised, but only if wished by the parents.

c. Schools.

As *for schools*, they considered the school as an essential part of the missionary work. For the school laid hold on the children. And without school it was not possible to give some teaching of the Bible. So the ultimate purpose with the heathens was that they should have both : the Word of God and Christian feeling. "Sound Christian confession as a complement and corrective of the heart-christendom."

NOTES

[1] K. MÜLLER, p. 301—303. F. AACHLIN, op. cit., p. 341. Article Missionspredigt.
[2] K. MÜLLER, p. 303.
[3] K. MÜLLER, cf. p. 307.
[4] K. MÜLLER, p. 311, 312.
[5] K. MÜLLER, p. 308—310, cf. AACHLIN, p. 342. Article Taufe und Tauflehre.

Par. V. Missionary Purpose.

a. The method.

There is a great difference between the method of preaching of the Danish Halle missionaries and the Hernhut missionaries. The former went to the missionfield laying much stress upon dogmatic principles when speaking to the heathen. True, in the early period the Hernhut brothers had the same method and could hardly see any success. But von Zinzendorf did not prescribe them a certain method. Your guide must not be human principles, he said but the *unction* or theopneustie. So there was more mobility than with the Pietists of Halle. They did not wish to see some result at any cost as the Pietists but went away from one place to another when they did not have any success.

"Denn mit der Idee gehen : ich muss etwas ausrichten, das ist pestilenzialisch vor einen Arbeiter, der in die Weite geht." Auch da wo der Arbeit der Erfolg nicht versagt blieb, blieb man sich dessen bewusst, dass es eine Arbeit auf lange Sicht war. "It is pestilential for any missionary to go with the idea I must reap some fruit ; also in those places where they met with some success they were conscious that it was the result of long labour." [1]

They considered themselves only as handymen of the Holy Ghost, who himself does the main work. Nothing but tools, instruments or eyewitnesses of things they had seen. "Before you speak to the heathens," says Von Zinzendorf, "you must listen to them as missionaries. You must sit down and be quiet and look at them, without saying a word. When a heathen comes to you and asks you to speak, then you must say a few words, but only in such a way that the heathen can feel that he stands in a very close connection with the Creator and that he is a real child of the Creator. In such a way you awaken love in a heathen and you can converse with him. Then you must take care that he does not make any connection with the Europeans and their way of living. You must advise him to let them alone until he can believe that the Creator is his Saviour."

A very important question was raised when some brothers asked whether they had to adapt themselves to customs of the different nations or that for all the nations the method of preaching should be the same.

This answer was given : "As the Gospel is the same and the faith is the same for all people we cannot make any difference in matters relating the heart. The Synod of Bethlehem in 1755 said : ,,Es ist unevangelisch und gegen die Lehre Jesu, wenn sich jemand dünken lässt, man müsste in Dingen einen Unterschied machen, die eigentlich des Herz angehen." And Von Zinzendorf said : "Ich erkenne absolut keinen Unterschied der Nationen in des Heilands Herzsachen. Einem Hottentotten muss werden wie einem Engeländer oder Deutschen, wenn er ein Kind Gottes wird, sonst ist er keins." [2]) I don't acknowledge any difference between the nations in matters relating to the heart. A Hottentot must become just the same as an Englishman or German when he becomes a child of God, otherwise he is not such a one.

So the *missionary purpose* of the Hernhut brothers becomes clear : the heathen must become a child of God or "in seiner Art ganz umgedrehte Kreatur" (a creature who changed totally his way of living). And the way to reach this purpose is according to Von Zinzendorf : "the personal contact with the individual heathen, who becomes the only care for the missionary." He advises too not to preach publicly but to address single souls, not teaching them all kinds of texts, songs, prayers. First of all the teaching must seize their hearts, it must be a personal testimony. The purpose must not be intellectual teaching, nor the establishment of schools, as many attended the schools only to have some education and then after having received it, went away without their heart being touched. But it must be spiritual teaching.

b. The organization of the congregations.

In the very beginning of the Moravian church Von Zinzendorf often states the principle that he only wishes to make some converts all over the world and that he does not like to establish churches just like the religions have now.

But later on he says that his ideas need correction. Then he declares that the missionary work has surpassed all expectation. Then he has to face the problem of the organisation of the churches. One of the main principles he puts down is that a missionary has to become superfluous. He wants to educate the natives to ministers and apostles of their nation. First of all they must be auxiliary workers. E.g. by means of buying slaves. But the great purpose behind this buying is the selfsupporting native church, which does not want the white man any longer but can be quite independent

"Wir wollen," says Von Zinzendorf, "mit Ernst dahin sehen, dass uns die Heiden nicht mehr brauchen, sondern ihre Sache allein fortführen können." [3]

NOTES

[1] K. MÜLLER, p. 297. AACHLIN, p. 341. Article Missionsmethode.
[2] K. MÜLLER, p. 299.
[3] K. MÜLLER, p. 312. AACHLIN, p. 341. Article Missionslehre.

CHAPTER III.

HIS MISSIONARY PRINCIPLES COMPARED WITH THOSE OF THE PIETISTS, ESPECIALLY THE MORAVIANS

PREFACE.

It is quite impossible to compare all the principles of William Carey with all those of the Pietists and Moravians. In the first place for this reason : William Carey has given a detailed description of his principles. He has shown his principles in his missionary work. In his Form of Agreement and in his Enquiry he gave special principles, as we stated before. All these principles are worth a careful examination. It would be possible to describe their origin, the method in which William Carey dealt with his own principles, their purpose, and their value. Then a comparison could be made with all the principles of the Pietists and Von Zinzendorf. But Von Zinzendorf differs materially from Von Spangenberg on important principles. To describe all these principles in one dissertation would not only be quite impossible, but it would be such an enormous task, that it would take many years before it would be finished.

To prevent crowding together of all those principles we must limit ourselves to a more modest task.

We will in the first place take only those principles which are of the highest importance and which are conspicuous to everybody. In the second place we will compare only those principles of the Pietists and William Carey which we described in this dissertation. Quite a lot could be added. But the main purpose must be, to see the principles of William Carey, not of other missionaries. So we omit principles of Von Spangenberg and we mainly will limit ourselves to William Carey's, some Pietists' and Von Zinzendorf's principles.

Par. I. Comparison of the motives of Mission.

It is not difficult to see that there is a difference between the principles of William Carey and those of the Pietists and the Moravians. The very title of Carey's famous Enquiry tells us already that he sees as the motive of missions the Commission of the Lord. He defines it as: "An Enquiry into the *obligations* of Christians". He uses the word: "obedience", "it is incumbent upon us", "it behoves us", "it becomes us", etc. He says: "Our blessed Lord has required us to pray that his Kingdom may come." He lays stress upon the fact that the Commission given by our Lord is still binding upon us. That the Lord commissioned his apostles to go and teach all nations. He lays stress upon the texts which order us to preach the Gospel to the heathens.

When we look at the motives of the Pietists and von Zinzendorf then we see first of all that the Lord moved them by means of the King of Denmark. That they laid full stress upon the people in misery. The motives of the Pietists are: conversion of the heathen. There may be some difference between the principles of the Pietists and those of von Zinzendorf, yet von Zinzendorf wishes - "Seelen für das Lamm zu werben," to gain souls for the Lamb. Later on, his motive changed, when he said that "the Unitas fratrum should be an instument to make visible the vera ecclesia." He lays stress upon being witnesses, fighters against the darkness, some of them among Roman Catholics, others among Christians adhering to different religions and still others among the heathens of all tongues. He warns against "Generalheiden-bekehrungen", general conversions of the heathen. He even says that it is not his intention to convert the heathens. He only wants to take a few souls for the Saviour.

So we see that William Carey asks what is the command of the Lord and that he listens to the authority of Holy Scripture, that his missionary work is founded on the firm, objective ground of the Word of God, while the Pietists lay much more stress upon the poor heathens, their darkness, their misery, their conversion etc. Because the heathens are poor people, we must be moved to help them. Their motives are more subjective. We also can put it in this way: William Carey sees that the principle must be in the first place obedience, while Pietists and Moravians are moved to compassion. William Carey listens in the first place

251

to the command of the Lord. Then he is moved to obedience and compassion. The Pietists and Moravians listen to the crying of the people from afar and are moved because their heart is full of richness which they will share with other people.

Still another difference must be mentioned here : William Carey lays much stress upon the work which must be done by ministers. After having reached his conclusions of his statistical survey he says : "all these things are loud calls to christians and especially to ministers, to exert themselves to the utmost in their several spheres of action, and to try to enlarge them as much as possible."

So William Carey will move the ministers and the ministers must move the people and so the whole of christianity must be in action.

But von Zinzendorf and the Pietists may try to revive dead orthodoxism but they don't wish to make of the whole church a missionary church. On the contrary : "Our plan goes no further than the firstlings," says von Zinzendorf and these must be won not by "religions" but only by the "bundle", the unitas fratrum. He does not move ministers by making much propaganda, as William Carey does, but he prays for the moving power of the Holy Ghost in the first place.

William Carey lays far more stress upon human work and human tasks, and human means, while Pietists and especially von Zinzendorf lays stress on the work of the Holy Ghost : we only have to gather souls in that bundle, who are prepared by the Holy Ghost.

We may state that Pietists and von Zinzendorf are more inspired priests, while William Carey is more prophet. When we ask which principle is right then we must acknow ledge that both, William Carey and the Pietists have had very great influence and that the Church in its pluriform appearance can never be grateful enough to these men. But we also must state that William Carey's motives were sounder than those of the Pietists, as conforming more to the word of God. He also lays stress upon the work of the Holy Ghost. All means without the Holy Ghost, he says, will be ineffectual. But he begins to listen to the Word and that Word of God is his guide. Von Zinzendorf mentions the Word only occasionaly. He is moved by the Lamb which he sees in the cross full of wounds and killed for his sins : ego pro te haec passus sum, te vero quid fecisti pro me ? The combination of these two men, Carey and von Zinzendorf would be : compassionate obedience. That would be the right principle. That is the principle of the Word of God. In St. John 3 : 16 we read : For God so loved the world, that he gave his only begotten Son, that whose over believeth in him, should not perish but have everlasting life. So behind the sending of the Son lies God's compassion. And behind the command of our Lord in St. Matthew 28 : 19 Go ye therefore, and make disciples of all the nations, baptizing them into the name of the Father, and of the Son and of the Holy Ghost, lies also divine compassion. We even can only understand St. Matthew 28 : 19 if we first understood St. John 3 : 16. So we must state that the cornerstone of the missionary work is the command of Christ, but we only can listen to that command if we are moved to compassion, which was in Him when He gave the command. Compassionate obedience must move the Church : all the Churches in their pluriformity. Even when heathen should not like our compassion then we still have to be compassionate, after the example of the Lord. And when that compassion dwindles away in the churches because they are too much introverted, then the command of the Lord may awaken their call and make them obey, which means : to have compassion with those who don't know the true Bread of Life. [1]

So we have to go back to the Word of God when we consider the motives of Mission. Our guide must not be subjective feelings towards poor people, nor the hard duty of a command, but compassionate obedience.

(Later on Von Spangenberg gave in his "Von der Arbeit der evangelischen Brüder unter den Heiden," a first trial to describe the motives of the missionary action, both from Old and New Testament. [2] But in this dissertation we only deal with the early beginning of the-Pietists and von Zinzendorf.)

Par. II. Comparison of the organs of Mission.

a. The task of the organs at home.

As one of the first duties of the organs at home William Carey mentions prayer, as basic for all missionary activities. But the task of the organs of the home base is not finished with praying, on the contrary : we must use the means, Carey says, for the obtaining of those things we pray for. He even draws a parallel between the trading companies of his time, exerting all powers and trying

253

all means to reach their aim. The best means for our missionary aim is the establishment of a Missionary Society. Such a Missionary Society must not confine itself to its own denomination. Before missionaries are sent to the field the task of the home base is to sit down and count the cost. Rich and poor must give their financial aid. Apart from some general rules he does not give a detailed description of the task of the Society at home.

The first task seen by Von Zinzendorf is also praying, but apart from that, he lays much stress upon the "Zeugentrieb", witness-drive, which "comes from irrational backgrounds." Later on that enthusiastic form goes away and Von Zinzendorf complains of lack of love. But he continues to send missionaries without knowledge of languages or conditions of the heathenland and without money. He does not sit down to count the cost ; on the contrary, they must trust that God will help them and when on the missionary field they must support themselves. The organ which sends them is the ,,church". And the church draws lots to decide who shall go and where they shall go etc. The task of the organisation at home became later on to help the missionaries as much as possible, before they reach the field. Trade was also a means of supporting them but later on he changed his opinion.

The difference between William Carey and Von Zinzendorf seems to be : William Carey desires a Society, Von Zinzendorf desires a church which performs the missionary task. But we must state here that when Pietism placed the missionary idea in the centre of religious life, it would not introduce new missionary principles at the same time : "The old orthodox opinion, that the state or in its place some company, had the right and the duty to send missionaries was maintained. And also the opinion that the church had the duty to commission the ordained ministers for the field.

These principles were not changed by the Pietism of Halle, which procured only ordained ministers or the Danish government. But yet there was a difference in practise in the Lutheran Church. According to the old orthodox standpoint the church was behind the missionary work, or some organ of the church, or some committee, which was nominated officially by the church.

Now Pietism did not change this theoretically, but practically. For behind the missionary work was no longer the church but the "conventicle", which means the ecclesiola in ecclesia. Moreover

Halle sent only such theologians which had received their education in their seminaries. And they did not think it sufficient that they were ordained, but they only were sent to the field, when they had received a special call and they were conscious of that call.

Here we see a shifting from the church towards the conventicle, from the objective confraternity to a subjective circle and its calling." [3])

Now Von Zinzendorf gave his conventicle its own character. He did not call it conventicle but church. It really was not a conventicle but a "church" which BETTERMANN called a "ver-kirchlichtes Konventikel", which gradually became a church. [4]) And in this way the Moravians and Von Zinzendorf turned from the pietistic idea and came back to the old opinion that the church as church must stand behind the missionary work. As the Moravian church subsisted on its own, means it could ordain missionaries. But Pietism, though a movement of laymen, was connected with the church and for that reason, they themselves could not send ordained laymen. The Moravians were free and so they could ordain and send out laymen. [5])

LÜTJEHARMS asserts that Pietism and the Moravians were much nearer to church missionary work than the later missionary societies and corporations, which claimed the rights of the church.

I think Lütjeharms is right. When we compare the organs used by Pietism and Von Zinzendorf, William Carey, then we must state that Von Zinzendorf was nearest to church missionary work. Of course his idea of church is different from ours. He sees his church as a "philadelphic congregation of mere regenerated people. But the foundation of his work was not the subjective sanctification of the individual members, but the belief in the salvation through Christ which the members have in common." [6])

Later on, about 1740 he made a difference between the Moravian Brother church and the philadelphic saviour-congregation ("Gemeine Jesu" or Unitas fratrum). The Moravian Brother church stands on the same line as all the other churches and on the other hand is the invisible church, not bound to any place or time, the Philadelphia, the Unitas fratrum. This Philadelphia is the vera ecclesia. It never can be realised in a certain confessional church as confessions made separations. The Moravian church is only means or instrument to realise the ecclesia vera or Unitas Fratrum. [7])

But whatever his idea of church may be, it is clear that he did not like to form a Society as William Carey did. Every member of his church was considered to be a worker for missionary work, either at home or abroad, and not merely some separate members belonging to some churches.

That William Carey established a Society may have been due to the fact that he could not rouse all the colleagues and church members as he wished, for we saw in his biography that he tried to do that, and to a certain extent he even succeeded in it. But he did not maintain the principle against all opposition that the *church* should do the missionary work. ADRIANUS SARAVIA (1531—1613) saw this great principle much better than Luther, Calvin and other Reformators except Bucer.

William Carey himself asserts that the commission of Christ cannot possibly be limited to the apostles as the promise: "and lo I am with you alway, even unto the end of the world", is looking much further into the future than the lifetime of the apostles. We don't know whether William Carey has seen that the church, which was built upon the foundation of the apostles was just for this reason, heir of the call of the apostles viz., to make disciples of all nations for Christ.

But at any rate not some government nor a conventicle or some society received the order of Christ to preach the Gospel to all nations. Sometimes they behaved as if they had had that call. And indeed they did quite a lot of marvellous work. Pietism and the church of Von Zinzendorf and the Society of William Carey stimulated missionary work in Europe very much. We cannot explain that these means had such a great result, at a time when the Church was in danger to separate itself from the world in an old Testament way. The heart of the Lord, however, was moved to mercy with the heathens. It is very shameful for the churches in Europe that not they, but Pietism, Moravians and Societies were the leading powers in missionary work. [8])

As for the special task of these organs, Pietists and Von Zinzendorf and also William Carey, they all lay much stress upon praying and the work of the Holy Ghost. After praying they all wish to exert their powers in the missionary work.

William Carey admires the example of the Moravian Missionaries especially their way of self support. But neither Pietists nor Von Zinzendorf nor William Carey describe the special task of the organs at home. They all agree that missionaries must have special qualifications : Pietists wish educated men, who are converted and who have a special calling, Von Zinzendorf wishes laymen with witness-drive, while William Carey wishes educated men. According to these wishes they see *their task* different. Pietists give their candidates a thorough education at the Francke's establishments, Von Zinzendorf doesnot give them a special education but looks for all kinds of handicraftmen, to support the mission. William Carey says that the home mission has to look for men of highest qualifications, but wants also handicraftmen according to the example of the selfsupporting Moravian missionaries. They all desire that the organs at home shall sit down and count the cost. In the early period, Pietists had financial help of the King of Denmark ; Von Zinzendorf did not like financial help and William Carey had only some pocket-money. But afterwards they all understood that the task of the organs at home was to look for financial help for the missionaries, at least until the time they arrived at the field. Later on we will deal separately with this subject.

It is a great pity, that the attitude of the missionaries towards the Committee at home was not described by William Carey. Von Zinzendorf gave special instructions and these instructions prevented the trouble which later on was detrimental for the Serampore mission.

They all agreed that the choice of the mission field was a task of the home-organisation and that the missionaries had the duty to report continuously about the progress of the work.

Pietists and Von Zinzendorf wished to inspect the missionaries too and if necessary would take disciplinarian measures, but William Carey's attitude was different. He considered the members of the Committee in England more or less as equals. Here especially we cannot agree with his opinion regarding the task of the home-organisation. William Carey had gradually become independent of the Committee at home and so he did not like examination of his work. Generally speaking we can say that one of the mistakes of William Carey was that he did not give a description of the task and functions of the organisation at home. Pietists and Von Zinzendorf better understood this province of work.

b. Qualifications of the missionaries.

As said in the preceding chapter : Pietists wished to send to the missionfield only qualified clergymen, who had received their education at one of the Halle institutions.

Von Zinzendorf only wished to send men and women with witness drive as a decisive qualification of the divine call. In the first years he did not ask any more : everybody is sent who possesses this qualification. Indeed, he sometimes sent educated men and women, but they were not sent on account of their education, but due to their spiritual qualifications. They wanted people of character. A doctor might be sent, but not because he was a doctor, but a helper of the people, who can do some missionary work too. At the same time he can help some natives.

William Carey has given a very detailed description of the qualifications necessary for a missionary : he must be pious, be able to preach and do handicraft work, must adhere to the idea of equality with the people, must become self-supporting as soon as possible, must be a man of calmness and evenness of temper, must show equality for each and pre-eminence to none, must try to understand the situation and disposition of the aboriginal inhabitants, set an infinite value upon immortal souls, must be well informed about the snares and delusions in which the heathen are held, bear the faults of the native brethren and conquer the heathens by their personal example and they must pray, secretly, fervently and with faith.

Now we saw that whatever these qualifications are, William Carey does not ask for educated men. And when later on he asks to send such men as described above, he himself tries to educate them. Neither the home base committee nor the church has this task, but he only wants men with the above mentioned qualifications and further they will receive their education on the missionfield itself.

William Carey saw the great importance of educated men very well, especially later, and so did the Pietists, but it is a pity that William Carey did not require them from the home base. It may be that here we meat with another influence of Von Zinzendorf.

Dr. A. M. Brouwer says in his "Hoe te prediken voor Heidenen en Mohammedanen" : the missionary-preacher must be a devoted personality, with excellent erudition and a world-wide vision.

Before all, he must be willing to be a pupil of the people among whom he labours etc. [9])

And Prof. Dr. G. Warneck also describes the necessity of a special education and thinks that the seminary education is the best way. [10])

And the Reformed Churches in Holland especially after the synod of Middelburg in 1896 understood, that only ministers can be sent who have had a special education in missionary branches. They need knowledge of the field, of the people, of the way of living, of the religions of the field, of the history of mission and the theory of mission. Moreover they want a thorough knowledge of the languages of the people with whom they have to deal. And not only well educated men must be sent, but also ordained men, those who are allowed to preach in the Name of the Lord and to baptize and celebrate Holy Supper.

Also for this reason the church and not a society must send missionaries A society is not allowed to ordain missionaries ; societies may assume this as a right but only the Church, as an institution is entitled to it.

There are of course excuses for William Carey but we must state that he did not lay enough stress upon the training of the missionaries at home, whatever may have been his accomplishments in India. In England he laid more stress upon the qualifications of character than upon their educational training, but when in India he gradually saw the necessity of educated missionaries from his own experience and their inadequacy, as we stated above.

Only the Pietists sent educated men, due to their connection with the official church. Generally speaking we can say that this principle of sending educated missionaries was not seen as essential neither by Von Zinzendorf, neither by William Carey. Later on they understood the importance of it.

c. The financial support of the missionaries.

The pecuniary task of the home committee was limited to the necessaries for the voyage and the first expenditure on the field. The missionaries were expected to support themselves as soon as possible. They did it in a very democratic way by pooling all the money into one purse. He adopted the Moravian method but with one difference : the Moravians desired a housefather to control dissensions etc., but Carey diverged from this scheme

259

by determining that there should be equality for each and pre-eminence to none.

Von Zinzendorf used all possible means to make the missionaries self-supporting and for that reason cobblers, tailors, carpenters, butchers, farmers and doctors etc. were sent to the field. Even trade was allowed if it contributed to support the mission.

Against this method we must state that missionaries have a right of being supported by the home base. Jesus himself says that "the workman is worthy of his meat" (St. Matthew 10 : 9) and St. Paul says : "Even so hath the Lord ordained that they which proclaim the Gospel should live of the Gospel" (1 Cor. 9 : 14).

St. Paul was an exception but he himself says that his practice is not the ordinary wary. [11]) The Reformed Church of Holland after the Synod of Middelburg always wished to follow this principle, that missionaries shoud be supported by the home base, preferable by voluntary contributions of all the churches in the country. This system proved to be not only useful but also benificial to the churches themselves.

d. Auxiliary missionaries.

It is rather difficult to describe what definition Von Zinzendorf and William Carey and also the Pietists gave of a missionary. And still more difficult is the definition of an auxiliary missionary. Especially as William Carey advocated the "democratic nonsense of every apprentice sent to him, being equal the moment he set foot on Bengal ground". Moreover he introduced the Moravian principle in Bengal that women-missionaries should be helpers too. He also laid stress on the help of the converted natives. As the Moravians had the same custom, he may have deduced this principle from their practice. At any rate it is very important that William Carey educated all these helpers : women, for whom he established educational schools and natives for whom he established educational schools and natives for whom he established his Serampore college. We stated above already how important this College was, and that it can be considered as an unique institution for native people. So we see that this man with world-wide-vision did much more for the education of the auxiliary-missionaries than e.g. the Moravians and Pietists. Actually they also gave them some education, but William Carey saw this great principle that Gospel preaching is done in the best way when done by the natives themselves. And contact with the female natives is made in the best way by women missionaries he says. This principle is nowadays not yet understood in all the Churches. It will be necessary that far more women act as auxiliary workers on the mission fields, and also workers at the home base.

NOTES

[1]) Prof. Dr. J. H. BAVINCK, Ons Zendingsboek, p. 5—7.
[2]) VON SPANGENBERG, Von der Arbeit der evangelischen Brüder unter den Heiden, Barby 1782.
[3]) Dr. W. LÜTJEHARMS, Het Philadelphisch oecumenisch streven der Hernhutters in de Nederlanden in de achttiende eeuw. Zeist 1935, p. 98.
[4]) Cf. W. BETTERMANN, Das Werden einer Kirche im 18. Jahrhundert, in Zwischen den Zeiten, 11. Jahrg. 1933, p. 514, cited by LÜTJEHARMS, p. 98.
[5]) LÜTJEHARMS, op. cit., p. 99.
[6]) Idem   p. 15.
[7]) Idem   p. 20—21.
[8]) Prof. Dr. J. H. BAVINCK, op. cit., p. 121—122.
[9]) Dr. A. M. BROUWER, Hoe te prediken voor Heidenen en Mohammedanen. Rotterdam 1916, p. 22—23.
[10]) Dr. G. WARNECK, Ev. Missionslehre. Die Organe p. 168—207.
[11]) Idem, cf. p. 168.

Par. III. Comparison of the management of mission.

a. Territory of the mission field.

The Danish Halle mission sent the missionaries to the Danish territory, but they also tried to find other fields. Von Zinzendorf at once grasps the idea of world mission.

William Carey sees the whole world open to him, except a few christian countries. The circumference of the missionfield is seen by Von Zinzendorf and William Carey according to the principle of Holy Scripture "make ye disciples of all nations". Even when governments are opposing them, they obeyed more the Lord than the rulers of this earth. This does not mean that they were not very careful in avoiding difficulties arising from going to fields where missionaries of other societies were working. But wherever they could send missionaries they tried to do this.

b. Missionary Territory.

1. SLAVE TRADE.

It is a great honour for the Friends (Quakers) in England that they were the first protesters against slave trade. Then followed the Baptists. Carey violently opposed this abomination.

He says in his Enquiry : "Arabian Mohammedanism has bled Africa to death through the slave trade of which Christian nations shared the guilt." And when a letter arrived reporting that the Cabinet decided to emancipate the West Indian slaves, it was such a source of great joy for him, that with tears in his eyes he thanked God and proposed special thankgivings for one month in all the meetings in Bengal. In no public question had he taken a deeper interest. Quite different is the attitude of the Moravians. Of course they disliked the behaviour of the slave owners and slave traders, but they did not wish to give freedom to all the slaves while Wilberforce and other men fought for it. We mentioned the motives, but it is pretty difficult to understand that they even quoted Holy Scripture to defend their standpoint. Slave trade and slavery are against the law of Christ, especially the second table of the ten commandments. Our Lord washes the feet of his disciples, he bears the cross and tells his disciples : "If any man would come after me, let him deny himself and take up his cross and follow me." Matth. 16 : 24. [1])

2. POLITICS.

According to the Enquiry William Carey will give the civil magistrate the "readiest obedience whether persecuted or protected." But William Carey disobeyed the Directors of the East India Company in going to India when not any missionary could get a license. The question here is this : Is Government justified in prohibiting the sending of missionaries to any missionary field and does not government exceed the limits of its power when it meddles with the affairs of the missionaries. The first question was answered by William Carey in a negative way and the second question was answered in this way that government should not prevent the missionary activities in so far as these activities don't purposely interfere with reasonable laws.

It is interesting that Von Zinzendorf strikes quite the same attitude : he states that the Moravians have a right to preach the Gospel everywhere and he says that it is not the method to deal with the conversion of the heathen with permission of the government.

Now a days this problem cannot be solved in such an easy way. But the main lines of William Carey are still of importance and are an in stand of his broad vision.

3. MILITARY SERVICE.

The principle of the Moravians was that they mostly refused to go into the forces. Carey hated militarism as a Baptist. He opposed the idea even more than Von Zinzendorf. Both were wrong. They did not make a difference between militarism and military service, between imperialism and the task of every country to defend itself against an attacking enemy. Just as militarism is onesided and lays too much stress on the significance of army and fleet so their attitude was onesided and they laid too much stress upon a fixed idea : a world in which there will be no war, if only there are no soldiers. Forgetting too much the ruinous influence of sin.

4. POLYGAMY.

Von Zinzendorf sees polygamy as a "schöpfungsmässige Gegebenheit". He finds arguments in the Old Testament for polygamy and the New Testament does not prohibit it. However he sees the ideal in this : that one man is married to one wife.

William Carey considers the problem more deeply and sees that many difficulties may arise by an easy solution. When he asks, what is to be done with converts whose wives would not join them, the answer is that the husband must use all means to induce the heathen wife to join him. If she refused they counted it as a sufficient reason for divorce and the christian is allowed to marry again.

On page 194 we gave another example of his dealing with this problem. We saw that he did not solve this problem in a quick and easy way.

Contrary to Von Zinzendorf we must state that monogamy is given by God in creation. And that the special cases on the missionary field must be dealt with in a special way. But three answers have been given to the question whether a polygamist should be baptised : a negative, a positive and an intermediary. But whatever the attitude may be, the ideal must be that polygamy must end as soon as possible. It may be that for some time it is allowed in special circumstances but the rule of creation and New Testament must be followed as soon as posible.

5. CLIMATIC AND NATIONAL DIFFERENCES.

As for the *climatic* problems, neither William Carey nor

Von Zinzendorf solved this problem. They took all respon-
sibilities without asking whether they could bear the strain of
other climatic conditions. As for the *national differences*, William Carey tries to solve this problem by establishing many
vernacular schools. Von Zinzendorf sees also the importance
of missionary schools. But William Carey tries to give to Bengal
a new culture. Von Zinzendorf, however, sees the schools more
as a means for knowing the Bible better. William Carey
tries to give another system of living : he will remove the caste
system, quite contrary to the principles of the Pietists. The
Danish missionaries had allowed the converts to retain their
caste, and caste distinctions were perpetuated within the Church
of Christ, but William Carey understood that such an attitude
does not agree with the principles of Scripture, which teaches
us that we are one in Christ and are brothers and sisters of one
body and washed by one blood and sanctified by one Holy Spirit.

Caste differences in the church is the ultimate undoing of the
Church. In this respect William Carey proved to be a man of
wider and deeper outlook than the Pietists. He laid down a
new foundation for a new national life, according to Christian
principles.

6. CULTURAL DIFFERENCES ON THE MISSION FIELD.

Von Zinzendorf states that first we have to evangelize then
civilize. William Carey clearly saw that the natives possessed
their own cultural life and that this life should be thoroughly
known by the missionaries. His principle is that the heathen
must first receive the Gospel and in this way he must be civilized.
So these two great men have the same principle on this point
but they elaborate it differently. William Carey will guide
the native life in such a way that it really makes the missionaries
superfluous and that all the treasures of the native culture are
christianized. Pietists in Tranquebar translated the Bible
too and they erected schools, but neither they nor Von Zinzendorf
had the ideas of William Carey of establishing a College for natives
in order to give them an opportunity to lead their own life according
to the principles of the Gospel. William Carey tried to conquer
the cultured life of the heathens for Christ by leading their
culture to the cross. There was abandoned what was contrary
to the Holiness of Christ and saved what could be used in order

to build up a total new culture. Pietists and Von Zinzendorf met with quite a different life and so it is not possible to compare their achievements with William Carey's. But generally speaking we can say that the achievements of William Carey surpass any other endeavour to lead the culture of the heathens to Christ.

Here we have to say something of adaptation too. This problem was solved in a very simple way by Von Zinzendorf. "I don't acknowledge any difference between the nations in matters relating to the heart. A Hottentot must lead exactiy just the same life as an Englishman or German." William Carey solved this problem in a better way. He adapted only these customs and forms of the Bengalees which were not contrary or hostile to the Gospel of Jesus Christ. He really wished to save their cultural life but not at the cost of the Gospel. The Roman Catholics sacrificed their principles in order the save the culture of the heathens. So did de Nobili in the 17th century. Pietists and Von Zinzendorf did not make this Roman mistake, and William Carey adapted the right method.

NOTE

[1] Au interesting book is J. VON WALTER, Die Sklaverei im Neuen Test.

Par. IV. Comparison of missionary instruments.

a. The preaching of the Word.

We described the colossal work of William Carey relating his translation of the Bible. We put forward his conviction that the Bible was the means. κατ᾽ εξοχην. Nearly all missionaries of that time and before him saw the importance of Holy Scripture. Ziegenbalg and Plütschau and Schwarz. Von Zinzendorf and Spangenberg, were all convinced that Scripture should be preached and translated and not only brought into the houses but also into the schools. The great question, however, is whether the Word is brought not as a means of personal conviction but as the particular revelation of God. Missionaries must be ministers of the Word and not minister the Word. They have to listen to the Word and bring its message to the people and not their personal insights. Missionaries are only servants of the Word, the Word has not to serve them.

And not only have they to serve the Word by preaching it but also by their deeds. A minister has to show by his example that he is a minister of the Word, but especially among the heathens.

Missionaries, who had much success were those who preached with their example. Not only by words.

As for the translation of the Bible : it is quite impossible that missionaries do this enormous task, except for some exceptional men. This task must be done by specialists of the Bible Societies. And we never can be grateful enough for what Bible Societies did and do. They should be supported far more than is done.

When the translation of the Bible is ready the preaching can begin. It must be done in a very tactful way. People who listen must be able to understand it. It must be done not in antithesis to the principles of the heathens. So Pietists did in the beginning. So Raymundus Lullus did in Africa. Heads grew warm and hearts grew cold. Also it should not be done in a sympathetic way. That means not in such a way that some of the pagan principles are accepted and that some doctrines are appreciated, though contrary to Christendom. The method should be thetic, that means : the Gospel must be preached. Christ must be seen. And in this way the heathen will gradually see the mistakes of his religion. Missionaries have to prevent as much as possible all kinds of antithetic discussions. This thetic principle is according to Scripture. St. Paul uses it. He does not blame the Ephesians for their Diana but he connects their service with his principles and gradually he teaches them the right religion. Hand. 19. [1])

Of course the preaching of the Word is not the preaching from the Pulpit. It should be done in a very tactful way. By means of missionary conversation. By means of missionary schools as mentioned. By means of education of the higher classes (cf. page 204 of this diss.). But in whatever way they may preach it always should be : Christ and Him cruficied and by showing the expiatory work of our Saviour. Gradually when the heathen take some interest, other doctrines can be taught. But in the very beginning this should be the central idea.

As we mentioned William Carey opened a great number of Sunday Schools and they proved to be very useful. Also boarding-schools were opened. We could not find any place which informed us he that took this idea of the Moravians or Pietists. William Carey used the same method. But if he did, it only tells us that the idea of preaching the Gospel was tried by him in every possible way and the blessing of these Sunday schools was enormous. Honour is due to both men, Von Zinzendorf and Carey, but also to the Pietists who all saw Holy Scripture as the most important means for the propaganda of Christendom.   But William Carey was a master in finding all kinds of methods in distributing the Word of God.

b. Baptism.

As we stated on page 211 William Carey never baptized children. Only adults who were immersed after having confessed their faith.   Von Zinzendorf and the Pietists baptised children.   But Von Zinzendorf only if wished by the parents.

It is a pity that William Carey did not agree with the principles of infant baptism.   Some arguments for infant baptism are: under the Old Covenant all the boys, when eight days old, were circumcised.   If the Lord intended to baptize only adults under the New Covenant he would have revealed this.

In the second place children are considered as believers in Holy Scripture.   So it is not necessary that the Word of God says explicitly that children must be baptized.

In Col. 2 : 11 and 12 we read : "in whom ye were also circumcised with a circumcision not made with hands, in the putting off of the body of flesh in the circumcision of Christ, having been buried with him in baptism, wherein ye were also raised with him through faith in the working of God who raised him from the dead."   So Baptism has come in stead of circumcision.   And as children were circumcised children must be baptized.

In the Old Testament we see that the Covenant is revealed in an organic and a historic way.   For that reason children are called an heritage of the Lord.   In the New Testament we see the same when the Lord called the children towards him, and he declared that of them was the Kingdom of heaven.   And the apostles teach that *ecclesia* took the place of the Old Covenant.   And the children belong to that ecclesia too.   Acts 2 : 39 cf Acts 11 : 14 and 16 : 31 and 16 : 15.38.

Anabaptists and Baptists don't make difference between the "habitus" of faith and the "actus" of faith.   Children may have the "habitus".   Adults when regenerated the "actus".   And when children possess the "habitus" then they are accepted in Christ to grace, just like the adults.

The whole question depends on this : are children in the Covenant of God and his congregation.   Scripture says : yes.   Children of the believers are under the covenant, and for that reason they have a right to baptism, i.e. a right to the symbol and assurance of the covenant. Christ does not claim of the children that they should understand the significance of baptism before they are baptised. So there is no difficulty at all. [2]) William Carey, who was a self-made man, who had given himself an education and who underwent the influence of Baptist preachers when he was a boy, has shown this influence during all the rest of his life. Yet we must honour him in this that not his Baptist principles, but Jesus Christ and his expiatory death was the centre of his preaching.

Pietists and Von Zinzendorf had a better understanding of baptism, but their understanding of the Covenant was not according to Scripture. At any rate, Von Zinzendorf baptized children when the parents were baptized and the parents wished it. We cannot agree with his opinion, but arguments against his opinion are not within the scope of this dissertation.

Par. V. Comparison of missionary Purpose.

a. The problem.

The glory of the Name of God should be the ultimate purpose of all work in the church. Missionary work either at home or abroad does not make any exception. The Saviour taught us to pray: Hallowed be thy Name, Thy kingdom come, Thy will be done on earth as it is in heaven. Not the honour of men is the purpose, but everything must be directed towards the God and Father of our Lord Jesus Christ, who created all things and who has reconciled with Himself this lost world in Jesus Christ. "For of him, and through him, and unto him, are all things. To him be the glory for ever." [3])

The mission report of the General Synod of Middelburg says: "The glory of God is shown at best, when it leads to the saving of lost people and when it makes shining the wondrous richness of the grace and mercy of God. But even if heathens are not saved but the hearts are hardened the same glorious end is reached."

This highest purpose is reached by preaching the Gospel and by establishing the church of Christ.

Now Von Zinzendorf wanted to preach the Gospel all over the world. But he does not like to establish churches "just like religions have now". Later on he corrected this idea and wishes to see a self-supporting native church, which does not want the white man any longer.

William Carey has the same purpose but he also sees this important principle : "we have availed ourselves of the help of native brethren ever since we had one who dared speak in the name of Christ and their exertions have chiefly been the immediate means by which our church has increased. But we have lately made a plan for rendering their labours more extensively useful ; namely that of sending them out, two and two without any European brother."

On page 213 and 214 we described his further purpose. But here we see already that his purpose and the purpose of Von Zinzendorf are almost the same. Von Zinzendorf said : "we like to reach this purpose that the heathens don't want us any longer, but that they can further their own business."

As for the self supporting of the churches we refer to what we said below. Both Pietists and William Carey had the same purpose, relating self support. The highest purpose was for both the same, only the method was different. William Carey used much more means on his way to the ultimate purpose, more modern means. He wishes to naturalize Christianity in India. For that reason he established his Serampore College. He established all kinds of schools even for women, which was not attempled any where else. He tried to change the whole life of India, caste, burning of widows, marriages of children, and above all he translated the Bible in all the different languages he knew and ordered other people to translate it into all the languages of the world. His method to reach the highest purpose has been more thorough, more modern than of any missionary but we also must acknow ledge that Von Zinzendorf saw these methods but he could not accomplish them. Summarizing we can say that William Carey did a colossal work. But Pietists and Von Zinzendorf have stimulated his work very much and he is also dependent for his method on them. William Carey had a much wider view, but almost the same principles were present as Von Zinzendorf. We conclude that the influence of the Moravians has been enormous and that William Carey has been one of the greatest missionaries of the world.

NOTES

[1] WARNECK, Sendungsmittel, p. 1—29, cf. Dr. J. H. BAVINCK, op. cit., p. 72.
[2] Dr. A. G. HONIG, Handboek voor de Gereformeerde Dogmatiek, p. 650 ff. Kampen 1938, cf. Hodge Systematic Theology. London 1880. Vol. III, p. 546—557.
[3] Prof. Dr. J. H. BAVINCK, p. 42 ff.

CHAPTER IV.

HIS MISSIONARY PRINCIPLES AND SOME CONCLUSIONS.

In this conclusive chapter, we like to give a summary of the main principles of the Dutch Reformed Churches as stated at the Synod of Middelburg in 1896 and applied in the Order of Mission at the Synod of Arnhem in 1902.

1. The purpose of Mission is the glorification of God ; the mission must serve God throughout.

2. Mission is the task of the Church ; not of the church as a collective idea, but of the local church, though the connection with other churches must have its rights.

3. Persons who are sent must be ordained officials ; the church can of course perform all kinds of work by not-ordained-officials, either on pedagogical, medical, architectural, juridical or financial domain, but in the administration of the Word of God, and of Baptism and of Holy Supper and in the execution of Church Discipline in short, when the keys of the kingdom of heaven are to be used, the church is here and everywhere bound to the office.

4. Mission is directed towards the whole world, but according to the providential guidance of God, the Netherlands have a special call relating their colonies. There the Mission has to direct itself towards the people and in this way to the individuals, but in relation with the whole people according to the example given by Christ and the apostles.

5. Contrary to the practice of the mediaeval time and of the Roman Catholics, when often violence and trickery was used, the method of mission must be convincing, in order to bring to belief those, who don't believe and to gather into churches, those who reveal themselves as believers.

6. The administration of the Word of God, the service of schools and the medical service, must not be in the hand of one person, but different persons must supervise these different domains. School-service and medical service are to be used as auxiliary services, that

means that the churches when they use the preparative and auxiliary means are never allowed to identify themselves with the office.

7. The mission must respect the government and take the right line of conduct towards government ; when touching the missionary labour of other denominations, it has to maintain the unity of the body of Christ, in order to show clearly to Islam e.g. the solidarity of all those who profess Christ as Son of God and Saviour.

Ad 1 William Carey sees as the purpose of mission to strive by every means possible to bring non-christians to the knowledge of the Saviour, to set an infinite value upon immortal souls, to spread the knowledge of the name of the Saviour.

Von Zinzendorf sees as purpose that the heathen may become a child of God hoping that he will completely change his way of living.

Both did not see the vertical line : the glory of God, at least they did not say it expressis verbis. Their ultimate purpose seemed to be more anthropocentric than theocentric.

Ad 2 William Carey suggests the establishment of a company of serious Christians, ministers and private persons, who form themselves into a Society to make a number of rules respecting the regulation of the missionary plan. That Society may be interdenominational, but it preferably amongst those of his own denomination : the particular baptist denomination.

Von Zinzendorf sees the "church" as the organ which sends missionaries to the field. Each of the "churches" of the Moravians has the task to be missionary church. On this idea "church", we declare that Von Zinzendorf saw this principle better than William Carey. William Carey tried to rouse the collective church, Von Zinzendorf the local church.

Ad 3 William Carey does not adhere to the idea that missionaries must be ordained officials. He says : they must be men of great piety, prudence, courage and forbearance etc. ; his idea of missionaries is not defined at all.

Von Zinzendorf lays stress upon spiritual qualifications necessary for a missionary who must also be a man of character. But the idea of a missionary is not fixed either. He may be a handicrafts-man, etc. They received some consecration, but the official ordination was not required.

Neither William Carey nor Von Zinzendorf saw the relation between the church — the missionary—and their task, and that the church is bound to the office.

Ad 4   William Carey purposely aims at world missionary action.   The very first words of his Enquiry are : Our Lord Jesus Christ commissioned his apostles to go and teach all nations.

Von Zinzendorf had the same purpose.   His practice may have been different , due to his opinion about "white nominal christians" and his fear to enter into competition with other missionary societies yet he also understood the commission of the Lord.

Ad 5   William Carey's method is that a non-christian must be won by the astonishing and all-constraining love shown in our Redeemer's propitiatory death.   We must only know Christ and Him crucified. Von Zinzendorf lays much stress upon this method that the heathen must know that the Creator is his Saviour.   Missionaries have to preach the expiatory death of Christ on the Cross.

So both disliked the mediaeval practice of violence or trickery and tried to move the feelings of the non-christians.

This does not exclude that they also would convince non-christians, not by logical arguments but by the thetic method as used by St. Paul.   In this method, however, William Carey surpassed Von Zinzendorf.   As for the gathering into churches William Carey wished to plant churches everywhere, while Von Zinzendorf did not like churches in his early period, but later on he established them, too.

Ad 6   William Carey understood very well the importance of medical help to the afflicted.   He even planned the establishment of a native hospital in Calcutta.   But he saw medical service subordinated, not coordinated to the central service i.e. the preaching of the Gospel.   Von Zinzendorf also wished medical help for his own missionaries and for the benifit. of the heathens.   But not as a special means for the Gospel preaching.

As for schools, William Carey did not see the schools and his famous Serampore college, a kind of Indian University for India, as subordinate to his preaching of the Gospel : the central service, he called the professors, the lecturers and the schoolmasters, missionaries.   He saw the school as coordinated with the central service.

Von Zinzendorf considered schools as an essential part of missionary work but subordinate to Gospel preaching.   Schools are means to teach the heathens the Word of God.

So we see that relating medical service the standpoint of William Carey and Von Zinzendorf does not differ materially.   They have however relating schools. William Carey did not, however, define the idea of missionary", for the teachers. Von Zinzendorf sees them as the same person.

Ad 7 William Carey did not agree with a government when it prohibited the sending of missionaries to India. He behaved, however, loyally towards Government, even when he was treated roughly and unjustly. He would never permit Government to touch his missionary work, as the spreading of the Gospel according to his view is the exclusive province of the missionaries in heathen countries.

He also maintained the idea that it always should be understood that the distance between christians and non-christians is much wider than the difference between the different denominations of Christians.

Von Zinzendorf states that the Moravians have a right to preach the Gospel everywhere and he says that it is not his method to deal with the conversion of the heathens with permission of the Government. Relating military service, he refused to go into the forces.

His attitude towards other christians differed materially from William Carey's. He stands very much aloof from them especially as he sees how detrimental the example of the name christian is to the conversion of the heathen.

In this attitude William Carey understood better than Von Zinzendorf that we have to cooperate as much as possible in our endeavour to make disciples of all nations, baptizing them into the name of the Father and of the Son and of the Holy Ghost.

APPENDIX. A.

THE BOND OF THE MISSIONARY BROTHERHOOD OF SERAMPORE.

The form of agreement printed at the Brethren's press, Serampore, in 1805, and reprinted at the Baptist Mission Press, Calcutta, in 1874 with this title-page :

Form of Agreement respecting the *great principles* upon which the Brethren of the Mission at Serampore think it is their duty to act in the work of instructing the Heathen, agreed upon at a meeting of the Brethren at Serampore, on Monday, October 7, 1805.

The *Redeemer*, in planting us in the heathen nation, rather than in any other, has imposed upon us the cultivation of peculiar qualifications. We are firmly persuaded that Paul might plant and Apollos water, in vain, in any part of the world, did not God give the increase. We are sure that only those who are ordained to eternal life will believe, and that God alone can add to the church such as shall be saved. Nevertheless we cannot but observe with admiration that Paul, the great champion for the glorious doctrines of free and sovereign grace, was the most conspicuous for his personal zeal in the work of persuading men to be reconciled to God. In this respect he is a noble example for our imitation. Our Lord intimated to those of His apostles who were fishermen, that He would make them fishers of men, intimating that in all weathers, and amidst every disappointment they were to aim at drawing men to the shores of eternal life. Solomon says : "He that winneth souls is wise", implying, no doubt, that the work of gaining over men to the side of God, was to be done by winning methods, and that it required the greatest wisdom to do it with success. Upon these points, we think it right to fix our serious and abiding attention.

First. In order to be prepared for our great and solemn work, it is absolutely necessary that we set an infinite value upon immortal souls ; that we often endeavour to affect our minds with the dreadful loss sustained by an unconverted soul launched into eternity.

It becomes us to fix in our minds the awful doctrine of eternal punishment, and to realise frequently the unconceivably awful conditions of this vast country, lying in the arms of the wicked one. If we have not this awful sense of the value of souls, it is impossible that we can feel aright in any other part of our work, and in this case it had been better for us to have been in any other situation rather than in that of a Missionary. Oh ! may our hearts bleed over these poor idolaters, and may their case lie with continued weight on our minds, that we may resemble that eminent Missionary, who compared the travail of his soul, on account of the spiritual state of those committed to his charge, to the pains of childbirth. But while we thus mourn over their miserable condition, we should not be discouraged, as though their recovery were impossible. He who raised the Scottish and brutalised Britons to sit in heavenly places in Christ Jesus, can raise these slaves of superstition, purify their hearts by faith, and make them worshippers of the one God in spirit and in truth. The promises are fully sufficient to remove our doubts, and to make us anticipate that not very distant period when He will famish all the gods of India, and cause these very idolaters to cast their idols to the moles and to the bats, and renounce for ever the work of their own hands.

Secondly. It is very important that we should gain all the information we can of the snares and delusions in which these heathen are held. By this means we shall be able to converse with them in an intelligible manner. To know their modes of thinking, their habits, their propensities, their antipathies, the way in which they reason about God, sin, holiness, the way of salvation, and a future state, to be aware of the bewitching nature of their idolatrous worship, feasts, songs, etc., is of the highest consequence, if we would gain their attention to our discourse, and would avoid to be barbarians to them. This knowledge may be easily obtained by conversing with sensible natives, by reading some parts of their works and by attentively observing their manners and customs.

Thirdly. It is necessary, in our intercourse with the Hindoos, that as far as we are able, we abstain from those things which would increase their prejudices against the Gospel. Those parts of English manner which are most offensive to them should be kept out of sight as much as possible. We should also avoid every degree of cruelty to animals. Nor is it advisable, at once to attack their prejudices by exhibiting with acrimony the sins of their gods ;

neither should we upon any account do violence to their images, nor interrupt their worship. The real conquests of the Gospel are those of love : "And I, if I be lifted up, will draw all men unto me". In this respect, let us be continually fearful lest one unguarded word, or one unnecessary display of the difference betwixt us, in manners, etc., should set the natives at a greater distance from us. Paul's readiness to become all things to all men, that he might by any means save some, and his disposition to abstain even from necessary comforts that he might not offend the weak, are circumstances worthy of our particular notice. This line of conduct we may be sure was founded on the wisest principles. Placed amidst a people very much like the hearers of the Apostle, in many respects, we may now perceive the solid wisdom which guided him as a missionary. The mild manners of the Moravians, and also of the Quakers—towards the North American Indians, have, in many instances, gained the affections and confidence of heathens in a wonderful manner. He who is too proud to stoop to others in order to draw them to him, though he may know that they are in many respects inferior to himself, is ill-qualified to become a Missionary. The words of a most successful preacher of a preacher still living, "that he would not care if the people trampled him under their feet, if he might become useful to their souls", are expressive of the very temper we should always cultivate.

Fourthly. It becomes us to watch all opportunities of doing good. A missionary would be highly culpable if he contented himself with preaching two or three times a week to those persons whom he might be able to get together into a place of worship. To carry on conversations with the natives almost every hour in the day, to go from village to village, from market to market, from one assembly to another, to talk to servants, labourers, etc., as often as opportunity offers, and to be instant in season and out of season- this is the life to which we are called in this country. We are apt to relax in these active exertions, especially in a warm climate ; but we shall do well always to fix in our minds, that life is short, that all around us are perishing, and that we incur a dreadful woe if we proclaim not the glad tiding of salvation.

Fifthly. In preaching to the heathen, we must keep to the example of St. Paul, and make the greatest subject of our preaching, Christ Crucified. It would be very easy for a missionary to preach nothing but truths, and that for many years together, without any well-grounded hope of becoming useful to one soul. The doctrine of Christ's expiatory death and all-sufficient merits had been, and must ever remain, the great means of conversion. This doctrine, and others immediately connected with it, have constantly nourished and sanctified the church. Oh that these glorious truths ever be the joy and strength of our own souls and then we will not fail to become the matter of our conversation to others. It was the proclaiming of these doctrines that made the Reformation from Popery in the time of Luther spread with such rapidity. It was these truths that filled the sermons of the modern Apostles, Whitefield, Wesley, etc., when the light of the Gospel which had been held up with such glorious effects by the Puritans was almost extinguished in England. It is a well-known fact that the most successful missionaries in the world at the present day make the atonement of Christ their continued theme. We mean the Moravians. They attribute all their success to the preaching of the death of our Saviour. So far as our experience goes in this work, we must freely acknowledge, that every Hindoo among us who has been gained to Christ, has been won by the astonishing and all-constraining love exhibited in our Redeemer's propitiatory death. O then may we resolve to know nothing among Hindoos and Mussulmans but Christ and Him crucified.

Sixthly. It is absolutely necessary that the natives should have an entire confidence in us, and feel quite at home in our company. To gain this confidence we must on all occasions be willing to hear their complaints ; we must give them the kindest advice, and we must decide upon everything brought before us in the most open, upright, and impartial manner. We ought to be easy of access,to condescend to them as much as possible, and on all occasions to treat them as our equals. All passionate behaviour will sink our characters exceedingly in their estimation. All force, and everything haughty, reserved and forbidding it becomes us ever to shun with the greatest care. We can never make sacrifices too great, when the eternal salvation of souls is the object except, indeed, we sacrifice the commands of Christ.

Seventhly. Another important part of our work is to build up, and watch over, the souls that may be gathered. In this work we shall do well to simplify our first instructions as much as possible, and to press the great principles of the Gospel upon the minds of the converts till they be thoroughly settled and grounded in the foundation of their hope towards God. We must be willing to spend some time with them daily, if possible, in this work. We must have much patience with them, though they may grow very slowly in divine knowledge.

We ought also to endeavour as much as possible to form them to habits of industry, and assist them in procuring such employments as may be pursued with the least danger of temptations to evil. Here too we shall have occasion to exercise much tenderness and forbearance, knowing that industrious habits are formed with difficulty by all heathen nations. We ought also to remember that these persons have made no common sacrifices in renouncing their connections, their homes, their former situations and means of support, and that it will be very difficult for them to procure employment with heathen masters. In these circumstances, if we do not sympathise with them in their temporal losses for Christ, we shall be guilty of great cruelty.

As we consider it our duty to honour the civil magistrate, and in every state and country to render him the readiest obedience, whether we be persecuted or protected, it becomes us to instruct our native brethren the same principles. A sense of gratitude too presses this obligation upon us in a peculiar manner in return for the liberal protection we have experienced. It is equally our wisdom and our duty also to show to the civil power, that it has nothing to fear from the progress of Missions, since a real follower of Christ must resist the example of his Great Master, and all the precepts the Bible contains on this subject, before he can become disloyal. Converted heathens, being brought over to the religion of their Christian Governors, if duly instructed, are much more likely to love them, and be united to them, than subjects of a different religion.

To bear the faults of our native brethren, so as to reprove them with tenderness, and set them right in the necessity of a holy conversation, is a very necessary duty. We should remember the gross darkness in which they were so lately involved, having never had any just and adequate ideas of the evil of sin, or its consequences. We should also recollect how backward human nature is in forming spiritual ideas, and entering upon a holy self-denying conversation. We ought not, therefore even after many falls, to give up and cast away a relapsed convert while he manifests the least inclination to be washed from his filthiness.

278

In walking before native converts, much care and circumspection are absolutely necessary. The falls of Christians in Europe have not such a fatal tendency as they must have in this country, because there the word of God always commands more attention than the conduct of the most exalted Christian. But here those around us, in consequence of their little knowledge of the Scriptures, must necessarily take our conduct as a specimen of what Christ looks for in His disciples. They know only the Saviour and His doctrine as they shine forth in us.

In conversing with the wives of the native converts, and leading them in to he ways of Christ, so that they may be an ornament to the Christian cause, and make known the Gospel to the native women, we hope always to have the assistance of the females who have embarked with us in the mission. We see that in primitive times the Apostles were very much assisted in their great work by several pious females. The great value of female help may easily be appreciated if we consider how much the Asiatic women are shut up from the men, and especially from men of another caste. It behoves us therefore, to afford to our European sisters all possible assistance in acquiring the language, that they may, in every way which Providence may open to them, become instrumental in promoting the salvation of the millions of native women who are in a great measure excluded from all opportunities of hearing the word from the mouths of European missionaries. A European sister may do much for the cause in this respect, by promoting the holiness, and stirring up the zeal, of the female converts. A real missionary becomes in a sense a father to his people. If he feels all the anxiety and tender solicitude of a father, all that delight in their welfare and company that a father does in the midst of his children, they will feel all that freedom with, and confidence in him which he can desire. He will be wholly unable to lead them on in a regular and happy manner, unless they can be induced to open their minds to him, and unless a sincere and mutual esteem subsist on both sides.

Eighthly. Another part of our work is the forming of our native brethren to usefulness, fostering every kind of genius, and cherishing every gift and grace in them. In this respect we can scarcely by too lavish of our attention to their improvement. It is only by means of native preachers that we can hope for the universal spread of the Gospel throughout this immense continent.

Europeans are too few, and their subsistence costs too much for us ever to hope that they can possibly be the instruments of the universal diffusion of the word amongst so many millions of souls spread over such a large portion of the habitable globe. Their incapability of bearing the intense heat of the climate in perpetual itineracies, and the heavy expenses of their journeys, not to say anything of the prejudices of the natives against the very presence of Europeans, and the great difficulty of becoming fluent in their languages, render it absolute duty to cherish native gifts, and to send forth as many native preachers as possible. If the practice of confining the ministry of the word to a single individual in a church be once established amongst us, we despair of the Gospel's ever making much progress in India by our means. Let us therefore use every gift, and continually urge on our native brethren to press upon their countrymen the glorious Gospel of the blessed God.

Still further to strengthen the cause of Christ in this country, and, as far as in our power, to give it a permanent establishment, even when the efforts of Europeans may fail, we think it our duty, as soon as possible, to advise the native brethren who may be formed in separate churches, to choose their pastors and deacons from amongst their own countrymen, that the word may be steadily preached, and the ordinances of Christ administered, in each church by the native minister, as much as possible without interference of the missionary of the district who will constantly superintend their affairs, give them advice in cases of order and discipline, and correct any errors into which they may fall, and who joying and beholding their order, and their steadfastness of their faith in Christ, may direct his efforts continually to the planting of new churches in other places, and to the spread of the Gospel throughout his district as much as in his power. By this means the unity of the missionary character will be preserved, all the missionaries will still form one body, each one movable as the good of the cause may require, the different native churches will also naturally have to care and provide for their ministers, for their church expense, the raising of places of worship, etc., and the whole administration will assume a native aspect, by which means the inhabitants will more readily identify the cause as belonging to their own nation, and their prejudices at falling into the hands of Europeans will entirely vanish. It may be hoped too that the pastors of these churches, and the members in general, will feed a new energy in attempting to spread the Gospel, when they shall thus freely enjoy the privileges of the Gospel amongst themselves.

Under the divine blessing, if, in the course of a few years, a number of native churches be thus established, from them the Word of God may sound out even to the extremities of India, and numbers of preachers being raised up and sent forth, may form a body of native missionaries, inured to the climate, acquainted with the customs, language, modes of speech and reasoning of the inhabitants ; able to become perfectly familiar with them, to enter their houses, to live upon their food, to sleep with them, or under a tree ; and who may travel from one end of the country to the other almost without any expense. These churches will be in no immediate danger of falling into errors of disorders, because the whole of their affairs will be constantly superintended, by a European missionary.

The advantages of this plan are so evident, that to carry it into complete effect ought to be our continued concern. That we may discharge the important obligations of watching over these infant churches when formed, and of urging them to maintain a steady discipline, to hold forth the clear and cheering light of evangelical truth in this region and shadow of death, and to walk in all respects as those who have been called out of the darkness into marvellous light, we should continually go to the Source of all grace and strength for it. If to become the shepherd of one church be a most solemn and weighty charge, what must it be to watch over a number of churches just raised from a state of heathenism, and placed at a distance from each other ?

We have thought it our duty not to change the names of native converts, observing from Scripture that the Apostles did not change those of the first Christians turned from heathenism, as the names Epaphroditus, Phebe, Fortunatus, Sylvanus, Apollos, Hermes, Junia, Narcissus, etc., prove. Almost all these names are derived from those of heathen gods. We think the great object which Divine Providence has in view in causing the Gospel to be promulgated in the world, is not the changing of the names, the dress, the food, and the innocent usages of mankind, but to produce a moral and divine change in the hearts and conduct of men. It would not be right to perpetuate the names of heathen gods amongst Christians, neither is it necessary or prudent to give a new name to every man after his conversion, as hereby the economy of families, neighbourhoods, etc., would be needlessly disturbed. In other respects, we think it our duty to lead our brethren by example, by mild persuasion, and by opening and illuminating their minds in a gradual way rather than use authoritative means. By this they learn to see the evil of a custom, and then to despise and forsake it ; whereas in cases wherein force is used, though they may leave off that which is wrong while in our presence, yet not having seen the evil of it, they are in danger of using hyprocrisy, and of doing that out of our presence which they dare not do in it.

Ninthly. It becomes us also to labour with all our might in forwarding translations of the sacred scriptures in the languages of Hindoostan. The help which God has afforded us already in this work is a loud call to us to "go forward". So far therefore, as God has qualified us to learn those languages which are necessary, we consider it our bounden duty to apply ourselves with unwearied assiduity in acquiring them. We consider the publication of the Divine Word throughout India as an object which we ought never to give up till accomplished, looking to the Fountain of all knowledge and strength to qualify us for this great work, and to carry us through it to the praise of His Holy Name.

It becomes to us to use all assiduity in explaining and distributing the Divine Word on all occasions, and by every means in our power to excite the attention and the reverence of the natives towards it, as the fountain of eternal truth and the Message of Salvation to men. It is our duty also to distribute, as extensively as possible, the different religious tracts which are published. Considering how much the general diffusion of the knowledge of Christ depends upon a liberal and constant distribution of the Word, and of these tracts, all over the country, we should keep this continually in mind, and watch all opportunities of putting even single tracts into the hands of those persons with whom we occasionally meet. We should endeavour to ascertain where large assemblies of the natives are to be found, that we may attend upon them, and gladden whole villages at once with the tidings of salvation.

The establishment of native free schools is also an object highly important to the future conquests of the Gospel. Of this very pleasing and interesting part of our missionary labours, we should endeavour not to be unmindful. As opportunities are afforded, it becomes us to establish, visit, and encourage these institutions, and to recommend the establishment of them to other Europeans. The progress of divine light is gradual, both as it respects individuals and nations. Whatever therefore tends to increase the body of holy light in these dark regions is "as bread cast upon the waters to be seen after many days." In many ways the progress of providential events in preparing the Hindoos for casting their idols to the moles and the bats, and for becoming a part of the chosen generation, the royal priesthood, the holy nation. Some parts of missionary labours very properly tend to present conversion of the heathen, and others to the ushering in the glorious period when "a nation shall be born in a day". Of the latter kind are native free schools.

Tenthly. That which, as a means, is to fit us for the discharge of these laborious and unutterably important labours, is the being instant in prayer, and the cultivation of personal religion. Let us ever have in remembrance the examples of those who have been most eminent in the work of God. Let us often look at Brainerd, in the woods of America, pouring out his very soul before God for the perishing heathen, without whose salvation nothing could make him happy. Prayer secret, fervent, believing prayer, lies at the root of all personal godliness. A competent knowledge of the languages current where a missionary lives, a mild and winning temper, and a heart given up in closet religion, these, these are the attainments which, more than all knowledge, or all other gifts, will fit us to become the instruments of God in the great work of Human Redemption. Let us then ever be united in prayer at stated seasons whatever distance may separate us, and let each one of us lay it upon his heart that we will seek to be fervent in spirit, wrestling with God, till He famish these idols and cause the heathen to experience the blessedness that is in Christ.

Finally. Let us give ourselves up unreservedly to this glorious cause. Let us never think that our time, our gifts, our strength, our families, or even the clothes we wear, are our own. Let us sanctify ourselves for His work! Let us ever shut out the idea of laying up a dowry for ourselves or our children. If we give up the resolution which was formed on the subject of private trade, when we first united at Serampore, the Mission is from that hour a lost cause. A wordly spirit, quarrels, and every evil work will succeed the moment it is admitted that each brother may do something on his own account. Woe to that man who shall ever make the smallest movement towards such a measure. Let us continually watch against a wordly spirit, and cultivate a Christian indifference towards every indulgence. Rather let us bear hardness as good soldiers of Jesus Christ, and endeavour to learn in every state to be content.

If in this way we are enabled to glorify God, with our bodies and spirits which are His,—our wants will be His care. No private family ever enjoyed a greater portion of happiness, even in the most prosperous gale of worldly prosperity, than we have done since we resolved to have all things in common, and that no one should pursue business for his own exclusive advantage. If we are enabled to persevere in the same principles, we may hope that multitudes of converted soulds will have reason to bless God to all eternity for sending His Gospel into this country.

To keep these ideas alive in our minds, we resolve that this Agreement shall be read publicly, at every station, at our three annual meetings, viz., on the first Lord's day in January, in May, and October.

APPENDIX. B.

We found in Hefte zur Missionskunde Nr 12 : "Die Wichtegsten Missionsinstruktionen Zinzendorf" Hernhut 1913, the instructions given to all kind of missionaries. We only give here the instructions "An einen Missionarium von der englischen Sozietät", as one of the oldest set of instructions, and in the second place "Instruktion an alle Heyden-Boten".

I. An einen Missionarium von der englischen Sozietät.

Uttendörfer informs us in the perface to these instructions that there are three copies of this first letter. On one copy is written : "Extract Schreibens nach Madras" on the other two : "Schreiben an den engl. Missionarium in Madras HE. Geistern". This letter is of importance as Von Zinzendorf made these principles before he sent the first missionaries.

Herrnhuth, am 12 April. 1732.

Mein lieber Bruder, gleichgültig ist mir es nicht gewesen, dasz ich sie nicht gesehen habe, und ich musz frey bekennen, dasz die grosze Gefahr, in welcher ich sie gesehen, mich recht sehr für sie beängstigt hat. Ich mache einen groszen Unterschied unter der Arbeit an Heiden und an sogenannten Christen ; die Arbeit an jenen ist vor den äusserlichen Menschen beschwerlicher, den innern aber weit leichter, wenn es in der Kraft Christi und nicht sowohl aus menschlicher Gewalt als aus innern Triebe zu Christo geschiehet. Es jammert mich sehr, wenn ich sehen musz, dasz die armen Heyden wieder su Sectirern (Anhängern bestimmter Kirchen) werden müssen, dasz man ihnen die Kirchen wieder aufputzet und sie fraget, von welcher der christlichen Religionen sie sind. O wie gut wäre es, wenn sie den Gekreuzigten kennen lernten und seine Gnade glaubten und seine Kraft fühlen mögten, gewies das Herz im Liebe möchte einem zerspringen, wenn man höret dasz ein Neubekehrter gestorben, zu dem man doch einige Hofnung gehabt, dasz er selig worden, und dort einer wegen seines liederlichen Lebenswandels aus der Anstallt gethan werden müssen. Wenn man an den Catecheten selbst als Raianaiacken und dergl. noch keine Spur des wahren Gemeinschaft mit J. Ch. siehet und sie ohngefehr mit der Predigt des Evangelii wie die ungerischen Studenten mit dem Disputiren umgehen, da man sich freuet, wenn man einen bessern Syllogismuss machen kan als der andere oder ein Sophisma, darüber der Respondente confus wird oder sich aus einem üblen Stande und gefährlichen Frage durch eine Aequivocation in die Antwort herausfindet. Gewisz l. Br., lieset man die apostolische Methoden, da ginge es anders zu. Ich schreibe diesen Brief in grosser Liebe, in geistlicher groszer Dürftigkeit ohne der geringsten Absicht mich über fremden Knechten aufzuhalten, ich weisz ja zur Genüge, wie ich gar nichts bin und meine Arbeit gegen der Brüder ihre Kinderspiel ist, aber ich schreibe es ihnen, M. l. Br., ganz kindlich und herzlich zur Nachricht und bitte, es niemanden zu weisen, sondern in aller Stille vor Gott durchzuarbeiten, ob nicht nachfolgendes gut wäre:

1. An keinem Heiden direkt zu arbeiten, in dem nicht eine glückliche Disposition zu einem recht schaffenen Wesen findet, weil es eben die sind ex Corn., Candacaei (von der Art des Kornelius oder des Kämmerers der Königin Candace) p., denen Christus seine Boten schicket, so jemand will den Willen thun.

2. Publice die Lehre von Jesu Christo und seinem Kreuz, dem Falle und der Wiedererstattung conjunctim der Lehre von der Schöpfung Erhaltung p. zu praemittiren und den Gott Menschen — und Gott offenbaret im Fleisch — d.i. Jesum Imanuel an die Herzen zu legen mit Bewegungs-Kräften, ohne etwan — (ohne dasz man viel mit den Philosophis disputire).

3. Müszte man aber ja mit ihnen disputiren, gesetzt, gründlich und definite geantwort. Qu. (Frage) Ist der Teufel so böse, warum schlägt ihn Gott nicht tod? Rp. (Antwort) Darum weil er nöthig und nützlich ist, die Treue der Seelen gegen ihren Erlöser zu üben und weil er niemand nicht schaden kan, der nicht selbst will.

4. Die allgemeine Erlösung des Menschlichen Geschlechts auf einmal et uno actu, wie sie allen Menschen recht wahrhaftig zu gute kommen und Christus nicht nur vor uns, sondern der ganzen Welt Sünde würklich gestorben sey, recht klar auszuwicklen und dasz eine jede Seele, wenn sie verdammt word, nicht um fremder Schuld willen, sondern um ihres eigenen neuen Falles willen zu Grunde gehe.

286

5. So zu reden, so allgemein, so christlich, dasz man weder mit der Schrift selbst zu streiten scheine noch mit allerley Irr-Geistern in einigen Streit gerathen möge, wo sie scheinbarer als wir über die Materie zu reden wissen, dasz man also alle Propositionen, wo man noch nicht stark und unüberwindlich genug ist, lieber suspendire als wage.

6. Einen fröhlichen und muntern Geist zu zeigen und im geringsten nicht äusserlich über die Heiden zu herschen, sondern mit Geistes Kraft sich in respect bei ihnen zu setzen, dem äussern nach aber sich soviel als möglich unter sie zu demüthigen. Die Pröbstin Ziegenbalg hat mir gesagt, die Missionarii machen sich mit den Heiden nicht gemein, es wäre ein sclavisches Volk, sie wüsten sich nicht darein zu schicken — so redet aber der Heiland nicht.

7. Mit den Bramanen nicht hochherfahrend zu reden, sondern ihre Gelehrsamkeit und Einsicht zu erkennen, aber zu zeigen, dasz alles auf Einfalt, Kraft und Erfahrung ankomme.

8. Menschliche Bücher, wenn sie nicht ganz exquisit, ihnen nicht sehr recommendiren, hingegen desto mehr Auszüge der Schrift, Lutheri herzhafte Reden, aber nicht unter seinem Namen.

9. Die ganze Sache mit Gebet zu tractiren und einen gemeinschaftlichen Umgang mit Gott zu suchen, dasz man ohne ihn keine Hand und Fusz rege, sondern mit ihm alles wage.

10. Wo keine reflexiones helfen, zu losen mit völliger indifferenz.

11. Im Privat Umgang die Menschen ganz kindlich zur Sinnes-Anderung bereden und sich mit ihnen vor dem unbekannten Gott im Gebet zu demüthigen, auch soviel möglich, sich ihren nicht irrigen, sondern incompleten Ideen zuu accomodiren sonderlich zukünftige Geheimnisze nicht ex hypothesi zu obtrudiren.

12. Die Sclavische Ehrerbietung vor Menschen und Lehrern aus ihrem Gemüthe zu reisen und alles auf der unsichtbaren Heiand zu führen, deszen Knechte wir, alle Engel und Kräfte wären.

INSTRUKTION AN ALLE HEYDEN-BOTEN.

Lieben Brüdern und Schwestern.

Es ist bey eures gleichen Verrichtungen schwer, eine Anweisung zu geben weils, überhaupt schwer ist, Brüder zu instruiren. Ein Bruder, der von hier nach Hanau gehen soll und weisz, was er da soll, dem kan es leicht schwerer gemacht werden, wenn man ihm dazu sagt, wie ers dort machen soll, denn es darf sich in den 3 Stunden nur ein Umstand ereignen, den wir nicht wüsten, so musz der Bruder einen Boten zurückschicken und um eine neue Anweisung bitten oder in Gefahr stehen, dasz er es versiehet. Es schreibt mir dieser Tage ein wichtiger Bruder : gespannt seyn und dienen ist einem jeden schwer. Man kan dencken wie genau eine Instruktion seyn müsse, wenn sie alle vorkommende Umständ sollte einschliessen, und wie allgemein, wenn sie einen Bruder nicht binden sollte.

Unserm ersten Boten nach Thomas gaben wir die Instruktion mit, allda eine Seele zum Heyland zu bringen, und was der Heyland sonst mehr geben würde. Denen nach Grönland, sie sollten sehen, of sie dem Pfarrer Egedi was helfen könnten, und das wars alles. Was soll man den Brüdern auf ein paar 1000 Meilen sagen, da man keine Seel kennt, zu denen sie kommen ? Die Instruction des Heylandes : gehet hin in alle Welt und prediget aller Creatur das Evangelium, war auch general ; und das siehet man an den Zwistigkeiten, die nach der Ausgiessung des Heil. Geistes über der Art und Weise entstanden sind. Unterdessen, damit sich die Brüder ein wenig und sonderlich, wenn sie schwermüthig sind, an die Gemeinen erinneren können und an ihren Sinn, so wollen wir etliche unsrer Gedancken schreiben.

I. Wenn an einem Orte gar keine Leute sind, die den Heyland kennen, oder die Leute, die den Heyland kennen, haben keine Art noch Sinn, das Erkannte von sich zu geben, so ists schwehr und natürlicher Weise unmöglich, das Erkenntnisz Jesus, an einen solchen Ort zu bringen. Ist aber nur jemand da und ist nur 14 Tage da, der Jesum kennt und es jemand anders sagt, so kan in 10 Jahren darnach eine Seele, mit der es wie mit Cornelio bewandt ist, durch die Weiszheit des Heylandes an den Menschen gebracht werden, der es von dem gehört hat, der nur 4 Wochen in demselben Land gelebet hat, und aus dem Waytzen-Körnlein, das daselbst in die Erde gefallen ist, kan eine grosse Erndte werden.

II. Die Leute in Indien reden über anderthalb 1000 Jahr von Apostel Thomas, und es stehet dahin, ob er sein Lebtage da gewesen ist, die die Mohren von Abraham, die Copten von Salomo und die Persianer von Adam. Kan nun eine fliegende Rede von etlichen solchen Menschen sich verewigen, wie soll nicht das Wort vom Jesu von Nazareth, dem Gecreutzigten, geredt zu seiner Ziet, ein unaussprechlichen Seegen haben können ? Und das ist nur von einem Waytzen-Körnlein gesagt, das sich auf einmahl verliert. Wie wirds mit den Senff-Körnern seyn, die der Heyland Jahr und Tag bleiben und sich ausbreiten läszt, das Vögelchen drunter nisten ? Daraus ist klar, dasz man in alle Welt Leute schicket, als dasz man keine schickt.

Es ist also nur vor folgenden Versuchungen zu warnen.

1. Die geringsten Händel mit den Geistlichen anzufangen.

2. Vor langer Weile neue Glaubens-Artickel machen.

3. Sich erst in den Ländern besinnen, was man dort will.

4. Seinen Beruf an die Heyden prüfen, wenn man unter ihnen ist.

5. Wegen Ausbleiben der Briefe wider die Gemeine eingenommen worden.

6. Wenn man um Rath gefragt hat, was man einem eingeben soll, der das hitzige Fieber hat und darüber gestorben ist, über der Gemeine ihre Langwierigkeit in Antworten klagen und, wenn sie ja kommt, applicatione facti machen, dasz es nicht so allenthalben zutrifft.

7. Melancholich werdeu über alte Sünden, Unlauterkeiten, unabgethane Händel oder sich einen Bann einbilden und die Arbeit darüber liegen lassen.

8. Den Schlusz machen, wenn eine Sache nicht geht, die Gemeine wüste sich die Leute nicht auszulesen, die es machen könnten, oder aber gar, die hätten rechten Paln gehabt.

9. Heimlich mit der Idee fortgehen, man werde zur Zucht oder aus Leichtsinn oder politique weggeschrickt, und es so lange verbeiszen, bisz man drinnen ist.

10. Sich mit seinen Cameraden brouilliren und die Sachen ihnen gleichsam zum Tort liegen lassen.

11. Sich ansäszig machen wollen und vergessen, dasz man sich auf der Wanderschaft befindet und ein Pilger under den Nationen ist.

12. Auch nur einen halben Gedancken haben, etwas zu gewinnen, etwas zu gelten oder sich dort erst durch gute Aspecten einnehmen lassen.

13. Wieder die Heyden eingenommen werden, dasz sie nicht fromm seyn, und darüber eiffern, dasz es so schlimm unter ihnen zugehet.

14. Sich einen Gedanken von Commoditäten einfallen lassen.

15. Uber den Plan der Gemeine andre um Rath fragen.

16. Sich treuhertzig machen lassen, andern su gestehen, dasz man den Plan vergeszen hat.

17. Die Gemeine drüber ausschelten, wenn man was versehen hat.

18. Die Gemeinschafft der Güter entweder nichs verstehen oder hassen oder unweizlich administriren und mit dem geringsten Schein einer Partheylichkeit, sonderlich für sich und die seinen, worunter der Geringste Vorzug, den man sich in etwas vor den andern Brüdern nimmt, mitzuzehlen ist, wenn sie es gleich einem antragen.

Sich die Zeit lang währen lassen und drüber krickeln, dasz keine apostolische Wunder geschehen, welches eben so viel ist, als wollen, dasz die Bekehrung in einem halben Jahre zu Stande kommen soll damit man in einem Jahre kann martyrisirt werden.

20. Gantze Diaria mit Schwürigkeiten anfüllen und die Wege des Heylandes aus den Schwürigkeiten heraus entweder gar nicht oder gantz seichte berühren.

21. Sich einige Vorstellung machen, dasz seine Sache so oder so seyn wird, die, wenns hernach nicht zutrifft, einen confus im Gemühte macht.

22. Den Weg des Raisonnierens erwehlen und dencken, weil man einmahl eine gescheute Antwort hat geben können, so ist man ein Philosoph worden und kan nun den Leuten demonstriren.

23. Vergessen, dasz man nicht so viel durch Worte als durch den mit der Benennung des Bluts, Todes, Creutzes, Verdienstes Christ verknüpfften Geist, Krafft und Sympathie mit dem Hertzen ausrichte.

24. Den Haupt-Plan der gantzen Gemeine vergessen.

25. Sich mit einigen Gegnern überwerffen.

26. Im geringsten Stück gegen die Policey handeln und die Obrigkeit ombragiren.

27. Die Mit-Arbeiter und sonderlich Vorgesetzte nach dem Innern examiniren und seine Harmonie mit ihnen in Amts-Sachen darnach einrichten, wie man mit ihnen zufrieden oder unzufrieden ist.

28. Bei sich selbst Knecht und Kind nicht unterscheiden.

29. Ohne Noth mit Verheyrathung untüchtiger Leute oder sonst einer Anvertrauung grosser und gefährlicher Dinge in unzuverläszige Hände allzusehr eilen und vergessen, dasz ein Haup-Mazime glücklicher Streiter ist, dasz sie unter den Unmöglichkeiten ausdauern und die Schwürigkeiten abwarten können und Sachen und Personen überleben.

30. Einen einzeitigen Eiffer kriegen, Leute, die gar nicht in unser Departement gehören, zu corrigiren, zu straffen d.d. die Säue

heraus zu fordern, dasz sie sich wenden und uns ein Knopffloch entzwey reissen sollen.

31. Mit reicher oder vornehmer Leute Bekehrung sich unzeitig zu thun oder mit ihnen Compagnie machen, das Werk des Herrn zu treiben, darüber man offt was gewisses fahren läszt und sich mit etwas ungewisses so lange martert, bis man endlich mit Schaden abziehen musz.

32. Seine Privat-Erfahrung bey 2 oder 3 Menschen zur Regel machen ausser oder gegevn den Plan der Oeconomie des Heylands.

33. Sich von einem Plan auf den andern bringen lassen und endlich so weit kommen, dasz einem die Wahl wehe thut und man das Decisum mit Aufhaltung der gantzen Sache endlich den Brüdern überlassen musz.

34. Ohne Noth lossen und loosen, wenn man melancholisch ist, oder über unmögliche Sache loosen oder zu decisiv oder zu eingeschränkt oder über künfftige Sachen oder über Dinge, die von anderm dependiren.

35. Zu eine grosse Idee haben vom Zweck seiner Expedition und die höchst geseegnete und göttliche Regel aus den Augen verlieren dasz wenn man in Einfalt und Liebe nicht mehr auf 3000 Meil-Weges thut, als wenn eine Bothe ein Stück Acten aus der Stadt ins Dorff trägt es dem Heylande und der Gemeine genug ist.

36. Ferner ist noch bey unserer Heyden-Sache sorgfältig zu vermeiden das Heimweh und die unzeitige Erinnerung der schönen Erweckung daheim.

37. Der Korah-Geist.

38. Die Fremdigkeit gegen den Heyland.

39. Die Streitigkeiten älter werden zu lassen als einen Tag.

40. Dasz man sich nicht gleich in alle Umstände schickt und wenn man ein viertel Jahr auf der See oder im Texel oder vor Ancker liegen musz, nicht gleich eine gehieme augenblickliche Conferenz mit den Engeln anfängt, bisz man wieder mit Menschen zu thun kriegt.

41. Dasz man nachdenckt und glaubt, wäre ich jetzt da und da, so stürbe ich nicht, so gienge mirs nicht so und so; und also vermuthen, dasz man des Heylandes Absicht und Rathschlusz über sich auf einigerley Art und Weise hätte vermeiden können.

42. Sich durch welcherley gute Vorstellung es auch sey in eine Speculation bringen lässet, die einen von der Arbeit abhält.

43. Unter was Praetext es auch sey und mit was Recht es nur

sey, dem Satan durch Kunst oder Confusion oder Bitterkeit im Gemüthe eine Gelegenheit giebt, uns zu überlisten, uns zu Boden zu werfen, uns aus den Frieden zu treiben.

44. Sich unterwegens den Plan ändern lässet, weiter gehet oder zurücke bleibet. Dazu füge ich noch 2 Remarquen :

45. Wenn was nicht fort will, so ists nich allemahl eine bösz Zeichen ; nur Gedult.

46. Ledige Brüder solle alle frommen Weibes-Personen (auch unter den Heyden) sobald es nur möglich ist Gott befehlen.

Marienborn, m. Aug. 1738.

APPENDIX. C.

THE BAPTIST CONFESSION OF FAITH OF 1688
(The Philadelphia Confession).

This confession is almost the same as the Westminster Confession. We only give the main differences.

In Chapter XX, "Of Christian Liberty and Liberty of Conscience", Art. 4 of the westminster Conf. is omitted.

In Chapter XXIII, "Of the Civil Magistrate", Arts. 3 and 4 of the Westminster Conf. are omitted and the following inserted.

Civil Magistrates being set up by God for the end aforesaid, subjection in all lawfull things commanded by them ought to be yielded by us in the Lord, not only for wrath, but for conscience sake ; and we ought to make supplications and prayers for kings and all that are in authority, that under them we may live a quiet and peaceable life, in all godliness and honesty.

In the Chapter "Of the Church" (Ch. XXV. W.C. ; Ch. XXVI of the Bapt. Conf. and Savoy Declaration) the changes are so great that we give the whole ;

1. The Catholicof Universal Church which (with respect to the eternal work of the Spirit and truth of grace) may be called invisible, consists of the whole number of the elcet, that have been, are or shall be gathered into one, under Christ, the head thereof : and is the spouse the body, the fullness of him that filleth all in all.

2. All persons throughout the world, professing the faith of the Gospel and obedience unto God by Christ according unto it, not destroying their own profession by any errors, averting the foundation, or unholiness of conversation, are and may be called visible saints ; and of such ought all particular congregations to be constituted.

3. The purest churches under heaven are subject to mixture

and error ; and some have so degenerated as to become no churches of Christ, but synagogues of Satan ; nevertheless Christ always hath had and ever shall have a kingdom in this world to the end thereof, of such as believe in him, and make professions of his name.

4. The lord Jesus Christ is the head of the Church, in whom, by the appointment of the Father, all power for the calling, institution, order or government of the Church is invested in a supreme and sovereign manner ; neither can the Pope of Rome, in any sense be head thereof, but is no other than Antichrist, that man of sin and son of perdition, that exalteth himself in the Church against Christ, and all that is called God : whom the Lord shall destroy with the brightness of his coming.

5. In the execution of this power wherewith he is so intrusted, the Lord Jesus calleth out of the world unto himself, through the ministry of his Word, by his Spirit, those that are given unto him by his Father, that they may walk before him in all the ways of obedience which he prescribeth to them in his Word. Those thus called he commandeth to walk together in particular societies or churches, for their mutual edification, and the due performance of that public worship which he requireth of them in the world.

6. The members of these churches are saints by calling, visibly manifesting and evidencing (in and by their profession and walking) their obedience unto that call of Christ ; and do willingly consent to walk together according to the appointment of Christ giving up themselves to the Lord and one to another, by the will of God, in the professed subjection to the ordinances of the gospel.

7. To each of these churches thus gathered, according to his mind, declared in his Word, he hath given all that power and authority which is in any way needful for their carrying on that order in worship and discipline which he hath instituted for them to observe, with commands and rules for the due and right exerting and executing of that power.

8. A particular church gathered and completely organized according to the mind of Christ consists of officers and members and the officers appointed by Christ to be chosen and set apart by the Church (so-called and gathered) for the peculiar administration of ordinances, and execution of power and duty, which he instrusts them with or calls them to, to be continued to the end of the world, are bishops or elders and deacons.

9. The way appointed by Christ for the calling of any person, fitted and gifted by the Holy Spirit, unto the office of bishop or elder in the church is that he be chosen thereunto by the common suffrage of the church itself, and solemnly set apart by fasting and prayer, with imposition of hands of the eldeship of the church, if there be any before constituted therein ; and of a deacon, that he be chosen by the like suffrage, and set apart by prayer, and the like imposition of hands.

10. The work of pastors being constantly to attend the services of Christ in his churches, in the ministry of the Word and prayer, with watching for their souls, as they that must give account to him, it is incumbent on the churches to whom they minister, not only to give them all due respect, but also to communicate to them of all their good things, according to their ability, so as they may have a comfortable supply, without being themselves entangled with secular affairs ; and may also be capable of exercising hospitality towards others ; and this is required by the law of nature, and by the express order of our Lord Jesus, who hath ordained that they that preach the gospel should live of the gospel.

11. Although it be incumbent on the bishops or pastors of the churches to be instant in preaching the Word by way of office, yet the work of preaching the Word is not so peculiarly confined to them but that others also, gifted and fitted by the Holy Spirit for it, and approved and called by the Church, may and ought to perform it.

12. As all believers are bound to join themselves to particular churches, when and where they have opportunity so do to, so all that are admitted unto the privileges of a church are also under the censures and government thereof, according to the rule of Christ.

13. No Church members, upon any offense taken by them, having performed their duty required of them towards the person they are offended at, ought to disturb any church order, or absent themselves from the assemblies of the church or administration of any ordinances upon the account of such offense at any of their fellow-members, but to wait upon Christ in the further proceeding of the Church.

14. As each church, and all the members of it, are bound to pray continually for the good and prosperity of all the churches of Christ, in all places, and upon all occasions to further it (every

one within the bounds if their places and callings, in the exercise of their gifts and graces) so the churches (when planted by the providences of God so as they may enjoy opportunity and advantage for it) ought to hold communion among themselves for their peace, increase of love and mutual edification.

15. In cases of difficulties or differences, either in point of doctrine or administration, wherein either the churches in general are concerned or any one church in their peace, and edification ; or any member or members of any church are injured, in or by any proceedings in censures not agreeable to truth and order ; it is according to the mind of Christ that many churches, holding communion together do by their message meet to consider and give their advice in or about that matter of difference, to be reported to all the churches concerned ; howbeit these messengers assembled are not intrusted with any church themselves, to exercise any censures either over any Churches of persons, to impose their determination on the churches or officers.

Instead of Chapter XXVII, "Of the sacraments", of the Westminster Confession, the following is given (Bapt. Conf. Ch. XXVIII)

1. Baptism and the Lord's Supper are ordinances of positive and sovereign institution, appointed by the Lord Jesus, the only Lawgiver, to be continued in his Church to the end of the world.
2. These holy appointments are to be administrated by those only who are qualified, and thereunto called, according to the commission of Christ.

Similarly (Ch. XXVIII. W. C. ; Ch. XXIX. B.C.) :

Of Baptism.

1. Baptism is an ordinance of the New Testament ordained by Jesus Christ to be unto the party baptized a sign of his fellowship with him in his death and ressurrection ; of his being engrafted into him ; of remission of sins ; and of his giving up unto God, through Jesus Christ, to live and walk in newness of life.
2. Those who do actually profess repentance towards God, faith in and obedience to our Lord Jesus, are the only proper subjects of this ordinance.
3. The outward element to be used in this ordinance is water,

wherein the party is to be baptized in the name of the Father, and the Son and of the Holy Spirit.

4. Immersion, or dipping of the person in water, is necessary to the due administration of this ordinance.

Chapters **XXX**, "Of Church Censures", and **XXXI**, "Of Synods and Councils", of the Westminster Confession are omitted. On the other hand, a chapter "Of the Gospel and the Extent of the Grace thereof" is added from the Savoy Declaration.

APPENDIX. D.

Vestgesetzte Regeln der Bruedersocietät zur Förderung des Evangelii unter den Heiden. From the work of August Gottlieb Spangenberg ,,Von der Arbeit der evangelischen Brueder unter den Heiden'', Barby 1782. cf. p. 149.

Da wir Endes Unterschriebene ueberzeugt sind, dass die Brueder-kirche einen besonderen Beruf von GOTT hat, die frohe Nachricht von der Erloesung unter die Heiden, und vorzueglich unter solche zu bringen welche von den Erloeser der Welt noch nichts gehoert haben, und da uns auch bekannt ist, dass viele Diener und Glieder besagter Kirche itzt wirklich in diesem gesegneten Werke angestellt sind, von deren Arbeit an vielen Orten sich der glückliche Erfolg und die Früchte zeigen ; und da wir selbst mit dieser Kirche in Verbindung stehen : so koennen wir nicht anders, als eifrigst wuen-schen, dieses grosse Werk GOTTES auf die uns moegliche Weise zu befördern.

Deswegen haben wir beschlossen, uns zu einer Gesellschaft unter dem Namen der Brüdersocietät zur Foerderung des Evangeliums unter den Heiden einzurichten, und haben uns ueber folgenden Artkeln, als ueber vestgesetzten Regeln dieser Societät, einmuthig verstanden.

Artikel I.

Die Societät ist nicht eingerichtet, um irgend einer andern von aehnlicher Beschaffenheit entgegen zu seyn, noch ihr in Absicht der milden Beysteuren Abbruch zu thun.

Artikel II.

Diese Societät soll aus Gliedern der Bruederkirche bestehen, und hat eigentlich hier in London ihren Sitz, wo sie gewöhnlich sich versamlen wird ; doch koennen auch Mitglieder erwehlt werden, welche sonst wo unter britischer Hoheit wohnen oder anderwerts.

Artikel III.

Ausser den eben gemeldeten Gliedern der Societät koennen aber auch Personen, die nicht zur Bruederkirche gehoeren, aber Freunde und Goenner der Foerderung des Evangelii unter den Heiden sind, als Ehrenmitglieder dieser Societät erwehlt werden, welchen von Zeit zu Zeit Nachrichten von dem Werke unsres HERRN unter den Heiden durch die Missionen der Brueder mitgetheilet werden ; und diese Ehrenmitglieder koennen gelegentlich zu den Versamlungen der Societät zugelassen werden.

Artikel IV.

Da unsere Absicht ist, solchen Missionarien und ihren Gehuelfen beyzustehen, welche von der Direction der Missionen der Bruederkirche zu den Heiden in verschiedene Welttheile gesendet werden ; so wollen wir unsren Beystand nicht blos auf milden Gaben und Beyträge zum Behuf dieser Missionen einschraenken ; sondern es wird uns zum groesten Vergnuegen gereichen, dieses angenehme Werk mit unsern Diensten in aller Absicht bestens zu foerdern, indem wir dieselben waehrend ihres Aufenthalts in England unterhalten, und sie auch mit allem nöthigen zu ihrer Reise nach den Oertern ihrer Bestimmung und waehrend ihres Aufenthalts an solchen Orten versehen.

Artikel V.

Obgleich unsre Hauptabsicht ist, das Evangelium zu befoerdern und den Missionarien unter brittischer Hoheit in America und andern Welttheilen behuelflich zu seyn : so sind wir doch auch willig, denen Bruedermissionen unter den Heiden in andern Gegenden alle moegliche Huelfe zu leisten.

Artikel VI.

Und da die Bruederunität schon seit mehrern Jahren Deputirte bestellt, und ihnen die Sorge fuer die Heidenmissionen und die Verwaltung der Beysteuern aufgetragen hat, welche zu den bey diesem Werk Gottes unvermeidlichen Ausgaben freywillig von Zeit zu Zeit, sowol von den Bruedergemeinen, als von andern gegeben werden : so wollen wir in Verbindung und Gemeinschaft mit diesen Deputirten handeln ; zu dem Ende hat der Secretair und andere

Brueder des Ausschusses einen bestaendigen Briefwechsel mit denselben unterhalten, damit wir von den Gelegenheiten, die unsern Beystand erfordern, benachrichtiget werden, und dazu bereit seyn moegen.

Artikel VII.

Und weil eben diese Deputirten der Bruederkirche allezeit einen correspondirenden Agenten haben, der sich in London aufhaelt, um ihre Aufträge zu bestellen ; so wollen wir allezeit bereit seyn, ihm darinn allen uns moeglichen Beystand zu leysten.

Artikel VIII.

Jeder von uns ist willig, sein Scherflein zu den milden Gaben beyzutragen, welche zu gewissen vestgesetzten Zeiten in den Bruedergemeinen zum Behuf der Missionen unter den Heiden gegeben werden. Ausserdem aber soll noch in den Zimmer, in welchem wir uns versamlen, eine Buechse, aufgestellt seyn, in welche jedes Glied der Societät zu jeder Zeit einlegen kan, was ihm beliebt, und alles, was sich da samlet, ist zum Behuf der Missionen anzuwenden. Der Ausschusz hat sowol ueber die Einnahme dieses und anderen Geldes das durch Geschenke, Vermächtnisse, oder sonst einkomt, als ueber dessen Ausgabe genaue Rechnung zu fuehren, und dieselbe vierteljaehrig der Societaet vorzulegen.

Artikel IX.

Solte diese Societaet oder eines oder mehrere Glieder derselben zu Trustees irgend eines Stueck Landes zu einer Niederlassung unter den Heiden bestellt werden ; so versprechen wir in diesem Falle, das auf uns gesetzte Vertrauen nicht zu missbrauchen, und nie fuer uns selbst einigen Anspruch auf dasjenige zu machen, was auf unsern Namen gesetzt und uns anvertraut ist.

Artikel X.

Die gewoehnliche Versamlung der Societät soll monatlich an einen von derselben zu bestimmenden Tage und Orte gehalten werden, und zwar sobald als es sich thun laeszt, nach dem Tage, an welchem Berichte von dem Fortgang des Evangelii, sonderlich unter den Heiden in der Bruedercapelle pflegen gelesen zu werden.

Artikel XI.

Die Societät hat einen Ausschuss von sechs Gliedern zu erwehlen, einen Secretair, einen oder zween Diener, einer aus dem Ausschuss ist zum Caszirer zu bestellen, und alle ordinirte Diener der Brueder-kirche, die in London anwesend sind, werden als Glieder des Ausschusses angesehen, deren dabey eine Stimme hat.

Artikel XII.

Die Glieder des Ausschusses haben als Deputirte der Societät zu handeln, und wochentlicht einmal, oder so oft als er zur Besorgung der Geschaefte fuer noetig erachtet wird, zusammen zu kommen, und viere von dem Ausschusz sind befugt, die Arbeit zu thun.

Artikel XIII.

Der Ausschuss kan, wenn es die Geschaefte erfordern, eine ausserordentliche Versammlung der Societät berifen.

Artikel XIV.

Der Ausschusz ist befugt, in irgend einem unvermutheten Falle im Namen der Societät eine Summe die nicht ueber funfzig Pfund Sterling ist, zu entlehnen.

Artikel XV.

In den ersten Societätsversamlung im Jahr sind die sechs Glieder des Ausschusses, der Secretär und die Diener entweder in ihren Aemtern zu bestätigen oder andere an ihre Stelle zu erwehlen.

Artikel XVI.

In dem Falle, wenn ein Glied des Ausschusses stirbt oder abgeht oder in jedem andern Falle, wo eine neue Wahl noethig ist, hat der Ausschusz eine Person oder Personen der Societät vorzuschlagen, welche derselbe zu dem Amte fuer schicklich haelt.

Artikel XVII.

Solche Personen sollen Glieder der Bruederkirche, von gutem Verstand und gutem Ruf sein, sowol under den Bruedern als ihren Mitbuergern.

Artikel XVIII.

Personen, welche von dem Ausschusse zu Gliedern desselben der Societät vorgeschlagen worden, sind durch die Mehrheit der Stimmen der anwesenden Societätsglieder zu erwehlen.

Artikel XIX.

Wenn ein oder mehrere neue Mitglieder der Societät vorgeschlagen werden sollen, do hat der Ausschusz vorher zu ueberlegen, ob die Person oder Personen der Societät in der Fortsetzung der virbemeldeten Absichtten nuetzlich seyn koennen, und wenn die von dem Ausschusz vorgeschlagen Personen durch einmuthige Wahl der Societät erwehlt werden, alsdann werden sie als Mitglieder aufgenommen.

Artikel XX.

Solte aber unter den Votis ein verneinendes gegen die Wahl der Vorgeschlagenen Personen seyn, so hat das Glied, oder die Glieder, die etwas dagegen einzuwenden haben, ihre Einwendung einem Mitgliede des Ausschusses zu eroefnen, wenn die Sache wieder in Ueberlegung zu nehmen ist. Und wenn die Einwendung zu Befriedigung dessen, der sie gemacht hat, gehoben werden kan, so kan die Person, oder die Personen abermals der Societät vorgeschlagen, und wenn kein neues verneinendes Votum bey der Wahl vorkommt, alsdann als Glieder angenommen werden.

Artikel XXI.

Kein Glied der Societät soll jemand benachrichtigen, weder dass er zum Societätsglied vorgeschlagen, noch dass er dazu erwehlt worden ; denn dieses muss durch den Secretair, oder nach Erforderung der Umstaende durch ein anderes dazu bestelltes Glied des Ausschusses geschehen.

Artikel XXII.

Niemand, der einmal in die Societät aufgenommen worden, soll anders als nach reifer Ueberlegung des Ausschusses und mit Genehmigung des groesten Theils der Societät davon ausgeschlossen werden. Und eine solche ausgeschlossene Person kan nicht anders als durch neue Wahl wieder angenommen werden.

Artikel XXIII.

Wenn neue Glieder aufgenommen werden, so muessen ihnen die Regeln der Societät vorgelesen werden ; und jedes neues Glied hat sie zu unterschreiben.

Artikel XXIV.

Die Societät kan, wie es die Umstaende kuenftig erfoedern, neue Artikel vest setzen, nur dasz die mit den bisherigen und den Wohlstand der Societät uebereinstimmen.

Artikel XXV.

Die bisherigen Artikel koennen nur nach reifer Ueberlegung in einer Versammlung der Societät durch die Mehrheit der Stimmen geaendert werden ; und vier Wochen vor irgend einer Aenderung soll von der Natur und dem Zweck der zu machenden Veraenderung Nachricht gegeben werden.

More detailed books about the labour of the Moravians are : "Von der Arbeit der evangelischen Brüder unter den Heiden", Barby 1782 and ,,Kurzgefaszte Historische Nachricht der gegenwärtigen Verfassung der evangelischen Brüderunität augpurgischer Confession. Zweite Auflage 1781, Barby.

SOME BOOKS AND ARTICLES ABOUT THE LIFE AND PRINCIPLES OF WILLIAM CAREY.

Allgemeine Missionszeitschrift. Vierzehnte Band. Gütersloh, 1887.

BERG, G. VAN DEN, Geschiedenis der Zending. Zeist, Avis, 1888.

BEUSEKOM, DR. IR. H. G. VAN, William Carey, De grondlegger der hedendaagsche zending. Voorhoeve, Den Haag, 1935.

CAREY, William, An Enquiry into the Obligations of Christians to use means for the conversion of the heathens. Hodder and Stoughton, London, 1891.

DAKIN, Arthur, B.D.D.D., William Carey, Shoemaker, Linguist, Missionary. London, 1942.

DALTON, L. H., William Carey of India, "Young man—sit down". Edinburgh, 1938.

DEAVILLE WALKER, F., William Carey, Missionary, Pioneer and Statesman. London, 1936. Student Christian Movement.

DOUWES JR., J., Leven en werken van Dr. William Carey. Groningen, Wolters, 1856.

DOUWES HOENDERLOO Z.S.R., Lichtstralen op den akker der wereld.

Evangelische Missionsgeschichte in Biographien von Rheinhold Vornbaum. Vierter Band. Elberfeld, 1860.

Evangelisches Missionsmagazin. Basel, 1892.

Handbook for Bible Classes, Short History of Christian Missions. Edinburgh, T. & T. Clark, 1884.

HOWELLS, George, M.A., Ph. D. and Members of the College Faculty. The Story of Serampore and its college. Serampore, 1927.

JACOB, E.P., B.A., B.L., India's Carey, A centenary Play. Serampore College, India.

LAIQUE, Un, Petite Histoire des Missions Chrétiennes. Paris, 1929.

MARSHMAN, John Clark, The life and times of Carey, Marshman and Ward, in two Volumes. London, 1859.

Mededeelingen vanwege het Nederl. zendelingsgenootschap. 61e deel, 3e stuk. Rotterdam, 1917.

MULLER, P. H., Gedenkt uwen voorgangers. Amsterdam, 1941.

MYERS, J. B., William Carey. London, Partridge, 1887.

NORTIER, C. W., Wegwijzer Schetsen van Kerk en Zendingsgeschiedenis. Theolog. school te Balewtyata te Malang.

OGILVIE, J. N., The apostles of India. Hodder and Stoughton, London.

PAYNE, E. A., The great Succession leaders of the Baptist Missionary Soc. during the 19th century. London, Carey Press, 1938.

PEARCE CAREY, S., Carey Portrait. London & Edinburgh: Marshall. Morgan & Scott 1936.

PEARCE CAREY, S., William Carey. London, 1942.

PEARCE CAREY, S., William Carey, (a great grandson of William Carey). London, The Carey Press. An up-to-date book with many letters and documents very useful for everyone who takes an interest in the life of William Carey.

PIERSON, Dr. Arthur, De Nieuwe handelingen der apostelen. In vertaling door G. A. VAN DER BRUGHEN. Nijmegen, Ten Hoet, 1898.

RICHTER, Dr., History of Christianity in India.

RICHTER, Julius, Die Evangelische Missionen. 11. Jahrgang 1905. Gütersloh.

SCHMIDT, B., William Carey, der Missionspionier in Indien. Kassel.

SCHOTT, G., William Carey, der Vater der gegenwärtigen Missionsbewegung. Barmen, 1915.

SCHUURMAN, M., William Carey, de groote apostel van Voor-Indië. Leiden, D. Donner.

SHERRING, M. A., Rev., History of Protestant Missions in Indië, 1707—1782, revised by Rev. E. STORROW. London, 1884.

SILEN, Elin, Den Moderna Världmissionsfader, Uppsala-Lindblads Forlag, 1934.

SMITH, George, Life of William Carey. London, 1885.

SPEER, Robert E., Some great Leaders in the World Movement among others William Carey. New York and London, Reveil 1911.

STOSCH, Georg, Zeugen Gottes aus allerlei Volk. William Carey. Berlin.

SVARD, Arvid, Mannen med Bibeln, Stockholm. B.M.'s Bokforlags A.B. 1934.

ZAHN, Dr. J. M., Dr. R. GRUNDEMANN, Dr. Gustav WARNECK, Allgemeine Missionszeitschrift. In Verbindung mit, Berlin, p. 97—123, 1887.

LIST OF SOME BOOKS USED.

(See also page 304 and 305)

ANDEL, Dr. H. A. v., ,,De Zendingsleer van Gisbertus Voetius''. Kok, 1912.
BAVINCK, Prof. Dr. J. H., Christus en de mystiek van het Oosten. Kampen, without date.
BAVINCK, Prof. Dr. J. H., Ons Zendingsboek. Zomer en Keunig, Wageningen 1940.
BAVINCK, Prof. Dr. J. H., Zending in een wereld in nood. Zomer en Keunig, Wageningen 1942.
BERG, G. v. d., Gesch. der zending. Avis, Zeist 1888.
BETTERMAN, W., Das Werden einer Kirche im 18 Jahrhundert inzwischen den Zeiten, 1933.
BEUSEKOM, Dr., William Carey. Voorhoeve, Den Haag 1935.
BIESTERFELD, P., Schets van de symboliek. Kampen 1912.
BROUWER, Dr. A. M., Hoe te prediken voor heidenen en Mohammedanen. Rotterdam 1916.
BROUWER, Dr. A. M., De opleiding onzer zendelingen. Hollandia Drukkerij. Without date.
BROWN, The Rev. George, The History of British and Foreign Bible Society.
BROWN MYERS, John, William Carey.
CAMBRIDGE, Modern History. Cambridge 1909.
CANTON, W., History of the British and Foreign Bible Society. London, John Murray 1904.
CAREY William, An enquiry Reprinted in Facsimile from the edition of 1792. London, Hodder and Stroughton 1901.
CARLITE, Dr. J. C., The story of the English Baptists. James Clarke en Co. London 1905.
CHANTEPIE DE LA SAUSSAYE, Ch., De godsdienstige bewegingen van dezen tijd naar oorsprong geschetst. Rotterdam 1863.
CRAMP D. D., J. M., History from the foundation of the christian church to the close of the eighteenth century p. p. 13—48. London, Elliot Stock 1868.
CRASHAW, W. H., The making of English Literature. London 1906.
DAKIN, Arthur D. D. D. D., William Carey, Shoemaker, Linguist, Missionary. Carey Press, 19 Furnival Street, London 1942.
DALTON, L. H., Young man sit down. Edinburgh 1938.
DALTON, L. H., William Carey of India. Edinburgh 1938.
DOUWER, J. Jr., Leven en werken van Dr. William Carey. Groningen 1856.
DOUWES, P. A., Lichtstralen op den akker der wereld. Hoenderloo Z.S.R. 1900.
DOWDEN, Edward, Puritan and Anglican. London 1900.
EVAN's Early English Baptist. Vol. I. Bunyan Library. Vol. VII.
EVAN's Early English Baptist. Vol. I Bunyan Library Vol.II. London 1862.
GISPEN, W. H., Alg. zendingstijdschrift ,,de Macedonier''. Leiden 1890. 8e jaarg.
GREEN, John Richard, History of the English people. London 1908.
HEILER, Prof. Dr. Friedrich. De Openbaring in de godsdiensten van Britsch Indië en de Christusverkondiging. Paris, Amsterdam 1931.
HEUSSI, Compendium der Kirchengeschichte. 1937.
HISTORISCH Document Zendingsrapport v.d. Geref. Kerken van Middelburg 1896. Bootsma, Utrecht.
HODGE Systematic Theology Vol. I, II, III. London 1875.
HONIG, Dr. A. G., Handboek v.d. Geref. Dogmatiek. Kampen 1938.

JONES, E. Stanley, The Christ of the Indian Road. London 1930.
KEMP, Mr. P. H. v. d., Mededeelingen v. h. N. Zend. Gen. Tijdschrift voor Zendings-wetenschap, 61e deel. M. Wyt en Zonen, Rotterdam 1917.
KOK's Christelijke Encyclopaedie, artikel: ,,Baptisten'' en ,,Die Religion in Geschich-te und Gegenwart'', art. ,,Baptiste''. 1925 f.
KRAEMER, Dr. H., Schets en leven van Dr. N. Adriani, Paris. Amsterdam 1935.
KRAEMER, Prof. Dr. H., The christian message in a non-christian world. London 1938.
KURZ, J. H., Lehrbuch der Kirchengesch. Mitau 1863.
LAIGUE, Un Petite Histoire des missions chrétiennes. Seconde édition 1929. Société des missions évangéliques, Paris.
LAVISSE et RAMBAUD, Histoire Générale. Paris 1896.
LEEUW, Prof. Dr., G. v. d., Godsdiensten der aarde. Hind. I. Meulenhoff, Amster-dam 1940.
LÜTJEHARMS, Dr. W., ,,Het Philadelphisch-oecomenisch streven der Hernhutters i. d. Nederlanden in de achttiende eeuw.'' Zeist 1935.
MARSHMAN, John Clark, The life and times of William Carey, Marshman and Ward, London 1859.
MONIER—WILLIAMS Sir, Hinduism. London 1897.
MYERS, J. B., William Carey. London, Partridge 1887.
MERKELIJN, A., 26 jaren op het zendingsveld. Herinneringen van een missionair predikant. Daamen, Den Haag 1941.
MORRIS, J. A., Memoirs of the life and writings of the Rev. Andrew Fuller. 1816.
MULDER, P. H., Gedenk Uw voorgangers. Bigot en v. Rossum, Amsterdam zonder jaartal.
MULLER, KARL, 200 Jahre Brüdermission. Das erste Mission Jahrhundert. Hern-hut 1931.
MULLER, TH., Een blik in de geschiedenis der Evangelische broedergemeente. Zeist 1925.
MYERS, JOHN BROWN, The shoemaker who became the father and founder of modern missions. Patridge and Co., London 1887.
NES, Dr. H. M. v., John Wesley. Nijkerk, Callenbach 1907.
NIERMEYER, Dr. H. A., Collectio Confessionum in ecclesiis reformatis publicata-rum. Leipzig 1840.
NOREL, Dr. O., John Wesly. Voorhoeve, Den Haag 1936.
NORTIER, C. W., Wegwijzer. Schetsen van kerk en zendingsgesch. W. Carey, Balewy-ata, Malang.
OGILVIE, J. N., The Apostles of India. Hodder and Stroughton, London without date.
PATON, Rev. W., Industralism and international Issue Vol. V. Oxford 1928. Je-rusalem 1928.
PATON, Rev. W., World Community. London 1938.
PEARCE CAREY, S. M. A., William Carey. London, The Carey Press 1923. Idem 1942 a different edition.
PIERSON, Dr. ARTHUR, De nieuwe Handelingen der Apostelen. Nijmegen 1898.
REPORT of the centenary Conference of the protestant missions of the world. Lon-don 1888. Vol. II.
RICHTER, JULIUS GÜTERSLOH, Die Evangelische Missionen 11 Jahrgang 1905.
RINN und JÜNGST, Kirchengeschichtliches Lesebuch. Tübingen 1906.
ROUSE, RUTH, God has a purpose. London 1935.
SCHAFF, PHILIPS, D.D. L.L.D., The creeds of Christendom. New York 1905.
SCHMIDT, B., KASSEL. W. Carey der Missionspionier in Indien.
SCHOTT, G., W.Carey, der Vater der gegenwärtigen Missionsbewegung. Barmen 1915.
SCHUURMAN, M., William Carey, de groote apostel van Voor-Indië. Leiden D. Donner.
SELL, KARL, Christentum und Weltgeschichte. Leipzig 1909.
SHERRING, M. A., History of Protestant Missions in India. W. Carey 1706—1782. London 1884.
SMITH, GEORGE, The life of William Carey. London 1885.
SOCIETY for promoting christian knowledge Life of Missionaries. London no date.

SPANGENBERG, AUG. GOTTLIEB von, Idea Fidei Fratrum. Utrecht 1782.
SPANGENBERG, AUG. GOTTLIEB von, „Leben des Herrn Nicolaus Ludwig, Grafen und Herrn von Linsendorf und Pottendorf". Barby 1772.
SPANGENBERG, AUG. GOTTLIEB von, Historische Nachricht. Barby 1781.
SPANGENBERG, A. G. von, Leben von Graf von Zinzendorf Brüdergemeinen 1774.
SPANGENBERG, A. G. von, Unterricht für die Brüder und Schwestern, welche den Heiden am Evangelie dienen. Gandau 1837.
SPANGENBERG, von, Von der Arbeit der evangelischen Brüder unter den Heiden. Barby 1782.
SPENER, PHILIPP JACOB, Pia Desideria. Kurt Aland, Berlin 1940.
SPUR, ROBERT E., D.D. Christ the leader of the missionary work of the church. World Missionary conference 1910. Vol. IX.
STACHLIN, F., Die Mission der Brüdergemeine I, II, III. Hernhut no date.
STEPHAN, LESLIE, English thoughts on the 18th Century. London 1881.
STOSCH, GEORG, Zeugen Gottes aus allerlei Volk. William Carey. Berlin.
THE christian mission in relation to rural problems. Jerusalem 1928. Vol. V.
THE church and the state. Vol. VI. Tambaram 1938.
TOWNSEND, W. J., WORKMAN and GEORGE EAYRS. A new History of Methodism. S. Hodder and Stroughton, London 1909.
TROELTSCH, ERNST, Die Soziallehren der kirchlichen Kirche und Gruppen. Tübingen 1923.
UNTERRICHT für die Brüder und Schwestern, welche den Heiden am Evangelie dienen. Zweite durchgesehene und vermehrte Ausgabe, Gandau 1837.
UTTENDÖRFER, von, Religiöse Grundgedanken. Hernhut 1935.
VEDDER, HENRY C., A short History of the Baptists. Revised edition. American Baptist Publication 1897.
VERSLAGEN der Nederl. afdeeling van het zendeling genootschap der Engelsche Baptisten in Serampore 1822.
VORNBAUM, REINHOLD, Evangelische Missionsgeschichte in Biographien. Elberfeld 1860.
VORBAUM, RHEINHOLD, Evangelische Missionsgeschichte in Biographien William Carey. Vierter Band. Elberfeld 1860.
VORNBAUM, REINHOLD, Berichten v.d. Utrechtsche Zendingsver. 1861 no. 9. Article relating David Brainerd, der Apostel der Indianer in Pensylvanien und New Yersey.
WALKER, F. DEAVILLE, William Carey Missionary, Pioneer and Staterman. Walker, London 1926.
WANTON, W., History of the British and Foreign Bible Society.
WARNECK, Dr. G., Abrisz der Geschichte der Protest. Mission von der Reformation bis auf Gegenwart (1882) 1913.
WARNECK, Dr. GUSTAV, Historische Schets der Protestantsche zendingen van den tijd der Kerkhervorming tot op heden. Utrecht 1882.
WARNECK, G., Evangelische Missionslehre. Erste Abt : Die Begründung der Sendung. Gotha, Fr. A. Perthes 1897.
WARNECK, G., Evangelische Missionslehre. Zweite Abt : Die Organe der Sendung. Gotha, Fr. A. Perthes 1897.
WARNECK, G., Evangelische Missionslehre. Dritte Abt : Der Betrieb der Sendung. Erste Hälfte. Gotha, Fr. A. Perthes 1902.
WARNECK, G., Evangelische Missionslehre. Der Betrieb der Sendung. Zweite Hälfte : Die Missionsmittel. Botha, Fr. A. Perthes 1905.
WARNECK, G., Evangelische Missionslehre. Der Betrieb der Sendung. Schluszabschnitt : Das Missionsziel. Gotha : Fr. A. Perthes 1903.
WANTON, W., History of the British and Foreign Bible Society.
WERELDGESCHIEDENIS. De geschiedenis der menschheid van de oudste tijden tot heden. Artikel Dr. J. S. Bartstra 18e eeuw. De Haan, Utrecht.
WUMKES, Dr. G. A., De opkomst en vestiging van het Baptisme in Nederland". Osinga, Sneek 1912.
ZENDELINGGENOOTSCHAP Ned. Mededeelingen van. William Carey. 61e deel 3e stuk. Rotterdam 1917.

INDEX OF NAMES.

Krishna Prasad, 85, 216.
Kuyper, Dr. Abraham, 107.

Latrobe, 72.
Law, 14.
Lawson, Mrs., 172.
Lawson, John, 96, 113.
Leeshman of Glasgow, 208.
Lessing, Gotthold Ephraim, 7.
Lewis, C. B., 53.
Löszner of Surinam, 241.
Lot's wife, 57.
Louis XVI, 33.
Loyola Ignatius, 47.
Lullus, Raymandus, 205, 266.
Luther, Maarten, 50, 131, 133, 161.
Lütjeharms, Dr., 255.
Lütkens, Dr., 50, 219, 220.

Macauly, Zachary, 192.
Mack of Edinburgh, 208.
Mack, Rev. John of Serampore, 121.
Mahomet (see Mohammed).
Mansfield, Lord chief Iustice, 191.
Marco Polo, 45, 56.
Mardon, Mr., 87.
Maria Antoinette, 6.
Mark, the Apostle, 64, 137.
Marshmann, John Clark, 72, 114, 180, 181, 192.
Marshmann, Joshua, 52, 68, 75, 80, 82, 94, 96, 101, 103, 104, 108, 110, 113, 114, 115, 117, 120, 160, 162, 165, 166, 167, 168, 169, 182, 185, 201, 208.
Marshman, Mrs. Hannah, 76, 171, 172.
Marshman, Rachel, 76.
Martin (English resident of Amboyna), 150, 151.
Martin, Byam, 98.
Martyn, Henry, 92, 99, 103, 200, 211.
Martyr, 133.
Matthew, the Apostle, 64.
Melanchton, 50, 131, 133.
Mellitus, 133.
Merkelijn, The Rev. A., 16, 18.
Methodius, 133.
Minto, Lord, 93, 94, 95, 96, 104.
Mohammed or Mahomet, 94, 135.
Moira, Lord (the Marquis of Hastings), 104.
Montesquieu, Charles de Secondat, baron de, 1, 6, 11.
Moore, 87.
Morris, J. W. at Clipstone, 144.
Muller, Mr., 218.
Müller, Professor, 122.
Munro, Sir Thomas, 184.
Myers, J. B., 201.

Naomi, 21.
Nestorius, 45.

Neumeister of Hamburg, 220.
Newton, John, 6, 43, 70.
Nichols, Clarke, 23.
Nitzschmann, David, 223.
Nommenson, 156.

Ogilvie, Dr., 46, 49, 56, 74, 79, 92, 166.
Old, Thomas, 25.
Oliver, Goldsmith, 2.
Olsen, Isaäk, 223.
Osgood, Dr. Howard, 126.

Palladius, 133.
Pantaenus of Alexandria, 45.
Paton, The Rev. W., 155.
Patrick, 133.
Paul, St., 15, 43, 106, 127, 132, 137, 143, 147, 152, 153, 154, 158, 186, 194, 204, 206, 233.
Paulinus, 133.
Pearce Jr., 113, 152.
Pearce, Mrs., 172.
Pearce, Samuel, 34, 70, 145.
Pelham, 10.
Penncy, Mr., 113.
Peros, 216.
Peter, the Apostle, 56.
Pelumber Sing, 83, 216.
Pick, Francis, 31.
Pitt, William, 7, 88.
Placket, Daniel, 57.
Placket, Dorothy, 26, 57, 59.
Placket, Katherine, 42, 59, 61.
Plütschau, Henry, 19, 36, 50, 223, 229.
Potter, J. G., 10, 120.
Pratapaditya, Raja, 211.
Pursur, John, 31.

Ramabai, Pundita, 182.
Rasoo, 216.
Rhumohr Count, of the Duchy of Schleswick, 84, 98.
Rhumohr, Fraulein Charlotte Emilia, 84, 121, 167.
Richard, Dr., 5.
Richard II, 20.
Ringletaube, The Rev. Tobias, 52.
Robert de Nobili(bus), 48, 50.
Robinson, William The Rev., 93, 97, 98, 120, 179.
Rogers, Prof., 192.
Ronaldshay, Lord, Governor of Bengal, 119.
Rousseau, Jean Jacques, 7, 191.
Rowe, Mr., 87, 169.
Ruffinian, 133.
Ryland, Dr. John, 28, 32, 33, 34, 37, 41, 102, 107, 112, 113, 115, 118, 122, 143, 162, 169.

311

INDEX OF SUBJECTS.

Doctor of Divinity, 97.
doctrines, 30, 106, 108, 128, 142, 226/228.
dogma, 15, 106, 108, 126, 142, 211.
Dominican friars, 45, 47.
Dominions, British in India, 54, 106.
down-pouring of the spirit, 132.
drawing, 26.
Dunkerk, 41.
Dutch, 28.
"Earl of Oxford", 40, 41.
Eating with Europeans, 76.
ecclesiola in ecclesia, 220.
economic management, 79, 164, 165, 166.
education, 11, 17, 21, 84, 105, 108, 161,
    162, 163, 171, 172, 192.
emotional (movement), 8, 9.
empirism, 6.
England, 19, 25, 44 et passim.
Enquiry into the obligations of Christians
    to use means for the conversion of
    the heathen, 30, 32, 129ff.
equality, 74, 158.
Ethiopia, 133.
etymology of the name Carey, 20.
Europe, 45, 46, 63, 107.
evangelisation, handmaid of, 105, 108.
examples, Paul and the discipels, 158.
excavations, 6.
excommunication, 85.
expect and attempt, 32.
expense, 59.
experiences, 128.
experimentalism, 6.
expiatory work of Christ, 206.
fall of Adam, 130.
fanatics, 95.
fashionable society, 11.
fasting, 24, 27.
female immolation (see also Sati), 83/84.
female population, 66, 110, 156.
finance, 37, 41, 72, 88, 103/104, 116, 146.
fire, 103, 119.
flood, 70, 115.
Formalism, 1.
Form of Agreement, 129, 152, 178.
Fort William, 6, 60.
Franciscan friars, 40, 47.
Franconia, 133.
France, 141.
Freedom, 3, 16, 110, 126.
freethinker, 11.
Friesland (West), 133.
Ganges, the, 77.
garden, Carey's, 115.
genealogical tree of Carey, 21.
General Assembly of the Church of
    Scotland, 43.
geographical studies, 29, 30.
Goa, 47.
Gospel, 1, 3 et passim.

Governor (Danish), 68, 75, 94.
Government (English), 56, 66, 70, 72,
    74, 99, 179, 181, 213, 242, 262.
grace, 153.
Grammar, 64, 86, 101, 102, 119.
Greek, 25, 28, 43.
Greenland, 132.
Halle, 219, 220, 221, 222, 223, 224.
heathen (see also pagan, pain), 13, 29,
    30, 129.
Hebrew, 25, 28.
Hernhut(ters), 12
highchurchmen, 9.
Hindoo-people, 190.
Hinduism, 46, 105, 154.
Hindustani, 29, 52, 64, 175.
historic (moment in the history of mis-
    sions), 32.
history, 30, 138, 140.
Home-circle, 98.
homefront, the (base), 97, 104, 138,
    141, 146, 215.
Hooghi, 42, 58, 74.
horticulture, 196.
hospital, 87, 202, 203.
housefathership, 149, 166.
hypocritical, 130, 180.
idolatry, 108, 131, 157.
ignorance, 4, 131.
immersion, 27.
immorality, 1, 5.
impossibility, natural, 132.
Incarnations, 64.
incumbent, 130.
independence, independent, 9, 27.
Indies, Dutch East, 174.
India (English East), 40, 41, 42, 44, 45, 68.
Indians, 30.
indigo factory, 61, 62, 63, 66, 67, 68,
    179, 215.
individual(ism), 9, 10, 11, 15.
indolence, 53, 131.
industry, 150, 155.
infanticide, 84, 185.
inhabitants of the world, 134/135.
initiative, 56.
insinuation, 111.
Institution (Benevolent) for the In-
    struction of indigent children, 208.
institutions, 127.
instructions, 145, 146, 171.
instructions to (Burmah) missionaries,
    101, 151, 152ff.
instruments, 198, 244ff, 265ff.
intellectual, 10.
Ireland, 133.
Isle of Wight, 41.
Israelites, 143.
Italian, 28.
itinerate, 58, 152, 185, 213.

ordinances, 127.
ordination, 28, 30.
organisation of the congregations, 216, 248.
organs, The organs of missions, 141,
    145, 232ff, 253, 254ff.
orthodoxy German, 220.
orthodoxy, 11.
pagan, 8, 77, 108.
painting, 26.
Pariah, 49.
Paris, 32.
Parliament, 54, 97, 100, 105, 111, 124,
    126, 179.
Parthia, 133.
patriarchs, 142.
peculiarity, 176.
Pentecost, 132/133.
perfection, 13.
persevere, 29, 44, 66, 97, 103.
Persian, 198.
Persic, 29.
philosophy, 46, 107.
philosophers, 10, 108.
Phrygia, 133.
Pia Desideria, 219.
Piddington, 40.
piety, pious, 12, 158 et passim.
Pietism, 6, 12, 14, 15, 128, 219 et passim.
Pilgrim's Progress of John Bunyan, 122.
plan of mission to Bengal, 54.
Plan of the Lord, 78.
plurality, 4.
poita, 82, 84, 85.
Polished before enlightened, 43.
political differences on the missionary
    field, 179.
politics, 74, 110, 195, 196, 242, 243, 262.
polygamy, 193, 194, 263.
polyglottes, 102, 103.
Pompeji, 6.
Pope, the, 47.
popish missionaries, 132.
population, 29.
Portugal, 45, 47, 133.
Portuguese language, 51, 52, 95.
practicability, 135, 138.
praedestination, 122, 127.
prayer, 24, 141, 146, 156, 157, 158.
prayer-meetings, 141.
preaching, 27, 163, 205, 244, 245.
Press (see printing).
prejudices, 158, 177.
principles of Mission, 129.
principles of the Moravians, 129.
principles of Pietists, 129, 216 et passim.
printing (press), 40, 64, 68, 69, 73, 74,
    75, 87, 94, 97, 103, 112.
prison, 2.
professor of languages in an Oriental
    college, 28, 78, 86, 101, 116.

profession of faith, 125.
profits, 136.
program, 145.
propagation of the Gospel, 11, 16, 108, 139.
Protestant missions in India, 50, 51.
Protestantismus, 15, 50, 135.
providence, 28, 56, 61, 78, 87, 104.
Puritans, 1, 9, 11, 14, 25, 143.
Purpose, missionary, 245, 247, 248, 268ff.
Quakers (or Friends), 132, 154, 191,
    261, 278.
Qualifications of the missionaries (see
    missionaries).
rationalism, 4, 6, 7.
Ramayana, The, epic, 86, 94, 102, 103.
reason, 6, 7, 9, 10.
redemption, 1.
Reformation, 4, 14, 50, 131.
relations, the ecclesiastical, 217.
religion, 1, 3, 6, et passim.
Renaissance, 8.
resolutions of Wilberforce, 53/54.
responsibility, 153.
revelation, 3.
Revolution (French), 6, 8, 9, 14, 15,
    32, 53, 65, 191, 192.
Rippon, 70.
rites, 127.
Rococo, 6.
Romanticism, 8, 9.
rope, 37, 72, 114.
Salary, 61, 79, 85.
Salvation (national), 1.
Sannyasi, 49.
Sanskaras, 83.
Sanskrit, 65, 78, 85, 101, 102, 103, 105,
    106, 107, 198, 204.
Sati or suttee, 83, 90, 110, 115, 116, 185.
satire, 205.
scepticism, 9, 11.
Schism Bill, 3.
schism, The, in Serampore, 110, 113,
    114, 120, 149, 152.
Scholasticism, 1.
schools, missionary, 17, 40, 63, 65, 69,
    77, 104, 105, 115, 150, 172, 207, 209, 246.
schoolmaster, 28.
School, Theological High, at Kampen, 125.
Scotland, 133.
Scriptures, Sacred, 4, 6, 27, 68, 69,
    103, 106, 133, 143, 172.
Scythia, 133.
secession, 12.
sectarian, 107.
seduction, 2.
Self-supporting, 58, 157, 164, 212, 237,
    238, 248, 254.
seminary (Baptist Theological at Ro-
    chester), 126.
Seniores, 110, 113, 169.